THE CHRISTIAN WRITERS
MARKET GUIDE
2023

THE CHRISTIAN WRITERS
MARKET GUIDE

2023

Your Comprehensive Resource for Getting Published

STEVE LAUBE

THE CHRISTIAN WRITERS MARKET GUIDE 2023

ISBN – 978-1-62184-2422 (paperback)
ISBN – 978-1-62184-2439 (ebook)

Cover design by Hannah Linder (*hannahlinderdesigns.com*)
Typesetting by Jamie Foley (*jamiefoley.com*)
Edited by Lin Johnson (*wordprocommunicationservices.com*)

Printed in the United States of America.

Visit The Christian Writers Institute at *www.ChristianWritersInstitute.com*.

E-mail: *admin@christianwritersmarketguide.com*

TABLE OF CONTENTS

FOREWORD

WHEN I WAS A BEGINNING WRITER, I INVESTED IN
guides like this one to:
- study the markets
- find a publisher
- avoid rejection slips

And later, when agents became common in the inspirational market, to:
- find an agent
- express my faith-based worldview in my writing

Thanks to publisher and industry insider Steve Laube, you'll find this book a treasure trove of opportunities, as well as ideas. I find my thinking expanded even by reading what publishers look for.

But we should talk about what publishers *don't* want to see.

It doesn't sound fair. It doesn't seem right. But here's a dirty little secret of the writing life: Veteran editors can tell within two minutes whether they're going to reject your manuscript.

"What?" you say. "Before I've had a chance to wow them, before my plot really takes off?"

Sorry.

Because the competition is so stiff and editors have so many manuscripts to read, you have only nanoseconds to grab them.

Am I saying editors look for reasons to reject your work? No, they're looking for the next Harry Potter. They want you to succeed!

Then how can they know so quickly that your manuscript won't cut it?

I've heard dozens of reasons, but let me give you three for fiction from my experience as both an editor and a publisher:

1. Too may characters introduced too quickly. Any time I see more than three characters within the first few pages, my eyes start to swim; and I quickly lose interest.

Your readers are trying to comprehend the story; and if you ask them to start cataloguing a cast of characters right away, you risk losing them. Keep things simple until the story has taken shape.

2. *Clichés, and not only words and phrases.* Clichéd situations exist, too, like starting your story with the main character waking to an alarm clock, a character describing herself while looking in a full-length mirror, and future love interests literally bumping into each other on first meeting.

Avoid, too, beginning with an evocative, dramatic scene and surprise, surprise, the main character wakes up to discover it's all been a dream. There's nothing wrong with dreams, but having them come as surprises has been used to death and takes all the air from the balloon of your story.

Another cliché is to have your main character feel his heart pound, race, thud, or hammer; and then he gasps, sucks wind, his breath comes short, etc. If you describe the scene properly, your reader should experience all that; and you shouldn't have to say what your character did. Put your character into a rough enough situation, and readers will know what he's feeling without having to be told—and hopefully share his distress.

3. *Simply bad writing.* Hollywood screenwriters coined the term *on the nose* for prose that exactly mirrors real life but fails to advance your plot. There's nothing wrong with the words themselves, except they could be synopsized to save the reader's time and patience. A perfect example is the banal greetings that precede meaningful dialogue. Rather, synopsize them this way: "After trading pleasantries," then get right to the good stuff.

Watch for those sales killers in your writing. And if *The Christian Writers Market Guide* plays a part in your selling your work in 2023, be sure to let Steve Laube and his team know.

— Jerry B. Jenkins
www.JerryJenkins.com

INTRODUCTION

WRITING IS A SERIOUS BUSINESS. It is also a serious calling. The privilege of having your words influence other people's thinking or inspiring their spirit is a gift from God. A number of publication opportunities for great writing from great authors exist. Traditional methods for publication remain, but the diversity of online opportunities are seemingly endless. In addition, independent-publication options have made it easier to see your byline on a book, on a blog post, or in an online magazine.

Since many Christian bookstores have closed, it may seem like the Christian publishing industry is shrinking; but it is not. It is simply changing. Therefore, you must research more effectively to find the best place for your work. The problem with online search engines is the immense number of results you receive. Then the results depend on that site's search-engine optimization and those who have paid to have their sites show at the top. *The Christian Writers Market Guide* has curated the information for you. Now you can find what is targeted specifically for the Christian market and your areas of interest.

One of the biggest mistakes a writer can make is to ignore the guidelines of an agent, an editor, or a publisher. In the past, some publications dropped their listings in this guide because writers failed to follow the instructions in it. Editors are looking for writers who understand their periodicals or publishing houses and their unique approaches to the marketplace. This book will help you be such a writer. With a little time and effort, you can meet an editor's expectations, distinguish yourself as a professional, and sell what you write.

If you can, I recommend you attend a writers conference, whether virtual or in person. (We have many listed inside.) It is good to meet new people and become familiar with the best teachers in the industry. If you cannot get to a conference, consider exploring the courses available online at *ChristianWritersInstitute.com.* There are more than 110 to choose from, and you can enjoy them at any time on any device.

If this is the first time you've used this guide, read the "How to Use This Book" section. If you run into an unfamiliar term, look it up in the "Publishing Lingo" section in back and learn the terminology.

Please be aware that the information in this guide is provided by the companies or individuals through online questionnaires and email inquiries, as well as their websites and writers guidelines. The companies or individuals do not pay to be listed in this guide. The entries are not endorsed by me or The Christian Writers Institute. We make every attempt to verify the accuracy of the information provided. The entries are for information only. Any transaction(s) between a user of the information and the individuals or companies listed is strictly between those parties.

May God bless your writing journey. We are on a mission to change the world, word by word. To that end, strive for excellence and make your work compelling and insightful. Great writing is still in demand. But it must be targeted, crafted, critiqued, edited, polished, and proofread until it shines.

My thanks go to Lin Johnson whose invaluable work makes this all possible. She keeps tabs throughout the year on market changes, so every listing is accurate to the best of our information at the time of publication. (Our online version of this guide, *ChristianWritersMarketGuide.com*, is updated regularly during the year.) As the administrator of the online and print editions, she is the genius behind the details. In addition, I would also like to acknowledge my wife, Lisa. Her love, support, and encouragement have been incalculable. We make a great team!

Steve Laube
President
The Christian Writers Institute
and
The Steve Laube Agency
24 W. Camelback Rd. A-635
Phoenix, AZ 85013
www.christianwritersinstitute.com
www.stevelaube.com

To update a listing or to be added to the next edition or online, go to *christianwritersmarketguide.com*. Click on the Get Listed tab, and fill out the form.

For direct-sales questions, email the publisher: *admin@christianwritersinstitute.com*.

For books and courses on the writing craft, visit The Christian Writers Institute: *www.christianwritersinstitute.com*.

HOW TO USE THIS BOOK

THE CHRISTIAN WRITERS MARKET GUIDE 2023 IS DESIGNED to make it easier for you to sell your writing. It will serve you well if you use it as a springboard to become thoroughly familiar with the markets best suited to your writing style and areas of interest and expertise.

As you look through this guide, you may run into words in the listings that you are not familiar with. If so, check "Publishing Lingo" at the back of the book.

GETTING ACQUAINTED WITH THIS BOOK

Start by getting acquainted with the setup of this guide.

Book Publishers

Part 1 lists traditional book publishers and anthology series with information about what they are looking for. Notice that many houses accept manuscripts only from agents or through meeting with their editors at a writers conference. If you need a literary agent, check the agent listings in Chapter 17.

Independent Book Publishing

Since independent book publishing is a viable option today, Part 2 provides resources to help you. Chapter 3 lists independent book publishers, many of which provide all the services you need as packages or à la carte options. If you decide to publish on your own, Chapters 4 and 5 list design, production, and distribution services. You'll also want to hire a professional editor and proofreader, so see Chapter 20 for help in this area.

Periodical Publishers

Part 3 lists periodical—magazine, newspaper, and newsletter—publishers. Chapter 6 will help you find markets by topics (e.g., marriage, evangelism) and types (e.g., how-to, poetry, personal experience). Although these lists are not comprehensive, they provide a shortcut for finding appropriate markets for your ideas.

Cross-referencing may be helpful. For example, if you have an idea for a how-to article on parenting, look at the lists in both the how-to and parenting categories. Also, don't overlook writing on the same topic for different periodicals, such as money management for a general adult magazine, a teen magazine, a women's newsletter, and a magazine for pastors. Each would require a different slant, but you would get more mileage from one idea.

Specialty Markets

In Part 4, "Specialty Markets," you'll find nonbook, nonperiodical markets like daily devotionals and drama. Here you can explore types of writing you may not have thought about but can provide a steady writing income.

Support for Writers

As a writer, you'll need support to keep going. Part 5 provides information for various kinds of support.

One of the best ways to get published today is to meet editors at writers conferences. Check out Chapter 18 for a conference or seminar near you or perhaps in a location you'd like to visit. Before deciding which conference to attend, check the websites for who is on faculty, what houses are represented, and what classes are offered that can help you grow your craft and writing business. You may also want to factor in the size of the conference. Don't be afraid to stretch outside your comfort zone.

For ongoing support and feedback on your manuscripts, join a writers group. Chapter 19 lists groups by state and internationally. If you can't find one near you, consider starting one or join an online group.

Since editors and literary agents are looking for polished manuscripts, you may want to hire a professional editor. See Chapter 20 for people who offer a variety of editorial services, including coaching.

Whether you publish your book with a royalty house or go the independent route, you'll need to do most, if not all, of the promotion. If you want to hire a specialist with contacts, check out Chapter 21, "Publicity and Marketing Services." And if you need accounting or legal help, check out Chapter 22.

One way to promote your message and your books is through speaking. If you need help in this area—and most writers do—see Chapter 23, "Speaking Services." There you will find organizations and conferences that train speakers and/or connect them with groups looking for speakers.

Since writers who stagnate don't get published, check out Chapter 24 for education resources to help you improve your writing style, write different types of manuscripts, and learn the business of writing and publishing. You'll find a variety of free and paid resources, including podcasts and classes.

Entering a writing contest can boost your sales, supplement your writing income, lead to publication, and sometimes give you valuable feedback on your writing. Check out Chapter 25 for a list of contests by genre. Many of them are not Christian oriented, but you can enter manuscripts with a Christian worldview.

USING THIS BOOK

Once you get acquainted with this guide, start using it. After you identify potential markets for your ideas and/or manuscripts, read their writers guidelines. If these are available on the website, the URL is included. Otherwise, email or send (with a SASE) for a copy. Also study at least one sample copy of a periodical (information to obtain one is given in most listings) or the book publisher's website to see if your idea truly fits there. Never send a manuscript without doing this market study.

Above all, keep in mind that this guide is only a starting point for your research and change is the one constant in the publishing industry. It is impossible for any market guide to be 100 percent accurate since editors move around, publications and publishing houses close, and new ones open. But this guide is an essential tool for getting published in the Christian market and making an impact on God's Kingdom with your words.

PART 1

TRADITIONAL BOOK PUBLISHERS

1

TRADITIONAL BOOK PUBLISHERS

Before submitting your query letter or book proposal, it's critical that you read and follow a publisher's guidelines exactly. In many cases, the guidelines are available on the website and a direct link is given in the listing. If you do not have a literary agent—and even if you do—check out a publisher thoroughly before signing a contract.

Note: Not all the imprints listed in imprint entries below are in this book, primarily since they are focused for the general market. Also, some may be in other sections.

1517 MEDIA
Augsburg Fortress, Beaming Books, Broadleaf Books, Fortress Press

ABINGDON PRESS
810 12th Ave. S, Nashville, TN 37203 | 615-749-6000
www.abingdonpress.com
Constance Stella, senior acquisitions editor
> **Denomination:** United Methodist
> **Parent company:** United Methodist Publishing House
> **Submissions:** Publishes 120 titles per year; receives 2,000 submissions annually. First-time authors: fewer than 5%. Bible: CEB. Submit proposal with sample chapters through the website.
> **Royalty:** minimum 7.5%
> **Types and topics:** Christian living/spirituality, leadership, theology, academic
> **Guidelines:** *www.abingdonpress.com/submissions*

Tip: Looking for "any young and new voices that have active speaking and conference engagements, as well as blog and social-media followers."

AMBASSADOR INTERNATIONAL

411 University Ridge, Ste. B14, Greenville, SC 29601 | 864-751-4844
www.ambassador-international.com
Katie Cruice Smith, senior editor

Mission statement: to spread the gospel of Christ and empower Christians through the written word

Submissions: Publishes 50 titles per year; receives 750 submissions annually. First-time authors: 50%. Length: minimum 144 pages. Submit proposal with sample chapters through the website. Responds in one month. Bible: KJV, NIV, ESV, NKJV, NASB.

Royalty: 15-20%, 25% for ebooks, no advance

Types and topics: biography, business, Christian living/spirituality, finances, theology, Bible studies, children, devotionals, fiction, teen/YA

Guidelines: *ambassador-international.com/get-published/submission-guidelines*

Tip: "We're most open to a book which has a clearly defined market and the author's total commitment to the project. We do well with first-time authors. We have full international coverage. Many of our titles sell globally."

AMERICAN CATHOLIC PRESS

16565 State St., South Holland, IL 60473-2025 | 708-331-5485
acp@acpress.org | *www.americancatholicpress.org*
Rev. Michael Gilligan, executive director

Denomination: Catholic

Submissions: Publishes four titles per year; receives ten submissions annually. Mail query first. No simultaneous submissions. Responds in two months. Bible: NAS.

Payment: $25–$100 flat fee

First print run: 3,000

Types and topics: liturgy, nonfiction

Guidelines: *www.americancatholicpress.org/faq.html#faq5*

Tip: "We publish only materials on the Roman Catholic liturgy. No poetry or fiction."

AMG PUBLISHERS

6815 Shallowford Rd., Chattanooga, TN 37421 | 423-894-6060

sales@amgpublishers.com | *www.amgpublishers.com*

Amanda Jenkins, sales manager

Parent company: AMG International

Mission statement: God's Word to you is our highest calling.

Submissions: Publishes ten titles per year; receives 200 submissions annually. First-time authors: 30%. Length: minimum 150 pages. Conference contact or email proposal with sample chapters. Responds in six months. Bible: any.

Royalty: 14–16%, sometimes gives advances

Types and topics: African-American, Bible study, Christian living/spirituality, Hispanic, Bible reference/commentaries, Bible studies, devotionals

Types of books: ebook, hardcover, offset paperback, POD

Imprints: AMG (reference, Bible studies, Bibles, devotionals), Living Ink (YA fiction), God and Country Press (military/history devotionals)

Guidelines: *amgpublishers.com/index.php/author-guidelines*

Tip: "Most open to an interactive workbook Bible study geared for small groups that effectively taps into a largely female audience. We are currently placing priority on books with strong bibliocentric focus."

ANCIENT FAITH PUBLISHING

PO Box 748, Chesterton, IN 46304 | 800-967-7377

khyde@ancientfaith.com | *www.ancientfaith.com/publishing*

Katherine Hyde, editorial director

Jane Meyer, children's project manager, jmeyer@ancientfaith.com

Denomination: Orthodox Christian

Parent company: Antiochian Orthodox Christian Archdiocese of North America

Mission statement: to embrace the fullness of the Orthodox Christian faith, encourage the discipleship of believers, equip the faithful for ministry, and evangelize the unchurched

Submissions: Publishes 12–16 titles per year; receives 100 submissions annually. First-time authors: 50%. Length: 40,000–100,000 words. Email query first. Responds in two months to proposal after requested. Bible: NKJV.

Royalty: 10–15%, no advance

First print run: 2,000

Types and topics: biography, Christian living/spirituality, church history, contemporary issues, family, marriage, memoir/personal narrative, theology, worship, Bible reference/commentaries, children, fiction, teen/YA

Guidelines: *www.ancientfaith.com/publishing#af-resources*

Tip: "Read and follow the guidelines. Look through our website to see the kinds of books we publish. Do not submit material that is not intended specifically for an Eastern Orthodox audience."

ANEKO PRESS

PO Box 652, Abbotsford, WI 54405 | 715-223-3013

jeremiah@lspbooks.com | *www.anekopress.com*

Jeremiah Zeiset, president

Parent company: Life Sentence Publishing, Inc.

Mission statement: to publish books for ministry

Submissions: Publishes 20 titles per year; receives 50 submissions annually. First-time authors: 20%. Length: 30,000–100,000 words. Submit proposal with complete manuscript through the website. Responds in two weeks. Bible: KJV, ESV, NKJV. Niche is publishing ministry-related books.

Royalty: 30%, no advance

First print run: 1,000–5,000

Types and topics: Christian living/spirituality

Types of books: audiobook, ebook, hardcover, offset paperback

Guidelines: *anekopress.com/write-for-us*

Tip: "The majority of our authors are in ministry as missionaries or other similar ministries."

ARMOUR BOOKS

PO Box 492, Corinda, QLD 4075, Australia

words@armourbooks.com.au | *www.armourbooks.com.au*

Anne Hamilton

Mission statement: to publish quality books with a "kiss from God at their heart"

Submissions: Publishes five titles per year; receives 50–100 submissions annually. First-time authors: 50%. Length: maximum 50,000 words. No simultaneous submissions. Responds in two to four weeks.

Royalty: 9–10%, sometimes offers advances

Types and topics: Christian living/spirituality; fiction: fantasy, science fiction

Types of books: POD

Tip: "The golden rule: Support other authors as you would like to be supported."

ASHBERRY LANE

13607 Bedford Rd. NE, Cumberland, MD 21502 | 866-245-2211

r.white@whitefire-publishing.com | *AshberryLane.com*

Roseanna White, senior fiction editor

Parent company: WhiteFire Publishing

Mission statement: Ashberry Lane is a romance line that specializes in "heartfelt stories of faith."

Submissions: Publishes five to ten titles per year; receives 50 submissions annually. First-time authors: 10%. Length: 60,000–110,000 words. Email proposal with sample chapters. Responds in three months.

Royalty: 50% for ebooks, 10% of retail for print, sometimes advance of $500–$2,000

Types and topics: fiction: historical romance, romance, romantic suspense

Types of books: POD

Guidelines: *ashberrylane.com/submissions*

Tip: "Please be familiar with our titles and mission."

ASPIRE PRESS

PO Box 3473, Peabody, MA 01961 | 800-358-3111

LynnettePennings@tyndale.com | *www.hendricksonrose.com*

Lynette Pennings, managing editor

Parent company: Hendrickson Publishing Group/Tyndale House Ministries

Submissions: Agent, conference contact, or *ChristianBookProposals. com.*

Types and topics: Christian living/spirituality, counseling

Tip: Publishes books that are "compassionate in their approach and rich with Scripture," giving "godly insight and counsel for those personally struggling and for believers who have a heart to minister and encourage others." Need credentials in helping others.

AUGSBURG FORTRESS

PO Box 1209, Minneapolis, MN 55440-1209

afsubmissions@1517.media | *www.augsburgfortress.org*

Suzanne Burke, director of development and senior editor

Denomination: Evangelical Lutheran Church in America

Parent company: 1517 Media

Submissions: Email proposal with sample chapters. Responds in 60 days, only if it fits publishing needs.

Types and topics: Bible study, Christian living/spirituality, leadership, worship

Guidelines: *ms.augsburgfortress.org/downloads/Submission%20 Guidelines.pdf*

AVE MARIA PRESS

PO Box 428, Notre Dame, IN 46556 | 800-282-1865, ext. 1

submissions@mail.avemariapress.com | *www.avemariapress.com*

Heidi Hess Saxton, senior acquisitions editor

Denomination: Catholic

Mission statement: to serve the spiritual and educational needs of individuals, groups, and the Church as a whole

Submissions: Publishes 40 titles per year; receives 350 submissions annually. First-time authors: 30%. Length: 20,000–60,000 words. Email or mail proposal with sample chapters. Responds in three to four weeks. Bible: RSV2CE, NABRE.

Royalty: 10%, minimum advance of $1,000

Types and topics: Advent, African-American, Christian living/ spirituality, death and dying, evangelism, faith formation, family, grief, healing, Hispanic, marriage, ministry, parenting, prayer, theology, curriculum, ministry resources, small-group study guides

Types of books: ebook, hardcover, offset paperback

Guidelines: *www.avemariapress.com/manuscript-submissions*

Tip: "Our most successful books identify and address a specific felt-need for a potential reader. We are eager to work with authors who have robust platforms and direct connections to their potential readers. There are a number of areas in which we do not accept unsolicited manuscripts: fiction (for adults or teens), children's books (fiction or nonfiction), poetry, and accounts of personal conversion or private revelation. If your manuscript falls in one of these categories, we advise you to seek a publisher active in your area of interest."

B&H KIDS

1 Lifeway Plaza, Nashville, TN 37023 | 615-251-2000
michelle.freeman@lifeway.com | *www.bhpublishinggroup.com/categories/kids*
Michelle Freeman, publisher
Anna Sargeant, associate publisher, anna.sargeant@lifeway.com

> **Denomination:** Southern Baptist
>
> **Parent company:** B&H Publishing/Lifeway Christian Resources
>
> **Mission statement:** to help kids develop a lifelong relationship with Jesus and to empower parents and church leaders to guide the spiritual growth of the next generation
>
> **Submissions:** Publishes 18–24 titles per year; receives hundreds of submissions annually. First-time authors: 10–20%. Length: depends on age group. Prefers agents. Email proposal with sample chapters or complete manuscript. Responds in one to three months. Bible: CSB. Any book for children or teens with a Christian message. Themes include but are not limited to adventure, attributes of God, Bible-story retellings, biblical virtues, church, community, diversity and inclusion, family, relationships, friendships, prayer, emotions, and theology.
>
> **Royalty:** 18–22%, gives advances
>
> **Types and topics:** Bible stories, board books, children, devotionals, fiction, first-chapter, middle grade, nonfiction, picture books, teen/ YA
>
> **Types of books:** audiobook, board books, ebook, hardcover, offset paperback, picture books
>
> **Tip:** "We are a conservative Christian publishing house that publishes Protestant authors. Note that illustrations for children's books are not necessary or suggested."

B&H PUBLISHING GROUP

1 Lifeway Plaza, Nashville, TN 37234
www.bhpublishinggroup.com
Ashley Gorman, acquisitions and development editor
Mary Wiley, Christian living and leadership

> **Denomination:** Southern Baptist
>
> **Parent company:** LifeWay Christian Resources
>
> **Submissions:** Publishes 90 titles per year; receives thousands of submissions annually. First-time authors: 10%. Agent only. Responds in two to three months. Bible: CSB.
>
> **Royalty:** gives advance

Types and topics: Bible study, Christian living/spirituality, church growth, evangelism, leadership, marriage, parenting, theology, women, worship, academic, Bible reference/commentaries, children

Imprints: B&H Publishing (trade books), B&H Kids (children), B&H Academic (textbooks), Holman Bibles, B&H Español (Spanish)

Tip: "Be informed that the market in general is very crowded with the book you might want to write. Do the research before submitting."

BAKER ACADEMIC

6030 E. Fulton Rd., Ada, MI 49301 | 616-676-9185

submissions@bakeracademic.com | *bakerpublishinggroup.com/bakeracademic*

Robert Hosack, senior acquisitions editor

Anna Moseley Gissing, acquisitions editor

Brandy Scritchfield, acquisitions editor

Parent company: Baker Publishing Group

Submissions: Publishes 50 titles per year. First-time authors: 10%. Agent preferred, conference contact, *ChristianBookProposals.com,* Writers Edge. Email proposal with sample chapters.

Royalty: gives advance

Types and topics: academic, professional

Guidelines: *bakerpublishinggroup.com/bakeracademic/contact/submitting-a-proposal*

BAKER BOOKS

6030 E. Fulton Rd., Ada, MI 49301 | 616-676-9185

bakerpublishinggroup.com/bakerbooks

Rebekah Guzman, editorial director

Brian Vos, senior acquisitions editor

Stephanie Duncan Smith, acquisitions editor

Patnacia Goodman, acquisitions editor

Parent company: Baker Publishing Group

Submissions: Agents or *ChristianBookProposals.com.*

Types and topics: apologetics, biography, business, Christian living/spirituality, church life, culture, family, leadership, marriage, memoir/personal narrative, ministry, parenting, spiritual growth, theology, Bible reference/commentaries

Guidelines: *bakerpublishinggroup.com/contact/submission-policy*

BAKER PUBLISHING GROUP

Baker Academic, Baker Books, Bethany House, Brazos Press, Chosen, Revell

BANNER OF TRUTH

PO Box 621, Carlisle, PA 17013 | 717-249-5747
info@banneroftruth.org | *banneroftruth.org*

Submissions: Email proposal with sample chapters.

Types and topics: biography, Christian living/spirituality, church life, history, ministry, theology, children, commentaries, devotionals

Types of books: ebook, hardcover, offset paperback

Guidelines: *banneroftruth.org/us/about/contact-us/submit-a-manuscript*

Tip: "What makes a Banner book? It must be a book worthy of publication irrespective of its likely commercial success; it must pass theological and doctrinal scrutiny; it must promote practical Christian living; it most likely has enduring application and will be as relevant in 100 years as it is today; it must be well written and carefully edited; it must be well produced."

BARBOUR PUBLISHING, INC.

PO Box 719, Uhrichsville, OH 44683 | 740-922-6045
submissions@barbourbooks.com | *www.barbourbooks.com*
Annie Tipton, senior acquisitions editor
Paul Muckley, senior acquisitions editor, Bible and reference
Rebecca Germany, senior editor and acquisitions, fiction

Mission statement: to inspire the world with the life-changing message of the Bible

Submissions: Agents only.

Types and topics: Christian classics, Christian living/spirituality, Hispanic, activities and puzzles, Bible reference/commentaries, Bible stories, children, devotionals, planners; fiction: Amish, contemporary, historical, romance, suspense/thriller

Imprints: Barbour Books (nonfiction), Barbour Fiction (novels), Barbour Reference, DayMaker (planners), Barbour Young Adult (nonfiction, devotionals), Barbour Kidz (children), Barbour Bibles, Casa Promesa (Spanish)

Guidelines: *www.barbourbooks.com/frequently-asked-questions*

BEAMING BOOKS

510 Marquette Ave., Minneapolis, MN 55403 | 800-960-9705
www.beamingbooks.com
Naomi Krueger, acquisitions editor

Denomination: Evangelical Lutheran Church in America

Parent company: 1517 Media

Submissions: Publishes 24 titles per year; receives 250 submissions annually. First-time authors: 50%. Length: 500 words for picture books. Agents only. Responds in three months. Bible: NIV, CEB. Publishes board books for ages birth–3, picture books for ages 3–8, activity books for ages 3–8, early-reader and first-chapter books for ages 5–9, nonfiction books for ages 5–9 and 8–12, fiction for ages 8–12, activity books for families, devotionals for children ages 0–12 and families.

Royalty: gives advance

Types and topics: activities and puzzles, children, devotionals, fiction, nonfiction

Tip: "Look at what we've published before. Read a few of our books."

BETHANY HOUSE PUBLISHERS

11400 Hampshire Ave. S, Bloomington, MN 55438 | 952-829-2500

bakerpublishinggroup.com/bethanyhouse

Andy McGuire, editorial director

David Long, nonfiction acquisitions editor

Jeff Braun, nonfiction acquisitions editor

Jennifer Dukes Lee, nonfiction acquisitions editor

Jessica Sharpe, fiction acquisitions editor

Rochelle Gloege, fiction acquisitions editor

Parent company: Baker Publishing Group

Mission statement: to publish high-quality writings that represent historical Christianity and serve the diverse interests and concerns of evangelical readers

Submissions: Publishes 75–85 titles per year. Bible: NIV. Agents or conference contact only.

Royalty: varies, gives advance

Types and topics: Christian living/spirituality, family, prayer, relationships, theology, devotionals; fiction: Amish, biblical, contemporary, fantasy, historical, Regency, romance, romantic suspense

Types of books: ebook, hardcover, offset paperback

Tip: "The best opportunities for new authors come via literary agencies, conferences, writing communities, and author referrals. Get connected."

BOLD VISION BOOKS

PO Box 2011, Friendswood, TX 77549-2011 | 832-569-4282

boldvisionbooks@gmail.com | *www.boldvisionbooks.com*

Karen Porter, managing editor

Rhonda Rhea, acquisitions editor, boldvisionbooks@gmail.com

Mission statement: to publish compelling, creative, and beautiful books to change the world and further the message of Christ through the written word

Submissions: Publishes 25 titles per year; receives 150 submissions annually. First-time authors: 85%. Length: 50,000–70,000 words. Email query or proposal with sample chapters. Responds in three to four months. Bible: any.

Royalty: 25–50%, gives advance of $1,000–$5,000

First print run: 2,000–10,000

Types and topics: arts, business, Christian living/spirituality, family, parenting, productivity, speaking, teaching, time management, writing, YA; fiction: adventure, contemporary, historical, humor, mystery, romance, teen/YA

Types of books: ebook, hardcover, offset paperback

Imprints: Nuts 'n Bolts (teaching, writing, speaking, painting, acting, business principles, productivity, time management), Optasia Books (fee-based for beloved pastors)

Guidelines: fiction: *www.boldvisionbooks.com/new-page-1;* nonfiction: *www.boldvisionbooks.com/new-page*

Tip: "To become a successful writer, learn the craft of writing and attend writers conferences and take courses to understand this industry. Keep your message firmly planted in the Word of God. Know your audience and what they need. Read and follow our guidelines, and send a professional proposal. We want to see timeless truth told in fresh creative language."

BRAZOS PRESS

6030 E. Fulton Rd., Ada, MI 49301 | 616-676-9185

submissions@brazospress.com | *bakerpublishinggroup.com/brazospress*

Katelyn Beaty, editorial director

Parent company: Baker Publishing Group

Mission statement: to draw upon the riches of the Christian story to deepen our understanding of God's world and inspire faithful reflection and engagement

Submissions: Authors typically hold advanced degrees and have established publishing platforms. Email proposal with sample chapters.

Types and topics: nonfiction

Guidelines: *bakerpublishinggroup.com/brazospress/submitting-a-proposal*

Tip: "We welcome book proposals from scholars, church leaders, activists, artists, and writers who have something to say and can write with both skill and passion, demonstrating that serious writing can also be lively and compelling."

BRIMSTONE FICTION

1440 W. Taylor St., Ste. 449, Chicago, IL 60607 | 224-339-4159
brimstonefiction@gmail.com | *www.brimstonefiction.com*
Rowena Kuo, CEO and executive editor

Submissions: Publishes 8–12 titles per year; receives 60 submissions annually. First-time authors: 60%. Length: 60,000–100,000 words. Agent or conference contact preferred. Email proposal with sample chapters or complete manuscript. Responds in six to eight weeks. Bible: NIV.

Royalty: 30% of profits, no advance

Types and topics: fiction: adventure, fantasy, historical, romantic suspense, science fiction, speculative, teen/YA, time travel, women's

Types of books: ebook, POD

Guidelines: *brimstonefiction.com/submission-guidelines*

Tip: "We welcome new and multipublished authors and/or authors with or without agents. If you have a good story, come and meet us at writers conferences or through our website."

BROADLEAF BOOKS

PO Box 1209, Minneapolis, MN 55440-1209 | 800-328-4648
submissions@broadleafbooks.com | *broadleafbooks.com*
Lil Copan, senior acquisitions editor
Valerie Weaver-Zercher, acquisitions editor

Denomination: Evangelical Lutheran Church in America

Parent company: 1517 Media

Submissions: Agent preferred or email proposal with sample chapters.

Types and topics: Christian living/spirituality, culture, social justice

Guidelines: *www.broadleafbooks.com/info/submissions*

Tip: "Please note that we receive a large volume of proposals. You will receive a response only if we see your proposal as a potential fit for our program."

BROADSTREET PUBLISHING

8646 Eagle Creek Cir., Ste. 210, Savage, MN 55378 | 855-935-2000

proposals@broadstreetpublishing.com | *www.broadstreetpublishing.com*

Tim Payne, editorial manager

Submissions: Publishes 100+ titles per year. Agents preferred or email proposal with sample chapters.

Types and topics: Bible promises, biography, Christian living/spirituality, coloring books, devotionals, fiction, journals

Imprints: Belle City Gifts (journals and planners)

Guidelines: *broadstreetpublishing.com/contact*

CASCADE BOOKS

199 W. 8th Ave., Ste. 3, Eugene, OR 97401 | 541-344-152

proposal@wipfandstock.com | *wipfandstock.com/search-results-grid/?imprint=cascade-books*

Parent company: Wipf and Stock

Submissions: Email proposal with sample chapters. Responds in one to two months.

Types and topics: religion, theology

Types of books: ebook, POD

Guidelines: *wipfandstock.com/submitting-a-proposal*

CASCADIA PUBLISHING HOUSE

126 Klingerman Rd., Telford, PA 18969

editor@CascadiaPublishingHouse.com | *CascadiaPublishingHouse.com*

Michael A. King, publisher and editor

Submissions: Looking for creative, thought-provoking, Anabaptist-related material. Email or mail query first.

Types and topics: denomination

Imprint: DreamSeeker Books

Guidelines: *www.cascadiapublishinghouse.com/submit.htm*

Tip: "All Cascadia books receive rigorous evaluation and some form of peer or consultant review."

CATHOLIC BOOK PUBLISHING CORP.

77 W. End Rd., Totowa, NJ 07572 | 973-890-2400

info@catholicbookpublishing.com | *www.catholicbookpublishing.com*
Anthony Buono, editor

Denomination: Catholic
Submissions: Mail query first. No simultaneous submissions. Responds in two to three months.
Royalty: negotiable, no advance
Types and topics: Christian living/spirituality, liturgy, prayer
Imprints: Resurrection Press (popular nonfiction)
Guidelines: *catholicbookpublishing.com/page/faq#manuscript*

CHALICE PRESS

483 E. Lockwood Ave., Ste. 100, St. Louis, MO 63119 | 800-366-3383
submissions@chalicepress.com | *chalicepress.com*
Brad Lyons, publisher

Mission statement: to publish resources inviting all people into deeper relationship with God, equipping them as disciples of Jesus Christ, and sending them into ministries as the Holy Spirit calls them
Submissions: Particularly interested in publishing content by and for women, young adults (age 18 to 35), and racial/ethnic cultures for our academic, congregational leadership, and general audiences. Submit through the website.
Types and topics: Christian education, Christian living/spirituality, discipleship, evangelism, leadership, ministry, missions, theology, academic, teen/YA
Guidelines: *chalicepress.com/pages/write-for-us*
Tip: "Our theological tradition is evangelistic (we share with others our experience of God), inclusive (we are guests at a table where everyone is welcome), and mission-oriented (our gratitude to God compels us to serve others)."

CHARISMA MEDIA

600 Rinehart Rd., Lake Mary, FL 32746 | 407-333-0600
Debbie.Marrie@CharismaMedia.com | *www.charismamedia.com*
Debbie Marrie, VP of book acquisitions and content development
Adrienne Gaines, developmental editor, Adrienne.Gaines@CharismaMedia.com

Denomination: Charismatic/Pentecostal
Parent company: Plus Communications, Inc.
Mission statement: to inspire people to encounter the power of the Holy Spirit
Submissions: Publishes 50–60 titles per year; receives 150–200

submissions annually. First-time authors: fewer than 10%. Length: 50,000–60,000 words/224–256 pages. Agents preferred or email proposal with sample chapters. Responds in one month. Bible: MEV.

Royalty: 16–25%, sometimes offers advance

Types and topics: African-American, Christian living/spirituality, end-times prophecy, fitness, health, Hispanic, spiritual warfare

Types of books: audiobook, ebook, hardcover, offset paperback, POD

Imprints: Charisma House (Christian living, Charismatic interest), Siloam (natural health remedies), FrontLine (current events, end-time prophecy)

Tip: "Three key areas we evaluate are the concept, the writing quality, and the author's platform."

CHOSEN

11400 Hampshire Ave. S, Bloomington, MN 55438 | 952-829-2500

bakerpublishinggroup.com/chosen

Kim Bangs, editorial director, kbangs@bakerpublishinggroup.com

David Sluka, senior acquisitions editor, dsluka@chosenbooks.com

Denomination: Charismatic

Parent company: Baker Publishing Group

Mission statement: to publish authors who recognize the gifts and active ministry of the Holy Spirit today

Submissions: Publishes 33 titles per year; receives 200 submissions annually. First-time authors: 45%. Length: 224 pages. Email query first with form from the website. Responds in one month. Bible: any.

Royalty: varies, gives advance sometimes

Types and topics: African-American, Asian, Charismatic, deliverance, dreams, Hispanic, Holy Spirit, prayer, prophecy, revival, spiritual warfare, supernatural, nonfiction

Types of books: audiobook, ebook, hardcover, offset paperback, POD

Guidelines: *bakerpublishinggroup.com/chosen/contact/preparing-a-proposal-for-chosen-books*

Tip: "Have a well-established platform on social media, enewsletter, etc."

CHRISM PRESS

13607 Bedford Rd. NE, Cumberland, MD 21502 | 301-876-4876

submissions@chrismpress.com | *www.chrismpress.com*

Karen Ullo, editor

Rhonda Ortiz, editor

Marisa Stokely, editor

William Gonch, editor

    Parent company: WhiteFire Publishing

    Mission statement: to publish stories informed by Catholic and Orthodox Christianity that may not be able to find a home in either mainstream secular or Christian (evangelical) presses

    Submissions: Publishes 6–12 titles per year; receives 50 submissions annually. First-time authors: 25%. Email query first. Length: 60,000–120,000 words. Responds in three months.

    Royalty: 50% for ebooks, 10% for print, sometimes gives advance

    Types and topics: all fiction, including teen/YA

    Types of books: audiobook, ebook, POD

    Guidelines: *www.chrismpress.com/submissions*

    Tip: "We are acquiring adult and young-adult fiction that reflects a Catholic or Orthodox Christian worldview and appeals to Catholic and/or Orthodox readers. Please read our submissions guidelines and FAQ at *chrismpress.com/submissions*."

CHRISTIAN FOCUS PUBLICATIONS

Geanies House, Fearn, Tain, Ross-shire IV20 1TW, Scotland, UK | 01862871011

submissions@christianfocus.com | *www.christianfocus.com*

Willie MacKenzie, director of publishing

Catherine Mackenzie, children's editor, Catherine.Mackenzie@christianfocus.com

    Submissions: Email or mail proposal with sample chapters.

    Types and topics: biography, Christian living/spirituality, church history, theology, academic, activities and puzzles, Bible reference/commentaries, children, crafts, fiction, game books

    Imprints: Christian Focus (popular adult titles), CF4K (children), Mentor (serious readers), Christian Heritage (classic writings from the past)

    Guidelines: *www.christianfocus.com/about/adult-guidelines;* children's: *www.christianfocus.com/about/childrens-guidelines*

    Tip: "Read our website please. Don't send us stuff we don't publish."

CHURCH PUBLISHING INCORPORATED

19 E. 34th St., New York, NY 10016 | 800-242-1918

astuart@cpg.org | *churchpublishing.org*

Airié Stuart, publisher

    Denomination: Episcopal

    Submissions: Email proposal with sample chapters.

Types and topics: Bible study, biography, counseling, death and dying, finances, leadership, memoir/personal narrative, prayer, social justice, theology, worship

Guidelines: *churchpublishing.org/manuscriptsubmission*

Tip: "CPI's core publishing program is structured around The Book of Common Prayer, The Hymnal 1982, and the specialized books and resources used in the liturgy, faith formation, governance, life, and mission of the Episcopal Church."

CKN CHRISTIAN PUBLISHING

cknchristianpublishing.com

Parent company: Wolfpack Publishing

Mission statement: to publish books that will help readers to rise and develop their understanding of God's Word and to apply it more abundantly to their lives

Submissions: Submit proposal with complete manuscript through the website. Responds in three months.

Royalty: up to 35%

Types and topics: fiction: Amish, historical, mystery, romance, westerns

Types of books: ebook, POD

Guidelines: *cknchristianpublishing.com/christian-manuscript-submissions*

Tip: "We enjoy seeing forgotten books come to life in a new and up-to-date way and watching the success. We will bring the book to life again with a new cover, marketing plan and promotion of the book in the best way we can. We will also work with you if you have a backlist that you have received the rights to."

CLADACH PUBLISHING

PO Box 336144, Greeley, CO 80633 | 970-371-9530

cathyl@cladach.com | *www.cladach.com*

Catherine Lawton, publisher and editor

Christina Slike, assistant editor

Submissions: Publishes four titles per year; receives 50 submissions annually. First-time authors: 50%. Length: 120–300 pages. Conference contact or email query first. Responds in three months. Bible: NIV, NRSV.

Royalty: 10–20%, gives advance of $100

Types and topics: healing, memoir/personal narrative, nature, devotionals, poetry; fiction: frontier, literary

Types of books: audiobook, ebook, offset paperback, POD

Guidelines: *cladach.com/authors*

Tip: "We are accepting very few unsolicited manuscripts."

CLC PUBLICATIONS

PO Box 1449, Fort Washington, PA 19034 | 215-542-1242

submissions@clcpublications.com | www.clcpublications.com

David Fessenden, editorial director

Dan Balow, publisher and acquisitions

Parent company: CLC Ministries International

Mission statement: to make evangelical Christian literature available to all nations so that people may come to faith and maturity in the Lord Jesus Christ

Submissions: Publishes 6–12 titles per year; receives 60 submissions annually. First-time authors: 30%. Agent preferred or email proposal with sample chapters through the website. Length: 20,000–80,000 words. Responds in one to three months. Bible: ESV.

Royalty: 12–16%, sometimes gives advance

Types and topics: Christian living/spirituality

Types of books: audiobook, ebook, offset paperback

Guidelines: *www.clcpublications.com/about/prospective-authors-submissions*

Tip: "Try to be both succinct and complete in your submission."

COLLEGE PRESS PUBLISHING

PO Box 1132, Joplin, MO 64801 | 800-289-3300

collpressbooks@gmail.com | www.collegepress.com

Denomination: Church of Christ

Submissions: Email proposal with sample chapters. Responds in two to three months.

Types and topics: apologetics, biography, Christian living/spirituality, academic, Bible reference/commentaries, Bible studies

Guidelines: *www.collegepress.com/pages/for-authors*

CONVERGENT BOOKS

1745 Broadway, New York, NY 10019 | 212-366-2724

kbaltzer@penguinrandomhouse.com | crownpublishing.com/archives/imprint/convergent-books

Keren Baltzer, VP, editorial director

Derek Reed, executive editor, dreed@penguinrandomhouse.com

*Becky Nesbitt, editorial director and executive editor, bnesbitt@
penguinrandomhouse.com*

Matthew Burdette, associate editor, mburdette@penguinrandomhouse.com

Parent company: Penguin Random House/The Crown Publishing Group

Mission statement: to seek out diverse viewpoints and honest conversations that shed light on the defining challenges facing people of faith today; to help readers ask important questions, find paths forward in disagreement, and shape the way faith is expressed in the modern world

Submissions: Publishes 12–16 titles per year; receives 100–150 submissions annually. First-time authors: 10%. Length: 204–300 pages, 45,000–65,000 words. Agent preferred or email proposal with sample chapters. Responds in a few weeks to two months. Bible: NIV, ESV.

Royalty: 10–15%, gives advance of $10,000–high six figures

Types and topics: African-American, Asian, Christian living/spirituality, deconstruction/reconstruction of faith, friendship, Hispanic, marriage, memoir/personal narrative, parenting, self-help, social issues, social justice, wellness, essays

Types of books: audiobook, ebook, hardcover, offset paperback

Tip: "Have a good agent and a good platform."

CROSSLINK PUBLISHING

1601 Mt. Rushmore Rd., Ste. 3288, Rapid City, SD 57701 | 888-697-4851

publisher@crosslink.org | www.crosslinkpublishing.com

Rick Bates, managing editor

Parent company: CrossLink Ministries

Submissions: Publishes 35 titles per year; receives 500 submissions annually. First-time authors: 85%. Length: 12,000–60,000 words. Submit through the website. Responds in one week.

Royalty: 10%, 20% for ebooks, no advance

First print run: 2,000

Types and topics: Christian living/spirituality, Bible studies, children, devotionals, fiction

Imprint: New Harbor Press

Guidelines: *www.crosslinkpublishing.com/submit-a-manuscript*

Tip: "We are particularly interested in providing books that help Christians succeed in their daily walk (inspirational, devotional, small groups, etc.)."

CROSSRIVER MEDIA GROUP

4810 Gene Field Rd. #2, St. Joseph, MO 64506 | 816-752-2171
deb@crossrivermedia.com | *www.crossrivermedia.com*
Debra L. Butterfield, editorial director

Mission statement: to publish high-quality books and materials that help women build a battle-ready faith

Submissions: Publishes four to eight titles per year; receives 60–75 submissions annually. First-time authors: 30–40%. Length: 50,000–80,000 words. Conference contact or email proposal with sample chapters through the website. Responds in 12–16 weeks. Bible: any except NIV.

Royalty: 8–12%, no advance

Types and topics: Bible study, Christian living/spirituality, family, inspirational, marriage; fiction: biblical, contemporary, historical, mystery, romance

Types of books: ebook, hardcover, POD

Guidelines: *www.crossrivermedia.com/guidelines*

Tip: "Read our website and follow the proposal guidelines."

CROSSWAY

1300 Crescent St., Wheaton, IL 60187 | 630-682-4300
submissions@crossway.org | *www.crossway.org*
Todd Augustine, director of acquisitions

Parent company: Good News Publishers

Mission statement: to publish gospel-centered, Bible-centered content that will honor our Savior and serve his Church. We seek to help people understand the massive implications of the gospel and the truth of God's Word, for all of life, for all eternity, and for the glory of God.

Submissions: Publishes 100 titles per year; receives 500 submissions annually. First-time authors: 1%. Length: 35,000 words minimum. Email query first. Responds in six to eight weeks if interested. Bible: ESV.

Royalty: varies, advance varies

First print run: varies

Types and topics: Bible study, Christian living/spirituality, contemporary issues, academic, Bible reference/commentaries

Types of books: audiobook, ebook, hardcover, offset paperback, POD

Guidelines: *www.crossway.org/submissions*

Tip: "A well-written, concise query is an essential component to create interest in your book. Be sure your book fits within the types of books Crossway publishes."

CSS PUBLISHING COMPANY, INC.

5450 N. Dixie Hwy., Lima, OH 45807-9559 | 419-227-1818

editor@csspub.com | www.csspub.com

David Runk, publisher

Mission statement: to help Protestant pastors and lay leaders share the Good News of Jesus Christ

Submissions: Publishes 20 titles per year; receives 50 submissions annually. First-time authors: 10%. Length: 80–240 pages, depending on subject matter. Email or mail proposal with sample chapters or complete manuscript. Responds in six months. Bible: NRSV, NIV, RSV, ESV, TLB.

Royalty: 7–10%, no advance, $350–500 for sermon books

Types and topics: Christian education, ministry, preaching, stewardship, worship, Bible studies, church resources, drama, ministry resources, sermons

Types of books: ebook, POD

Guidelines: *store.csspub.com/page.php?Custom%20Pages=10*

Tip: "Use solid biblical research."

DAVID C. COOK

4050 Lee Vance Dr., Colorado Springs, CO 80918 | 719-536-0100

www.davidccook.org

Michael Covington, VP of publishing and acquisitions for pastors and leaders

Susan McPherson, acquisitions, women and leadership

Stephanie Bennett, acquisitions, students and youth

Luke McKinnon, acquisitions, apologetics and worldview

Laura Derico, acquisitions, children's

Mission statement: to equip the Church with Christ-centered resources for making and teaching disciples

Submissions: Publishes 40 titles per year; receives 1,200 submissions annually. First-time authors: 10%. Length: 45,000–50,000 words. Agent only or conference contact. Responds in one month.

Royalty: 12–22%, advance varies

Types and topics: Christian living/spirituality, discipleship, family, leadership, marriage, men, parenting, women, Bible reference/ commentaries, Bible studies, church resources, devotionals, teen/YA

Types of books: ebook, hardcover, offset paperback, POD

Imprints: Esther Press (women)

Guidelines: *shop.davidccook.org/pages/frequently-asked-questions*

Tip: "We look for significant platform, excellent writing, and relevant content."

DOVE CHRISTIAN PUBLISHERS

PO Box 611, Bladensburg, MD 20710 | 240-342-3293

editorial@dovechristianpublishers.com | *www.dovechristianpublishers.com*

Raenita Wiggins, acquisitions editor

Parent company: Kingdom Christian Enterprises

Mission statement: to entertain, edify, equip, and encourage people through products that glorify and honor Jesus Christ and His kingdom and to provide new and emerging Christian authors with a forum for their creative and Kingdom-building voices

Submissions: Publishes ten titles per year; receives 300 submissions annually. First-time authors: 95%. Length: 100–220 pages. Submit proposal with sample chapters through the website. Responds in four to six weeks. Bible: NIV.

Royalty: 10–25%, no advance

Types and topics: Christian living/spirituality, church life, discipleship, ministry, prayer, Bible studies, children, devotionals; fiction: fantasy, historical, humor, mystery, romance, science fiction, suspense/ thriller

Types of books: ebook, hardcover, POD

Guidelines: *www.dovechristianpublishers.com/publish-with-us*

Tip: "Author should establish a platform and familiarize themselves with book marketing and promotion prior to submission."

EERDMANS BOOKS FOR YOUNG READERS

4035 Park East Ct. SE, Grand Rapids, MI 49546 | 800-253-7521

kmerz@eerdmans.com | *www.eerdmans.com/youngreaders*

Kathleen Merz, editorial director

Courtney Zonnefeld, assistant editor

Parent company: Wm. B. Eerdmans Publishing Co.

Mission statement: to engage young minds with books—books that are honest, wise, and hopeful; books that delight us with their storyline, characters, or good humor; books that inform, inspire, and entertain

Submissions: Publishes 12–18 titles per year; receives 1,500 submissions annually. First-time authors: 5–10%. Length: picture books, 1,000 words; middle-grade books, 15,000–30,000 words. Mail proposal with sample chapters or complete manuscript. Responds in four months if interested.

Royalty: gives advance

Types and topics: African-American, animals, history, multicultural, nature, social issues, humor, middle grade, picture books, teen/YA

Types of books: audiobook, ebook, hardcover

Guidelines: *www.eerdmans.com/Pages/Item/2237/EBYR-Guidelines. aspx*

Tip: "We are always looking for well-written picture books and novels for young readers. Make sure that your submission is a unique, well-crafted story, and take a look at our current list of titles to get a sense of whether yours would be a good fit for us."

WM. B. EERDMANS PUBLISHING CO.

4035 Park East Ct. SE, Grand Rapids, MI 49546 | 800-253-7521

submissions@eerdmans.com | *www.eerdmans.com*

Andrew Knapp, acquisitions editor

Lisa Ann Cockrel, acquisitions editor

Submissions: Publishes 100 titles per year. Email proposal with sample chapters or complete manuscript. Responds in two months.

Royalty: gives advance sometimes

Types and topics: biography, Christian living/spirituality, contemporary issues, ethics, history, ministry, theology, academic, Bible reference/commentaries

Imprints: Eerdmans Books for Young Readers (children and teens)

Guidelines: *www.eerdmans.com/Pages/Item/2068/Submission-Guidelines.aspx*

Tip: "Review submission guidelines carefully and check recent catalogs for suitability. Target readerships range from academic to semipopular. We are publishing a growing number of books in Christian life, spirituality, and ministry."

ELK LAKE PUBLISHING, INC.

35 Dogwood Dr., Plymouth, MA 02360-3166 | 508-746-1734

Deb@ElkLakePublishingInc.com | *ElkLakePublishingInc.com*

Deb Haggerty, publisher and editor in chief

Les Stobbe, acquisitions editor, lhstobbe123@gmail.com

Mission statement: to captivate our readers and carry them to places of escape, encouragement, education, and entertainment—to broaden their horizons and urge them to new heights

Submissions: Publishes 70–100 titles per year; receives 350 submissions annually. First-time authors: 60%. Length: fiction, 80,000–90,000 words, 300 pages; speculative fiction, 80,000–130,000 words; nonfiction, 40,000–60,000 words. Agent preferred, conference contact, or email proposal with sample chapters through the website. Responds in two weeks or less. Bible: NASB, NLT.

Royalty: 40%, no advance

Types and topics: Bible study, Christian living/spirituality, middle grade, YA; fiction: contemporary, juvenile, mystery, speculative, suspense, women's

Types of books: audiobook, ebook, hardcover, POD

Guidelines: *tinyurl.com/2s3zyuyb*

Tip: Submit "letter perfect proposals, well-edited manuscripts."

EMANATE BOOKS

PO Box 141000, Nashville, TN 37214-1000 | 615-889-9000
Janene.MacIvor@harpercollins.com | *www.thomasnelson.com/emanatebooks*
Janene MacIvor, senior editor

Parent company: Thomas Nelson Publishers/HarperCollins Christian Publishing

Mission statement: to reflect the work of the Holy Spirit, feed His church, and help a new generation hear from God and grow in their spiritual journey

Submission: Agents only or conference contact.

Types and topics: Christian classics, nonfiction

Types of books: audiobook, ebook, hardcover, offset paperback

ENCLAVE PUBLISHING

24 W. Camelback Rd. A-635, Phoenix, AZ 85013
acquisitions@enclavepublishing.com | *www.enclavepublishing.com*
Steve Laube, publisher and acquisitions editor

Parent company: Oasis Family Media

Mission statement: to publish out-of-this-world stories that are informed by a coherent theology

Submissions: Publishes 12–18 titles per year; receives 200

submissions annually. First-time authors: 20–30%. Length: 80,000–140,000 words. Conference contact, author referral, or submit proposal with sample chapters through the website. Responds in 60–90 days.

Royalty: industry standard, no advance

First print run: 2,000–5,000

Types and topics: fiction: allegory, fantasy, science fiction, speculative, supernatural

Types of books: audiobook, ebook, hardcover, offset paperback

Imprint: Enclave Escape (YA)

Guidelines: *www.enclavepublishing.com/guidelines*

Tip: "Keep word count above 80,000 words and below 140,000. Too often we are sent books that are either far too short or extremely long."

END GAME PRESS

PO Box 206, Nesbit, MS 38651 | 901-590-6584

hope@endgamepress.com | *www.endgamepress.com*

Hope Bolinger, managing and acquisitions editor

Michelle Medlock Adams, children's acquisitions

Mission statement: to leverage all of its resources to make the greatest positive impact possible by holding a high standard for the books it publishes in both design and quality, while also making the experience a good one for each of the authors in the End Game Press family

Submissions: Publishes 20 titles per year; receives 300 submissions annually. First-time authors: 25%. Agent only or conference contact. Then email proposal with sample chapters. Length: depends on the genre. Responds in two to three months. Bible: any.

Royalty: 20–25%, advance

Types and topics: Christian living/spirituality, faith, marriage, parenting, prayer, board books, fiction, middle grade, picture books, teen/YA

Types of books: audiobook, ebook, hardcover

Imprint: Wren and Bear Books (children and YA)

Guidelines: *www.endgamepress.com/submissions*

Tip: "Make a personal connection and have a clean manuscript/proposal with well-thought-out marketing ideas."

EXEGETICA PUBLISHING

312 Greenwich #112, Lee's Summit, MO 64082 | 816-269-8505

editor@exegeticapublishing.com | *www.exegeticapublishing.com*

Mission statement: to encourage Christians and non-Christians alike to engage with the Bible, to understand the world around them, and to "taste and see that the Lord is good," as Psalm 34:8 exhorts

Submissions: Publishes ten titles per year; receives 30 submissions annually. First-time authors: 10%. Length: 200–300 pages. Email proposal with sample chapters. Responds in three to four weeks. Bible: NASB, NKJV, ESV.

Royalty: 10%, no advance

Types and topics: Bible, Christian living/spirituality, theology, academic, nonfiction

Types of books: ebook, offset paperback

Imprint: Grace Acres Press

Guidelines: *exegeticapublishing.com/submit-a-proposal*

Tip: "Follow submission guidelines with solid biblical resources."

EXPANSE BOOKS

15 Lucky Ln., Morrilton, AR 72110 | 501-548-2736

expansebooks@gmail.com | *expansebooks.pub*

Erin R. Howard, acquisitions editor

Parent company: Scrivenings Press, LLC

Submissions: Length: 50,000–100,000 words. Submit through the website. Responds in four to six weeks.

Royalty: 12%, 50% ebook, 40% pages read in Kindle Unlimited, no advance

Types and topics: fiction: speculative

Types of books: ebook, POD, hardcover

Guidelines: *expansebooks.pub/submissions*

Tip: "We only accept proposals for *clean* fiction. No sexual content, foul language (including euphemisms), crudeness, vulgarity, abuse, or graphic violence will be permitted in our books. Stories do not have to include a religious theme or content; but if they do, we will not accept proposals for books that are 'preachy' in nature. Stories that do include a religious theme must be nondenominational so that anyone who embraces a Christian worldview can enjoy them."

FAITHWORDS

1 Franklin Park, 6100 Tower Cir., Ste. 210, Franklin, TN 37067 | 615-221-0996

www.faithwords.com

Beth Adams, acquisitions editor
Sean McGowan, editor and acquisitions
India Hunter, associate editor and acquisitions
> **Parent company:** Hachette Book Group
> **Submissions:** Agents only.
> **Royalty:** minimum 10%, gives advance
> **Types and topics:** African-American, Christian living/spirituality, Hispanic, marriage, parenting, social issues
> **Types of books:** ebook, hardcover, offset paperback
> **Tip:** "Have a clear, well-written proposal and a solid platform."

FIRST STEPS PUBLISHING
PO Box 571, Gleneden Beach, OR 97388 | 541-961-7641
publish@firststepspublishing.com | *www.FirstStepsPublishing.com*
Suzanne Fyhrie Parrott, publisher
> **Submissions:** Publishes three to five titles per year. Agents only.
> **Types and topics:** fiction: adventure, historical, mystery, suspense/thriller
> **Guidelines:** *www.firststepspublishing.com/get-published*
> **Tip:** "We are looking for well-written books by new authors, taking them from raw manuscript to well-marketed and designed masterpieces people want to read."

FLYAWAY BOOKS
100 Witherspoon St., Louisville, KY 40202-1396
submissions@flyawaybooks.com | *www.flyawaybooks.com*
Jessica Miller Kelley, acquisitions editor
> **Denomination:** Presbyterian
> **Parent company:** Westminster John Knox Press/Presbyterian Publishing Corporation
> **Submissions:** Email proposal with complete manuscript. Responds in six weeks or not interested.
> **Types and topics:** picture books
> **Types of books:** picture books
> **Guidelines:** *www.flyawaybooks.com/submissions*
> **Tip:** "Flyaway Books embraces diversity, inclusivity, compassion, care for each other, and care for our world. Many of our books explore social justice and other contemporary issues. Some retell familiar religious stories in new ways, while others carry universal themes appealing to those with any, or no, religious background."

FOCUS ON THE FAMILY

8605 Explorer Dr., Colorado Springs, CO 80995 | 719-531-5181

www.focusonthefamily.com

Larry Weeden, editor in chief

> **Submissions:** Agents only, *ChristianBookProposals.com*, Writers Edge.
> **Types and topics:** family, marriage, parenting
> **Types of books:** ebook, hardcover, offset paperback
> **Other Information:** Books are published by Tyndale House Publishers.

FORTRESS PRESS

PO Box 1209, Minneapolis, MN 55440-1209

gaedel@fortresspress.com | *www.fortresspress.com*

Beth Gaede, senior acquisitions editor, professional and ministry resources

Ryan Hemmer, acquisitions editor, theology, culture, biblical studies, ethics, and philosophy, hemmerr@fortresspress.com

Yvonne D. Hawkins, acquisitions editor, ministry, hawkinsy@fortresspress.com

Laura Gifford, acquisitions editor, ministry, giffordl@fortresspress.com

Bethany Dickerson, associate acquisitions editor, theology, culture, literature, religious history, and biblical studies, dickersonb@fortresspress.com

> **Denomination:** Evangelical Lutheran Church in America
> **Parent company:** 1517 Media
> **Submissions:** Email proposal with sample chapters.
> **Types and topics:** Bible study, Christian living/spirituality, culture, history, ministry, social justice, theology, academic, Bible reference/ commentaries
> **Types of books:** hardcover, offset paperback
> **Guidelines:** *www.fortresspress.com/info/submissions*

FORWARD MOVEMENT

412 Sycamore St., Cincinnati, OH 45202-4110 | 800-543-1813

editorial@forwardmovement.org | *www.forwardmovement.org*

Richelle Thompson, managing editor

> **Denomination:** Episcopal
> **Mission statement:** to offer resources that strengthen and support discipleship and evangelism
> **Submissions:** Email proposal with sample chapters. Responds in four to six weeks.
> **Types and topics:** Bible study, discipleship, evangelism, leadership, prayer

Types of books: ebook, offset paperback

Guidelines: *www.forwardmovement.org/Pages/About/Writers-Guidelines.aspx*

THE FOUNDRY PUBLISHING

PO Box 419527, Kansas City, MO 64141 | 800-877-0700

RMcFarland@thefoundrypublishing.com | *www.thefoundrypublishing.com*

René McFarland, submissions editor

Bonnie Perry, editorial director

Denomination: Nazarene

Mission statement: to empower people with life-changing ways to engage in the mission of God

Submissions: Email proposal with sample chapters. Responds in two months.

Types and topics: Christian living/spirituality, ministry

Guidelines: *www.thefoundrypublishing.com/book-manuscript-submission-faqs.html*

Tip: "Because we are a denominational publisher of holiness literature, our books reflect an evangelical Wesleyan stance in accord with the Church of the Nazarene. We seek practical as well as serious treatments of issues of faith consistent with the Wesleyan tradition."

FOUR CRAFTSMEN PUBLISHING

PO Box U, Lakeside, AZ 85929-0585 | 928-367-2076

info@fourcraftsmen.com | *www.fourcraftsmen.com*

CeCelia Jackson, editor in chief

Mission statement: to publish truth that works for Christian readers

Submissions: Publishes four to six titles per year; receives five submissions annually. First-time authors: 100%. Length: 40,000–80,000 words. Email or mail proposal with sample chapters or complete manuscript. Responds in two weeks. Bible: NASB, NKJV, TLB, TEV.

Royalty: 10% print, 50–60% ebook, no advance

First print run: 500

Types and topics: Bible study, Christian living/spirituality, finances, spiritual warfare, testimony

Types of books: ebook, hardcover, offset paperback, POD

Guidelines: *fourcraftsmen.com/additional-info*

Tip: "Original work, not compilation of source quotes. Necessary quotes correctly attributed and permissions provided."

FRANCISCAN MEDIA

28 W. Liberty St., Cincinnati, OH 45202 | 513-241-5615
proposal@FranciscanMedia.org | *www.FranciscanMedia.org*
Christopher Heffron, editorial director

Denomination: Catholic
Submissions: Publishes 20–30 titles per year. Email proposal with sample chapters. Responds in six to eight weeks. Bible: NRSV. Seeks manuscripts that inform and inspire adult Catholics, other Christians, and all who are seeking to better understand and live their faith. Goal is to help people "Live in love. Grow in faith."
Royalty: 10–14%, advance of $1,000–$3,000
Types and topics: Christian living/spirituality, spiritual growth, fiction
Guidelines: *www.franciscanmedia.org/writers-guidelines*
Tip: "Special consideration will be given to book proposals that show how the book relates to one or more of the teachings of St. Francis or the Franciscan charism."

FREE GRACE PRESS

815 Exchange Ave., Ste. 101, Conway, AR 72034 | 501-214-9663
submissions@freegracepress.com | *www.freegracepress.com*
Liz Smith, managing editor

Denomination: Reformed Baptist
Mission statement: to glorify God by assisting others in obtaining a deeper knowledge and a greater enjoyment of the Lord Jesus Christ
Submissions: Publishes 24 titles per year; receives 20 submissions annually. First-time authors: 50%. Length: 50,000–75,000 words. Email proposal with sample chapters. No agents. Responds in two months. Bible: ESV.
Royalty: 12%, no advance
Types and topics: Christian living/spirituality, ministry, theology
Types of books: ebook, hardcover, offset paperback, POD
Tip: "Authors should generally have a social-media presence and be willing to market their book on their various platforms."

GOOD & TRUE MEDIA

1520 S. York Rd., Gastonia, NC 28053 | 704-865-1256
info@goodwillpublishers.com | *www.goodwillpublishers.com*
Fred Gallagher, editor in chief

Parent company: Good Will Publishers

Mission statement: Guiding principles: Educate the Imagination; Move the Heart; Deepen the Mind; Strengthen the Soul.
Submissions: Publishes 10–20 titles per year.
Types and topics: children, picture books
Tip: Looking for books that "have a strong moral foundation and will also foster virtue in children while entertaining them and nurturing their imagination."

THE GOOD BOOK COMPANY

1805 Sardis Rd. N, Ste. 102, Charlotte, NC 28270 | 866-244-2165
submissions@thegoodbook.com | *www.thegoodbook.com*
Brian Thomasson, VP of editorial

Mission statement: to promote, encourage, and equip people to serve our Lord and Master Jesus Christ
Submissions: Email or mail proposal with sample chapters.
Types and topics: Bible study, Christian living/spirituality, evangelism, children, devotionals, teen/YA
Guidelines: *www.thegoodbook.com/authors*
Tip: "Our aim with all our resources is to get people directly interacting with the Bible. So we expect our authors to facilitate that process, rather than just commenting on their own view of what the Bible says. A primary question we ask of any resource submitted to us is: Does it handle the Bible well (i.e., taking note of the context of each passage), and is it helping people understand its message?"

GRACE ACRES PRESS

PO Box 22, Larkspur, CO 80118 | 303-681-9995
Anne@graceacrespress.com | *www.GraceAcresPress.com*
Anne R. Fenske, publisher

Parent company: Exegetica Publishing
Mission statement: to grow your faith one page at a time
Submissions: Publishes six titles per year; receives 20 submissions annually. First-time authors: 75%. Length: 100–300 pages. Email or mail query first. Responds in one month. Bible: NKJV, NIV.
Royalty: 10–15%, no advance
First print run: 500–2,000
Types and topics: Bible study, biography, discipleship, evangelism, missions, nonfiction
Types of books: ebook, hardcover, offset paperback, POD
Tip: "Explain your contribution as a copartner in marketing your book."

GRACE PUBLISHING

PO Box 1233, Broken Arrow, OK 74013-1233 | 918-346-7960
editorial@grace-publishing.com | *www.grace-publishing.com*
Terri Kalfas, publisher

Mission statement: to develop and distribute—with integrity and excellence—biblically based resources that challenge, encourage, teach, equip, and entertain Christians young and old in their personal journeys

Submissions: Publishes four to eight titles per year; receives 75 submissions annually. First-time authors: 10–20%. Length: 40,000–60,000 words. Conference contact or email or mail query or proposal with sample chapters. Responds in three to six months. Bible: any.

Royalty: varies, sometimes give variable advance

Types and topics: Bible study, Christian living/spirituality, anthologies, Bible studies, nonfiction

Types of books: ebook, POD

Imprint: Jomaga House (Christian worldview but not necessarily overtly Christian)

Guidelines: *grace-publishing.com/manuscript-submission*

Tip: "We're looking for material that is presented in a manner relevant to today's Christian without going outside the boundaries of orthodox Christianity. No fluff."

GROUP PUBLISHING, INC.

1515 Cascade Ave., Loveland, CO 80538 | 970-669-3836
submissions@group.com | *www.group.com*

Mission statement: to create experiences that help people grow in relationship with Jesus and each other

Submissions: Publishes 30 titles per year; receives 200 submissions annually. First-time authors: 10%. Length: 128–250 pages. Email or mail proposal with sample chapters. Responds in three months. Bible: NLT.

Royalty: 8–10%, sometimes gives advance of $2,000

First print run: 3,000

Types and topics: Christian education, family, leadership, parenting, activities and puzzles, church resources, curriculum

Types of books: ebook, hardcover, offset paperback

Guidelines: *grouppublishingps.zendesk.com/hc/en-us/articles/211878258-Submissions*

Tip: "Most open to a practical resource that will help church leaders change lives; innovative, active/interactive learning. Tell our readers something they don't already know, in a way that they've not seen before."

GUIDEPOSTS BOOKS

110 William St., Ste. 901, New York, NY 10038 | 212-251-8100
bookeditors@guideposts.org | www.guideposts.org
Jane Haertel, fiction editor, jhaertel@guideposts.org
Carolyn Mandarano, devotional auditions, nonfiction needs, cmandarano@ guideposts.org
Tarice Gray, acquisitions, devotionals, TGray@guideposts.org

Submissions: Publishes 20–30 titles per year. Agents only.
Types and topics: Christian living/spirituality, memoir/personal narrative, devotionals; fiction: contemporary, women's
Tip: "For new Guideposts writers, devotionals require an audition by sending in three sample devotions. We select only a few new writers each year. Contributors write on a work-for-hire basis. Guideposts holds the copyright. For more information or to submit devotional auditions, please email Carolyn Mandarano."

HARBOURLIGHT BOOKS

PO Box 1738, Aztec, NM 87410
customer@harbourlightbooks.com | www.pelicanbookgroup.com
Nicola Martinez, editor-in-chief

Parent company: Pelican Book Group
Mission statement: to publish quality books that reflect the salvation and love offered by Jesus Christ
Submissions: Length: 25,000–80,000 words. Submit through the website. Responds in three to four months. Bible: NIV, NAB.
Royalty: 40% on download, 7% on print, sometimes gives advance
Types and topics: fiction: adventure, crime, family saga, mystery, suspense, westerns, women's
Types of books: audiobook, ebook, hardcover, offset paperback, POD
Guidelines: *tinyurl.com/22zruzzw*

HARPERCHRISTIAN RESOURCES

501 Nelson Pl., Nashville, TN 37214
www.harperchristianresources.com

Parent company: HarperCollins Christian Publishing
Mission statement: to equip people to understand the Scriptures, cultivate spiritual growth, and live an inspired faith with Bible study and video resources from today's most trusted voices
Submissions: Agents only.
Types and topics: Bible studies, ministry programs, small-group study guides
Types of books: offset paperback, video

HARPERCOLLINS CHRISTIAN PUBLISHING

HarperChristian Resources

Thomas Nelson: Emanate Books, Nelson Books, Thomas Nelson Fiction, Thomas Nelson Gift, Tommy Nelson, W Publishing Group

Zondervan: Zonderkidz, Zondervan, Zondervan Academic, Zondervan Fiction, Zondervan Gift, Zondervan Reflective

HARPERONE

353 Sacramento St. #500, San Francisco, CA 94111-3653 | 415-477-4400

gideon.weil@harpercollins.com | *harperone.com*
Gideon Weil, editorial director

Parent company: HarperCollins Publishing
Mission statement: to publish books for the world we want to live in
Submissions: Publishes 75 titles per year; receives 10,000 submissions annually. First-time authors: 5%. Length: 160–256 pages. Agents only. Responds in three months.
Royalty: 7.5–15%, gives advance
Types and topics: Christian living/spirituality, nonfiction
Types of books: ebook, hardcover, offset paperback
Imprint: Shelf-Seekers (millennials)

HARVEST HOUSE PUBLISHERS

PO Box 41210, Eugene, OR 97404-0322 | 800-547-8979
harvesthousepublishers.com
Steve Miller, acquisitions editor, nonfiction
Ruth Samsel, acquisitions editor, gifts
Kyle Hatfield, acquisitions editor, children and family
Emma Saisslin, acquisitions editor, nonfiction

Submissions: Agents only, *ChristianBookProposals.com,* or Writers Edge.

Types and topics: Christian living/spirituality, family, relationships, Bible reference/commentaries, Bible studies, children, gift

Imprint: Harvest Kids (children)

HENDRICKSON PUBLISHERS

PO Box 3473, Peabody, MA 01961-3473 | 800-358-3111

panders@tyndale.com | *www.hendricksonrose.com*

Patricia Anders, editorial director

Parent company: Tyndale House Ministries

Mission statement: to meet the publication needs of the religious studies academic community worldwide and to produce thoughtful books for thoughtful Christians

Submissions: Publishes 16 titles per year; receives 50–100 submissions annually. First-time authors: 40%. Length: trade, 75,000–100,000 words; academic, 100,000–200,000 words. Agent only or conference contact. Responds in two to three months.

Royalty: 12–14%, sometimes gives advance

First print run: varies

Types and topics: archaeology, church history, culture, marriage, ministry, parenting, theology, academic, Bible reference/ commentaries, biblical studies, language studies

Types of books: audiobook, ebook, hardcover, offset paperback

Imprints: Hendrickson Publishers (trade books), Hendrickson Academic (academic), Rose Publishing (Bible reference for everyone), RoseKidz (children), Aspire Press (counseling), Hendrickson Bibles (Bibles)

Tip: "Please be sure to look at our website to see what kind of books we publish."

INTERVARSITY PRESS

430 Plaza Dr., Westmont, IL 60559 | 630-734-4000

mail@ivpress.com | *ivpress.com*

Al Hsu, senior editor and acquisitions

Ethan McCarthy, editorial assistant and acquisitions

Jon Boyd editorial director, IVP Academic

Elissa Schauer, managing editor and IVP Kids editor

Parent company: InterVarsity Christian Fellowship

Mission statement: to publish thoughtful Christian books that shape both the lives of readers and the cultures they inhabit, speaking boldly into important cultural moments, providing timeless tools for spiritual growth, and equipping Christians for a vibrant life of faith

Submissions: Publishes 100 titles per year; receives 800 submissions annually. First-time authors: 20%. Length: 30,000–1000,000 words. Agent only or conference contact. Responds in three months. Bible: NIV.

Royalty: 14–18%, sometimes gives advance

Types and topics: African-American, Asian, Bible study, Christian living/spirituality, church leadership, Hispanic, spiritual formation, theology, academic, Bible reference/commentaries, Bible studies, children

Types of books: audiobook, ebook, hardcover, offset paperback, POD

Imprints: IVP Academic (undergraduate and graduate students, professors, scholars), IVP Formatio (spiritual formation), IVP Praxis (church leadership), IVP Kids (children)

Tip: "We accept submissions only from agents or from authors who have had direct contact with an editor."

IRON STREAM MEDIA

100 Missionary Ridge, Birmingham, AL 35242 | 888-811-9934
submissions@ironstreammedia.com | *www.ironstreammedia.com*

Submissions: Publishes 20–25 titles per year; receives 150 submissions annually. First-time authors: 30%. Length: 50,000–90,000 words. Agents preferred, conference contact, or email proposal with sample chapters. Responds in three months. Bible: NASB.

Royalty: escalating, gives advance

Types and topics: African-American, Christian living/spirituality, family, leadership, memoir/personal narrative, parenting, relationships, women, Bible studies, devotionals; fiction: romance, romantic suspense, speculative, suspense, westerns

Types of books: audiobook, ebook, offset paperback, POD

Imprints: Iron Stream (nonfiction), Iron Stream Fiction (novels), Iron Stream Kids (board and picture books, Bible storybooks), Harambee Press (books that feature diversity), Brookstone Publishing Group (independent publishing), Life Bible Study (digital Bible study curriculum direct to churches)

Guidelines: *www.ironstreammedia.com/submission-process*

Tip: "Focus on hook, comps, and marketing sections in book proposal. Also, provide a great list of influencers."

JOURNEYFORTH

1700 Wade Hampton Blvd., Greenville, SC 29614 | 864-546-4600

journeyforth@bju.edu | www.bjupress.com/books/journeyforth

Charlotte Bradley, acquisitions editor

- **Parent company:** BJU Press/Bob Jones University
- **Mission statement:** to provide well-written, biblically sound resources for readers of varying reading abilities and interests— books with a Christian worldview and excellent in every facet of their presentation
- **Submissions:** Publishes two to five titles per year; receives 100–150 submissions annually. First-time authors: 45%. Length: ages 6–8, 8,000 to 10,000 words; ages 9–12, 30,000 to 40,000 words; ages 12 and up, 40,000 to 60,000 words. Email or mail proposal with sample chapters. Responds in four to six months. Bible: KJV, NKJV, ESV, NASB.
- **Royalty:** 10–15%, sometimes gives variable advance
- **Types and topics:** Bible study, Christian living/spirituality, youth fiction, Bible studies, first-chapter, middle grade, teen/YA
- **Types of books:** ebook, offset paperback
- **Guidelines:** *www.bjupress.com/books/freelance.php*
- **Tip:** "We use in-house authors for short stories, picture books, rhyming text, and poetry. Our market is not open to stories that include profanity or minced oaths, magic or witchcraft, time travel, and characters who engage in unscriptural activities without a biblical consequence."

JUDSON PRESS

1075 First Ave., King of Prussia, PA 19406 | 800-458-3766

acquisitions@judsonpress.com | www.judsonpress.com

- **Denomination:** American Baptist
- **Parent company:** American Baptist Home Mission Societies
- **Mission statement:** to produce Christ-centered leadership resources for the transformation of individuals, congregations, communities, and cultures
- **Submissions:** Publishes 12 titles per year; receives 300 submissions annually. First-time authors: 25%. Length: 128–244 pages. Email or mail query or proposal with sample chapters. Responds in three to six months. Bible: NRSV.
- **Royalty:** 10–15%, sometimes gives advance
- **First print run:** 2,500

Types and topics: African-American, Asian, Christian education, Christian living/spirituality, Hispanic, history, ministry, church resources, devotionals, ministry resources

Types of books: ebook, offset paperback, POD

Guidelines: *www.judsonpress.com/Pages/Info/For-Authors.aspx*

Tip: "Most open to practical books that are unique and compelling, for a clearly defined niche audience. Theologically and socially we are a moderate publisher. And we like to see a detailed marketing plan from an author committed to partnering with us."

KREGEL PUBLICATIONS

2450 Oak Industrial Dr. NE, Grand Rapids, MI 49505 | 616-451-4775

KPacquisitions@kregel.com | *www.kregel.com*

Lindsay Danielson, editorial coordinator

Janyre Tromp, acquisitions editor, fiction, women's

Robert Hand, academic director

Submissions: Agent only, conference contact, *ChristianBookProposals. com,* or Writers Edge.

Types and topics: Bible study, biography, Christian living/spirituality, church life, discipleship, family, marriage, ministry, parenting, theology, women, Bible reference/commentaries, Bible studies, children, devotionals, teen/YA; fiction: historical, romance, romantic suspense, teen/YA

Guidelines: *www.kregel.com/contact-us/submissions-policy*

LEAFWOOD PUBLISHERS

ACU, Box 29138, Abilene, TX 79699 | 325-674-2720

manuscriptsubmissions@groupmail.acu.edu | *www.leafwoodpublishers.com*

Jason Fikes, director

Rebecka Scott, managing editor

Denomination: Church of Christ

Parent company: Abilene Christian University

Mission statement: to explore Scripture, Christian identity, spiritual formation, and our current cultural context

Submissions: Publishes 25 titles per year; receives 110+ submissions annually. First-time authors: 20%. Length: 50,000–75,000 words. Agent preferred or submit through the website. Responds in nine months if unsolicited. Bible: NIV, ESV.

Royalty: 14–25%, gives advance

Types and topics: Bible study, Christian education, Christian living/

spirituality, history, social issues, spiritual formation, theology

Types of books: audiobook, ebook, offset paperback

Guidelines: *store.acupressbooks.com/pages/author-resources*

Tip: "Solid proposals combine three elements: a compelling hook, a carefully crafted summary of their active platform, and great writing samples.

"Our editorial team enjoys working with authors to elevate their teaching voice and message, but every author has to bring their own platform to the table. Authors should be mindful that while we can support their plans, we cannot create platform out of thin air. We can only make a limited number of investments in authors, and platform (or lack thereof) is often a determining factor.

"First-time authors need to build a multistep and, in many cases, multiyear plan to grow their audience so that by the time of their book release they are hitting on all cylinders. While many would like to rush the publishing process, it takes time to do this work correctly. Have patience with yourself and try to be discerning about the right partners that you need in your work."

LEXHAM PRESS

1313 Commercial St., Bellingham, WA 98225

editor@lexampress.com | www.lexhampress.com

Jesse Myers, publisher and acquisitions

Deborah Keiser, acquisitions editor, Kirkdale Press, submissions@ kirkdalepress.com

Parent company: FaithLife Corporation, makers of Logos Bible Software

Submissions: Submit proposal with sample chapters through the website. Responds in eight weeks or not interested. Publishes innovative resources for Logos Bible Software.

Types and topics: Bible study, ministry, theology, academic, Bible reference/commentaries

Imprints: Kirkdale Press (general)

Guidelines: *www.lexhampress.com/manuscript-submission*

LIGHTHOUSE PUBLISHING

754 Roxholly Walk, Buford, CA 30518 | 770-709-2268

info@lighthousechristianpublishing.com | www.lighthousechristianpublishing.com

Andy Overett

Parent company: Lighthouse eMedia and eMusic

Mission statement: to provide high-quality original works at the least possible prices

Submissions: Publishes 30 titles per year; receives 200 submissions annually. First-time authors: 80%. Length: fiction, 300–320 pages. Email proposal with sample chapters. Responds in four to six weeks.

Royalty: 50%, no advance

Types and topics: African-American, all nonfiction topics, Hispanic, fiction

Types of books: audiobook, ebook, POD

Guidelines: *lighthouseebooks.com/custom.html*

Tip: Looking for unique stories.

LIGHTHOUSE TRAILS PUBLISHING, LLC

PO Box 387, Talent, OR 97540 | 541-897-0341

david@lighthousetrails.com | *www.lighthousetrails.com*

David Dombrowski, acquisitions editor

Mission statement: to bring clarity and light to areas of spiritual darkness or deception

Submissions: Publishes two to four titles per year; receives 50–75 submissions annually. First-time authors: 30%. Length: 160–300 pages. Email or mail proposal with sample chapters. Responds in two months. Bible: KJV.

Royalty: 12–17% of net, 20% of retail

Types and topics: biography, memoir/personal narrative, missionaries, fiction

Guidelines: *www.lighthousetrails.com/content/11-submit-manuscript*

Tip: "Any book we consider will not only challenge the more scholarly reader, but also be able to reach those who may have less experience and comprehension. Our books will include human interest and personal-experience scenarios as a means of getting the point across. Read a couple of our books to better understand the style of writing we are looking for. We also have a doctrinal statement on our website that helps to define us."

LIGUORI PUBLICATIONS

1 Liguori Dr., Liguori, MO 63057-9999 | 800-325-9521

manuscript_submission@liguori.org | *www.liguori.org*

Elizabeth Gebhart, director of editorial

Denomination: Catholic

Submissions: Proposal with sample chapters. No simultaneous submissions. Responds in 8-12 weeks.

Types and topics: sacraments, saints, Bible studies, biography, devotionals

LION HUDSON

John Eccles House Science Park, Robert Robinson Ave., Littlemore, Oxford OX4 4GP, United Kingdom

www.lionhudson.com

Parent company: SPCK Group

Submissions: Receives 400 submissions annually. Submit proposal with sample chapters through the website. If no response in three months, consider it a rejection.

Types and topics: Christian living/spirituality, children

Imprints: Lion Books (adults), Lion Children's Books (children), Lion Fiction (Christian worldview to general market), Candle Books (children), Monarch Books (co-published with organizations)

Guidelines: *www.lionhudson.com/authors-and-illustrators/prospective-authors*

LITTLE LAMB BOOKS

PO Box 211724, Bedford, TX 76095 | 817-505-8719

subs@littlelambbooks.com | *www.littlelambbooks.com*

Rachel Pellegrino, publisher and managing editor

Parent company: Lamb Publishing, LLC

Mission statement: to shepherd the next generation of faithful readers

Submissions: Publishes three to five titles per year; receives 200-250 submissions annually. First-time authors: 85%. Length: picture books, 500 words; chapter books, 1,500-5,000; middle grade, 30,000-60,000 words; young adult, 50,000-80,000 words. Agent preferred, conference contact, or email proposal with sample chapters. Responds in three to four months. Bible: NIV. Accepts unsolicited submissions only during announced acceptance dates.

Royalty: varies, no advance

Types and topics: animals, belonging, courage, friendship, holidays, multicultural, nature, prayer, self-confidence, sports, travel, values, devotionals, first-chapter, middle grade, picture books, teen/YA; fiction: adventure, contemporary, mystery, romance, suspense

Types of books: ebook, hardcover, offset paperback, POD

Guidelines: *littlelambbooks.com/subs*

Tip: "We're seeking evergreen content that is diverse and original from a biblical worldview. Your story should entertain without being preachy; should inspire without being sappy; and should have original concepts, strong characters, interesting settings, and curious plots. Your pitch should hook us from the beginning, and your query should follow our guidelines."

LITURGICAL PRESS

PO Box 7500, Collegeville, MN 56321-7500

submissions@litpress.org | www.litpress.org

Denomination: Catholic

Submissions: Submit through the website.

Types and topics: Bible, liturgy, prayer, theology, nonfiction

Guidelines: *www.litpress.org/Authors/submit_manuscript*

LOVE INSPIRED

195 Broadway, 24th floor, New York, NY 10007 | 212-207-7900

www.LoveInspired.com

Tina James, executive editor

Melissa Endlich, senior editor

Emily Rodmell, editor

Shana Asaro, editor

Caroline Timmings, assistant editor

Besarta Sinanovic, editorial assistant

Katie Gowrie, associate editor

Parent company: Harlequin/HarperCollins Publishers

Mission statement: to uplift and inspire through stories

Submissions: Publishes 144 titles per year; receives 500–1,000 submissions annually. First-time authors: 15%. Length: 55,000 words. Submit through the website. Responds in three months. Bible: KJV.

Royalty: on retail, gives advance

Types and topics: fiction, romance, romantic suspense

Types of books: mass-market paperback

Imprints: Love Inspired (contemporary romance), Love Inspired Suspense (contemporary romantic suspense)

Guidelines: *harlequin.submittable.com/submit*

Tip: "We're looking for compelling stories with engaging characters, a sustained conflict, and an emotionally satisfying romance."

LOVE2READLOVE2WRITE PUBLISHING, LLC

PO Box 103, Camby, IN 46113 | 317-550-9755
editor@love2readlove2writepublishing.com |
www.love2readlove2writepublishing.com
Michele Israel Harper, acquisitions editor

Submissions: Publishes four to six titles per year; receives 150–200 submissions annually. First-time authors: 20%. Length: 60,000–90,000 words. Agents only. Responds in two to three months. Bible: NKJV.

Royalty: 50%, $50 advance

Types and topics: fiction: fantasy, speculative, teen/YA

Types of books: POD

Guidelines: *www.love2readlove2writepublishing.com/submissions*

Tip: "Be professional, be succinct, and know your audience."

LOYOLA PRESS

8770 W. Bryn Mawr Ave., Chicago, IL 60631-3515 | 773-281-1818
submissions@loyolapress.com | *www.loyolapress.com*
Vinita Wright, managing editor, trade books

Denomination: Catholic

Submissions: Publishes 20 titles per year; receives 500 submissions annually. Length: 25,000–75,000 words or 150–300 pages. Email proposal with sample chapters. Responds in four to six weeks. Bible: NRSV (Catholic Edition).

Royalty: gives advance

Types and topics: Christian living/spirituality

Guidelines: *www.loyolapress.com/general/submissions*

Tip: "Looking for books and authors that help make Catholic faith relevant and offer practical tools for the well-lived spiritual life."

MOODY PUBLISHERS

820 N. LaSalle Blvd., Chicago, IL 60610 | 800-678-8812
randall.payleitner@moody.edu | *www.moodypublishers.com*
Randall Payleitner, editorial director
Judy Dunagan, acquisitions editor, women and Bible study,
    judy.dunagan@moody.edu
John Hinkley, acquisitions editor, marriage, family, relationships,
    John.Hinkley@moody.edu
Trillia Newbell, acquisitions director, Trillia.Newbell@moody.edu

Catherine Strode Parks, acquisitions editor

Parent company: Moody Bible Institute

Mission statement: to resource the church's work of discipling all people

Submissions: Publishes 50–60 titles per year; receives thousands of submissions annually. First-time authors: 20%. Agent only, conference contact, or author referral. Then email proposal with sample chapters. Responds in one to two months. Bible: NASB, ESV, NKJV. Books need to fit one of these categories: marriage and family resources—how to be a better mom, dad, grandparent, etc.; church leaders—pastors, community care, leading in a church context; Bible study materials—how to better study God's Word, primarily for women and young people; Christian living—how to help people take that next step in the Christian life; and ministry partners—those who work to make a better world in some way from orphan care to responsible finances.

Royalty: advances begin at $500

Types and topics: Bible study, Christian living/spirituality, church life, family, marriage, parenting, women, Bible reference/commentaries

Guidelines: *www.moodypublishers.com/About/faq/submitting-proposals*

Tip: "Most open to books that (1) have a great idea at the core, (2) are executed well, and (3) can demonstrate an audience clamoring for the content."

MOUNTAIN BROOK FIRE

mountainbrookink@gmail.com | fire.mountainbrookink.com

Alyssa Roat, managing editor

Parent company: Mountain Brook Ink

Mission statement: We're dedicated to quality worldbuilding, spellbinding plots, and high-stakes adventures with a whole lot of heart for middle grade, young adult, and adult audiences.

Submissions: Length: minimum 75,000 words. Email query or proposal with sample chapters. Responds in two months. Bible: KJV, NKJV, NIV.

Royalty: 30–40%, $25 advance

Types and topics: fiction: middle grade, YA, dystopian, fantasy, science fiction, speculative, supernatural

Types of books: audiobook, ebook, POD

Guidelines: *fire.mountainbrookink.com/submission-guidelines*

Tip: "Manuscripts need not be explicitly 'Christian'; we are equally happy with general market. However, we're looking for fiction that is clean. Books having a Christian worldview without having a faith thread will work as well."

MOUNTAIN BROOK INK

submissions@mountainbrookink.com | www.mountainbrookink.com
Miralee Ferrell, lead acquisitions editor

Mission statement: to publish fiction you can believe in that embodies restoration and/or renewal

Submissions: Publishes 12 titles per year; receives 50+ submissions annually. First-time authors: 75%. Length: minimum 75,000 words. Email query or proposal with sample chapters. Responds in two months. Bible: KJV, NKJV, NIV.

Royalty: 30–40%, $25 advance

Types and topics: fiction: contemporary, historical, mystery, romance, romantic suspense, suspense/thriller, women's

Types of books: audiobook, ebook, POD

Imprints: Mountain Brook Fire (speculative fiction)

Guidelines: *mountainbrookink.com/submission-guidelines-for-inquiries*

Tip: "Send the best work you've done, preferably that's been edited so it shines."

MT ZION RIDGE PRESS, LLC

295 Gum Springs Rd. NW, Georgetown, TN 37336 | 423-458-4256
mtzionridgepress@gmail.com | mtzionridgepress.com
Tamera Lynn Kraft, managing editor
Michelle Levigne, managing editor

Mission statement: to publish Christian books off the beaten path: fiction with a Christian worldview that doesn't fit the mold, nonfiction that goes deeper in Scripture than the bubblegum Christianity you find elsewhere

Submissions: Publishes seven titles per year; receives 30 submissions annually. First-time authors: 50%. Length: 50,000–100,000 words. Conference contact or email query first. Responds in two months. Bible: KJV for historical, ESV, NIV, NKJV.

Royalty: 30% books, 20% audiobooks, no advance

Types and topics: African-American, Asian, Bible study, Christian living/spirituality, Hispanic, Bible studies, devotionals; fiction: biblical, contemporary, historical, mystery, romance, suspense/

thriller, westerns, women's

Types of books: audiobook, ebook, POD

Guidelines: *mtzionridgepress.com/about*

Tip: "Make sure it has a strong Christian worldview and is a little bit different from the norm."

MY HEALTHY CHURCH

1445 N. Boonville Ave., Springfield, MO 65802 | 417-831-8000

newproducts@myhealthychurch.com | *www.myhealthychurch.com*

Denomination: Assemblies of God

Parent company: Gospel Publishing House

Submissions: Agent only. Responds in two to three months.

Types and topics: Bible studies, church resources

Guidelines: *myhealthychurch.com/store/startcat.cfm?cat=tWRITGUID*

Tip: "The content of all our books and resources must be compatible with the beliefs and purposes of the Assemblies of God."

NAVPRESS

3820 N. 30th St., Colorado Springs, CO 80904

inquiries@navpress.com | *www.navpress.com*

Caitlyn Carlson, acquisitions editor

Deborah Gonzalez, associate acquisitions and developmental editor

Parent company: The Navigators

Submissions: Publishes 20 titles per year; receives 1,000 submissions annually. First-time authors: 40%. Length: 40,000 words. Agent only or author referral. Responds in two months.

Royalty: 16–22%, gives advance

Types and topics: Christian living/spirituality, counseling, discipleship, family, leadership, marriage, parenting, prayer, relationships, spiritual growth, women, Bible studies

Guidelines: *www.navpress.com/faq*

Tip: "Proposals with strong discipleship elements are preferred. Authors should have a ministry platform that supports their discipleship elements. NavPress does not accept unsolicited manuscripts."

NELSON BOOKS

PO Box 141000, Nashville, TN 37214-1000 | 615-889-9000

www.thomasnelson.com/nelsonbooks

Jenny Baumgartner, senior acquisitions editor

Jennifer Smith, acquisitions

Parent company: Thomas Nelson Publishers/HarperCollins
Christian Publishing
Submissions: Agents only.
Types and topics: biography, business, Christian living/spirituality,
leadership, spiritual growth, devotionals
Types of books: audiobook, ebook, hardcover, offset paperback

NEW GROWTH PRESS

PO Box 4485, Greensboro, NC 27404 | 336-378-7775
submissions@newgrowthpress.com | www.newgrowthpress.com
Rush Witt, acquisitions editor and manager

Mission statement: to reach every church and home with gospel-
centered resources that point to Jesus and help every person grow
closer to Christ
Submissions: Email proposal with sample chapters. Responds in six
weeks or not interested.
Types and topics: Christian living/spirituality, counseling, family,
parenting, relationships, Bible studies, children, devotionals,
fiction, teen/YA
Guidelines: *newgrowthpress.com/submissions*

NORTHWESTERN PUBLISHING HOUSE

N16W23379 Stone Ridge Dr., Waukesha, WI 53188-1108 |
800-662-6022
submissions@nph.wels.net | online.nph.net
John Braun

Denomination: Wisconsin Evangelical Lutheran Synod
Mission statement: to deliver biblically sound, Christ-centered
resources within the Wisconsin Evangelical Lutheran Synod and
beyond
Submissions: Mail proposal with sample chapters.
Types and topics: family, history, theology, Bible reference/
commentaries, devotionals
Guidelines: *online.nph.net/manuscript-submission*

OLIVIA KIMBRELL PRESS

PO Box 470, Fort Knox, KY 40121-0470 | 859-577-1071
admin@oliviakimbrellpress.com | myokpress.com
Heather McCurdy, editor
Gregg Bridgeman, editor-in-chief

Mission statement: We specialize in previously unpublished authors who write about contemporary life and the challenges Christians face in our very secular fallen world.

Submissions: Email proposal with complete manuscript. Specializes in true-to-life, meaningful Christian fiction and nonfiction titles intended to uplift the heart and engage the mind. Primary focus on "Roman Road" small-group guides or reader's guides to accompany nonfiction and fiction.

Types and topics: Christian living/spirituality, family, health, social issues, devotionals; fiction: biblical, fantasy, historical romance, romantic suspense, science fiction, speculative

Imprints: CAVË (historical fiction around the time of Christ), Sign of the Whale (biblical and speculative fiction), House of Bread (nutrition)

Guidelines: *myokpress.com/editorial-standards/submission-guidelines*

Tip: "Must meet our stated editorial standards. Follow our submission guidelines. Fiction series preferred over standalone titles. Complete manuscripts only."

OUR DAILY BREAD PUBLISHING

3000 Kraft Ave. SE, Grand Rapids, MI 49507 | 616-974-2210

dawn.anderson@odb.org | ourdailybreadpublishing.org

Dawn Anderson, executive editor

Joyce Dinkins, executive editor, VOICES, Joyce.dinkins@odb.org

Katara Patton, senior editor and acquisitions, Katara.patton@odb.org

Parent company: Our Daily Bread Ministries

Mission statement: to feed the soul with the Word of God

Submissions: Publishes 24–36 titles per year; receives 100 submissions annually. First-time authors: fewer than 10%. Length: approximately 192 pages. Agent preferred or conference contact. Responds in three months. Bible: NIV, NLT, ESV.

Royalty: 12–18%, no advance

First print run: 3,000–50,000

Types and topics: African-American, Asian, Bible study, Christian living/spirituality, contemporary issues, Hispanic, men, pop reference, prayer, social issues, women, children, devotionals

Types of books: audiobook, board books, ebook, hardcover, offset paperback

Tip: "We look for strongly Bible-based content with practical application for everyday living."

OUR SUNDAY VISITOR, INC.

200 Noll Plaza, Huntington, IN 46750-4303 | 260-356-8400

www.osv.com

Denomination: Catholic

Mission statement: to assist Catholics to be more aware and secure in their faith and capable of relating their faith to others

Submissions: Publishes 30–40 titles per year; receives 500 submissions annually. First-time authors: 10%. Query first through the website. Responds in six to eight weeks.

Royalty: 10–12%, $1,500 advance

Types and topics: apologetics, biography, Christian living/spirituality, church life, culture, evangelism, family, history, marriage, ministry, parenting, prayer, devotionals, prayer guides

Imprints: OSV Kids (children and teens)

Guidelines: *osv.submittable.com/submit*

Tip: "All books published must relate to the Catholic Church; unique books aimed at our audience. Give as much background information as possible on author qualification, why the topic was chosen, and unique aspects of the project. Follow our guidelines. We are expanding our religious-education product line and programs."

P&R PUBLISHING

1102 Marble Hill Rd., PO Box 817, Phillipsburg, NJ 08865 | 908-454-0505

submissions@prpbooks.com | *www.prpbooks.com*

David Almack, acquisitions director

Amanda Martin, editorial director

Melissa Craig, children's editor

Denomination: Reformed

Mission statement: to serve Christ and His church by producing clear, engaging, fresh, and insightful applications of Reformed theology to life

Submissions: Publishes 40 titles per year; receives 200 submissions annually. First-time authors: 10–15%. Length: 40,000–50,000 words. Email proposal with sample chapters through the website. Responds in three months. Bible: ESV.

Royalty: 14–16%, sometimes gives advance

First print run: 3,000–5,000

Types and topics: Christian living/spirituality, counseling, parenting, prayer, theology, women, academic, children, devotionals

51

Types of books: audiobook, ebook, hardcover, offset paperback
Guidelines: *www.prpbooks.com/manuscript-submissions*
Tip: "We are looking for authors with a Reformed theological conviction, and we utilize the Westminster Confession of Faith as a guideline."

PACIFIC PRESS

PO Box 5353, Nampa, ID 83653-5353 | 208-465-2500
booksubmissions@pacificpress.com | *www.pacificpress.com*
Scott Cady, acquisitions editor

Denomination: Seventh-Day Adventist
Mission statement: to provide readers with a wide variety of books that connect them with God and help them develop a relationship with Him; provide information about God, His character, and His ways; and encourage and uplift them in the struggles of life
Submissions: Publishes 35–40 titles per year; receives 500 submissions annually. First-time authors: 5%. Length: 40,000–90,000 words or 128–320 pages. Email query first. Responds in one to three weeks.
Royalty: 12–16%, $1,500 advance
Types and topics: Bible study, biography, Christian living/spirituality, contemporary issues, health, history, marriage, memoir/personal narrative, parenting, prayer, theology, children, fiction
Guidelines: *www.pacificpress.com/authors___artists/books*
Tip: "Most open to spirituality, inspirational, and Christian living. Our website has the most up-to-date information, including samples of recent publications. For more information, see *www.adventistbookcenter.com*. Do not send full manuscript unless we request it after reviewing your proposal."

PARACLETE PRESS

PO Box 1568, Orleans, MA 02653-1568 | 508-255-4685
submissions@paracletepress.com | *www.paracletepress.com*

Denomination: Catholic, Protestant
Submissions: Publishes 40 titles per year. Agent only or prior relationship, then email proposal with sample chapters. Responds in one month.
Types and topics: Advent/Christmas picture books, Christian living/spirituality, grief, Lent/Easter picture books, prayer, children; fiction: contemporary, fantasy, horror, science fiction
Imprints: Raven (fiction)
Guidelines: *www.paracletepress.com/pages/submission-guidelines*

PARAKLESIS PRESS

113 Winn Ct., Waleska, GA 30183 | 404-274-8615
submissions@paraklesispress.com | *ParaklesisPress.com*
Sally Apokedak, editor

Mission statement: to delight children with fun language; smart, humble, comical, relatable characters; charming illustrations; and exciting plots, all while also giving these young minds plenty of food for thought

Submissions: Publishes four titles per year; receives 75 submissions annually. First-time authors: 50%. Length: 32–400 pages. Email proposal with complete manuscript. Responds in three months. Bible: ESV.

Royalty: 10–50%, gives advance

Types and topics: Bible study, children, picture books; fiction: contemporary, fantasy, mystery

Types of books: POD, hardcover

Guidelines: *paraklesispress.com/submit-to-us*

Tip: "Write something interesting and entertaining that doesn't need a ton of editing and that is not offensive to Christians and you'll have a good chance of getting published here."

PARSONS PUBLISHING HOUSE, LLC

PO Box 410063, Melbourne, FL 32941 | 850-867-3061
info@parsonspublishinghouse.com | *www.parsonspublishinghouse.com*
Diane Parsons, owner and senior editor

Submissions: Publishes four to eight titles per year; receives 20 submissions annually. First-time authors: 15%. Length: 140 pages. Email proposal. No agents. Responds in one month.

Royalty: no advance

Types and topics: nonfiction

Types of books: ebook, hardcover, offset paperback, POD

Tip: "Present the positive message of Christ in an uplifting and understandable way."

PAULINE BOOKS & MEDIA

50 Saint Paul's Ave., Boston, MA 02130-3491 | 617-522-8911
editorial@paulinemedia.com | *pauline.org/PBMPublishing*

Denomination: Catholic

Parent company: Daughters of St. Paul

Submissions: Publishes 20 titles per year; receives 300+ submissions annually. First-time authors: 10%. Length: 10,000–60,000 words. Email proposal with sample chapters. Responds in two months. Bible: NRSV.

Royalty: 5–10%, gives advance

Types and topics: Christian living/spirituality, evangelism, family, prayer, spiritual formation, theology, activities and puzzles, board books, first-chapter, middle grade, picture books, prayer guides, teen/YA fiction and nonfiction

Types of books: ebook, paperback

Imprints: Pauline Kids, Pauline TEEN

Guidelines: *tinyurl.com/mr2e8zny*

PAULIST PRESS

997 Macarthur Blvd., Mahwah, NJ 07430-9990

submissions@paulistpress.com | www.paulistpress.com

Trace Murphy, editorial director

Denomination: Catholic

Submissions: Email proposal with sample chapters. Responds in six to eight weeks.

Types and topics: academic, children, nonfiction

Guidelines: *www.paulistpress.com/Pages/Center/auth_res_0.aspx*

PELICAN BOOK GROUP

Harbourlight Books, Prism Book Group, Pure Amore, Watershed Books, White Rose Publishing

PRAYERSHOP PUBLISHING

PO Box 10667, Terre Haute, IN 47802 | 812-238-5504

jon@prayershop.org | prayershop.org

Jonathan Graf, publisher

Parent company: Harvest Prayer Ministries, Church Prayer Leaders Network

Mission statement: to encourage and equip individuals and local-church prayer leaders to grow prayer in their spheres of influence

Submissions: Publishes six to eight titles per year; receives 15–25 submissions annually. First-time authors: 25%. Length: 80–144 pages. Email or mail proposal with sample chapters or complete manuscript. Responds in six to ten weeks. Bible: NIV. "We are looking for prayer topics that would move believers from just praying for their own needs to prayer that is focused on growing God's

Kingdom."

Royalty: 10–15%, no advance

First print run: 1,000–5,000

Types and topics: prayer, revival, devotionals, prayer guides

Types of books: ebook, offset paperback

Tip: "Currently looking for book manuscripts, booklets, and materials that can be formatted via CD and print into training kits. We are mostly interested in products that will in some way enhance the prayer life of a local church."

PRISM BOOK GROUP

PO Box 1738, Aztec, NM 87410

customer@prismbookgroup.com | *www.prismbookgroup.com*

Jacqueline Hopper, acquisitions editor, jhopper@prismbookgroup.com

Paula Mowery, acquisitions editor, pmowery@prismbookgroup.com

Parent company: Pelican Book Group

Mission statement: to publish quality books that reflect the salvation and love offered by Jesus Christ

Submissions: Length: 25,000–80,000 words. Submit query or proposal with sample chapters through the website. Responds in three to four months. Bible: NIV, NAB.

Royalty: 40% download, 7% print, sometimes gives advance

Types and topics: fiction: contemporary, fantasy, historical, mystery, romance, romantic suspense, science fiction, suspense/thriller, teen/YA

Types of books: ebook, POD

Imprints: Prism Lux (Christian), Prism CW (clean and wholesome)

Guidelines: *pelicanbookgroup.com/ec/index.php?main_page=page&id=76*

Tip: "Our books offer clean and compelling reads for the discerning reader. We will not publish graphic language or content and look for well-written, emotionally charged stories, intense plots, and captivating characters."

PURE AMORE

PO Box 1738, Aztec, NM 87410

customer@pelicanbookgroup.com | *pelicanbookgroup.com*

Nicola Martinez, editor-in-chief

Parent company: Pelican Book Group

Mission statement: to publish quality books that reflect the salvation and love offered by Jesus Christ

Submissions: Length: 40,000–45,000 words. Submit proposal with sample chapters through the website. Responds in one to four months. Only contemporary Christian romance. Pure Amore romances are sweet in tone and in conflict. These stories are the emotionally driven tales of youthful Christians between the ages of 21 and 33 who are striving to live their faith in a world where Christ-centered choices may not fully be understood.

Royalty: 40% download, 7% print, sometimes gives advance

Types and topics: fiction: romance

Types of books: ebook, POD

Guidelines: *pelicanbookgroup.com/ec/index.php?main_page=page&id=69*

Tip: "Pure Amore romances emphasize the beauty in chastity, so physical interactions, such as kissing or hugging, should focus on the characters' emotions, rather than heightened sexual desire; and scenes of physical intimacy should be integral to the plot and/or emotional development of the character or relationship."

RANDALL HOUSE

PO Box 17306, Nashville, TN 37217 | 615-361-1221

books@randallhouse.com | *D6family.com*

Dr. Danny Conn, director of editorial and strategic projects

Denomination: Free Will Baptist

Mission statement: to build believers through church and home

Submissions: Publishes 8–12 titles per year; receives 40 submissions annually. First-time authors: 20%. Length: 20,000–100,000 words. Conference contact or email proposal with sample chapters. Responds in three months. Bible: ESV, NIV, KJV.

Royalty: 15–20%, sometimes gives advance

Types and topics: Christian living/spirituality, discipleship, family, Free Will Baptist history and doctrine, Hispanic, theology

Types of books: ebook, hardcover, offset paperback

Guidelines: *rhpweb.s3.amazonaws.com/Book-Proposal-Guide.pdf*

Tip: "Provide insightful material with practical application on a subject that fits our genres."

RESOURCE PUBLICATIONS

199 W. 8th Ave., Ste. 3, Eugene, OR 97401 | 541-344-1528

proposal@wipfandstock.com | *wipfandstock.com/search-results/*
?imprint=resource-publications

Parent company: Wipf and Stock
Submissions: Email proposal with sample chapters. Responds in one to two months.
Types and topics: biography, fiction, poetry, sermons
Types of books: ebook, POD
Guidelines: *wipfandstock.com/submitting-a-proposal*

RESURRECTION PRESS

77 West End Rd., Totowa, NJ 07572 | 973-890-2400

info@catholicbookpublishing.com | *www.catholicbookpublishing.com*

Anthony Buono, editor

Denomination: Catholic
Parent company: Catholic Book Publishing Corp.
Submissions: Mail proposal with sample chapters. Responds in four to six weeks.
Types and topics: Christian living/spirituality, healing, ministry, prayer
Guidelines: *www.catholicbookpublishing.com/page/faq#manuscript*

REVELL

6030 E. Fulton Rd., Ada, MI 49301 | 616-676-9185

bakerpublishinggroup.com/revell

Andrea Doering, editorial director

Kelsey Bowen, fiction acquisitions editor

Rachel McRae, senior acquisitions editor

Grace Cho, nonfiction acquisitions editor

Parent company: Baker Publishing Group
Submissions: Agent only, conference contact, or *ChristianBookProposals.com*.
Types and topics: apologetics, Bible study, biography, Christian living/spirituality, church life, culture, family, marriage, memoir/personal narrative, children, fiction, teen/YA
Guidelines: *bakerpublishinggroup.com/contact/submission-policy*

ROSE PUBLISHING

PO Box 3473, Peabody, MA 01961 | 800-358-3111

lpennings@tyndale.com | *www.hendricksonrose.com*

Lynette Pennings, managing editor

> **Parent company:** Hendrickson Publishing Group/Tyndale House Ministries
>
> **Mission statement:** to make the Bible and its teachings easy to understand
>
> **Types and topics:** Bible, Bible reference/commentaries, charts

ROSEKIDZ

PO Box 3473, Peabody, MA 01961 | 800-358-3111

kmcgraw@tyndale.com | *www.hendricksonrose.com*

Karen McGraw, managing editor

> **Parent company:** Hendrickson Publishing Group/Tyndale House Ministries
>
> **Mission statement:** to help kids grow closer to God in a hands-on way
>
> **Submissions:** Submit by email.
>
> **Types and topics:** activities and puzzles, children, crafts, devotionals, fiction
>
> **Types of books:** offset paperback

SALEM BOOKS

300 New Jersey Ave. NW, Ste. 500, Washington, DC 20001

www.regnery.com/custom/salem-books

Tim Peterson, publisher and acquisitions

> **Parent company:** Regnery Publishing/Salem Media Group
>
> **Mission statement:** to enrich the lives of Christians and proclaim the gospel of Jesus to the world through the written word
>
> **Submissions:** Agents only.
>
> **Types and topics:** apologetics, Christian living/spirituality, culture, memoir/personal narrative, men, women, worldview

SCEPTER PUBLISHERS

PO Box 360694, Strongsville, OH 44136 | 212-354-0670

info@scepterpublishers.org | *www.scepterpublishers.org*

Nathan Davis, editor

> **Denomination:** Catholic
>
> **Mission statement:** to help people find God in ordinary life and realize sanctity in work, family life, and everyday activities; to assist people in their quest to live an integrated life where every moment, even the most ordinary, is offered up like a prayer; to immerse

people in the contemplative life even while living in the midst of the world, so that they might learn the will of God

Submissions: Publishes 8–18 titles per year. Query through the website.

Types and topics: Christian living/spirituality, nonfiction

Guidelines: *scepterpublishers.org/pages/publishing-services*

SCRIVENINGS PRESS

15 Lucky Ln., Morrilton, AR 72110 | 501-548-2736

scriveningspress@gmail.com | scriveningspress.com

Linda Fulkerson, owner and acquisitions

Mission statement: to champion debut and newer novelists by helping them develop their manuscripts and grow their careers

Submissions: Publishes 36 titles per year; receives 100 submissions annually. First-time authors: 40%. Length: 55,000–100,000 words. Email proposal with sample chapters or complete manuscript through the website. Also conference contact. Responds in four to six weeks. Bible: any.

Royalty: 12% print, 50% ebook, 40% pages read in Kindle Unlimited, no advance

Types and topics: general nonfiction, writing craft, devotionals; fiction: middle-grade, novella collections, YA, historical, mystery, romance, romantic suspense, speculative, women's

Types of books: ebook, POD, hardcover

Imprints: Scrivenings Press (general fiction), Expanse Books (speculative fiction), MGM (middle-grade fiction), Ideas to Books (writing craft), Impart (general nonfiction)

Guidelines: *scriveningspress.com/submissions*

Tip: "We are a small publishing house, and we try to keep a family feel among our staff and authors. We encourage all our authors to encourage one another and to cross-promote books from other authors within our company."

SMYTH & HELWYS BOOKS

6316 Peake Rd., Macon, GA 31210-3960 | 478-757-0564

proposal@helwys.com | www.helwys.com

Leslie Andres, editor

Submissions: Email or mail proposal with sample chapters. Responds in several weeks.

Types and topics: Bible study, Christian living/spirituality, leadership, ministry

Guidelines: *www.helwys.com/submit-a-manuscript*

SPRINKLE PUBLISHING

2270 Ferguson Rd., Ste. 116, Ontario, OH 44906-5200 | 419-709-1435

Dr.Sprinkle@wsministries.ws | *www.wsministries.ws/home/sprinkle-publishing*

Dr. Wanda J. Sprinkle, editor

> **Parent company:** Wanda Sprinkle Ministries, LLC
>
> **Mission statement:** to make publishing affordable through our ministry as we specialize in first-time authors
>
> **Submissions:** Publishes seven titles per year; receives 20 submissions annually. First-time authors: 95%. Length: maximum 200 pages. Conference contact, writers attending Sprinkle Publishing Workshops, or email or mail proposal with sample chapters. No agents. No simultaneous submissions. Responds in two weeks.
>
> **Royalty:** 50–60%, no advance
>
> **First print run:** minimum 100
>
> **Types and topics:** autobiography, biography, Christian living/spirituality, inspirational, spiritual maturity, devotionals, fiction, poetry
>
> **Types of books:** hardcover, offset paperback, spiral binding
>
> **Tip:** "Must agree to our doctrinal absolutes of Scripture alone, Christ alone, faith alone, grace alone, and glory to God alone."

THOMAS NELSON FICTION

PO Box 141000, Nashville, TN 37214-1000 | 615-889-9000

www.thomasnelson.com/fiction

Becky Monds, editorial director

Kimberly Carlton, acquisitions editor

Laura Wheeler, acquisitions editor

> **Parent company:** Thomas Nelson Publishers/HarperCollins Christian Publishing
>
> **Mission statement:** to inspire the world by meeting the needs of people with content that promotes biblical principles and honors Jesus Christ
>
> **Submissions:** Agents only.
>
> **Types and topics:** biography, business, Christian living/spirituality, leadership, spiritual growth; fiction: historical, humor, mystery, romance, suspense/thriller
>
> **Types of books:** audiobook, ebook, offset paperback
>
> **Tip:** "What we are looking for: great writers who are passionate about

their stories, a willingness to work hard and engage with readers—coupled with a true love of readers, a unique angle on or a unique connection to their story matter, a great attitude."

THOMAS NELSON GIFT

PO Box 141000, Nashville, TN 37214-1000 | 615-889-9000

www.thomasnelson.com/gift

Adria Haley, acquisitions editor

> **Parent company:** Thomas Nelson Publishers/HarperCollins Christian Publishing
>
> **Mission statement:** to inspire the world by meeting the needs of people with content that promotes biblical principles and honors Jesus Christ
>
> **Submissions:** Agents only.
>
> **Types and topics:** devotionals, gift
>
> **Types of books:** ebook, hardcover, offset paperback
>
> **Tip:** "A gift book is designed to be shared. It's a beautiful keepsake that makes an ideal gift, a way to mark a special occasion or holiday, a message of the heart, and it usually satisfies a strong felt need. Featuring two or four-color interiors, sometimes photography or illustrations, and beautiful covers complete with special effects like foil, fabric, gilding, and padding, gift books are as much an experience as a collection of words to be read."

THOMAS NELSON PUBLISHERS

Emanate Books, Grupo Nelson, Nelson Books, Thomas Nelson Fiction, Thomas Nelson Gift, Tommy Nelson, W Publishing, WestBow Press

TOMMY NELSON

PO Box 141000, Nashville, TN 37214-1000 | 615-889-9000

www.tommynelson.com

Mackenzie Howard, associate publisher

> **Parent company:** Thomas Nelson Publishers/HarperCollins Christian Publishing
>
> **Mission statement:** to expand children's imaginations and nurture their faith while pointing them to a personal relationship with God
>
> **Submissions:** Agents only or conference contact.
>
> **Types and topics:** Bible storybooks, board books, devotionals, first-chapter, middle grade, picture books, teen/YA
>
> **Types of books:** board books, hardcover, offset paperback, picture books

THE TRINITY FOUNDATION

PO Box 68, Unicoi, TN 37692 | 423-743-0199
tjtrinityfound@aol.com | *www.trinityfoundation.org*
Thomas W. Juodaitis, president

Mission statement: to promote the Christian religion

Submissions: Publishes two or three titles per year; receives five submissions annually. First-time authors: 5%. Length: 100–200 pages. Email or mail proposal with sample chapters. Responds in two weeks. Bible: KJV, NKJV.

Royalty: none, flat fee of $1,500–$2,000, no advance

First print run: 1,000–1,500

Types and topics: philosophy, theology

Types of books: ebook, offset paperback

Tip: "Follow content on website."

TULIP PUBLISHING

PO Box 3150, Lansvale, NSW 2166, Australia | +61 2 9055 2195
submissions@tulippublishing.com.au | *tulippublishing.com.au*
Brett Lee-Price, general manager

Denomination: Reformed

Mission statement: to equip the Church with resources that will help stretch and grow readers in their spiritual formulation, development, and knowledge

Submissions: Publishes four titles per year; receives 20 submissions annually. First-time authors: 40%. Length: 250–350 pages. Email proposal with sample chapters or submit through the website. Responds in two to three months. Bible: ESV.

Royalty: 30–40%, no advance

First print run: 1,000

Types and topics: Christian living/spirituality, theology

Types of books: ebook, hardcover, offset paperback

Guidelines: *tulippublishing.com.au/about/submissions*

Tip: "Be concise and succinct in your proposal; have your manuscript read and proofed by others, like family or friends, before submission."

TULPEN PUBLISHING

11043 Depew St., Westminster, CO 80020 | 303-438-7276
TulpenPublishing.com
Sandi Rog, acquisitions editor

Mission statement: to provide Christian stories that take readers beyond what they can find on the bookshelves

Submissions: Length: novellas, 15,000–55,000 words; novels, 60,000–80,000 words; historical novels, 65,000–110,000 words. Email query first.

Royalty: 10%, 50% ebook

Types and topics: devotionals, self-help, chapter books; fiction: contemporary, fantasy, historical, science fiction, teen/YA

Types of books: ebook, paperback

Guidelines: *www.tulpenpublishing.com/submission-guidelines.html*

Tip: "All stories must have a Christian worldview or a moral worldview pleasing to our heavenly Father. Please, no preaching and no conversion scenes, *unless* baptism by immersion for the forgiveness of sins is used (Acts 2:38). Don't use miracles and/or mysticism to resolve conflicts or to 'fix' a difficult plot. Miracles may be used only in biblical fiction. No profanity please. By the end of the story, the main character should have experienced spiritual and/or character growth."

TYNDALE HOUSE PUBLISHERS

351 Executive Dr., Carol Stream, IL 60188 | 630-668-8300

www.tyndale.com

Jon Farrar, acquisitions director, nonfiction

Elizabeth Jackson, acquisitions editor

Jillian Schlossberg, senior acquisitions editor, nonfiction

Kara Leonino, acquisitions editor, nonfiction

Jan Stob, senior editor, fiction and acquisitions

Mission statement: to help readers discover the life-giving truths of God's Word

Submissions: Publishes 100+ titles per year. First-time authors: 5%. Length: fiction, 75,000–100,000. Agent, conference contact, or author referral. Responds in three to six months. Bible: NLT.

Types and topics: biography, Christian living/spirituality, counseling, family, finances, leadership, marriage, memoir/personal narrative, parenting, children, devotionals; fiction: teen/YA, biblical, children, contemporary, futuristic, historical, romance, suspense/thriller, teen/YA

Types of books: audiobook, ebook, hardcover, offset paperback

Imprints: Tyndale Kids (children), Wander (YA), Tyndale Español (Spanish), Tyndale Refresh (health and wellness), Tyndale Momentum (nonfiction), Hendrickson Publishers (nonfiction), Rose

Publishing (Bible study helps)

TYNDALE KIDS

351 Executive Dr., Carol Stream, IL 60188 | 630-668-8300
kidsandwandersubmissions@tyndale.com | *www.tyndale.com/kids*
Linda Howard, associate publisher and acquisitions
Alyssa Clements, acquisitions editor

Parent company: Tyndale House Publishers

Mission statement: to bring kids and families closer to God through publishing books with excellent content, creative formats, and outstanding design

Submissions: Publishes 10–15 titles per year; receives 300–400 submissions annually. First-time authors: 5%. Length: varies according to the age group. Responds in two to three months. Bible: NLT. Agent preferred or conference contact. Email proposal with sample chapters or full manuscript.

Royalty: 10–24%; gives advance that varies according to platform, previous sales history, and uniqueness of proposal

Types and topics: African-American, Asian, Hispanic, Bible stories, board books, devotionals, fiction, first-chapter, middle grade, nonfiction, picture books, YA

Types of books: audiobook, ebook, hardcover, offset paperback, POD

Imprints: Wander (YA fiction and nonfiction)

Tip: "Looking for a solid, well-written proposal; strong platform; excellent writing."

W PUBLISHING

PO Box 141000, Nashville, TN 37214-1000 | 615-889-9000
www.thomasnelson.com/wpublishing
Kyle Olund, senior acquisitions editor
Dawn Hollomon, acquisitions

Parent company: Thomas Nelson Publishers/HarperCollins Christian Publishing

Submissions: Agents only.

Types and topics: Christian living/spirituality, memoir/personal narrative

Types of books: audiobook, ebook, hardcover, offset paperback

Tip: "W prides itself on the ability to provide authors a nurturing, faith-friendly, boutique style publishing experience."

WARNER CHRISTIAN RESOURCES

2902 Enterprise Dr., Anderson, IN 46013 | 765-644-7721
editors@warnerpress.org | *www.warnerpress.org*
Robin Fogel Loisch, product editor

Denomination: Church of God

Mission statement: to equip the church, to advance the Kingdom, and to give hope to future generations

Submissions: Publishes three to five titles per year; receives 50+ submissions annually. First-time authors: 50%. Responds in six to eight weeks. Bible: KJV, NIV, ESV, NKJV. Email complete manuscript.

Royalty: based on the author and type of book, sometimes gives advance

Types and topics: Bible studies, small-group resources, small-group study guides

Types of books: ebook, offset paperback

Guidelines: *www.warnerpress.org/submission-guidelines*

Tip: "Do your research and visit our website to view what we already produce."

WATERBROOK & MULTNOMAH

10807 New Allegiance Dr. #500, Colorado Springs, CO 80921 | 719-590-4999
info@waterbrookmultnomah.com | *www.waterbrookmultnomah.com*
Jamie Lapeyrolerie, acquisitions editor
Paul Pastor, editor and acquisitions, pastoral, spiritual growth
Sara Rubio, children's editor
Bunmi Ishola, children's editor

Parent company: Crown Publishing Group/Penguin Random House

Submissions: Publishes 60 titles per year; receives 300 submissions annually. First-time authors: 15%. Length: 208–400 pages. Agent only or conference contact. Responds in one to two months.

Royalty: gives advance

Types and topics: Christian living/spirituality, home and lifestyle, memoir/personal narrative, relationships, spiritual growth, Bible studies, children, devotionals; fiction: Amish, historical, romantic suspense

Types of books: audiobook, ebook, hardcover, offset paperback, POD

Imprints: Ink & Willow (gifts)

Tip: "We recommend working with an agent whose clientele aligns with your strengths as a writer."

WATERSHED BOOKS

PO Box 1738, Aztec, NM 87410

customer@pelicanbookgroup.com | *www.pelicanbookgroup.com*

Nicola Martinez, editor-in-chief

Parent company: Pelican Book Group

Mission statement: to publish quality books that reflect the salvation and love offered by Jesus Christ

Submissions: Length: 25,000–65,000 words. Email proposal with sample chapters or submit through the website. Responds in three to four months. Bible: NIV, NAB. Interested in series ideas.

Royalty: 40% on download, 7% on print, sometimes gives advance

Types and topics: fiction: teen/YA, adventure, coming-of-age, crime, mystery, romance, science fiction, supernatural, suspense, westerns

Types of books: POD

Guidelines: *pelicanbookgroup.com/ec/index.php?main_page=page&id=60*

Tip: "We want to see something other than dystopian."

WESTMINSTER JOHN KNOX PRESS

100 Witherspoon St., Louisville, KY 40202-1396

submissions@wjkbooks.com | *www.wjkbooks.com*

David Dobson, publisher and acquisitions

Jessica Miller Kelley, editor, Flyaway Books

Denomination: Presbyterian

Parent company: Presbyterian Publishing Corporation

Submissions: Publishes 60 titles per year. Email proposal with sample chapters. Responds in two to three months.

Types and topics: Bible study, culture, ethics, ministry, theology, worship, academic

Types of books: hardcover, offset paperback

Imprints: Flyaway Books (children), Geneva Press (Presbyterian Church USA)

Guidelines: *www.wjkbooks.com/Pages/Item/1345/Author-Relations.aspx*

WHITAKER HOUSE

1030 Hunt Valley Cir., New Kensington, PA 15068 | 724-334-7000

publisher@whitakerhouse.com | *www.whitakerhouse.com*

Christine Whitaker, acquisitions editor

Denomination: Charismatic/Pentecostal

Parent company: Whitaker Corporation

Submissions: Publishes 75–100 titles per year; receives 200 submissions annually. First-time authors: 30%. Length: 50,000–80,000 words. Agent preferred. Email proposal with sample chapters. Responds in one to six months. Bible: KJV.

Royalty: 15–18%, sometimes gives advance

Types and topics: African-American, Asian, Charismatic, Christian living/spirituality, Hispanic, children, devotionals, fiction

Types of books: audiobook, ebook, hardcover, offset paperback, POD

Imprints: Whitaker Playhouse (parents of young children)

Guidelines: *tinyurl.com/z9cdmece*

Tip: "Follow the questions and suggestions on our submission guidelines."

WHITE ROSE PUBLISHING

PO Box 1738, Aztec, NM 87410

customer@pelicanbookgroup.com | *www.pelicanbookgroup.com*

Nicola Martinez, editor-in-chief

Parent company: Pelican Book Group

Mission statement: to publish quality books that reflect the salvation and love offered by Jesus Christ

Submissions: Length: short stories, 10,000–20,000 words; novelettes, 20,000–35,000 words; novellas, 35,000–60,000 words; novels, 60,000–80,000 words. Submit proposal with sample chapters through the website. Responds in three to four months. Bible: NIV, NAB.

Royalty: 40% on download, 7% on print, sometimes gives advance

Types and topics: fiction, romance

Types of books: ebook, POD

Guidelines: *pelicanbookgroup.com/ec/index.php?main_page=page&id=58*

Tip: "The setting for White Rose books can be contemporary, historical or futuristic. They can be straight romances or include other factors, such as mystery, suspense, or supernatural elements, etc.; however, an element of faith must be present in all White Rose stories—without becoming overbearing or preachy. Please specify in your proposal if your story includes elements beyond simple romance."

WHITECROWN PUBLISHING

13607 Bedford Rd. NE, Cumberland, MD 21502 | 866-245-2211
marisa@whitecrownpublishing.com | *www.whitefire-publishing.com*
Marisa Stokley, acquisitions editor
Janelle Leonard, acquisitions editor, janelle@whitecrownpublishing.com

Parent company: WhiteFire Publishing

Mission statement: to combine faith and inspiration with a deep-seated love of what is noble and regal, bringing readers royal stories for teens and adults

Submissions: Publishes 4–12 titles per year. First-time authors: 50%. Length: 60,000–120,000 words. Email query first or conference contact. Responds in one to three months. Bible: KJV for historicals.

Royalty: 50% on ebooks, 10% on print, sometimes gives advance

Types and topics: fiction: royalty

Types of books: audiobook, ebook, hardcover, POD

Imprints: Royal Fiction (princess stories)

Guidelines: *whitecrownpublishing.com/submissions*

Tip: "We're looking for strong hooks and creative takes on 'princess stories.'"

WHITEFIRE PUBLISHING

13607 Bedford Rd. NE, Cumberland, MD 21502 | 866-245-2211
r.white@whitefire-publishing.com | *www.whitefire-publishing.com*
Roseanna White, managing editor

Mission statement: to publish books that shine the Light of God into the darkness and embrace the motto of "Where Spirit Meets the Page"

Submissions: Publishes 24 titles per year; receives 200 submissions annually. First-time authors: 20%. Length: 60,000–100,000 words. Email query first. Responds in three months. Bible: KJV for historicals.

Royalty: 50% on ebooks, 10% on print, $1,500–$2,000 advance

Types and topics: all nonfiction topics; fiction: contemporary, general, historical, romance, suspense, women's

Types of books: audiobook, ebook, POD

Imprints: WhiteSpark (young readers), Ashberry Lane (romance), WhiteFire (nonfiction and fiction), Chrism Press (Catholic and Orthodox fiction)

Guidelines: *whitefire-publishing.com/submissions*

Tip: "Familiarize yourself with our titles and mission."

WHITESPARK PUBLISHING

13607 Bedford Rd. NE, Cumberland, MD 21502 | 866-245-2211
r.white@whitefire-publishing.com | *www.whitefire-publishing.com*
Roseanna White, managing editor

> **Parent company:** WhiteFire Publishing
> **Mission statement:** to engender a love of reading in kids with faith-based books
> **Submissions:** Publishes five to ten titles per year; receives 100 submissions annually. First-time authors: 10%. Email query first. Responds in three months.
> **Royalty:** 50% on ebooks, 10% on print, sometimes gives advance of $200–$1,000
> **Types and topics:** all topics, middle grade, picture books, YA
> **Types of books:** audiobook, ebook, picture books, POD
> **Guidelines:** *whitespark-publishing.com/submissions*
> **Tip:** "Come with fresh ideas on how to reach the young readership."

WILD HEART BOOKS

14250 Hwy. 55 W, Blacksburg, SC 29702 | 704-363-0360
submissions@wildheartbooks.org | *wildheartbooks.org*
Misty M. Beller, managing editor

> **Mission statement:** to provide the kind of exciting historical stories readers love, complete with heroes to make them swoon, strong heroines, and inspirational messages to encourage their faith
> **Submissions:** Publishes 12 titles per year; receives 50 submissions annually. First-time authors: 10%. Length: minimum 50,000 words, ideally 55,000–75,000 words. Conference contact or email proposal with sample chapters. Responds in two to three weeks. Bible: KJV.
> **Royalty:** 40–50%, no advance
> **Types and topics:** African-American, Asian, Hispanic, Native American; fiction: historical romance
> **Types of books:** ebook, large print, POD
> **Guidelines:** *www.wildheartbooks.org/submissions.html*
> **Tip:** "Our focus is Christian historical romance, so make sure your book fits the specifics of what we prefer on our submissions page. If you don't hear back from us, within four weeks of submission, please don't hesitate to contact Misty."

WILLIAM CAREY PUBLISHING

10 W. Dry Creek Cir., Littleton, CO 80120 | 720-372-7036
submissions@WCLBooks.com | *www.missionbooks.org*
Denise Wynn, director of publishing

Parent company: Frontier Ventures
Mission statement: to publish resources that edify, equip, and
  empower disciples of Jesus to make disciples of Jesus
Submissions: Email query first. Responds in three to six months.
Types and topics: biography, ethnography, missions, academic
Guidelines: *missionbooks.org/submissions*
Tip: "We want our books to sound like the intelligent conversation you
  have with friends over dinner. You may site statistics and research
  (like you might reference an article in a reputable source), but
  you are sharing it in the context of a story that makes the research
  matter to real people doing Kingdom work."

WINGED PUBLICATIONS

PO Box 8047, Surprise, AZ 85374 | 623-910-4279
cynthiahickey@outlook.com | *www.wingedpublications.com*
Cynthia Hickey, CEO/president
Gina Welborn, acquisitions editor
Christina Rich, acquisitions editor
Patty Smith Hall, acquisitions editor

Mission statement: Where Your Stories Take Flight
Submissions: Publishes 50 titles per year. First-time authors: 25%.
  Length: minimum 20,000 words. Conference contact or email
  proposal with sample chapters. Responds in two weeks. Bible: NIV.
Royalty: 60%, no advance
Types and topics: memoir/personal narrative; fiction: humor, fantasy,
  historical romance, mystery, romance, romantic suspense, science
  fiction, suspense/thriller, teen/YA, women's
Types of books: ebook, POD
Imprints: Soaring Beyond (stories of hope, devotionals, self-help),
  Aisling Books (fantasy, science fiction), Jurnee Books (young adult,
  juvenile fiction), Gordian Books (mystery, suspense, thriller), Forget
  Me Not Romances (contemporary and historical romances), Take
  Me Away Books (women's fiction, comedy)
Guidelines: *wingedpublications.com/what-were-looking-for*
Tip: "Send the cleanest proposal you can."

WIPF AND STOCK PUBLISHERS

199 W. 8th Ave., Ste. 3, Eugene, OR 97401-2960 | 541-344-1528

rodney@wipfandstock.com | *www.wipfandstock.com*

Rodney Clapp, editor

> **Submissions:** Publishes 500+ per year in all imprints titles. Email proposal with sample chapters. Responds in two months.
>
> **Types and topics:** Bible, church history, ethics, history, ministry, philosophy, theology, academic
>
> **Types of books:** ebook, offset paperback
>
> **Imprints:** Resource Publications (leaders, pastors, educators), Cascade Books (academic)
>
> **Guidelines:** *wipfandstock.com/submitting-a-proposal*
>
> **Tip:** "It is your responsibility to submit a manuscript that has been fully copyedited by a professional copy editor."

WORTHY KIDS

6100 Tower Cir., Ste. 210, Franklin, TN 37067 | 615-221-0996

idealsinfo@hbgusa.com | *www.worthykids.com*

Rebekah Moredock, assistant editor

Melinda Rathjen, senior editor

> **Parent company:** Worthy Publishing/Hachette Book Group
>
> **Mission statement:** to create books that are much more than just words and pictures—they're an opportunity for a moment of joy between a child and his or her loved one
>
> **Submissions:** Publishes 30–35 titles per year; receives 200 submissions annually. First-time authors: fewer than 10%. Length: maximum 200 words for board books, 600 words for picture books. Agent preferred or conference contact. Email or mail proposal with complete manuscript. Responds in one month. Bible: NLT.
>
> **Royalty:** varies, sometimes gives advance, sometimes various flat fees
>
> **First print run:** 10,000
>
> **Types and topics:** holidays, board books, fiction, first-chapter, middle grade, nonfiction, picture books, juvenile
>
> **Types of books:** audiobook, board books, ebook, hardcover, offset paperback, picture books
>
> **Tip:** "Carefully study the types of books our house has published and submit proposals that show an understanding of the marketplace, includes recent competitive titles, and identifies what sets your book apart."

WORTHY PUBLISHING

6100 Tower Cir., Ste. 210, Franklin, TN 37067 | 615-932-7600
www.worthypublishing.com
Beth Adams, acquisitions editor
Sean McGowan, editor and acquisitions
India Hunter, associate editor and acquisitions

Parent company: Hachette Book Group
Mission statement: to publish books that combine faith, creativity, and culture while establishing the next generation of voices who believe that living faith can transform the world
Submissions: Publishes 36 titles per year. Agents only.
Types and topics: biography, Christian living/spirituality, contemporary issues, culture, spiritual growth, devotionals, fiction, gift
Imprints: Worthy Books (broad spectrum of genres), Worthy Kids (children, holiday magazines), Ellie Claire (gifts)

YWAM PUBLISHING

PO Box 55787, Seattle, WA 98155 | 800-922-2143
books@ywampublishing.com | www.ywampublishing.com
Tom Bragg, publisher

Parent company: Youth With A Mission
Submissions: Email or mail proposal with sample chapters.
Types and topics: evangelism, leadership, missions, relationships, Bible studies, devotionals
Guidelines: *www.ywampublishing.com/topic.aspx?name=submission*

ZONDERKIDZ

3900 Sparks Dr. SE, Grand Rapids, MI 49512 | 616-698-6900
ZonderkidzSubmissions@harpercollins.com | www.zonderkidz.com
Katherine Easter, senior acquisitions editor

Parent company: Zondervan/HarperCollins Christian Publishing
Mission statement: to inspire young lives through imagination and innovation
Submissions: Agents only.
Types and topics: Bibles, children, fiction, nonfiction, teen/YA
Tip: "We are seeking fresh fiction and nonfiction for children ages 0–18. Under our Zonderkidz and Zondervan imprints, we look for engaging picture books and board books, timeless storybook

Bibles, faith-centric fiction from established authors, and nonfiction from key voices in the Christian sphere."

ZONDERVAN

www.zondervan.com

Andy Rogers, nonfiction acquisitions editor

Carolyn McCready, executive editor and trade acquisitions

Kyle Rohane, acquisitions editor

Parent company: HarperCollins Christian Publishing

Submissions: Publishes 120 titles per year. Bible: NIV. Agents only.

Types and topics: biography, Christian living/spirituality, church life, contemporary issues, family, finances, marriage, ministry, academic, Bible reference/commentaries, gift; fiction: contemporary, fantasy, historical, mystery, romance, science fiction, suspense/thriller

Imprints: Zondervan Books (nonfiction), Zondervan Reflective (leadership, ministry, faith and culture), Zondervan Fiction (novels), Zonderkidz (children, teens), Zondervan Academic (textbooks, Bible reference), Zondervan Gift (gift books), WestBow Press (independent publishing)

Guidelines: *www.harpercollinschristian.com/write-for-us*

ZONDERVAN ACADEMIC

3900 Sparks Dr. SE, Grand Rapids, MI 49512 | 616-698-6900

submissions@zondervan.com | *www.zondervanacademic.com*

Katya Covrett, executive acquisitions editor

Parent company: HarperCollins Christian Publishing

Mission statement: to reflect the breadth and diversity—both theological and global—within evangelical scholarship while maintaining our commitment to the heart of orthodox Christianity

Submissions: Email query. Responds in six weeks or not interested. Bible: NIV.

Types and topics: academic, Bible reference/commentaries

Types of books: ebook, hardcover, offset paperback

Guidelines: *www.harpercollinschristian.com/authors/manuscript-information*

ZONDERVAN REFLECTIVE

3900 Sparks Dr. SE, Grand Rapids, MI 49512 | 616-698-6900

submissions@zondervan.com | *www.zondervan.com/zondervanreflective*

Stan Gundry, editor-in-chief

Parent company: HarperCollins Christian Publishing

Mission statement: to provide guidance and inspiration for effective leadership in business and ministry

Submissions: Email query. Responds in six weeks or not interested. Bible: NIV.

Types and topics: contemporary issues, culture, leadership, ministry, nonfiction

Types of books: ebook, hardcover, offset paperback

Guidelines: *www.harpercollinschristian.com/authors/manuscript-information*

Tip: "The authors are expected to have demonstrable expertise on the subject being addressed."

2

BOOK ANTHOLOGY SERIES

CHICKEN SOUP FOR THE SOUL
PO Box 700, Cos Cob, CT 06807
www.chickensoup.com
Amy Newmark, publisher and editor-in-chief
> **Parent company:** Chicken Soup for the Soul Publishing, LLC
> **Purpose:** to share happiness, inspiration, and hope
> **Submissions:** Only accepts complete manuscript through the website. Also takes submissions from children and teens for some books.
> **Upcoming books:** *www.chickensoup.com/story-submissions/possible-book-topics*
> **Types of manuscripts:** theme-related personal experience, poetry
> **Length:** 1,200 words maximum
> **Payment:** $250 plus ten copies of the book, one month after publication
> **Guidelines:** *www.chickensoup.com/story-submissions/story-guidelines*
> **Tip:** "A Chicken Soup for the Soul story is an inspirational, true story about ordinary people having extraordinary experiences. . . . These stories are personal and often filled with emotion and drama. . . . Poems tell a story; no rhyming. . . . The most powerful stories are about people extending themselves, or performing an act of love, service, or courage for another person."

DIVINE MOMENTS
PO Box 1233, Broken Arrow, OK 74013-1233 | 918-346-7960
terri@grace-publishing.com | grace-publishing.com
Terri Kalfas, complier and editor
> **Parent company:** Grace Publishing
> **Purpose:** to show the possibility of changing someone's life, heart, or mind
> **Submissions:** Email complete manuscript as attachment. Responds in

two weeks to two months. Accepts 150–200 manuscripts per year.

Upcoming books: *Lost Moments, Questionable Moments, Favorite Moments, Divine Detours, Unexpected Kindness, Patriotic Moments, Christmas*

Types of manuscripts: theme-related personal experience, poetry, fiction, humorous, uplifting

Length: 500–2,000 words

Rights: first, reprint

Payment: copy of book; royalties are donated to Samaritan's Purse

Guidelines: *grace-publishing.com/manuscript-submission/divine-moments-guidelines*

Tip: "Submit uplifting, optimistic stories that keep to the theme of the book."

SHORT AND SWEET

PO Box 1233, Broken Arrow, OK 74013-1233 | 918-346-7960

shortandsweettoo@gmail.com | grace-publishing.com

Susan King, compiler and editor

Parent company: Grace Publishing

Purpose: to show readers and writers that good storytelling doesn't have to use big, long words

Submissions: Email complete manuscript as attachment. Responds in two weeks to two months. Accepts 150 manuscripts per year.

Upcoming books: *Memorable Mutts, A Feline in the Family, Facing Fear, Mishaps and Misadventures: Vacations that Took an Unexpected Turn Along the Way*

Types of manuscripts: theme-related personal experience, poetry, fiction

Length: 500–1,000 words

Rights: first, reprint

Payment: copy of book; royalties are donated to World Christian Broadcasting

Guidelines: *grace-publishing.com/manuscript-submission/short-and-sweet-guidelines*

Tip: "The story must be uplifting and engage the reader with a Christian worldview. It does not have to have an overt Christian message or theme."

PART 2

INDEPENDENT BOOK PUBLISHING

3

INDEPENDENT BOOK PUBLISHERS

PUBLISHING A BOOK YOURSELF NO LONGER CARRIES THE STIGMA self-publishing has had in the past—if you do it right. Even some well-published writers are now hybrid authors, with independently published books alongside their royalty books. Others have built their readerships with traditional publishers, then moved to independent publishing where it is possible to make more money per sale.

Independent book publishers require the author to pay for part of the publishing costs or to buy a certain number of books. They call themselves by a variety of names, such as book packager, cooperative publisher, self-publisher, custom publisher, subsidy publisher, or simply someone who helps authors get their books printed. Services vary from including different levels of editing and proofreading to printing your manuscript as is.

Whenever you pay for any part of the production of your book, you are entering into a nontraditional relationship. Some independent publishers also offer a form of royalty publishing, so be sure you understand the contract they give you before signing it.

Some independent publishers will publish any book, as long as the author is willing to pay for it. Others are as selective about what they publish as a royalty publisher is. Some independent publishers will do as much promotion as a royalty publisher—for a fee. Others do none at all.

If you are unsuccessful in placing your book with a royalty publisher but feel strongly about seeing it published, an independent publisher can make printing your book easier and often less expensive than doing it yourself. POD, as opposed to a print run of 1,000 books or more, could save you upfront money, although the price per copy is higher. Having your manuscript produced only as an ebook is also a less-expensive option.

Entries in this chapter are for information only, not an endorsement of publishers. For every complaint about a publisher, several other authors may sing the praises of it. Before you sign with any company, get more than one bid to determine whether the terms you are offered are competitive.

A legitimate independent publisher will provide a list of former clients as references. Also buy a couple of the publisher's previous books to check the quality of the work: covers, bindings, typesetting, etc. See if the books currently are available through any of the major online retailers.

Get answers before committing yourself. You may also want someone in the book-publishing industry to review your contract before you sign it. Some experts listed in the "Editorial Services" chapter review contracts.

If you decide not to use an independent publisher but do the work yourself, at least hire an editor, proofreader, cover designer, and interior typesetter-designer. The "Editorial Services" and "Design and Production Services" chapters will help you locate professionals with skills in these areas, as well as printing companies. Plus the "Distribution Services" and "Publicity and Marketing Services" chapters can help you solve one of the biggest problems of independent publishing: getting your books to readers.

ACW PRESS

4854 Aster Dr., Nashville, TN 37211 | 615-498-8630
acwriters@aol.com | *www.acwpress.com*
Reg A. Forder, publisher

> **Types:** ebooks, gift books, hardcover, offset paperback, POD
> **Services:** copyediting, design, manuscript evaluation, proofreading, substantive editing
> **Production time:** four to six months
> **Books per year:** three to ten
> **Tip:** "Must be biblically sound."

AMPELOS PRESS

951 Anders Rd., Lansdale, PA 19446 | 484-991-8581
mbagnull@aol.com | *writehisanswer.com/ampelospress*
Marlene Bagnull, publisher

> **Types:** ebooks, POD
> **Services:** copyediting, design, manuscript evaluation, proofreading, substantive editing
> **Production time:** six months
> **Books per year:** two
> **Tip:** "Especially interested in issues fiction and nonfiction, as well as books about missions and the needs of children. Author pays a one-time fee, maintains all rights, and receives 100% royalty from Amazon KDP."

BELIEVERS BOOK SERVICES

2329 Farragut Ave., Colorado Springs, CO 80907 | 719-641-7862
dave@believersbookservices.com | *believersbookservices.com*
Dave Sheets, owner

> **Types:** ebooks, gift books, hardcover, offset paperback, picture books, POD
> **Services:** à la carte options, author websites, copyediting, design, distribution, manuscript evaluation, packages of services, proofreading, substantive editing
> **Production time:** three months
> **Books per year:** 45-50
> **Tip:** "Start thinking about strategy for publishing, marketing, and launching as soon as possible in the process. This strategy process will help produce a stronger book."

BK ROYSTON PUBLISHING

PO Box 4321, Jeffersonville, IN 47131 | 502-802-5385
bkroystonpublishing@gmail.com | *www.bkroystonpublishing.com*
Julia A. Royston, CEO

> **Types:** audiobooks, ebooks, hardcover, offset paperback, picture books, POD
> **Services:** copyediting, design, distribution, manuscript evaluation, online bookstore, packages of services, promotional materials, proofreading
> **Production time:** four to six months
> **Books per year:** 50
> **Tip:** "1. Please do at least spell-check before you submit a manuscript. 2. Be active on social media 3. Be passionate about the book that you're writing or have written. 4. After multiple drafts, edits, reviews, you eventually have to let the book go to the next level or it will never be published."

BOOKBABY

7905 N. Crescent Blvd., Pennsauken, NJ 08110 | 877-961-6878
info@bookbaby.com | *www.bookbaby.com*

> **Types:** comic book, ebooks, gift books, hardcover, offset paperback, picture books, POD
> **Services:** copyediting, design, distribution, manuscript evaluation, online bookstore, proofreading, social-media ads, substantive editing
> **Production time:** varies
> **Tip:** Has ebook and printed-book distribution network for self-published authors around the globe.

BRIDGE LOGOS, INC.

17750 NW 115th Ave., Bldg. 200, Ste. 220, Alachua, FL 32615 |
386-462-2525

info@bridgelogos.com | *www.bridgelogos.com*

Peggy Hildebrand, acquisitions editor

Types: ebooks, hardcover, paperback

Services: copyediting, design, distribution, proofreading, substantive
editing

Books per year: 40

Also does: royalty contracts

Tip: Traditional house that requires new Bridge Logos authors and
authors with no established marketing platform to purchase 1,000–
3,000 books. "Looking for well-written, timely books that are aimed
at the needs of people and that glorify God. Have a great message,
a well-written manuscript, and a specific plan and willingness to
market your book. Looking for previously published authors with an
active ministry who are experts on their subject."

BROWN CHRISTIAN PRESS

16250 Knoll Trail Dr., Ste. 205, Dallas, TX 75248 | 972-381-0009

publishing@brownbooks.com | *www.brownbooks.com/brown-christian-press*

Types: audiobooks, ebooks, gift books, hardcover, paperback

Services: author websites, copyediting, design, distribution,
ghostwriting, indexing, marketing, proofreading, substantive editing

Production time: six months

Tip: "We are a relationship publisher and work with our authors from
beginning to end in the journey of publishing."

CALLED WRITERS CHRISTIAN PUBLISHING

1900 Rice Mine Rd. N. 401, Tuscaloosa, AL 35406 | 205-872-4509

shannon@calledwriters.com | *CalledWriters.com*

Shannon McKinney, relationship builder

Types: offset paperback, POD

Services: à la carte options, copyediting, design, manuscript evaluation,
marketing, packages of services, proofreading, substantive editing

Production time: six months

Books per year: two

Also does: royalty contracts

Tip: "God will open the right doors for you at the right time. Don't give
up."

CARPENTER'S SON PUBLISHING

307 Verde Meadow Dr., Franklin, TN 37067 | 615-472-1128
larry@christianbookservices.com | *carpenterssonpublishing.com*
Larry Carpenter, president-CEO, editor

Types: audiobooks, ebooks, gift books, hardcover, offset paperback, picture books, POD
Services: à la carte options, author websites, copyediting, design, distribution, indexing, manuscript evaluation, marketing, promotional materials, proofreading, substantive editing
Production time: three to six months
Books per year: 100
Tip: "Make sure someone is selling your book to the bookstores."

CASTLE GATE PRESS

244 E. Glendale Rd., St. Louis, MO 63119 | 314-962-1940
p.wheeler@castlegatepress.com | *castlegatepress.com*
Phyllis Wheeler, owner

Types: audiobooks, ebooks, POD
Services: à la carte options, copyediting, design, manuscript evaluation, proofreading, substantive editing
Production time: depends on manuscript editing needs
Books per year: one or two
Tip: "Castle Gate Press was a traditional publisher from 2013–2018. One of our books is an Amazon genre bestseller, and another won a Selah Award for Christian fiction in the speculative category. Yet another was a finalist for Selah and also for the Realm Award, and another a finalist for the Grace Award. In short, we provide award-winning editing."

CHRISTIAN FAITH PUBLISHING

832 Park Ave., Meadville, PA 16335 | 800-955-3794
Chris@christianfaithpublishing.com | *www.Christianfaithpublishing.com*
Chris Rutherford, president

Types: ebooks, hardcover, offset paperback, POD
Services: à la carte options, copyediting, design, distribution, indexing, manuscript evaluation, marketing, packages of services, promotional materials
Production time: eight to ten months
Books per year: 1,200
Also does: royalty contracts

Tip: "Be mindful of the fact that it is quite challenging to publish a book and have commercial success."

CLM PUBLISHING

PO Box 1217, Bodden Town, Grand Cayman, Cayman Islands KY-11108 | 345-926 2507

production@clmpublishing.com | *www.clmpublishing.com*

Types: ebooks, gift books, hardcover, offset paperback, picture books, POD

Services: author websites, copyediting, design, distribution, indexing, manuscript evaluation, marketing, online bookstore, promotional materials, proofreading, substantive editing

Production time: three to six months

Books per year: eight

Tip: "Be willing to do some marketing."

COLEMAN JONES PRESS

info@colemanjonespress.com | *colemanjonespress.com*

Tracee and Ross Jones, owners

Types: audiobooks, curriculum, ebooks, hardcover, picture books, POD

Services: author websites, design, distribution, marketing, packages of services, promotional materials

Production time: three to six months

Tip: "Write for the sake of getting the gospel out, not for the money. When choosing a cover or illustrator, make sure your design looks like something that is in major retail stores."

COVENANT BOOKS

11661 Hwy. 707, Murrells Inlet, SC 29576 | 843-507-8373

contact@covenantbooks.com | *www.covenantbooks.com*

Denice Hunter, president

Types: ebooks, hardcover, offset paperback, POD

Services: à la carte options, copyediting, design, distribution, marketing, online bookstore, packages of services

Production time: six months

Books per year: 1,000

Also does: royalty contracts

Tip: "Publishing a book can be a fun and enlightening process. Take your time, and choose a publisher you feel comfortable with."

CREATIVE ENTERPRISES STUDIO

1507 Shirley Way, Ste. A, Bedford, TX 76022-6737 | 817-312-7393

AcreativeShop@aol.com | CreativeEnterprisesStudio.com

Mary Hollingsworth, publisher

> **Types:** audiobooks, ebooks, gift books, hardcover, offset paperback, picture books, POD
> **Services:** author websites, book trailer, coaching, copyediting, design, ghostwriting, marketing, proofreading, substantive editing, warehousing
> **Production time:** seven months, depending on type and length of book
> **Books per year:** varies
> **Tip:** "Contact us by email to set a phone conference to discuss your work before proceeding otherwise."

CREDO HOUSE PUBLISHERS

2200 Boyd Ct. NE, Grand Rapids, MI 49525-6714

publish@credocommunications.net | www.credohousepublishers.com

Timothy J. Beals, publisher

> **Types:** offset paperback
> **Services:** à la carte options, author websites, copyediting, design, distribution, indexing, manuscript evaluation, marketing, online bookstore, packages of services, promotional materials, proofreading, substantive editing
> **Production time:** three months
> **Books per year:** 30
> **Tip:** "Come prepared. Be persistent. Get published."

DCTS PUBLISHING

PO Box 40216, Santa Barbara, CA 93140 | 805-570-3168

dennis@dctspub.com | www.dctspub.com

Dennis Hamilton, publisher

> **Types:** ebooks, offset paperback, picture books
> **Services:** design, manuscript evaluation, promotional materials, proofreading, substantive editing
> **Production time:** three months
> **Books per year:** five
> **Tip:** "Place as many eyes on your manuscript as possible."

DEEP RIVER BOOKS, LLC

PO Box 310, Sisters, OR 97759 | 541-549-1139

andy@deepriverbooks.com | *www.deepriverbooks.com*

Andy Carmichael, publisher

> **Types:** audiobooks, ebooks, hardcover, offset paperback, POD
>
> **Services:** copyediting, design, distribution, manuscript evaluation, marketing, online bookstore, packages of services, promotional materials, royalty contract, substantive editing
>
> **Production time:** 9–14 months
>
> **Books per year:** 30-35
>
> **Also does:** royalty contracts
>
> **Tip:** "Check our website on how we work with authors before you submit."

DEEPER REVELATION BOOKS

PO Box 4260, Cleveland, TN 37320-4260 | 423-478-2843

pastormikeshreve@gmail.com | *www.deeperrevelationbooks.org*

Mike Shreve, founder, president

> **Types:** ebooks, gift books, hardcover, offset paperback, picture books, POD
>
> **Services:** author websites, copyediting, design, distribution, manuscript evaluation, marketing, online bookstore, promotional materials, proofreading, substantive editing
>
> **Production time:** four months
>
> **Books per year:** 15
>
> **Tip:** Imprints: Deeper Revelation Books (nonfiction), Pure Heart Publications (fiction), Children of Promise (children), Pivotal Publications (success and social issues). "One book that is well written and published with excellence can change the world."

DESTINY IMAGE PUBLISHERS

167 Walnut Bottom Rd., Shippensburg, PA 17257 | 717-532-3040

manuscripts@norimediagroup.com | *norimediagroup.com/pages/publish-with-us*

> **Types:** ebooks, paperback
>
> **Services:** copyediting, design, manuscript evaluation, marketing, proofreading, substantive editing
>
> **Production time:** 12 months
>
> **Tip:** Traditional publisher that requires prepurchase of 500 to 3,000 copies. "Focuses on Spirit-empowered themes: supernatural God encounters, healing/deliverance, prophecy and prophetic ministry,

gifts of the Holy Spirit, prayer and intercession, the presence and glory of God, and dreams/dream interpretation."

EABOOKS PUBLISHING

1136 W. Winged Foot Cir., Winter Springs, FL 32708 | 407-712-3431

Cheri@eabookspublishing.com | *www.eabookspublishing.com*

Cheri Cowell, founder and publisher

> **Types:** audiobooks, ebooks, gift books, hardcover, POD
> **Services:** à la carte options, author websites, copyediting, design, distribution, indexing, manuscript evaluation, marketing, packages of services, promotional materials, proofreading, substantive editing
> **Production time:** six months
> **Books per year:** 50
> **Also does:** royalty contracts
> **Tip:** "Contact for a free consultation to see if we can partner with you to make your publishing dreams come true."

EBOOK CONVERSION AND LISTING SERVICES

PO Box 57, Glenwood, MD 21738 | 443-280-5077

sales@taegais.com | *ebooklistingservices.com*

Amy Deardon, CEO

> **Types:** audiobooks, ebooks, POD
> **Services:** à la carte options, design, distribution, marketing, packages of services, promotional materials
> **Production time:** one to three months
> **Books per year:** 20
> **Tip:** "We empower independent authors to become successful. Unlike most other independent publishers, we set you up so you are the publisher, rather than publishing through the independent company. You can create your own publishing company name and logo, and we help you with that. You remain fully in charge of all decisions, rights, and profits from start to forever. Once your book is published, you can buy as few or as many books as you want at the lowest printer's price (a 200-page book costs less than $3.50); and books are delivered in a week or two through Amazon. We also have additional packages that can list your book with the Library of Congress and help you rank higher on Amazon's search engines so readers can actually find your book and buy it. We provide you with ownership of your book and work with you to make that succeed."

ELECTRIC MOON PUBLISHING, LLC

PO Box 466, Stromsburg, NE 68666 | 402-366-2033

laree@emoonpublishing.com | *www.emoonpublishing.com*

Laree Lindburg, owner

Types: audiobooks, ebooks, gift books, hardcover, offset paperback, picture books, POD

Services: à la carte options, author websites, copyediting, design, distribution, indexing, manuscript evaluation, promotional materials, proofreading, substantive editing

Production time: nine months

Books per year: 8-12

Tip: "Feel free to ask questions of the services and publishing models offered. We are here to help and would enjoy an initial conversation with you."

ESSENCE PUBLISHING

20 Hanna Ct., Belleville, ON K8P 5J2, Canada | 800-238-6376, 613-962-2360

s.brunton@essence-publishing.com | *www.essence-publishing.com*

Sherrill Brunton, publishing manager

Types: ebooks, gift books, offset paperback, picture books, POD

Services: copyediting, design, distribution, indexing, manuscript evaluation, marketing, online bookstore, promotional materials, proofreading, substantive editing

Production time: three to five months

Books per year: 100–150

Tip: "Submit a copy of your manuscript for your free evaluation."

FAIRWAY PRESS

5450 N. Dixie Hwy., Lima, OH 45807-9559 | 419-227-1818

david@csspub.com | *www.fairwaypress.com*

David Runk, president

Types: ebooks, hardcover, offset paperback, POD

Services: à la carte options, copyediting, design, manuscript evaluation, proofreading

Production time: 6-12 months

Books per year: 10-15

Tip: "No derogatory racist content. Christian content preferred."

FAITH BOOKS & MORE

PO Box 1024, Athens, OH 45701 | 678-232-6156

publishing@faithbooksandmore.com | *www.faithbooksandmore.com*

Nicole Antoinette Smith, owner

> **Types:** hardcover, offset paperback, POD
> **Services:** copyediting, design, manuscript evaluation, proofreading
> **Production time:** three months
> **Books per year:** five
> **Tip:** "Write, rewrite, write, and rewrite again until you're 100% satisfied with your manuscript."

FIESTA PUBLISHING

PO Box 44984, Phoenix, AZ 85064 | 602-795-5868

julie@fiestapublishing.com | *www.fiestapublishing.com*

Julie Castro, owner

> **Types:** ebooks, hardcover, offset paperback, POD
> **Services:** à la carte options, copyediting, distribution, marketing, promotional materials, proofreading, substantive editing
> **Production time:** four to six months
> **Books per year:** five to seven
> **Tip:** "Be willing to listen to an established publisher and act accordingly. There is a difference between a book and a great book! Look for publisher integrity and their purpose for having the publishing company."

FOUNTAIN PRESS

119/13 Pengamuck West, Thrissur, Kerala, India 680544 | +91-992-394-7792

pupaulson@gmail.com | *www.fountainpress.org*

Dr. Paulson Pulikottil

> **Types:** ebooks, offset paperback
> **Services:** copyediting, distribution, indexing, online bookstore, proofreading
> **Production time:** three months
> **Books per year:** ten
> **Also does:** royalty contracts
> **Tip:** "Published in India for distribution at affordable Indian prices. Selected books will also be translated into major Indian languages. The titles are available in all online bookstores globally."

FRUITBEARER PUBLISHING, LLC

PO Box 777, Georgetown, DE 19947 | 302-856-6649

cfa@candyabbott.com | *www.fruitbearer.com*

Elizabeth Boerner, author liaison

> **Types:** ebooks, gift books, hardcover, offset paperback, picture books, POD
>
> **Services:** à la carte options, copyediting, design, distribution, manuscript evaluation, marketing, online bookstore, packages of services, promotional materials, proofreading, substantive editing
>
> **Production time:** four to six months
>
> **Books per year:** 12+
>
> **Also does:** royalty contracts
>
> **Tip:** "We're looking for manuscripts that would receive a nod of approval from God. The book doesn't have to be religious, but it does need to be wholesome. Fruitbearer's chief concern is to keep in step with the Holy Spirit and exemplify the Fruit of the Spirit. If you're looking for a publisher who will walk you through the publishing process and not put you on an assembly line, we might be a good fit."

FUSION HYBRID PUBLISHING

PO Box 206, Nesbit, MS 38651 | 901-590-6584

victoria@endgamepress.com | *www.endgamepress.com/fusion*

Alice, acquisitions editor

> **Types:** audiobooks, ebooks, gospel tracts, hardcover, offset paperback, picture books, POD
>
> **Services:** à la carte options, copyediting, design, distribution, indexing, manuscript evaluation, marketing, online bookstore, packages of services, promotional materials, proofreading, substantive editing
>
> **Production time:** 6-12 months
>
> **Books per year:** three to four
>
> **Tip:** "Fusion is a great option for those who are excited to get to market faster than traditional houses and have a great audience already."

HARRISON HOUSE

167 Walnut Bottom Rd., Shippensburg, PA 17257 | 717-532-3040

manuscripts@norimediagroup.com | *norimediagroup.com/pages/publish-with-us*

> **Types:** ebooks, paperback
>
> **Services:** copyediting, design, manuscript evaluation, marketing, proofreading, substantive editing

Production time: 12 months
Also does: royalty contracts
Tip: Traditional publisher that requires prepurchase of 500 to 3,000 copies.

HEALTHY LIFE PRESS

3004 Shelby St. #316, Bristol, TN 37620 | 276-608-2086
healthylifepress@gmail.com | *www.HealthyLifePress.com*
Judy Johnson, publisher

    Types: ebooks, gift books, POD
    Services: design, online bookstore
    Also does: royalty contracts
    Production time: six months
    Tip: "If you have a book manuscript that is what used to be called 'camera ready,' i.e., the text is finished, needing no more than minor editing or proofing, we can take it from there to published form (printed book and electronic formats) very quickly. Our philosophy is to share expenses (authors subsidize these) and the net proceeds equitably. We will provide a copy of a sample contract upon request."

HONEYCOMB HOUSE PUBLISHING

315 3rd St., New Cumberland, PA 17070 | 215-767-9600
dave@fessendens.net | *www.davefessenden.com/honeycomb-house-publishing-llc*
David Fessenden, publisher

    Types: POD
    Services: à la carte options, author websites, copyediting, design, distribution, manuscript evaluation, marketing, packages of services, promotional materials, proofreading, substantive editing
    Production time: three to six months
    Books per year: one or two
    Tip: "Prepare a book proposal even if you plan to self-publish/subsidy publish."

IMMORTALISE

PO Box 656, Noarlunga Centre, SA 5168 Australia
toastercide@gmail.com | *www.immortalise.com.au*
Ben Morton, editor

    Types: ebooks, hardcover, offset paperback, picture books
    Services: à la carte options, copyediting, design, manuscript evaluation, online bookstore, packages of services, promotional materials,

proofreading, substantive editing
Production time: varies
Tip: "All our services are optional and there is no cost for enquiries. We will publish any book so long as the content is not likely to get anyone sued."

INSCRIPT BOOKS

PO Box 611, Bladensburg, MD 20710 | 240-342-3293
inscript@dovechristianpublishers.com | inscriptpublishing.com
Raenita Wiggins, acquisitions editor

Types: ebooks, hardcover, offset paperback, picture books, POD
Services: à la carte options, copyediting, design, distribution, indexing, marketing, online bookstore, packages of services, proofreading, substantive editing
Production time: one to two months
Books per year: ten
Tip: "We receive new proposals via our online form only. Carefully review publishing guidelines on website."

MORGAN JAMES

5 Penn Plaza, 23rd Floor, New York City, NY 10001 | 516-900-5711
terry@morganjamespublishing.com | www.morganjamespublishing.com
W. Terry Whalin, acquisition editor

Types: audiobooks, ebooks, hardcover, offset paperback, picture books, POD
Services: design, distribution, marketing, online bookstore, promotional materials
Production time: three to six months
Books per year: 180–200, 25–30 in the faith division
Also does: royalty contracts
Tip: "General-market publisher with a Christian division. Our books have been on *The New York Times* bestseller list more than 25 times (broad distribution). For nonfiction, requires authors to purchase 3,000 copies at print costs plus $3 over lifetime of agreement. Pays 20–30% royalties on sales; pays small advance. Email proposal with sample chapters or full manuscript. Only 30% of authors have agents."

NORDSKOG PUBLISHING

2716 Sailor Ave., Ventura, CA 93001 | 805-642-2070
jerry@nordskogpublishing.com | *nordskogpublishing.com*
Michelle Shelfer, editor

> **Types:** hardcover, paperback
> **Services:** copyediting, design, marketing
> **Tip:** "Looking for the best in sound theological and applied Christian-faith books, both nonfiction and fiction."

PARSON PLACE PRESS, LLC

PO Box 8277, Mobile, AL 36689-0277 | 251-643-6985
MLWhite@parsonplacepress.com | *www.parsonplacepress.com*
Michael L. White, founder and managing editor

> **Types:** ebooks, hardcover, POD
> **Services:** distribution, proofreading, substantive editing
> **Production time:** three to four months
> **Books per year:** one to four
> **Also does:** royalty contracts
> **Tip:** "Content must conform to biblical Christian orthodoxy. Review publisher's website for FAQ and other details."

REDEMPTION PRESS

1602 Cole St., Enumclaw, WA 98022 | 360-226-3488
Athena@redemption-press.com | *www.redemption-press.com*
BJ Garrett, acquisitions manager

> **Types:** audiobooks, ebooks, gift books, hardcover, offset paperback, picture books, POD
> **Services:** à la carte options, author websites, coaching, copyediting, design, distribution, ghostwriting, indexing, manuscript evaluation, marketing, online bookstore, promotional materials, proofreading, rewrites, substantive editing
> **Production time:** 6–12 months
> **Books per year:** 75
> **Tip:** "Don't skip the all-important involvement of an author coach or professional editor. Redemption Press is known for publishing award-winning books because we work with our authors to create a product of excellence."

SALVATION PUBLISHER AND MARKETING GROUP

PO Box 40860, Santa Barbara, CA 93140 | 805-252-9822

opalmaedailey@aol.com

Opal Mae Dailey, editor

> **Types:** ebooks, hardcover, offset paperback
> **Services:** copyediting, design, manuscript evaluation, proofreading, substantive editing
> **Production time:** six to nine months
> **Books per year:** five to seven
> **Tip:** "Turning taped messages into book form for pastors is a specialty of ours. We do not accept any manuscript we would be ashamed to put our name on."

SERMON TO BOOK

424 W. Bakerview Rd., Ste. 105 #215, Bellingham, WA 98226 | 360-223-1877

info@sermontobook.com | *www.sermontobook.com*

Caleb Breakey, lead book director

> **Types:** audiobooks, ebooks, offset paperback, POD
> **Services:** author websites, copyediting, design, distribution, indexing, manuscript evaluation, marketing, online bookstore, packages of services, promotional materials, proofreading, substantive editing
> **Production time:** seven to nine months
> **Books per year:** 60
> **Tip:** "Check out our materials at *SermonToBook.com*."

STONE OAK PUBLISHING

PO Box 2011, Friendswood, TX 77549 | 832-569-4282

stoneoakpublishing@gmail.com | *stoneoakpublishing.com*

Karen Porter, acquisitions

> **Types:** ebooks, hardcover, offset paperback, POD
> **Services:** à la carte options, copyediting, design, distribution, indexing, manuscript evaluation, marketing, packages of services, promotional materials, proofreading, substantive editing
> **Production time:** six to eight months
> **Books per year:** ten
> **Also does:** royalty contracts
> **Tip:** "Send us a well-thought-out email detailing the information about your book."

STRONG TOWER PUBLISHING

PO Box 973, Milesburg, PA 16863 | 814-206-6778

strongtowerpubs@aol.com | *www.strongtowerpublishing.com*

Heidi L. Nigro, publisher

Types: ebooks, POD

Services: copyediting, design, manuscript evaluation, online bookstore, proofreading, substantive editing

Production time: three to four months

Books per year: one or two

Tip: Specializes in books on end-times topics from the prewrath rapture perspective. Pays 25% royalty on sales.

TEACH SERVICES, INC.

11 Quartermaster Cir., Fort Oglethorpe, GA 30742-3886 | 800-367-1844

T.Hullquist@TEACHServices.com | *www.teachservices.com*

Timothy Hullquist, author advisor

Types: ebooks, gift books, hardcover, offset paperback, picture books, POD

Services: à la carte options, author websites, copyediting, design, distribution, indexing, manuscript evaluation, marketing, online bookstore, packages of services, promotional materials, proofreading, substantive editing

Production time: one to four months

Also does: royalty contracts

Tip: "We specialize in marketing our titles to Seventh-day Adventists."

TMP BOOKS

3 Central Plaza, Ste. 307, Rome, GA 30161 | 678-600-4617

info@tmpbooks.com | *www.TMPbooks.com*

Tracy Ruckman, publisher

Types: audiobooks, ebooks, hardcover, picture books, POD

Services: à la carte options, copyediting, design, manuscript evaluation, marketing, packages of services, promotional materials, proofreading, substantive editing

Production time: four to six months

Books per year: six to eight

Tip: "We are a subsidy press, but we offer affordable package options from full service to those that teach authors the process so they can publish the book themselves and keep 100% of the royalties. We also offer consultations and à la carte services."

TRACT PLANET

1275 Bennett Dr., Unit 119, Longwood, FL 32750 | 877-778-7228

support@tractplanet.com | *www.tractplanet.com*

Andy Lawniczak, owner

Types: gospel tracts
Services: design, promotional materials
Production time: varies
Tip: "We focus on Gospel tracts that follow the Way of the Master method of evangelism."

TRAIL MEDIA

PO Box 1285, Orange, CA 92856

admin@ChisholmTrailMedia.com | *www.chisholmtrailmedia.com*

Christine "CJ" Simpson, publishing director

Types: ebooks, gift books, picture books, POD
Services: à la carte options, copyediting, manuscript evaluation, marketing, packages of services, promotional materials, proofreading, substantive editing
Production time: negotiable
Tip: "Our goal is to help new authors publish their work by coordinating the services needed with experts in the field and publishing in a co-op fashion under the Trail Media imprint, so 100% of the revenue generated goes to ministry of the authors. In many cases, we find scholarships and grants to help missionaries and those in the persecuted church. Trail Media is a ministry of modified tentmaking models."

TRILOGY CHRISTIAN PUBLISHING

PO Box A, Santa Ana, CA 92711 | 855-214-2665

www.trilogy.tv

Types: ebooks, hardcover, POD
Services: copyediting, design, illustrations, marketing, online bookstore
Also does: royalty contracts
Tip: "The Trinity Broadcasting Family of Networks is blazing a trail worldwide, with fresh, innovative programs that entertain, inspire, and change lives. In addition to the 8,000 cable and satellite affiliates that reach over 100 million homes across America and every inhabited continent, the TBN Family of Networks will continue to aggressively expand their reach as they deliver content

across all social media and digital platforms. As part of your book release TBN will use its social media platforms such as Facebook (1.2 million Likes), Twitter (80,000 Followers) and Instagram (133,000 Followers) to promote it. From there, all of the social media strength of Trilogy Christian Publishing will be deployed."

VIDE PRESS

videpress.com

Tom Frieling, publisher

Types: ebooks, paperback
Services: copyediting, design, distribution, marketing, proofreading
Tip: "We are always searching for new voices, articulate Christian writers who have the courage to confront the issues challenging today's culture and our faith."

WARNER HOUSE PRESS

1325 Lane Switch Rd., Albertville, AL 35951 | 256-660-0232

robert@warner.house | warner.house

Robert Warner, managing editor

Types: ebooks, hardcover, offset paperback, picture books
Services: à la carte options, author websites, copyediting, distribution, manuscript evaluation, online bookstore, proofreading, royalty contract, substantive editing
Production time: three months
Books per year: eight
Tip: "Everyone has a story in them! No matter what stage of writing you're at, we can help."

WESTBOW PRESS

1663 Liberty Dr., Bloomington, IN 47403 | 844-714-3454

www.westbowpress.com

Types: audiobooks, ebooks, gift books, hardcover, offset paperback, POD
Services: book trailer, copyediting, design, distribution, illustrations, indexing, manuscript evaluation, marketing, Spanish translation, substantive editing
Tip: Independent publishing division of Thomas Nelson and Zondervan.

WORD ALIVE PRESS

119 De Baets St., Winnipeg, MB R2J 3R9, Canada | 866-967-3782

jen@wordalivepress.ca | www.wordalivepress.ca

Jen Jandavs-Hedlin, publishing consultant

> **Types:** audiobooks, ebooks, gift books, hardcover, offset paperback, picture books, POD
>
> **Services:** à la carte options, copyediting, design, distribution, indexing, manuscript evaluation, marketing, online bookstore, packages of services, promotional materials
>
> **Production time:** three to six months
>
> **Books per year:** 100
>
> **Also does:** royalty contracts
>
> **Tip:** "Start with a manuscript evaluation from a reputable editor or publisher. They will help you to identify and address any big-picture trouble spots prior to investing in copyediting or publishing."

XULON PRESS

2301 Lucien Way, Ste. 415, Maitland, FL 32751 | 407-339-4217, 866-381-2665

www.xulonpress.com

Donald Newman, executive director of publishing

> **Types:** ebooks, hardcover, offset paperback, POD
>
> **Services:** à la carte options, book trailer, copyediting, design, ghostwriting, illustrations, manuscript evaluation, marketing, online bookstore, packages of services, promotional materials, substantive editing
>
> **Production time:** three to six months

YOUR BACKYARD

PO Box 127, Cottondale, FL 32431 | 615-613-5040

ybbmedia@gmail.com | yourbackyard.us

shELAH, publisher

> **Types:** ebooks, hardcover, offset paperback, picture books, POD
>
> **Services:** à la carte options, author websites, coaching, design, distribution, indexing, manuscript evaluation, packages of services, proofreading, substantive editing
>
> **Production time:** 3–12 months
>
> **Books per year:** three
>
> **Tip:** "Study to shew [show] thyself approved unto God, a workman that needeth not to be ashamed, rightly dividing the word of truth" (2 Timothy 2:15, KJV).

ZOË LIFE PUBLISHING

PO Box 871066, Canton, MI 48187 | 734-578-6703

sabrina.adams@zoelifepub.com | www.zoelifebooks.org

Sabrina Adams, publisher

Types: ebooks, hardcover, offset paperback, picture books

Services: à la carte options, author websites, copyediting, design, distribution, manuscript evaluation, marketing, online bookstore, packages of services, proofreading, substantive editing

Production time: three to six months

Books per year: 12–24

Tip: "Plan, plan, plan, then write."

Note: See "Editorial Services" and "Publicity and Marketing Services" for help with these needs.

4

DESIGN AND PRODUCTION SERVICES

829 DESIGN | LINNÉ GARRETT
8749 Cortina Cir., Roseville, CA 95678-2940 | 408-410-8072
linne@829design.com | *www.829design.com*
> **Contact:** website contact form
> **Services:** book-cover design, book-interior design, ebook conversion, printing, typesetting, website design
> **Charges:** custom, flat fee, hourly rate, retainer
> **Credentials/experience:** "Over 30 years branding and graphic-design experience with a penchant for print. Please visit us online to learn more about our services and custom design."

BACK•DOOR DESIGN
backdoordesign99@gmail.com | *backdoordesign99.wixsite.com/info*
> **Contact:** email, website contact form
> **Services:** book-cover design, book-interior design, ebook conversion, illustrations, typesetting
> **Charges:** custom, flat fee
> **Credentials/experience:** "At back•door DESIGN, our mission is to create high-quality book designs at DIY prices. We are all about book design, from front cover to back cover and everything in between. Adobe Certified Associate in Print & Digital Publication Using Adobe InDesign."

BELIEVERS BOOK SERVICES | DAVE SHEETS
2329 Farragut Ave., Colorado Springs, CO 80907 | 719-641-7862
dave@believersbookservices.com | *www.believersbookservices.com*
> **Contact:** email
> **Services:** book-cover design, book-interior design, ebook conversion, illustrations, printing, typesetting, website design

Charges: custom

Credentials/experience: "Our team has decades of experience in traditional publishing (Tyndale, Multnomah, Harvest House, NavPress), book wholesaling (STL Distribution), book distribution (Advocate Distribution Solutions), book printing (Bethany Press, Snowfall Press), book retailing (Glen Eyrie Bookstore), and independent publishing (Believers Press, BelieversBookServices). We know how to help our clients achieve their goals, while maintaining control over their own book project. We have helped hundreds of authors successfully publish, both in the United States, and around the world."

BETHANY PRESS INTERNATIONAL

6820 W. 115th St., Bloomington, MN 55438 | 888-717-7400
info@bethanypress.com | *www.bethanypress.com*

Contact: email, phone, website contact form
Services: printing
Charges: flat fee
Credentials/experience: Printer for the majority of Christian publishing houses since 1997. "We partner with publishers and ministries to create, produce, and distribute millions of life-changing Christian books each year."

BLUE LEAF BOOK SCANNING | DON O'DANIEL

618 Crowsnest Dr., Ballwin, MN 63021 | 314-606-9322
blue.leaf.it@gmail.com | *www.blueleaf-book-scanning.com*

Contact: email
Services: audiobook, document scanning, ebook conversion
Charges: custom
Credentials/experience: "We have been providing low-cost scanning services since 2008."

BREADBOX CREATIVE | ERYN LYNUM

1437 N. Denver Ave. #167, Loveland, CO 80538 | 970-308-3654
eryn@breadboxcreative.com | *www.breadboxcreative.com/creators*

Contact: website contact form
Services: website design
Charges: flat fee
Credentials/experience: "At Breadbox Creative, we have more than twenty years of experience in web design. The owner, Eryn Lynum, is an author herself and marries her passion for writing with her

passion for web design to come alongside writers and speakers and help them further spread the messages God has laid on their hearts. Breadbox Creative works with businesses, writers, and speakers by creating professional WordPress websites, as well as assisting with SEO and social-media platforms. We also offer assistance with preparing book proposals and writing consulting."

BROOKSTONE CREATIVE GROUP | JOHN HERRING
100 Missionary Ridge, Birmingham, AL 35242 | 302-514-7899
www.brookstonecreativegroup.com

Contact: phone
Services: book-cover design, book-interior design, logo design, printing, promotional materials, website design
Charges: flat fee
Credentials/experience: "Brookstone Creative Group is changing the landscape for how writers, authors, speakers, pastors, musicians, and other creatives navigate the ever-changing landscape of platform development. Through true and tested solutions, training, and community-building, Brookstone Creative Group guides their clients in the who, where, when, and how to inspirational success."

BUTTERFIELD EDITORIAL SERVICES | DEBRA L. BUTTERFIELD
4810 Gene Field Rd., Saint Joseph, MO 64506 | 816-752-2171
deb@debralbutterfield.com | *themotivationaleditor.com*

Contact: email
Services: book-cover design, book-interior design, ebook conversion
Charges: flat fee
Credentials/experience: "Over six years of experience."

byBRENDA | BRENDA WILBEE
4631 Quinn Ct. #202, Bellingham, WA 98226 | 360-389-6895
Brenda@BrendaWilbee.com | *www.BrendaWilbee.com*

Contact: email
Services: book-cover design, book-interior design, illustrations, printing, promotional materials, typesetting
Charges: flat fee
Credentials/experience: "My clients have included Habitat for Humanity, Windstar Cruise Lines, Whatcom Community College, Edirol, Lions Club International, and other organizations. I currently specialize in cover design and spin-off marketing products like bookmarks and flyers."

CASTELANE, INC. | KIM MCDOUGALL

Whitehall, PA | 647-281-1554
kimm@castelane.com | *www.castelane.com*

Contact: email
Services: book-cover design, book-interior design, ebook conversion
Charges: flat fee
Credentials/experience: "I have made more than five hundred book video trailers and three hundred book covers since 2009. Samples and references are available on the website."

CELEBRATION WEB DESIGN | BRUCE SHANK

PO Box 471068, Kissimmee, FL 34747 | 610-989-0402
bruce@celebrationwebdesign.com | *CelebrationWebDesign.com*

Contact: email, phone, website contact form
Services: website design
Charges: custom
Credentials/experience: "Celebration Web Design develops handcrafted websites, branding packages, and marketing solutions. Since 2002, our expert staff has been helping individuals and organizations enhance their online presence. Celebration Web Design's team is enthusiastic with focused analysts, developers, and designers who have a passion for technology and online marketing solutions. We consider it a privilege to serve God, by helping individuals and organizations with their website and online marketing needs."

CHRISTIANPRINT.COM

6820 W. 115th St., Bloomington, MN 55438 | 888-201-1322
info@bethanypress.com | *www.christianprint.com*

Contact: phone
Services: printing
Charges: flat fee
Credentials/experience: A division of Bethany Press, founded in 1997. Prints ancillary products, such as business cards, brochures, booklets, banners, postcards, posters, and signs.

DESIGN BY INSIGHT | ERIN ULRICH

PO Box 80282, Simpsonville, SC 29680
erin@designbyinsight.net | *designbyinsight.net*

Contact: website contact form
Services: book-cover design, book-interior design, ebook conversion, website design

Charges: flat fee

Credentials/experience: "In today's world, your website matters more than ever. You need an online space designed to help you reach your goals. Sometimes that's easier said than done. We're here to listen to what you hope to achieve and develop a website strategy that gets results. We have been designing and building WordPress sites for over 12 years. Our clients include writers, small-business owners, nonprofits, and more. Whether you're starting from scratch or ready to take your web presence to the next level, we want to partner with you to see your vision become a reality. We also provide book layout and formatting services for self-publishing authors."

DESIGN CORPS | JOHN WOLLINKA

1370 Carlson Dr., Colorado Springs, CO 80910 | 719-260-0500
general@designcorps.us | *designcorps.us*

    Contact: email, phone, website contact form

    Services: book-cover design, book-interior design, ebook conversion, illustrations, typesetting

    Charges: flat fee

    Credentials/experience: "Design Corps has been serving the Christian community for over 20 years. Our publishing clients have ranged from big publishers (such as Zondervan and Moody Publishers) to self-publishers. We have a love for the Word that we bring with extensive experience in design to covers, interiors, page composition, illustration, and production (printed books and ebooks)."

THE DESIGN IN YOUR MIND | MARY C. FINDLEY

Tulsa, OK | 918-805-0669
mjmcfindley@gmail.com | *findleyfamilyvideopublications.com/the-design-in-your-mind*

    Contact: email, website contact form

    Services: book-cover design, book-interior design, ebook conversion, illustrations

    Charges: flat fee

    Credentials/experience: "More than ten years video and graphic design experience, book covers, formatting, and trailers."

DIGGYPOD | KEVIN OSWORTH

301 Industrial Dr., Tecumseh, MI 49286 | 877-944-7844
kosworth@diggypod.com | *www.diggypod.com*

    Contact: phone, website contact form

Services: book-cover design, printing
Charges: custom
Credentials/experience: "DiggyPOD has been printing books since 2001. All facets of the book printing take place in our facility."

EAH CREATIVE | EMILIE HANEY

1070 Terrace Lake Rd., Columbus, IN 47201 | 661-904-9409
emilie.eahcreative@gmail.com | *www.eahcreative.com*

Contact: email
Services: book-cover design, book-interior design
Charges: custom, flat fee
Credentials/Experience: "Emilie has worked as a graphic designer since 2016 and enjoys creating eye-catching, marketable covers for independent authors and traditional houses. She specializes in fantasy and science-fiction genres but enjoys designing for all fiction and nonfiction categories."

EDENBROOKE PRODUCTIONS | MARTY KEITH

615-415-1942
johnmartinkeith@gmail.com | *www.edenbrookemusic.com/booktrailers*

Contact: email
Services: book trailer
Charges: flat fee
Credentials/experience: "Edenbrooke Productions believes your story deserves a unique soundtrack. We've produced music for everyone from CBS Television to Discovery Channel, and now we want to give your story the star treatment."

FISTBUMP MEDIA, LLC | DAN KING

115 E. 4th Ave., Ste. 212, Mount Dora, FL 32757 | 941-780-4179
dan@fistbumpmedia.com | *fistbumpmedia.com*

Contact: email
Services: book-cover design, book-interior design, ebook conversion, website design
Charges: flat fee, hourly rate
Credentials/experience: "We've been helping writers with their websites and self-publishing needs for over ten years. And we do it because that's who we are. Our team is filled with experienced writers/bloggers who understand firsthand what you're going through and what you need done. And we're always happy to lift up your arms to help you achieve your goals!"

THE FORWORD COLLECTIVE | MOLLY HODGIN

1726 Charity Dr., Brentwood, TN 37027 | 615-497-4322
info@theforwordcollective.com | *www.theforewordcollective.com*

Contact: email, phone, website contact form
Services: book-cover design
Charges: flat fee, hourly rate
Credentials/experience: "The Foreword Collective was founded
by Molly Hodgin, a publishing professional with two decades of
experience. Most recently, she served as the Associate Publisher
for the Specialty Division of HarperCollins Christian Publishing,
working to acquire and create gift books, children's books, and
new media products with authors and brands."

HANNAH LINDER DESIGNS | HANNAH LINDER

hannah@hannahlinderdesigns.com | *www.hannahlinderdesigns.com*

Contact: email, website contact form
Services: book-cover design, book-interior design
Charges: custom, flat fee
Credentials/experience: "Hannah Linder Designs specializes in
professional book-cover design with affordable prices. Having
designed for both traditional publishing houses and individual
authors, including *New York Times*, *USA Today*, national, and
international bestsellers, Hannah understands the importance of
an attractive book cover and the trends of today's industry. Also,
Hannah is a *magna cum laude* Graphic Design Associates Degree
graduate and an award-winning book-cover designer."

HEADSHOTS OF CHICAGO | JIM MUELLER

66 Grove Ct. #1155, Elgin, IL 60120 | 847-220-4239
jim@headshotsofchicago.com | *headshotsofchicago.com*

Contact: email, phone, website contact form
Services: PR photo
Charges: flat fee
Credentials/experience: "I am an award-winning photographer
with 20+ years of experience with a concentration on people.
Over the years I've photographed a diverse range of faces—a wide
array of backgrounds, emotions, and aspirations—with the goal
of delighting my clients with best-in-class service and excellent
images."

INKSMITH EDITORIAL SERVICES | LIZ SMITH

Mebane, NC | 336-514-2331
liz@inksmithediting.com | inksmithediting.com

> **Contact:** email
> **Services:** book-interior design, ebook conversion, typesetting
> **Charges:** hourly rate
> **Credentials/experience:** "In addition to editing and indexing services, Liz Smith offers interior book design (formatting, typesetting) and ebook conversion. She has helped dozens of self-publishing authors go from raw manuscript to polished and published book. Her portfolio and client testimonials can be found on her website."

INKSNATCHER | SALLY HANAN

Austin, TX | 512-265-6403
inkmeister@inksnatcher.com | inksnatcher.com

> **Contact:** website contact form
> **Services:** book trailer, book-cover design, book-interior design, ebook conversion, self-publishing coach, typesetting, website design
> **Charges:** custom
> **Credentials/experience:** "Inksnatcher has been providing self-publishing services for many writers since 2007. As a published author of five books herself, Sally has a unique understanding of everything needed to publish a book with excellence."

KELLIE BOOK DESIGN | KELLIE PARSONS

Unit 1, 23 Apara Way, Nollamara, WA 6061, Australia | 0412 591 687
kellie@kelliemaree.com | www.kelliemaree.com

> **Contact:** website contact form
> **Services:** book-cover design, book-interior design, ebook conversion, typesetting
> **Charges:** flat fee
> **Credentials/experience:** "Book designer for over six years, graphic designer for over ten years. Experience with various software, including Vellum for ebook conversion. Primarily working with self-publishers."

MARTIN PUBLISHING SERVICES | MELINDA MARTIN

Palestine, TX | 903-948-4893
martinpublishingservices@gmail.com | melindamartin.me

> **Contact:** email, phone, website contact form
> **Services:** book-cover design, book-interior design, ebook conversion,

typesetting

Charges: flat fee

Credentials/experience: "More than five years of working with clients' manuscripts to achieve a design that is best for their platforms."

MISSION AND MEDIA | MICHELLE RAYBURN

11510 County Highway M, New Auburn, WI 54757

info@missionandmedia.com | missionandmedia.com

Contact: email, website contact form

Services: book-cover design, book-interior design, ebook conversion, typesetting

Charges: flat fee, free consultation, hourly rate

Credentials/experience: "Michelle works with indie and self-published authors to design a quality book cover and interior. She also coaches those who want to create their own imprint with full control of their own publishing process. Her area of specialty is with Amazon KDP. Michelle has more than 20 years of experience on the writing and editing side of publishing. Portfolio and additional information are available on the website."

PAGE & PIXEL PUBLICATIONS | SUSAN MOORE

La Crosse, WI | 608-780-3400

pageandpixelpublications@gmail.com | pageandpixelpublications.com

Contact: email

Services: book-cover design, book-interior design, ebook conversion, typesetting

Charges: hourly rate

Credentials/experience: "Over 25 years of experience with Christian publishers and independent authors. Offering individual attention, taking into consideration the client's preferences and matching the design with the theme of the material. Attention to detail. Satisfaction guaranteed. Also offer editorial services. Your one-stop shop for the independent author."

PRAIRIE FALLS BOOKS | DEBRA L. BUTTERFIELD and TAMARA CLYMER

St. Joseph, MO

deb@prairiefallbooks.com | prairiefallsbooks.com

Contact: website contact form

Services: book-cover design, book-interior design, ebook conversion, website design

Charges: flat fee

Credentials/experience: "Our professional designers have a wide variety of experience in book design, interior layout, catalogs, and magazines in both freelance and traditional publishing."

PROFESSIONAL PUBLISHING SERVICES | CHRISTY CALLAHAN

PO Box 1164, Frankston, TX 75763 | 912-388-1898

professionalpublishingservices@gmail.com | *professionalpublishingservices.us*

Contact: website contact form

Services: book-cover design, book-interior design, ebook conversion, typesetting

Charges: custom, flat fee

Credentials/experience: "Christy graduated Phi Beta Kappa from Carnegie Mellon University, where she first learned how to use Adobe software and worked as an assistant in the Language Learning Resource Center and the psychology department. While she earned her MA in Intercultural Studies from Fuller Seminary, she edited sound files for distance-learning classes for the Media Center and designed ads as Women's Concerns Committee chairperson. Christy is an Adobe Certified Associate in Print & Digital Publication Using Adobe InDesign, leveraging her expertise as an editor and proofreader and extensive knowledge of *Chicago* style to create professional-looking book covers and interior layouts."

RANEY DAY CREATIVE | KEN RANEY

1848 Georgia St., Cape Girardeau, MO 63701 | 316-737-9724

kenraney@mac.com | *kenraney-design.blogspot.com*

Services: book-cover design, book-interior design, ebook conversion, illustrations, typesetting

Charges: flat fee, hourly rate

Credentials/experience: "Over 40 years of experience as an illustrator and graphic designer."

REDEMPTION PRESS | ATHENA DEAN HOLTZ

1602 Cole St., Enumclaw, WA 98022 | 360-226-3488

athena@redemption-press.com | *www.redemption-press.com*

Contact: website contact form

Services: audiobook, website design

Charges: custom
Credentials/experience: "Redemption Press partners with the pioneers of Christian audiobook creation and distribution. We offer author narrated at approved studios, professional narration, as well as digitally narrated."

RICK STEELE EDITORIAL SERVICES | RICK STEELE

26 Dean Rd., Ringgold, GA 30736 | 706-937-8121
rsteelecam@gmail.com | *steeleeditorialservices.myportfolio.com*

Contact: email, website contact form
Services: book-interior design, ebook conversion, printing, typesetting
Charges: flat fee
Credentials/experience: "Rick Steele Editorial Services provides an array of editorial and publication services for individual clients and publishers. Visit my website for more information about services and pricing, or email me."

ROSEANNA WHITE DESIGNS | ROSEANNA WHITE

roseannamwhite@gmail.com | *www.RoseannaWhiteDesigns.com*

Contact: email, website contact form
Services: book-cover design, book-interior design, ebook conversion, illustrations, typesetting
Charges: custom, flat fee, hourly rate
Credentials/experience: "Roseanna has been designing and typesetting books for nearly ten years, combining her keen eye and artistic skills with her insider knowledge of the industry. As an author herself, she knows how important it is for the appearance of a book to match the words and strives to bring your story to life at a single glance. She has worked for publishing houses and independently for some of Christian fiction's top authors."

SCOTT LA COUNTE

Anaheim, CA | 714-404-7182
Roboscott@gmail.com | *scottdouglas.org/coaching*

Contact: website contact form
Services: audiobook, book-cover design, book-interior design, ebook conversion, printing, typesetting, website design
Charges: flat fee
Credentials/experience: "I have 15+ years publishing experience and have helped sell over 2,000,000 indie books. My specialty is helping new authors find their audience and sell more books."

SUZANNE FYHRIE PARROTT

PO Box 571, Gleneden Beach, OR 97388

author@suzannefyhrieparrott.com | *www.SuzanneFyhrieParrott.com*

> **Contact:** website contact form
> **Services:** book-cover design, book-interior design, ebook conversion
> **Charges:** custom, flat fee, hourly rate
> **Credentials/experience:** "Suzanne graduated from the University
> of Washington in 1981 and has earned several Montana Addy
> Awards for design excellence, working with such clients as
> Yellowstone Park, Old West Trail, Columbia Paint, Winston Fly
> Rod Company, and Montana Power Company. She is currently the
> lead designer for First Steps Publishing, Fireside Press, Penman
> Productions, and several other publishing companies. Her primary
> design focus is book design and publication, producing original
> layouts/designs in print and digital (ebook/audio), as well as
> creating a complete marketing plan for your publication success."

TLC BOOK DESIGN | TAMARA DEVER

Austin, TX

tamara@tlcgraphics.com | *www.TLCBookDesign.com*

> **Contact:** email
> **Services:** book-cover design, book-interior design, ebook conversion,
> printing, typesetting
> **Charges:** custom
> **Credentials/experience:** "TLC provides award-winning book design,
> editorial, printing, and guidance with a personal touch that takes
> the stress out of book creation and gives serious authors and
> publishers high-quality books they are proud to represent. The
> recipients of over 200 industry awards, we've been joyfully serving
> the publishing industry for twenty-five years."

TRILION STUDIOS | BRIAN WHITE

Lawrence, KS | 785-841-5500

hello@TriLionStudios.com | *www.TriLionStudios.com*

> **Contact:** email, phone
> **Services:** book-cover design, illustrations, logo design, website design
> **Charges:** flat fee, hourly rate
> **Credentials/experience:** Twenty years in the design/web design/
> branding industry. Has worked with nonprofits and churches for
> more than fifteen years.

VIVID GRAPHICS | LARRY VAN HOOSE
2273 Snow Hill Rd., Galax, VA 24333 | 276-233-0276
info@vivid-graphics.com | *www.vivid-graphics.com*

Contact: email, phone, website contact form
Services: book-cover design, book-interior design, ebook conversion, website design
Charges: custom, flat fee, hourly rate
Credentials/experience: "Publish and design magazines, literature, ads, websites, billboards; client consultant developing effective marketing and advertising programs; write and edit copy for literature, videos, ads, and training materials."

WRITER'S TABLET AGENCY | TERRI WHITEMORE
4371 Roswell Rd. #315, Marietta, GA 30062 | 770-648-4101
WritersTablet@gmail.com | *www.Writerstablet.org*

Contact: email, website contact form
Services: book-cover design, book-interior design, ebook conversion, illustrations, typesetting
Charges: flat fee
Credentials/experience: "Becoming a published author requires a lot more than a knack for writing and a great story. Partnering with the Writer's Tablet Agency will put you on the fast-track to seeing your name in print. Learn how to navigate the complex world of publishing alongside passionate published authors with years of experience. From polishing your final manuscript to launching your book, Writer's Tablet simplifies the Road to Publication."

YO PRODUCTIONS, LLC | YOLANDA SANDERS
PO Box 1543, Reynoldsburg, OH 43068 | 614-452-4920
info_4u@yoproductions.net | *www.yoproductions.net*

Contact: email
Services: book-cover design, book-interior design, typesetting
Charges: custom
Credentials/experience: "We work side-by-side with our clients to understand your needs and then to produce a quality product that meets them, using the most up-to-date software versions available. Don't have a solid design idea? Don't worry! We will help you brainstorm as well, if needed. We treat every project as if it were our own, and give the time and attention needed to make it a masterpiece."

Note: See "Editorial Services" and "Publicity and Marketing Services" for help with these needs.

5

DISTRIBUTION SERVICES

AMAZON MARKETPLACE (SELLER CENTRAL)
sell.amazon.com

Marketplace has two selling plans: individual for 99¢ per book and professional for $39.99 per month. Both plans have other selling fees as well. You can manage inventory, update pricing, communicate with buyers, contact support, and add new products all from the Seller Central website.

NOVELLA DISTRIBUTION
Unit 35 Currumbin Ct., Capalaba, QLD 4157 Australia | +61 07 3167 6519

info@novelladistribution.com.au | bookstores.novelladistribution.com.au

Provides warehousing and distribution to trade bookstores (Christian and general market), as well as library and educational suppliers and major online retailers. Also operates a specialist division that is the supplier of choice for many Christian schools in Australia. Must have a minimum of four new titles per year.

PATHWAY BOOK SERVICE
34 Production Ave., Keene, NH 03431 | 800-345-6665

pbs@pathwaybook.com | www.pathwaybook.com

Provides warehousing, order fulfillment, and trade distribution. It is a longtime distributor to Ingram and Baker & Taylor, the vendors of choice for most bookstores. Pathway uploads new-title spreadsheets to Ingram and Baker & Taylor, as well as to *Amazon.com*, Barnes & Noble, and Books-A-Million on a weekly basis. Distribution outside of North America is available through Gazelle Book Services in the United Kingdom. Also provides the option of having Pathway add titles to its Amazon Advantage account, which is at a lower discount and often a lower shipping cost per book than individual accounts.

STONEWATER BOOKS

email through the website | www.stonewaterbooks.com

Stonewater Books is a go-between service for indie authors. Each year Stonewater puts writers together in two sales cycles of books and sells those books through Anchor Book distributor, where bookstores and online retailers can order them.

PART 3

PERIODICAL PUBLISHERS

6

TOPICS AND TYPES

This chapter is not an exhaustive list of types of manuscripts and topics editors are looking for, but it is a starting place for some of the more popular ones. For instance, almost all periodicals take manuscripts in categories like Christian living, so they are not listed here. Plus writers guidelines tend to outline general areas, not every specific type and topic an editor will buy.

CONTEMPORARY ISSUES

Anglican Journal
Catholic Sentinel
Celebrate Life Magazine
The Christian Century
Christianity Today
Columbia
The Covenant Companion
Faith Today
Ministry
Now What?
Our Sunday Visitor
Presbyterians Today
St. Anthony Messenger
War Cry

DEVOTION

Eternal Ink
Focus on the Family
Gather
Gems of Truth
Mature Living

ParentLife
Power for Living
Words for the Way

ESSAY

America
The Canadian Lutheran
The Christian Century
Commonweal
Ekstasis
Faith Today
Image
Ink & Quill Quarterly
Love Is Moving
The Lutheran Witness
Our Sunday Visitor
Poets & Writers Magazine
Relief
U.S. Catholic
The Writer
The Writer's Chronicle
Writer's Digest

EVANGELISM

Blue Ridge Christian News
Christian Herald
Christian Research Journal
CommonCall
Evangelical Missions Quarterly
Faith on Every Corner
Just Between Us
Mature Living
Net Results
New Identity Magazine
Outreach
War Cry

FAMILY

Boundless
Brio
Columbia
CommonCall
Creative Inspirations
Faith & Friends
Focus on the Family
Focus on the Family Clubhouse
Focus on the Family Clubhouse Jr.
Guideposts
HomeLife
Homeschooling Today
Influence
Joyful Living Magazine
Light
Mature Living
Ministry
The Mother's Heart
Parenting Teens
ParentLife
St. Anthony Messenger
Vibrant Life

FICTION

See Short Story.

FILLER

Angels on Earth
Bible Advocate
Blue Ridge Christian News
Eternal Ink
Focus on the Family Clubhouse
Focus on the Family Clubhouse Jr.
Guideposts
LIVE
The Mother's Heart
Words for the Way
yOur Backyard

FINANCES/MONEY

Columbia
Joyful Living Magazine
Just Between Us

HOW-TO

Blue Ridge Christian News
Canada Lutheran
Canadian Mennonite
Celebrate Life Magazine
Christian Herald
Christian Standard
CommonCall
Evangelical Missions Quarterly
Faith Today
Focus on the Family
HomeLife
Homeschooling Today
InSite
The Journal of Adventist Education
Joyful Living Magazine

Just Between Us
Leading Hearts
Light
LIVE
The Lutheran Witness
Mature Living
Ministry
The Mother's Heart
Mutuality
Net Results
New Identity Magazine
Outreach
ParentLife
Parish Liturgy
Poets & Writers Magazine
Prayer Connect
SAConnects
Story Embers
Teachers of Vision
Vibrant Life
Words for the Way
The Writer Writer's Digest
WritersWeekly.com
Writing Corner
yOur Backyard

INTERVIEW/PROFILE

The Arlington Catholic Herald
Brio
byFaith
Cadet Quest
Canada Lutheran
Catholic Sentinel
Celebrate Life Magazine
Charisma
The Christian Century
Christian Herald
Christianity Today
Columbia

CommonCall
The Covenant Companion
Creation
DTS Magazine
Evangelical Missions Quarterly
Faith & Friends
Faith Today
Focus on the Family Clubhouse
Focus on the Family Clubhouse Jr.
Friends Journal
Guide
Homeschooling Today
Image
InSite
Joyful Living Magazine
Leading Hearts
The Lutheran Witness
Nature Friend
Our Sunday Visitor
Outreach
Peer
Poets & Writers Magazine
Point
Power for Living
St. Anthony Messenger
testimony/ENRICH
Today's Christian Living
U.S. Catholic
Vibrant Life
War Cry
The Writer
The Writer's Chronicle
Writer's Digest

LEADERSHIP/MINISTRY

CommonCall
Evangelical Missions Quarterly
Holiness Today
InSite

Just Between Us
Love Is Moving
Ministry
Outreach

MARRIAGE

Boundless
Faith & Friends
Focus on the Family
HomeLife
Joyful Living Magazine
Mature Living
St. Anthony Messenger

NEWSPAPER

Anglican Journal
The Arlington Catholic Herald
Blue Ridge Christian News
Catholic Sentinel
Christian Courier
Christian Herald
Christian News Northwest
The Good News
The Messianic Times
New Frontier Chronicle
Our Sunday Visitor

PARENTING

Columbia
Faith on Every Corner
Focus on the Family
HomeLife
Just Between Us
Light
Mature Living
The Mother's Heart
Parenting Teens
ParentLife

PERSONAL EXPERIENCE

Angels on Earth
Anglican Journal
Bible Advocate
Blue Ridge Christian News
The Breakthrough Intercessor
Café
Canada Lutheran
Catholic Sentinel
Celebrate Life Magazine
The Covenant Companion
Creation Illustrated
DTS Magazine
Ekstasis
Eternal Ink
Faith & Friends
Faith on Every Corner
Friends Journal
Gather
Guide
Guideposts
Highway News
Holiness Today
The Journal of Adventist Education
Joyful Living Magazine
Just Between Us
Leading Hearts
LEAVES
LIVE
The Lutheran Witness
Mature Living
The Mother's Heart
Mutuality
Mysterious Ways
New Identity Magazine
Now What?
Point
Power for Living

SAConnects
Standard
Teachers of Vision
testimony/ENRICH
Today's Christian Living
Vibrant Life
War Cry
Words for the Way
yOur Backyard

POETRY

America
Bible Advocate
The Christian Century
Christian Courier
Creation Illustrated
Creative Inspirations
Ekstasis
Eternal Ink
Faith on Every Corner
Focus on the Family Clubhouse Jr.
Friends Journal
Gather
Gems of Truth
Image
LEAVES
LIVE
Love Is Moving
The Lutheran Witness
Mutuality
Power for Living
Relief
Sharing
Sojourners
St. Anthony Messenger
Teachers of Vision
Time Of Singing
U.S. Catholic

Words for the Way
yOur Backyard

PROFILE

See Interview.

REVIEW

Anglican Journal
byFaith
Canadian Mennonite
Celebrate Life Magazine
Charisma
The Christian Century
Christian Courier
Christian Herald
The Christian Journal
Christian Librarian
Christian Research Journal
Christianity Today
CommonCall
Evangelical Missions Quarterly
Faith & Friends
Faith on Every Corner
Faith Today
The Journal of Adventist Education
Leading Hearts
LEAVES
Light
Love Is Moving
The Messianic Times
Ministry
The Mother's Heart
Mutuality
New Frontier Chronicle
Sojourners
Time Of Singing
Words for the Way
The Writer

SHORT STORY/FICTION

Blue Ridge Christian News
Brio
Cadet Quest
Creation Illustrated
Faith on Every Corner
Focus on the Family Clubhouse
Focus on the Family Clubhouse Jr.
Gems of Truth
Image
LIVE
Mature Living
Nature Friend
Relief
St. Anthony Messenger
Sharing
yOur Backyard

TAKE-HOME PAPER

Gems of Truth
Guide
LIVE
Our Little Friend
Power for Living
Primary Treasure
Standard

THEOLOGY

byFaith
The Canadian Lutheran
Christianity Today
Faith & Friends
Mature Living
Ministry
Presbyterians Today

7

ADULT MARKETS

AMERICA

106 W. 56th St., New York, NY 10019-3803 | 212-581-4640

articles@americamedia.org | *www.americamagazine.org*

Matt Malone, S.J., editor in chief

Denomination: Catholic

Parent company: America Media, Jesuit Conference of the United States and Canada

Type: monthly digital and print magazine, circulation 46,000

Audience: primarily Catholic, two-thirds are laypeople, college educated

Purpose: to provide a smart Catholic take on faith and culture

Submissions: Only accepts complete manuscript through the website. Unsolicited freelance: 100%. Response in two weeks.

Types of manuscripts: articles, essays, poetry

Length: 800–2,500 words; poetry, 30 lines maximum

Topics: Christian living/spirituality, culture, trends

Rights: electronic, first

Payment: on acceptance, competitive rates

Guidelines: *www.americamagazine.org/submissions*

Tip: "We are known across the Catholic world for our unique brand of excellent, relevant, and accessible coverage. From theology and spirituality to politics, international relations, arts and letters, and the economy and social justice, our coverage spans the globe."

ANGELS ON EARTH

110 William St., Ste. 901, New York, NY 10038 | 212-251-8100

www.shopguideposts.org/angels-on-earth-magazine.html

Colleen Hughes, editor-in-chief

Parent company: Guideposts

Type: bimonthly digital and print magazine, circulation 550,000

Audience: general

Purpose: to tell true stories of heavenly angels and earthly ones who find themselves on a mission of comfort, kindness, or reassurance

Submissions: Only accepts complete manuscript through the website at *guideposts.org/tell-us-your-story*. Unsolicited freelance: 90%. Response in two months or isn't interested.

Types of manuscripts: personal experience

Length: 1,500 words maximum

Topic: angels

Rights: all

Payment: on publication, $25–$500

Kill fee: 20%

Manuscripts accepted per year: 40–60

Sample: 7x10" envelope with four stamps

Guidelines: *www.guideposts.org/writers-guidelines*

Tip: "We are not limited to stories about heavenly angels. We also accept stories about human beings doing heavenly duties."

ANGLICAN JOURNAL

80 Hayden St., Toronto, ON M4Y 3G2, Canada | 416-924-9199
editor@national.anglican.ca | *www.anglicanjournal.com*
Tali Folkins, editor

Denomination: Anglican

Parent company: Anglican Church of Canada

Type: monthly digital and print newspaper, circulation 123,000, advertising accepted

Audience: denomination

Purpose: to share compelling news and features about the Anglican Church of Canada and the Anglican Communion and religion in general

Submissions: Only accepts email as attachment. Query first. Response in two weeks.

Types of manuscripts: news, personal experience, reviews

Length: 500–1,000 words

Topics: Christian living/spirituality, denomination, events, issues

Rights: first

Payment: on acceptance, $75–$100

Seasonal submissions: two months in advance

Preferred Bible version: NRSV

Guidelines: *www.anglicanjournal.com/about-us/writers-guidelines*

Sample: on the website

Tip: Looking for "local church/parish news stories, book reviews, spiritual reflection."

THE ARLINGTON CATHOLIC HERALD

200 N. Glebe Rd., Ste. 600, Arlington, VA 22203 | 703-841-2590
editorial@catholicherald.com | www.catholicherald.com
Ann Augherton, managing editor

Denomination: Catholic
Parent company: Arlington, Virginia, Diocese
Type: weekly digital and print newspaper, circulation 70,000, advertising accepted
Audience: denomination
Purpose: to support the Church's mission to evangelize by providing news from a Catholic perspective
Submissions: Only accepts email. Query first.
Types of manuscripts: news, feature articles, profiles
Sample: on the website

BIBLE ADVOCATE

PO Box 33677, Denver, CO 80233 | 303-452-7973
bibleadvocate@cog7.org | baonline.org
Sherri Langton, associate editor

Denomination: Church of God
Type: bimonthly digital and print magazine, circulation 13,000
Audience: denomination, general
Purpose: to advocate the Bible and represent the Church of God (Seventh Day)
Submissions: Only accepts complete manuscript by email. Unsolicited freelance: 25–30%. Response in four to ten weeks.
Types of manuscripts: filler, personal experience, poetry, teaching, testimony
Length: 600–1,300 words
Topics: Christian living/spirituality, theme-related
Rights: electronic, first, onetime, reprint (with info on where/when previously published)
Payment: on publication; articles, $25–$65; poems and fillers, $20
Manuscripts accepted per year: 10–20
Preferred Bible version: NIV, NKJV
Guidelines: *baonline.org/write-for-us*
Sample: 9x12" envelope with three stamps

Theme list: available on website

Tip: "Please read past issues of the magazine before you submit and become familiar with our style. No snail mail submissions or PDFs. No Christmas or Easter manuscripts."

BLUE RIDGE CHRISTIAN NEWS

261 Oak Ave., Spruce Pine, NC 28777 | 828-413-0506

cathy@brcnews.com | *blueridgechristiannews.com*

Cathy Pritchard, editor

Parent company: The Ninevah Productions, Inc.

Type: monthly digital and print newspaper; circulation 16,000 print, 3,000 digital; advertising accepted

Audience: people seeking to know more about God

Purpose: to share the good news of Jesus and other positive, uplifting, and good news from around the world

Submissions: Only accepts email. Unsolicited freelance: 10%. Response in one week.

Types of manuscripts: column, filler, how-to, personal experience, short story

Length: 1,000 words

Topics: Christian living/spirituality, evangelism

Rights: all, electronic, first, reprint (with info on where/when previously published)

Payment: none

Manuscripts accepted per year: 100

Seasonal submissions: one month in advance

Preferred Bible version: KJV, NKJV, NASB

Sample: $3, email request

Guidelines: not available

Tip: "Looking for positive, uplifting, good news."

THE BREAKTHROUGH INTERCESSOR

PO Box 121, Lincoln, VA 20160-0121 | 540-338-4131

breakthrough@intercessors.org | *www.intercessors.org*

Claudette Ammons, managing editor

Parent company: Breakthrough

Type: quarterly digital and print magazine, circulation 4,000

Audience: adults interested in growing their prayer lives

Purpose: to encourage people to pray and to equip them to do so more effectively

Submissions: Only accepts complete manuscript. Email or mail.

Types of manuscripts: personal experience, teaching
Length: 600–1,000 words
Topic: prayer
Rights: electronic, first, onetime
Payment: none
Guidelines: *www.intercessors.org/media/downloads/Guidelines%20 &%20PermissionForm.pdf*
Sample: on the website

byFAITH

1700 N. Brown Rd., Ste. 105, Lawrenceville, GA 30043 | 678-825-1005
editor@byfaithonline.wpengine.com | *byfaithonline.com*
Richard Doster, editor

Denomination: Presbyterian
Type: quarterly digital and print magazine, advertising accepted
Audience: denomination
Purpose: to provide news of the Presbyterian Church in America, to equip readers to become a more active part of God's redemptive plan for the world, and to help them respond biblically and intelligently to the questions our culture is asking
Submissions: Only accepts complete manuscript by email.
Types of manuscripts: news, profile, reviews, teaching
Length: 500–3,000 words
Topics: Christian living/spirituality, culture, denomination, theology
Guidelines: *byfaithonline.com/about*
Tip: "Theologically, the writers are Reformed and believe the faith is practical and applicable to every part of life. Most of our writers (though not all) come from the PCA."

CAFÉ

8765 W. Higgins Rd., Chicago, IL 60631 | 800-638-3522
cafe@elca.org | *www.boldcafe.org*
Elizabeth McBride, editor

Denomination: Evangelical Lutheran Church in America
Parent company: Women of the Evangelical Lutheran Church in America
Type: monthly website
Audience: Lutheran women ages 18–35+
Purpose: to share stories written by bold, young women who write about faith, relationships, advocacy, and more

Submissions: Send complete manuscript by email or query with clips by email. Simultaneous submissions OK. Responds only if interested.

Type of manuscripts: personal experience

Length: 700–1,000 words

Topics: theme-related

Rights: first, onetime, reprint (with info on where/when previously published)

Payment: $20 per 100 published words, excluding biblical text

Seasonal submissions: seven months

Preferred Bible version: NRSV

Guidelines: *www.boldcafe.org/add-voice-boldcafe*

Sample: see the website

Tip: "We ask particular established authors to write on specific themes far in advance of publication. We publish very few articles that originated as unsolicited manuscripts or queries. Those we do accept are most likely to be accepted from Christian women (though we accept queries from men) that include stories about women or reflections that especially speak to young adult women."

CANADA LUTHERAN

600–177 Lombard Ave., Winnipeg, MB R3B 0W5, Canada | 888-786-6707

editor@elcic.ca | canadalutheran.ca

Kenn Ward, editor

Rachel Genge, British Columbia Synod, csynodeditor@gmail.com

Richard Janzen, Synod of Alberta and the Territories, cleditor.richard@gmail.com

Anno Bell, Saskatchewan Synod, clsaskeditor@gmail.com

Rev. R. David Lowe, Manitoba/Northwestern Ontario Synod, mnoeditor@gmail.com

Liz Zehr, Eastern Synod, ezehr@elcic.ca

Denomination: Evangelical Lutheran Church in Canada

Type: monthly print magazine, circulation 14,000

Audience: denomination

Purpose: to engage the Evangelical Lutheran Church in Canada in a dynamic dialogue in which information, inspiration, and ideas are shared in a thoughtful and stimulating way

Submissions: Only accepts email.

Types of manuscripts: documentary, how-to, personal experience, profile

Length: 700–1,200 words

Topics: Christian living/spirituality, denomination, seasonal

Rights: onetime

Tip: "As much as is possible, the content of the magazine is chosen from the work of Canadian writers. The content strives to reflect the Evangelical Lutheran Church in Canada in the context of our Canadian society."

THE CANADIAN LUTHERAN

3074 Portage Ave., Winnipeg, MB R3K 0Y2, Canada | 800-588-4226
editor@lutheranchurch.ca | *www.canadianlutheran.ca*
Matthew Block, editor
Michelle Heumann, regional news

> **Denomination:** Lutheran
> **Type:** bimonthly digital and print magazine, circulation 20,000
> **Audience:** denomination
> **Purpose:** to inspire, motivate, and inform
> **Submissions:** Only accepts complete manuscript by email.
> **Types of manuscripts:** essay, news, teaching
> **Topics:** culture, denomination, theology
> **Rights:** first
> **Payment:** none
> **Guidelines:** *www.canadianlutheran.ca/editors-and-submissions*
> **Sample:** *issuu.com/thecanadianlutheran*
> **Tip:** "All feature articles with doctrinal content must go through doctrinal review to ensure fidelity to the Scriptures. As a result, authors may occasionally be asked to rewrite some sections of their article before publication."

CANADIAN MENNONITE

490 Dutton Dr., Unit C5, Waterloo, ON N2L 6H7, Canada | 519-884-3810
submit@canadianmennonite.org | *www.canadianmennonite.org*
Ross W. Muir, managing editor

> **Denomination:** Mennonite
> **Parent company:** Canadian Mennonite Publishing Service
> **Type:** biweekly digital and print magazine, circulation 8,500, advertising accepted
> **Audience:** denomination
> **Purpose:** to report news and viewpoints of the people and churches of the Mennonite Church Canada
> **Submissions:** Only accepts email; query first. Unsolicited freelance: few. Response in one week. To get an assignment, be acquainted with the magazine and its readership.
> **Types of manuscripts:** how-to, news, opinion, reviews

Length: 500–800 words
Topics: theme-related
Rights: first, onetime, reprint (with info on where/when previously published)
Payment: none
Manuscripts accepted per year: few; publish primarily the writing of correspondents and related organizations
Seasonal submissions: three months
Theme list: available on website
Guidelines: *canadianmennonite.org/submissions*
Sample: on the website
Tip: "Writers for our magazine need to know and understand the interests and concerns of Mennonites in Canada."

CATHOLIC SENTINEL
2838 E. Burnside, Portland, OR 97214 | 503-281-1191
edl@CatholicSentinel.org | *www.CatholicSentinel.org*
Ed Langlois, managing editor

Denomination: Catholic
Parent company: Archdiocese of Portland
Type: bimonthly print newspaper, advertising accepted
Audience: Catholics who live in Oregon
Purpose: to feature Oregon people and Oregon issues that relate to Catholics
Submissions: Only accepts email. Query first.
Types of manuscripts: personal experience, profile
Length: 600–1,500 words
Topics: Christian living/spirituality, issues
Payment: variable rates
Guidelines: *catholicsentinel.org/Content/About-Us/About-Us/Article/Article-Submission/15/60/11770*

CELEBRATE LIFE MAGAZINE
PO Box 1350, Stafford, VA 22555 | 540-659-4171
clmag@all.org | *www.clmagazine.org*
Susan Ciancio, editor

Denomination: Catholic
Parent company: American Life League
Type: quarterly digital and print magazine, circulation 7,500, advertising accepted
Audience: pro-life

Purpose: to inspire, encourage, and educate pro-life activists
Submissions: Only accepts complete manuscript, email as attachment. Unsolicited freelance: 25%. Response in one to two months.
Types of manuscripts: how-to, interview, personal experience, reviews, teaching
Length: 800–1,800 words
Topics: ethics, issues; see list of possible topics in the guidelines
Rights: first
Payment: on publication, 10–25¢/word
Kill fee: sometimes
Manuscripts accepted per year: six
Seasonal submissions: six months ahead
Preferred Bible version: NJB
Guidelines: *www.clmagazine.org/submission-guidelines*
Sample: email for copy
Tip: "Most in need of timely investigative reports and personal experiences."

CHARISMA

600 Rinehart Rd., Lake Mary, FL 32746 | 407-333-0600
robert.caggiano@charismamedia.com | *www.charismamag.com*
Robert Caggiano, managing editor

Denomination: Charismatic
Parent company: Charisma Media
Type: monthly digital and print magazine, circulation 207,000, advertising accepted
Audience: passionate, Spirit-filled Christians
Purpose: to empower believers for life in the Spirit
Submissions: Only accepts email. Query first. Unsolicited freelance: 20%. Response in two to three months.
Types of manuscripts: features, interviews, profiles, reviews
Length: 700–2,600
Topics: Christian living/spirituality, Christmas, Easter, prayer, prophecy, seasonal, spiritual warfare
Rights: all
Payment: on publication
Seasonal submissions: five months in advance
Preferred Bible version: MEV
Guidelines: *charismamag.com/about/write-for-us*
Sample: on the website

Tip: "Please take time to read—even study—at least one or two of our recent issues before submitting a query. Sometimes people submit their writing without ever having read or understood our magazine or its readers, and sometimes people will have read our magazine years ago and think it's the same as it has always been, but magazines undergo many changes through the years."

THE CHRISTIAN CENTURY

104 S. Michigan Ave., Ste. 1100, Chicago, IL 60603-5901 | 312-263-7510

submissions@christiancentury.org | *www.christiancentury.org*

Steve Thorngate, managing editor

Jill Peláez Baumgaertner, poetry, poetry@christiancentury.org

Type: monthly print magazine, advertising accepted

Audience: ecumenical, mainline ministers, educators, and church leaders

Purpose: to explore what it means to believe and live out the Christian faith in our time

Submissions: Only accepts email, query letter. Unsolicited freelance: 90%. Response in four to six weeks.

Types of manuscripts: essay, humor, interview, opinion, poetry, review

Length: articles, 1,500–3,000 words; poetry, to 20 lines

Topics: culture, issues, justice

Rights: all, reprint (with info on where/when previously published)

Payment: on publication; articles, $100–$300, poems, $50, reviews, to $75

Manuscripts accepted per year: 150

Seasonal submissions: four months in advance

Preferred Bible version: NRSV

Guidelines: *www.christiancentury.org/submission-guidelines*

Sample: *www.christiancentury.org/magazine*

Tip: "Keep in mind our audience of sophisticated readers, eager for analysis and critical perspective that goes beyond the obvious. We are open to all topics if written with appropriate style for our readers."

CHRISTIAN COURIER

2 Aiken St., St. Catherines, ON L2N 1V8, Canada | 800-969-4838

editor@christiancourier.ca | *www.christiancourier.ca*

Angela Reitsma Bick, editor-in-chief

Amy MacLachlan, features, features@christiancourier.ca

Brian Bork, reviews, reviews@christiancourier.ca

Denomination: Christian Reformed

Type: biweekly digital and print newspaper, circulation 2,500, advertising accepted

Purpose: to connect Christians with a network of culturally savvy partners in faith for the purpose of inspiring all to participate in God's renewing work with his creation

Submissions: Email complete manuscript or query letter. Simultaneous submissions OK. Response in one to two weeks, only if accepted.

Types of manuscripts: column, feature, news, opinion, poetry, review

Length: articles, 700–1,200 words; reviews, 750 words

Rights: onetime, reprint (with info on where/when previously published)

Payment: on publication; articles, $50–$70; reviews, $30–$70; poetry, $45; reprints, none

Seasonal submissions: three months in advance

Preferred Bible version: NIV

Guidelines: *www.christiancourier.ca/write-for-us*

Sample: *www.christiancourier.ca/past-issues*

Tip: "Suggest an aspect of the theme which you believe you could cover well, have insight into, could treat humorously, etc. Show that you think clearly, write clearly, and have something to say that we should want to read. Have a strong biblical worldview and avoid moralism and sentimentality."

CHRISTIAN HERALD

PO Box 68526, Brampton, ON L6R 0J8, Canada | 905-874-1731
info@christianherald.ca | christianherald.ca
Fazal Karim, Jr., publisher and editor-in-chief

Type: monthly digital and print newspaper, circulation 20,000, advertising accepted

Audience: Christians living in Southern Ontario, Canada

Purpose: to cover news and events of interest to Christians living in Southern Ontario

Submissions: Email as attachment or in body of message, or mail submissions. Gives assignments; to get one, send résumé with location and preferred subjects. Query first. Unsolicited freelance: 5-10%. Response in one week.

Types of manuscripts: event coverage, feature, how-to, interview, news, profile, review

Length: 300–1,200 words

Topics: culture, current events, education, evangelism, politics, pro-life,

religious freedom, technology
Rights: first, reprint (with info on where/when previously published)
Payment: on publication, 10–15¢/word
Kill fee: sometimes
Manuscripts accepted per year: 10
Seasonal submissions: three months
Theme list: available via email
Sample: email for digital copy
Guidelines: by email
Tip: "Product reviews pay less but are an easy way to build a relationship. Look for events/stories in your local city/region, but which might be broadly of interest."

THE CHRISTIAN JOURNAL

1032 W. Main, Medford, OR 97501 | 541-773-4004
info@thechristianjournal.org | thechristianjournal.org
Chad McComas, editor

Parent company: Set Free Christian Fellowship
Type: monthly digital and print magazine, circulation 1,200
Audience: both Christians and non-Christians
Purpose: to provide inspiration and encouragement with the body of Christ in the Rogue Valley, Oregon
Submissions: Accepts complete manuscript or query letter. Email only. Response in two weeks.
Types of manuscripts: children's story, feature, profile, review
Length: 300–500 words, average around 400
Topics: Christian living/spirituality, theme-related
Rights: onetime
Payment: none
Seasonal submissions: one month in advance
Preferred Bible version: NIV
Theme list: available on website
Guidelines: *thechristianjournal.org/writers-information/guidelines-for-writers*
Sample: on the website
Tip: "Call or email with your idea."

CHRISTIAN LIBRARIAN

PO Box 4, Cedarville, OH 45314 | 937-766-2255
trobinson@whitworth.edu | www.acl.org/index.cfm/publications/the-christian-librarian
Tami Robinson, managing editor

Craig Kubic, book reviews, ckubic@swbts.edu

    Parent company: Association of Christian Librarians

    Type: bimonthly online and print journal

    Audience: primarily Christian librarians in institutions of higher learning

    Purpose: to publish articles, provide a membership forum, and encourage writing

    Submissions: Only accepts complete manuscript; email as attachment.

    Types of manuscripts: bibliography, review, teaching

    Length: 1,000–5,000 words + 100-word abstract

    Topics: library science

    Rights: first

    Payment: none

    Guidelines: *www.acl.org/index.cfm/publications/the-christian-librarian/ guidelines-for-authors*

CHRISTIAN NEWS NORTHWEST

710 E. Foothills Dr., Ste. 103C, Newberg, OR 97132 | 503-537-9220

cnnw@cnnw.com | cnnw.com

Tim Hirsch, editor and publisher

    Parent company: Salt Media, LLC

    Type: monthly digital and print newspaper, circulation 26,000, advertising accepted

    Audience: evangelical Christian community in western and central Oregon and southwest Washington

    Purpose: to encourage and inform the evangelical Christian community in our part of the Pacific Northwest

    Submissions: Accepts complete manuscript. Email as attachment or in body of message, mail, or submit through the website. Gives assignments.

    Types of manuscripts: news, opinion

    Preferred Bible version: NIV

    Sample: on the website

CHRISTIAN RESEARCH JOURNAL

PO Box 8500, Charlotte, NC 28271-8500 | 704-887-8200

response@equip.org | www.equip.org/category/christian-research-journal

Melanie Cogdill, managing editor

    Parent company: Christian Research Institute

    Type: quarterly print journal

Audience: thoughtful laypeople, academics, scholars

Purpose: to equip Christians to discern errors in doctrine, biblical interpretation, and reasoning; to evangelize people of other faiths and belief systems; and to present a strong defense of Christian beliefs and ethics

Submissions: Accepts complete manuscript or query letter only by email. Response in four months.

Types of manuscripts: feature, news, opinion, review

Length: 1,700–3,500 words

Topics: apologetics, cults and new religions, evangelism

Rights: first, reprint

Payment: $175–$325

Kill fee: 50%

Guidelines: *www.equip.org/wp-content/uploads/2021/08/Writers-Guidelines.AUGUST-2021.pdf*

Tip: "Almost nothing can better prepare you to write for the *Christian Research Journal* than familiarity with the *Journal* itself. If you are not a regular reader of the *Journal*, you should read all the articles in recent issues that correspond to the type of article you wish to write."

CHRISTIAN STANDARD

16965 Pine Ln., Ste. 202, Parker, CO 80134 | 800-543-1353

cs@christianstandardmedia.com | *www.christianstandard.com*

Michael C. Mack, editor

Denomination: Christian Churches, Churches of Christ

Parent company: Christian Standard Media

Type: bimonthly digital and print magazine

Audience: paid and volunteer leaders

Purpose: to leverage the power of our unity and to resource Christian churches to fulfill Christ's commission

Submissions: Send query letter by email as attachment. Unsolicited freelance: 5%, 95% assigned. Response in one to three months.

Types of manuscripts: how-to, communion meditations for website

Length: maximum 1,800 words, prefers 500–1,200 words

Topics: theme-related

Rights: first, reprint (with info on where/when previously published)

Payment: on acceptance, $50–$250

Kill fee: sometimes

Manuscripts accepted per year: 15

Seasonal submissions: six to eight months

Preferred Bible version: NIV

Theme list: available on website
Guidelines: *christianstandard.com/writersguidelines*
Sample: on the website

CHRISTIANITY TODAY

465 Gundersen Dr., Carol Stream, IL 60188-2498 | 630-260-6200
editor@christianitytoday.com | *www.christianitytoday.com*
Andy Olsen, managing editor
Ted Olsen, director of editorial development
Matt Reynolds, books editor, mreynolds@christianitytoday.com

Parent company: Christianity Today International
Type: monthly digital and print magazine; circulation 110,000, 2.2 million page views/month; advertising accepted
Audience: Christian leaders throughout North America
Purpose: to equip Christians to renew their minds, serve the church, and create culture to the glory of God
Submissions: Only accepts query letter through the website. Unsolicited freelance: few.
Types of manuscripts: feature, interview, profile, review
Length: 300–1,800 words
Topics: Christian living/spirituality, culture, issues
Rights: first
Payment: on acceptance, varies
Preferred Bible version: NIV
Guidelines: *help.christianitytoday.com/hc/en-us/ articles/360047411253-How-do-I-write-for-CT-*
Sample: articles are on the website
Tip: "We are most interested in stories of Christians living out their faith in unique ways that impact the world for the better and communicate truth in a way that is deep, nuanced, and challenging."

COLUMBIA

1 Columbus Plaza, New Haven, CT 06510-3326 | 203-752-4398
columbia@kofc.org | *www.kofc.org/en/news-room/columbia/index.html*
Alton J. Pelowski, editor

Denomination: Catholic
Parent company: Knights of Columbus
Type: monthly digital and print magazine, circulation 1.7 million
Audience: general Catholic family
Submissions: Email or mail query letter first.

Types of manuscripts: feature, profile
Length: 700–1,500 words
Topics: current events, family, finances, health, issues, parenting, trends
Rights: electronic, first
Payment: on acceptance, varies
Seasonal submissions: six months in advance
Guidelines: *www.kofc.org/en/news-room/columbia/guidelines.html*
Sample: *www.kofc.org/en/columbia/cover/201610.html*

COMMONCALL: THE BAPTIST STANDARD MAGAZINE

PO Box 259019, Plano, TX 75025 | 214-630-4571
kencamp@baptiststandard.com | *www.baptiststandard.com*
Ken Camp, managing editor, news, features, book reviews
Eric Black, editor, opinion articles, sermons, eric.black@baptiststandard.com

Denomination: Baptist
Parent company: Baptist Standard Publishing
Type: quarterly print magazine
Audience: denomination
Purpose: to provide information relevant to the growth and welfare of Baptist people, support ministries conducted by Texas Baptists and cooperating churches and organizations, develop a fuller understanding of Baptist doctrines, encourage high moral standards and spiritual formation among all peoples, and help Christians fulfill their calling
Types of manuscripts: how-to, profile
Topics: evangelism, family, leadership, ministry, missions, Texas Baptist history
Guidelines: *www.baptiststandard.com/submissions*
Tip: "Looking for stories about everyday Christians who are putting their faith into action."

COMMONWEAL

475 Riverside Dr., Rm. 405, New York, NY 10115 | 212-662-4200
editors@commonwealmagazine.org | *www.commonwealmagazine.org*
Dominic Preziosi, editor

Denomination: Catholic
Type: monthly digital and print magazine, circulation 20,000, advertising accepted
Audience: liberal Catholics

Purpose: to provide a forum about faith, public affairs, and the arts, centered on belief in the common good

Submissions: Only accepts complete manuscript through the website. Response in ten weeks. Articles fall into three categories: "Upfronts," 1,500–2,500 words, newsy and reportorial, giving facts, information, and some interpretation behind the headlines of the day. Longer articles, 2,500–5,000 words, are more reflective and detailed, bringing new information or a different point of view to a subject, raising questions, and/or proposing solutions to the dilemmas facing the world, nation, church, or individual. The "Last Word" column, 750–1,300 words, is a more personal reflection on some aspect of the human condition: spiritual, individual, political, or social.

Types of manuscripts: essay, news, opinion

Length: 750–5,000 words

Topics: literature and the arts, public affairs

Rights: first

Payment: on publication, varies

Manuscripts accepted per year: 30 poems

Guidelines: *commonweal.submittable.com/submit*

Sample: request by email

THE COVENANT COMPANION

8303 W. Higgins Rd., Chicago, IL 60631 | 773-907-3328
Cathy.NormanPeterson@covchurch.org | *covenantcompanion.com*
Cathy Norman Peterson, editorial director

Denomination: Evangelical Covenant Church

Type: biannual print magazine

Audience: denomination

Purpose: to inform, stimulate thought, and encourage dialogue on issues that impact the church and its members

Submissions: Email or mail.

Types of manuscripts: news, personal experience, profile

Length: 1,200–1,800 words

Topics: Christian living/spirituality, church, church outreach, denomination, issues, justice

Rights: onetime

Payment: on publication

Payment: $35–$100 two months after publication

Tip: "We are interested in what is happening in local churches, conferences, and other Covenant institutions and associations, as well as reports from missionaries and other staff serving around the world. Human interest stories are also welcome."

CREATION

PO Box 4545, Eight Mile Plains, QLD 4113, Australia | 073 340 9888
m.wieland@creation.info | *creation.com/creation-magazine*
Dr. Don Batten, Dr. Tas Walker, Dr. Jonathan Sarfati, editors

> **Parent company:** Creation Ministries International
> **Type:** quarterly digital and print magazine, circulation 40,000
> **Audience:** families, homeschoolers, age 9 to adulthood
> **Purpose:** to support the effective proclamation of the Gospel by providing credible answers that affirm the reliability of the Bible, in particular its Genesis history
> **Submissions:** Only accepts complete manuscript; cover letter required. Email as attachment. Unsolicited freelance: 20%. Response in one week. Accepts submissions from teens.
> **Types of manuscripts:** interview, teaching
> **Length:** maximum 1,500 words
> **Topics:** creation science, evolution's errors
> **Rights:** will be requested
> **Payment:** none
> **Manuscripts accepted per year:** more than 100
> **Seasonal submissions:** six months in advance
> **Preferred Bible version:** ESV
> **Guidelines:** *creation.com/creation-magazine-writing-guidelines*
> **Sample:** on the website
> **Tip:** "Looking for articles on creation/evolution debate."

CREATIVE INSPIRATIONS

PO Box 19051, Kalamazoo, MI 49009 | 269-348-5712
creativeinspirations01@gmail.com | *creativeinspirationspp.blogspot.com*
MJ Reynolds, publisher and editor

> **Type:** bimonthly digital magazine
> **Audience:** poets and people who appreciate poetry
> **Purpose:** to publish inspirational poetry
> **Submissions:** Accepts email as attachment, email in body of message, and mail. Unsolicited freelance: 100%. Response in one to two weeks. Also accepts submissions from teens.
> **Type of manuscripts:** poetry
> **Topics:** Christian living/spirituality, family, nature
> **Rights:** onetime

Payment: none
Manuscripts accepted per year: varies
Preferred Bible version: NIV
Guidelines: by email
Sample: request by email
Tip: "Follow the submission guidelines."

DTS MAGAZINE

3909 Swiss Ave., Dallas, TX 75204 | 800-387-9673
magazine@dts.edu | *www.dts.edu/magazine*

Parent company: Dallas Theological Seminary (DTS)
Type: quarterly digital and print magazine, circulation 35,000
Audience: evangelical laypeople, students, alumni, donors, and
friends
Purpose: to apply biblical truth to life as a ministry to friends of
Dallas Theological Seminary
Submissions: Only accepts email; query first. Response in six to eight
weeks.
Types of manuscripts: personal experience, profile, teaching
Length: 1,500–2,000 words
Topics: Christian living/spirituality
Rights: first, reprint
Payment: $300, $100 for reprints
Seasonal submissions: six months in advance
Guidelines: *voice.dts.edu/magazine/editorial-policies*
Sample: *voice.dts.edu/magazine*
Tip: "*DTS Magazine* is a ministry of Dallas Theological Seminary. We
prefer articles written by our alumni, faculty, students, staff, board
members, donors and their families."

EKSTASIS

465 Gundersen Dr., Carol Stream, IL 60188 | 416-912-7454
editor@ekstasismagazine.com | *www.ekstasismagazine.com*
Conor Sweetman, editor in chief

Parent company: Christianity Today International
Type: monthly digital magazine + annual print, digital newsletter;
circulation 10,000, advertising accepted
Audience: 22- to 35-year-olds interested in arts, academia, Kingdom,
and culture
Purpose: to revive the Christian imagination
Submissions: Only accepts email as attachment. Simultaneous

submissions OK. Unsolicited freelance: 45%. Response in one month.

Types of manuscripts: historical, narrative, personal experience, poetry

Length: essays, 2,000 words

Topics: academia, arts, culture, Kingdom

Rights: first

Payment: on publication; $75 digital, $150 print

Kill fee: sometimes

Manuscripts accepted per year: 100 essays, 500 poems

Guidelines: *www.ekstasismagazine.com/submit*

Sample: buy on website

Tip: "*Ekstasis* publishes work that slants toward the triumphant and glorious aspects of life in Christ, framed through the arts and literature. *Ekstasis* is based in the work of Beautiful Orthodoxy, as defined by Christianity Today."

ETERNAL INK

4706 Fantasy Ln., Alton, IL 62002 | 618-466-7860

sonsong@charter.net

Mary-Ellen Grisham, editor

Type: biweekly e-zine, circulation 450

Audience: general

Purpose: to inspire, edify, and enlighten

Submissions: Only accepts email in body of message. Unsolicited freelance: 5–10%. Response in two weeks.

Types of manuscripts: devotion, humor, personal experience, filler, poetry

Length: 400–600 words

Topics: Christian living/spirituality, seasonal

Rights: onetime, reprint

Payment: none

Manuscripts accepted per year: 200

Seasonal submissions: two months

Preferred Bible version: NIV

Guidelines: by email

Sample: by email

Tip: Looking for "scriptural studies, verses or passages, clearly focused and easy to understand."

EVANGELICAL MISSIONS QUARTERLY

PO Box 398, Wheaton, IL 60187 | 678-392-4577

EMQ-Editor@MissioNexus.org | missionexus.org/emq

Heather Pubols, editorial director

David Dunaetz, book review editor

Parent company: Missio Nexus

Type: quarterly digital journal

Audience: missionaries, mission agency executives, mission professors, missionary candidates, students, mission pastors, mission-minded church leaders, mission supporters, and agency board members

Purpose: to increase the effectiveness of the evangelical missionary enterprise

Submissions: Only accepts complete manuscript; email as attachment.

Types of manuscripts: how-to, profile, review

Length: 2,000–3,000 words

Topics: church planting, culture, discipleship, evangelism, leadership, missions, trends

Rights: first

Guidelines: *missionexus.org/emq/submit-an-article-to-emq*

Tip: "We are not a scholarly journal written for academics, but desire material that is academically respectable, reflecting careful thought and practical application to missions professionals, and especially working missionaries. We like to see problems not only diagnosed, but solved either by way of illustration or suggestion."

FAITH & FRIENDS

The Salvation Army, 2 Overlea Blvd., Toronto, ON M4H 1P4, Canada | 416-422-6226

faithandfriends@can.salvationarmy.org | salvationist.ca/editorial/faith-and-friends

Giselle Randall, features editor

Denomination: The Salvation Army

Type: monthly digital and print magazine, circulation 50,000+

Audience: general

Purpose: to show Jesus Christ at work in the lives of real people and to provide spiritual resources for those who are new to the Christian faith

Submissions: Only accepts email as attachment. Query first.

Types of manuscripts: personal experience, review, testimony, profile
Length: 750–1,200 words
Topics: Christian living/spirituality, family, marriage, theology
Rights: first, reprint
Payment: none
Preferred Bible version: TNIV
Guidelines: *salvationist.ca/files/salvationarmy/Magazines/FAITH-FRIENDS.pdf*
Sample: on the website
Tip: "Looking for stories about people whose lives have been changed through an encounter with Jesus: conversion, miracles, healing, faith in the midst of crisis, forgiveness, reconciliation, answered prayers, and more. Profiles of people who have found hope and healing through their ministries, including prisoners, hospital patients, nursing-home residents, single parents in distress, addicts, the unemployed, or homeless."

FAITH ON EVERY CORNER

159 Hudson Cajah Mountain Rd., Hudson, NC 28638 | 828-305-8571
team@faithoneverycorner.com | *www.faithoneverycorner.com/magazine*
Craig Ruhl, managing editor
Karen Ruhl, publisher and editor in chief

Parent company: Faith On Every Corner, LLC
Type: monthly digital magazine, circulation 2,500
Audience: families, seekers
Purpose: to inspire, educate, and show how everyday people are making a difference in their communities through acts of faith and service
Submissions: Only accepts email as attachment. Simultaneous submissions OK. Unsolicited freelance: 85%. Response in one week. Also accepts submissions from teens.
Types of manuscripts: essay, feature, how-to, news, profile, review
Length: 250–1,000 words
Topics: Christian living/spirituality, evangelism, humor, parenting
Rights: first
Payment: none
Manuscripts accepted per year: 400
Seasonal submissions: one to two months
Preferred Bible version: KJV, NKJV, ESV, NIV, NLT, NASB, CSB
Guidelines: *www.faithoneverycorner.com/submission-guidelines.html*
Sample: on the website
Theme list: available on website and by email

Tip: "Feel free to pitch ideas for articles, stories or other content by email."

FAITH TODAY

9821 Leslie St., Ste. 103, Richmond Hill, ON L4B 3Y4, Canada | 866-302-3362

editor@faithtoday.ca | www.faithtoday.ca

Bill Fledderus, senior editor

Karen Stiller, senior editor

Parent company: The Evangelical Fellowship of Canada

Type: bimonthly digital and print magazine; circulation 12,000 print, 5,000 online; advertising accepted

Audience: Canadian evangelicals

Purpose: to connect, equip, and inform Canada's four million evangelical Christians from Anglican and Baptist to Pentecostal and The Salvation Army

Submissions: Only accepts email, query letter with clips. Unsolicited freelance: 10%. Response in one week.

Types of manuscripts: essay, feature, how-to, news, profile, review

Length: 350–1,800 words

Topics: church, issues, trends

Rights: electronic, first, onetime, reprint (with info on where/when previously published)

Payment: on acceptance, 15–25¢ CAD/word

Kill fee: sometimes

Manuscripts accepted per year: 100

Seasonal submissions: four months

Guidelines: *www.faithtoday.ca/writers*

Sample: *www.faithtoday.ca/digital*

Tip: "What is the Canadian angle? How does your approach include diverse Canadian voices from different churches, regions, generations, etc.?"

FOCUS ON THE FAMILY

8605 Explorer Dr., Colorado Springs, CO 80920 | 800-232-6459

FocusMagSubmissions@family.com | www.focusonthefamily.com/magazine

Andrea Gutierrez, managing editor

Parent company: Focus on the Family

Type: bimonthly print magazine

Audience: parents, primarily of ages 4–12

Purpose: to encourage, teach, and celebrate God's design for the family

Submissions: Email complete manuscript or query letter. Response in eight weeks or not interested.

Types of manuscripts: devotion, how-to, teaching

Length: 50–1,500 words

Topics: family, marriage, parenting

Rights: first

Payment: on acceptance; 25¢/word, $50 for short pieces

Guidelines: *www.focusonthefamily.com/magazine/call-for-submissions*

Sample: articles are on the website

Tip: "Looking for stories about how parents have dealt with challenges and come up with active, practical ways (beyond explaining or talking) of solving those problems."

FRIENDS JOURNAL

1216 Arch St., Ste. 2A, Philadelphia, PA 19107 | 215-563-8629

martink@friendsjournal.org | *www.friendsjournal.org*

Martin Kelly, senior editor

Denomination: Religious Society of Friends

Type: monthly digital and print magazine

Audience: denomination

Purpose: to communicate Quaker experience in order to connect and deepen spiritual lives

Submissions: Only accepts email through the website. Departments, around 1,500 words or fewer: Celebration, Earthcare, Faith and Practice, First-day School, Friends in Business, History, Humor, Life in the Meeting, Lives of Friends, Pastoral Care, Q&A, Reflection, Religious Education, Remembrance, Service, Witness.

Types of manuscripts: personal experience, profile, poetry, teaching

Length: 1,200–2,500 words

Topics: theme-related

Rights: first

Payment: none

Guidelines: *www.friendsjournal.org/submissions*

Sample: articles are on the website

Theme list: available on the website

GATHER

8765 W. Higgins Rd., Chicago, IL 60631 | 844-409-0576
gather@elca.org | *www.gathermagazine.org*
Elizabeth Hunter, editor

> **Denomination:** Evangelical Lutheran Church in America
> **Parent company:** Women of the Evangelical Lutheran Church in America
> **Type:** monthly digital and print magazine
> **Audience:** Lutheran women
> **Purpose:** to help readers grow in faith and engage in ministry and action
> **Submissions:** Email as attachment or in body of message. Query with clips first. Simultaneous submissions OK. Response only if interested.
> **Type of manuscripts:** personal experience
> **Topics:** theme-related
> **Rights:** first, onetime, reprint (with info on where/when previously published)
> **Payment:** on publication
> **Seasonal submissions:** seven months
> **Guidelines:** *www.gathermagazine.org/write-for-gather*
> **Sample:** article samples are on the website
> **Tip:** "Please know that most of what we publish is assigned—we ask particular established authors to write on specific themes far in advance of publication. We publish very few articles that originated as unsolicited manuscripts or queries. We rarely, if ever, publish freelance poetry or devotions."

GEMS OF TRUTH

7407–7415 Metcalf Ave., Overland Park, KS 66204 | 913-432-0331
www.heraldandbanner.com
Gordon L. Snider, editor of publications

> **Denomination:** Church of God
> **Parent company:** Herald and Banner Press
> **Type:** weekly Sunday school take-home paper
> **Audience:** denomination
> **Submissions:** Only accepts through the website.
> **Types of manuscripts:** biography, devotion, poetry, short story, teaching
> **Length:** fiction, 1,000–2,000 words

Topics: Christian living/spirituality
Seasonal submissions: six to eight months in advance
Preferred Bible version: KJV
Sample: download from website

THE GOOD NEWS

PO Box 670368, Coral Springs, FL 33067 | 954-564-5378
ShellyP@goodnewsfl.org | *www.goodnewsfl.org*
Shelly Pond, editor

Parent company: Good News Media Group, LLC
Type: monthly digital and print newspaper; circulation 80,000 print, 30,000 digital; advertising accepted
Audience: Dade, Broward and Palm Beach, Florida areas
Submissions: Only accepts query letter with clips via email.
Types of manuscripts: article
Length: 500–800 words
Payment: 10¢/word
Sample: on the website

GUIDEPOSTS

110 William St., Ste. 901, New York, NY 10038 | 212-251-8100
emiller@guideposts.org | *www.guideposts.org/brand/guideposts-magazine*
Evan Miller, senior editor

Type: bimonthly digital and print magazine
Audience: general
Purpose: to inspire people to believe that all things are possible with faith, hope, and prayer; to encourage, inform, entertain, and tell true stories of personal change; to affirm the positive, unite rather than divide, and meet people where they are on their spiritual journeys
Submissions: Only accepts query via email. Unsolicited freelance: 40%. Response in two months or not interested. Short anecdotes similar to full-length articles, 50–250 words, for departments: "Someone Cares," stories of kindness and caring, *sc@guideposts. com*; "Mysterious Ways," "Family Room," "What Prayer Can Do." Also takes inspiring quotes for "The Up Side," *upside@guideposts. com*.
Type of manuscript: personal experience
Length: articles, 1,500 words; department anecdotes, 50–250 words
Rights: all

Payment: on acceptance, $100–$500
Kill fee: 20% but not to first-time freelancers
Manuscripts accepted per year: 40–60
Guidelines: *www.guideposts.org/writers-guidelines*
Tip: "*Guideposts* magazine stories are about personal change. Narrators face challenges in their lives that they resolve through leaning on faith and God. The challenge can cover everything from relationships to life transitions—such as caregiving, divorce, retirement, or job loss—to life-threatening events. Our true stories deliver hope and inspiration with a clear spiritual point that readers can apply to everyday difficulties in their own lives. We want to be a source of spiritual well-being for our readers."

HEARTBEAT

PO Box 9, Hatfield, AR 71945 | 870-389-6196
heartbeat@cmausa.org | *cmausa.org/Resources/Heartbeat*
Misty Bradley, editor

Parent company: Christian Motorcyclists Association
Type: monthly digital and print magazine
Audience: motorcyclists
Purpose: to inspire leaders and members to be the most organized, advanced, equipped, financially stable organization, full of integrity in the motorcycling industry and the Kingdom of God
Submissions: Only accepts complete manuscript by email.
Type of manuscripts: article
Topics: motorcycling

HIGHWAY NEWS

1525 River Rd., Marietta, PA 17547 | 717-426-9977
editor@transportforchrist.org | *tfcglobal.org/highway-news/current-issue*
Ron Fraser, executive editor

Parent company: Transport for Christ, International
Type: monthly digital magazine, circulation 18,000–20,000
Audience: truck drivers and their families
Purpose: to lead truck drivers, as well as the trucking community, to Jesus Christ and help them grow in their faith
Submissions: Send complete manuscript by email. Unsolicited freelance: 10-20%.
Types of manuscripts: news, personal experience
Length: 800–1,000 words

Topic: trucking life
Rights: first, reprint
Payment: none
Seasonal submissions: six months in advance
Preferred Bible version: ESV
Guidelines: by email
Sample: download from the website
Tip: "Articles submitted for publication do not have to be religious in nature; however, they should not conflict with or oppose guidelines and principles presented in the Bible."

HOLINESS TODAY

17001 Prairie Star Pkwy., Lenexa, KS 66220 | 913-577-0500
holinesstoday@nazarene.org | *www.holinesstoday.org*
Nate Gilmore, content editor

Denomination: Nazarene
Type: bimonthly digital and print magazine, circulation 11,000, advertising accepted
Audience: denomination
Purpose: to keep readers connected with the Nazarene experience and provide tools for everyday faith
Submissions: Only accepts complete manuscript; email as attachment. Unsolicited freelance: 30%. Also accepts submissions from children and teens.
Types of manuscripts: column, personal experience
Length: 700–1,100 words
Topics: denomination, ministry, teaching
Rights: first, reprint (with info on where/when previously published)
Payment: on publication, $135
Kill fee: yes
Manuscripts accepted per year: six to eight
Preferred Bible version: NIV
Theme list: available via email
Guidelines: by email
Tip: "We are always interested in hearing from Nazarene pastors, lay leaders, and experts in their fields. We are a Nazarene publication that wants our articles to be relevant and applicable to real-life scenarios and the world we live in."

HOMELIFE

1 Lifeway Plaza, Nashville, TN 37234-0172 | 615-251-2196
homelife@lifeway.com | *www.lifeway.com/en/product-family/home-life-magazine*
David Bennett, managing editor

Denomination: Southern Baptist
Parent company: LifeWay Christian Resources
Type: monthly print magazine, circulation 250,000
Audience: parents
Purpose: to address all things faith, family, and life
Submissions: Only accepts complete manuscript; email as attachment. Gives assignments. Unsolicited freelance: 10%. Response in several weeks.
Types of manuscripts: column, how-to, narrative
Length: 1,500–7,500 words
Topics: faith, living on mission, marriage, parenting
Rights: first
Payment: on publication, $100–$400
Manuscripts accepted per year: 20
Seasonal submissions: four months in advance
Preferred Bible version: CSB
Guidelines: by email
Sample: on the website
Tip: "Include full bio, church name, and denomination with submission."

HOMESCHOOLING TODAY

PO Box 1092, Somerset, KY 42502 | 606-485-4105
editor@homeschoolingtoday.com | *homeschoolingtoday.com*
Ashley Wiggers, co-executive editor
Kay Chance, co-executive editor

Parent company: Paradigm Press
Type: triannual digital and print magazine, circulation 5,000–6,000, advertising accepted
Audience: homeschooling parents
Purpose: to encourage the hearts of homeschoolers and give them tools to instill a love of learning in their children
Submissions: Only accepts complete manuscript; email as attachment. Response in six months or not interested. Feature articles include information about a topic, unit study,

encouragement, challenge, or an interview, 900–1,200 words. Departments: "Faces of Homeschooling," true stories about real homeschooling families, 600–900 words; "The Home Team," physical education, 600–900 words; "Homeschooling around the World," 600–900 words; "Language Learning," foreign languages, 600–900 words; "Thinking," logic, critical thinking, 600–900 words; "Unit Study," 800–1500 words; "Family Math," 600–900 words.

Types of manuscripts: how-to, interview, lesson plans, profile
Length: 600–1,500 words
Topics: education, homeschooling
Rights: electronic, first, reprint
Payment: 10¢/published word
Guidelines: *homeschoolingtoday.com/write-for-us*

IMAGE

3307 Third Ave. W., Seattle, WA 98119 | 206-281-2988
jkasmith@imagejournal.org | *imagejournal.org*
James K.A. Smith, editor-in-chief
Lauren F. Winner, creative nonfiction editor, lwinner@imagejournal.org

Type: quarterly print journal
Audience: people interested in art and literature
Purpose: to demonstrate the continued vitality and diversity of contemporary art and literature that engage with the religious traditions of Western culture
Submissions: Accepts complete manuscript and query letter through the website. Simultaneous submissions OK. Response in five months.
Types of manuscripts: essay, interview, short story, poetry
Length: 3,000–6,000 words
Topics: literature and the arts
Rights: first
Payment: $25/published page; $3/line for poetry; minimum $100, maximum $400
Guidelines: *imagejournal.org/journal/submit*
Tip: "All the work we publish reflects what we see as a sustained engagement with one of the western faiths–Judaism, Christianity, or Islam. That engagement can include unease, grappling, or ambivalence as well as orthodoxy; the approach can be indirect or allusive, but for a piece to be a fit for *Image*, some connection to faith must be there."

INFLUENCE

1445 N. Boonville Ave., Springfield, MO 65802 | 417-862-2781
editor@influencemagazine.com | influencemagazine.com
Christina Quick, lead editor

Denomination: Assemblies of God
Parent company: The General Council of the Assemblies of God
Type: quarterly digital and print magazine
Audience: pastors and other leaders
Purpose: to provide a Christ-centered, Spirit-empowered perspective that propels people to engage their faith—as individuals, in community, and with the global Church
Submissions: Email complete manuscript or query letter.
Type of manuscripts: articles
Length: 700–1,000 words
Topics: career, community, current events, family
Rights: first
Guidelines: *influencemagazine.com/submission-guidelines*
Sample: *influencemagazine.com/en/issues*
Tip: "Both online and in print, we aim to unite and edify the Church through content marked by integrity and creativity. Our approach to the Christian life is holistic, offering a faith-based context for cultural and current events, as well as providing practical insight for your family, daily life, career and community."

INSITE

PO Box 62189, Colorado Springs, CO 80962-2189 | 719-260-9400
editor@ccca.org | www.ccca.org/ccca/Publications.asp

Parent company: Christian Camp and Conference Association
Type: bimonthly digital and print magazine, circulation 5,800
Audience: camp and conference-center leaders
Purpose: to maximize ministry for member camps and conference centers
Submissions: Only accepts emailed query letter. Unsolicited freelance: 1–2%. Response in one week.
Types of manuscripts: how-to, interview, profile, sidebar
Length: 1,000–1,500 words
Topics: business, camping ministry, discipleship, facilities, leadership, legal, relationships
Rights: all
Payment: on publication, $300

Kill fee: sometimes
Seasonal submissions: six months ahead
Preferred Bible version: NIV
Guidelines: *www.ccca.org/ccca/Publications.asp*
Sample: via email
Theme list: available on website
Tip: "All articles must be applicable to camps and conference centers."

THE JOURNAL OF ADVENTIST EDUCATION

12501 Old Columbia Pike, Silver Spring, MD 20904-6600 | 301-680-5069
mcgarrellf@gc.adventist.org | jae.adventist.org
Faith-Ann McGarrell, editor

Denomination: Seventh-day Adventist
Parent company: General Conference of Seventh-day Adventists
Type: quarterly digital journal, circulation 10,000-16,000, advertising accepted
Audience: educators and administrators
Purpose: to aid professional teachers and educational administrators worldwide, kindergarten to higher education
Submissions: Only accepts complete manuscript through the website. Unsolicited freelance: 10%. Response in four to six weeks.
Types of manuscripts: how-to, personal experience, sidebar, review
Length: 1,500–2,500 words
Topic: Christian education
Rights: first, reprint (with info on where/when previously published)
Payment: on publication, varies
Manuscripts accepted per year: 32
Seasonal submissions: six months in advance
Preferred Bible version: NIV
Guidelines: *jae.adventist.org/calls-for-manuscripts*
Sample: download from the website
Tip: Wants "articles on best practices for teaching and pedagogy that can be applied in education settings both nationally and internationally."

JOYFUL LIVING MAGAZINE

PO Box 311, Palo Cedro, CA 97073 | 530-247-7500
joyfullivingmagazineredding@gmail.com | joyfullivingmagazine.com
Cathy Jansen, editor in chief

Type: quarterly digital magazine, advertising accepted
Audience: general

Purpose: to share encouragement and hope, to help readers grow spiritually and emotionally, and to help them in their everyday lives with practical issues

Submissions: Only accepts complete manuscript; email as attachment.

Types of manuscripts: how-to, personal experience, profile, recipe

Length: 200–700 words

Topics: aging, Christian living/spirituality, depression, family, finances, health, marriage, singleness, work

Payment: none

Guidelines: *joyfullivingmagazine.com/writers-info.html*

Sample: *www.joyfullivingmagazine.com/issues*

Tip: "Joyful Living is dedicated to sharing encouragement and hope to people of all ages. That encouragement finds its way through articles of hope, love, caring, sharing. Also we have articles on health, finance and other subjects that help us grow in maturity and in our daily living."

JUST BETWEEN US

777 S. Barker Rd., Brookfield, WI 53045 | 262-786-6478
submissions@justbetweenus.org | *www.justbetweenus.org*
Shelly Esser, executive editor

Parent company: Elmbrook Church

Type: quarterly print magazine, circulation 8,000

Audience: women

Purpose: to encourage and equip women for a life of faith and service

Submissions: Only accepts complete manuscript; email as attachment. Response in six to eight weeks or not interested.

Types of manuscripts: how-to, personal experience, testimony

Length: articles, 1,000–1,200 words; testimonies, 450 words

Topics: Christian living/spirituality, evangelism, faith, finances, friendship, ministry, parenting, prayer, relationships, spiritual warfare

Payment: none

Preferred Bible version: NIV

Guidelines: *justbetweenus.org/magazine/writers-guidelines-for-just-between-us*

Sample: *justbetweenus.org/magazine-sample-issue*

Tip: "Articles should be personal in tone, full of real-life anecdotes as well as quotes/advice from noted Christian professionals, and be biblically based. Articles need to be practical and have a distinct Christian and serving perspective throughout."

LEADING HEARTS

PO Box 6421, Longmont, CO 80501 | 303-835-8473

amber@leadinghearts.com | *leadinghearts.com*

Amber Weigland-Buckley, editor

Parent company: Right to the Heart Ministries

Type: bimonthly digital magazine, circulation 60,000, advertising accepted

Audience: women who lead hearts at home, church, work, and community; ages 35–50

Submissions: Articles on assignment only. To audition for an assignment, email an article of 1,200 words maximum and a short résumé. Gives preferred consideration to members of AWSA.

Types of manuscripts: how-to, personal experience, profile, review

Length: 800 words maximum; columns, 250–500 words

Topics: theme-related

Rights: first, reprint

Payment: none

Preferred Bible version: NIV

Theme list: not available

Guidelines: *leadinghearts.com/wp-content/uploads/2014/06/ WritersGuidelines.pdf*

Sample: download from the website

LEAVES

PO Box 87, Dearborn, MI 48121-0087 | 313-561-2330

editor.leaves@mariannhill.us | *www.mariannhill.us/leaves.html*

Rev. Thomas Heier, editor-in-chief

Denomination: Catholic

Parent company: Marianhill Mission Society

Type: bimonthly print magazine, circulation 10,000

Audience: Catholics, primarily in the Detroit, Michigan, area

Purpose: to promote devotion to God and testimony of His blessings

Submissions: Only accepts complete manuscript; email or mail.

Types of manuscripts: personal experience, poetry, review, testimony

Length: 250 words

Topics: Christian living/spirituality, prayer

Rights: first, reprint

Payment: none

Manuscripts accepted per year: 40

Preferred Bible version: RSV Catholic edition

Sample: articles are on the website
Tip: Greatest need is for personal testimonies.

LIGHT

901 Commerce St., Ste. 550, Nashville, TN 37203 | 615-244-2495
nicolet@erlc.com | erlc.com/resource-libary/light-magazine-issues
Lindsay Nicolet, managing editor

Denomination: Southern Baptist
Parent company: The Ethics and Religious Liberty Commission
Type: biannual digital and print journal, circulation 10,000, advertising accepted
Audience: church and ministry leaders
Purpose: to bear witness to the gospel by speaking to congregations and consciences with a thoroughly Christian moral witness
Submissions: Only accepts complete manuscript; email as attachment. Unsolicited freelance: 10%. Response in one week.
Types of manuscripts: column, how-to, news, review
Length: 1,500 words
Topics: culture, ethics, family, justice, parenting, politics
Rights: all
Payment: depends on article and writer
Manuscripts accepted per year: ten
Preferred Bible version: CSB
Guidelines: not available
Sample: email request
Tip: "Looking for articles tied to current events and focus on local church ministry."

LIVE

1445 N. Boonville Ave., Springfield, MO 65802-1894 | 417-862-2781
wquick@ag.org | myhealthychurch.com
Wade Quick, editor

Denomination: Assemblies of God
Parent company: Gospel Publishing House
Type: weekly Sunday school take-home paper, circulation 40,000
Audience: denomination
Purpose: to encourage Christians in living for God through stories that apply biblical principles to everyday problems
Submissions: Only accepts email as attachment. Unsolicited freelance: 100%.

Types of manuscripts: filler, how-to, personal experience, poetry, short story

Length: 200–1,200 words; poetry, 12–25 lines

Topic: Christian living/spirituality

Rights: first, reprint

Payment: on acceptance; 10¢/word for first rights, 7¢/word for reprint, $42–60 for poetry

Seasonal submissions: 18 months

Preferred Bible version: NLT

Guidelines: *myhealthychurch.com/store/startcat.cfm?cat=tWRITGUID*

Tip: "Stories should be encouraging, challenging, and/or humorous. Even problem-centered stories should be upbeat. Stories should not be preachy, critical, or moralizing. They should not present pat, trite, or simplistic answers to problems. No Bible fiction or sci-fi. Make sure the stories have a strong Christian element, are written well, have strong takeaways, but do not preach."

THE LUTHERAN WITNESS

1333 S. Kirkwood Rd., St. Louis, MO 63122-7226 | 800-248-1930

lutheran.witness@lcms.org | *witness.lcms.org*

Roy S. Askins, managing editor

Denomination: Lutheran, Lutheran Church Missouri Synod

Type: monthly print magazine, circulation 120,000

Audience: denomination

Purpose: to interpret the contemporary world from a Lutheran perspective

Submissions: Only accepts complete manuscript through the website.

Types of manuscripts: Bible study, essay, how-to, humor, personal experience, poetry, profile, teaching

Length: 500, 1,000, or 1,500 words

Topics: theme-related

Rights: electronic, first

Payment: on acceptance, based on both article length and complexity and author's credentials

Preferred Bible version: ESV

Theme list: available on website

Guidelines: *witness.lcms.org/contribute*

Tip: "Because of the magazine's long lead time, and because many features are planned at least six months in advance of the publication date, your story should have a long-term perspective that keeps it relevant several months from the time you submit it."

MATURE LIVING

1 Lifeway Plaza, MSN 136, Nashville, TN 37234-0175 | 615-251-2000

debbie.dickerson@lifeway.com | *www.lifeway.com/en/product-family/mature-living-magazine*

Debbie Dickerson, managing editor

Denomination: Southern Baptist
Parent company: LifeWay Christian Resources
Type: monthly print magazine
Audience: ages 55 and older
Purpose: to equip mature adults as they live a legacy of leadership, stewardship, and discipleship
Submissions: Assignment only. Email for possible assignment.
Types of manuscripts: devotion, how-to, personal experience, puzzle, recipe, short story
Topics: caregiving, evangelism, marriage, parenting, relationships, theology
Preferred Bible version: CSB
Sample: on the website
Tip: Open for "Kicks and Grins," fun stories of your grandkids, 25-125 words; challenging biblical word search puzzles; and crossword puzzles.

THE MESSENGER

440 Main St., Steinbach, MB R5G 1Z5, Canada | 204-326-6401

messenger@emconference.ca | *emcmessenger.ca*

Rebecca Roman, editor

Denomination: Mennonite
Type: bimonthly digital and print magazine, circulation 2,700
Audience: members and adherents of churches within the Evangelical Mennonite Conference
Purpose: to inform concerning events and activities of the denomination, instruct in godliness and victorious living, and inspire to earnestly contend for the faith
Submissions: Only accepts emailed query letter. Unsolicited freelance: 50%. Response in two weeks.
Type of manuscripts: features
Length: 800–1,500 words
Topics: wide variety
Rights: first
Payment: on publication, $100–$150

Kill fee: always
Manuscripts accepted per year: few, mostly assigned
Seasonal submissions: six months in advance
Preferred Bible version: NIV
Guidelines: *emcmessenger.ca/submission-guidelines*
Sample: *issuu.com/emcmessenger*
Tip: "Always query first. A lead article involves a mixture of teaching, interpretation, and opinion. Effective writers 'inform, instruct, and inspire.' They display an informed opinion, a balance in approach, a Christ-centered focus, and concern for the well-being of the Church. The writer is expected to observe and comment on conference trends and issues as deemed fit. The purpose of a lead article is not to create controversy, but to motivate thought and action."

THE MESSIANIC TIMES

50 Alberta Dr., Amhurst, NY 14226 | 866-612-7770
editor@messianictimes.com | *www.messianictimes.com*
Kayla Levy, editorial coordinator

Denomination: Messianic
Parent company: Times of the Messiah Ministries
Type: bimonthly digital and print newspaper, advertising accepted
Audience: Messianic community
Purpose: to provide accurate, authoritative, and current information to unite the international Messianic Jewish community, teach Christians the Jewish roots of their faith, and proclaim that Yeshua is the Jewish Messiah
Submissions: Only accepts emailed query letter.
Types of manuscripts: analysis, news, opinion, review
Sample: on the website

MINISTRY

12501 Old Columbia Pike, Silver Spring, MD 20904 | 301-680-6518
ministrymagazine@gc.adventist.org | *www.ministrymagazine.org*
Pavel Goia, editor

Denomination: Seventh-day Adventist
Type: monthly digital and print magazine, circulation 18,000+
Audience: pastors, professors, administrators, chaplains, pastoral students, lay leaders
Purpose: to deepen spiritual life, develop intellectual strength, and increase pastoral and evangelistic effectiveness of all ministers in the

context of the three angels' messages of Revelation 14:6-12

Submissions: Only accepts complete manuscript; email as attachment.

Types of manuscripts: Bible study, how-to, review, teaching

Length: 1,500-2,000 words; reviews, 600 words maximum

Topics: family, issues, ministry, pastoral/preaching, relationships, theology

Rights: all

Payment: on acceptance, determined on amount of research done and other work needed to prepare manuscript

Guidelines: *www.ministrymagazine.org/about/article-submission*

Sample: articles are on the website

Tip: "Because *Ministry*'s readership includes individuals from all over the world, you will want to use words, illustrations, and concepts that will be understood by readers in various parts of the world. Avoid illustrations that are understood in one country but may be confusing in others."

THE MOTHER'S HEART

PO Box 275, Tobaccoville, NC 27050 | 336-775-8519

KymAWright@gmail.com | *www.the-mothers-heart.com*

Kym A. Wright, publisher and editor

Parent company: alWright! Publishing

Type: bimonthly digital magazine, circulation 100,000

Audience: moms at home, homeschoolers, large families, homesteaders, DIYers

Purpose: to serve and encourage mothers in the many facets of staying at home and raising a family

Submissions: Email as attachment or in body of message. Query first. Gives assignments; email to get one. Simultaneous submissions OK. Unsolicited freelance: 20%. Response in two months.

Types of manuscripts: column, filler, how-to, personal experience, review

Length: 750-1,000 and 1,250-1,750 words

Topics: adoption story, Christian living/spirituality, DYI, family, fostering, gardening, homeschooling, hospitality, organization, parenting, special needs, time management

Rights: electronic, first

Payment: on publication, $10-$100

Manuscripts accepted per year: 30

Seasonal submissions: six months in advance

Preferred Bible version: any

Guidelines: *tmhmag.com/Writers%20Guidelines%202016-2019.pdf*
Sample: *tmhmag.com/subscribe.htm*
Tip: "Break in with an adoption story, homeschool, gardening, parenting, DIY."

MUTUALITY

122 W. Franklin Ave., Ste. 218, Minneapolis, MN 55404 | 612-872-6898
mutuality@cbeinternational.org | *www.cbeinternational.org/publication/*
mutuality-blog-magazine
Sarabeth Marcello, editor

> **Parent company:** Christians for Biblical Equality
> **Type:** quarterly digital and print magazine, circulation 1,200
> **Audience:** Christian leaders, women in ministry, seminary and university students, and laity interested in gender, the Bible, and issues of justice
> **Purpose:** to provide inspiration, encouragement, and information on topics related to a biblical view of mutuality between men and women in the home, church, and world
> **Submissions:** Only accepts complete manuscript; email as attachment. Response in one month or more.
> **Types of manuscripts:** how-to, personal experience, poetry, review
> **Length:** articles, 800–1,800 words; reviews, 500–800 words
> **Topics:** theme-related
> **Rights:** electronic, first
> **Payment:** print, $40 gift card; digital, $20 gift card; plus subscription for both
> **Preferred Bible version:** NIV
> **Guidelines:** *www.cbeinternational.org/content/write-mutuality*
> **Sample:** *www.cbeinternational.org/content/mutuality-sample-issue*
> **Theme list:** available on website

MYSTERIOUS WAYS

110 William St., Ste. 901, New York, NY 10038 | 212-251-8100
www.guideposts.org/brand/mysterious-ways-magazine
Diana Aydin, editor

> **Parent company:** Guideposts
> **Type:** bimonthly digital and print magazine
> **Audience:** general
> **Purpose:** to encourage through true stories of extraordinary moments and everyday miracles that reveal a spiritual force at work in our lives

Submissions: Only accepts complete manuscript through the website.

Type of manuscript: personal experience

Length: 750–1,500 words; departments, 50–350 words

Rights: all

Payment: varies

Guidelines: *www.guideposts.org/tell-us-your-story*

Tip: "Looking for true stories of unexpected and wondrous experiences that reveal a hidden hand at work in our lives. The best stories are those that present a credible, well-detailed account that can even leave skeptics in awe and wonder. A typical *Mysterious Ways* story is written in dramatic style, with an unforeseen twist that inspires the reader to look for miracles in his or her own life. It may be told from a 1st-person or 3rd-person perspective, and can be your own experience or someone else's story. We are also on the lookout for recent experiences."

NET RESULTS

308 West Blvd. N, Columbia, MO 65203 | 888-470-2456

subs@netresults.org | netresults.org

Bill Tenny-Brittian, managing editor

Parent company: The Effective Church Group, LLC

Type: bimonthly digital magazine, circulation 500, advertising accepted

Audience: clergy, church leaders

Purpose: to provide workable, good ideas to pastors/church leaders for growing their churches

Submissions: Only accepts email as attachment. Send query letter first. Simultaneous submissions OK. Unsolicited freelance: 50%. Response in two days. Also accepts submissions from teens.

Length: 1,500–3,000 words

Topics: church growth, evangelism

Rights: reprint

Payment: subscription

Manuscripts accepted per year: 50

Seasonal submissions: four months in advance

Preferred Bible version: NIV

Theme list: available on website

Guidelines: *netresults.org/writers*

Sample: email request

Tip: "A good query goes a long way towards a good working relationship. We are always looking for competent writers who are willing and able to write within the themes and our specific how-to slant. We prefer articles from church leaders who are writing from experience rather than from research; tell us what you've done (even if it failed!) and what you learned. The best articles follow a general format of (1) We did this—and why we did this; (2) This is how we did this; (3) This was the result; (4) This is what we learned; (5) This is how the reader can adopt and adapt what we did."

NEW FRONTIER CHRONICLE

30840 Hawthorne Blvd., Rancho Palos Verde, CA 90275 | 562-491-8343
karen.gleason@usw.salvationarmy.org | www.newfrontierchronicle.org
Karen Gleason, senior editor
Hillary Jackson, managing editor, hillary.jackson@usw.salvationarmy.org

Denomination: The Salvation Army
Parent company: The Salvation Army Western Territory
Type: monthly print newspaper
Audience: denomination in the territory
Purpose: to empower Salvationists to communicate and engage with the Army's mission
Submissions: Only accepts query letter.
Types of manuscripts: article, review
Topics: denomination
Sample: *issuu.com/newfrontierpublications*
Tip: "Shares information from across The Salvation Army world, reports that analyze effective programs to identify the unique features and trends for what works, tips to help local congregations better engage in the issues of today, and influential voices on relevant (and sometimes controversial) matters."

NEW IDENTITY MAGAZINE

PO Box 1002, Mount Shasta, CA 96067 | 310-947-8707
submissions@newidentitymagazine.com | www.newidentitymagazine.com
Cailin Briody Henson, editor-in-chief

Type: quarterly digital and print magazine
Audience: new believers
Purpose: to provide diverse, Bible-centered content to help lead new believers and seekers to a fuller understanding of the Christian faith
Submissions: Only accepts complete manuscript through the website. Response in two to three weeks. Departments: "Grow," teaching new believers and seekers about different Christian

perspectives on topics, understanding Christian concepts, jargon, disciplines, practical application of Scripture, etc.; "Connect," encouraging new believers and seekers with testimonies, articles about relationships, fellowship, church, community, discussions and expressions of faith; "Live," engaging new believers and seekers to live out their faith in the real world, with stories of people actively pursuing God and their passions, organizations and resources to apply one's gifts, talents and desires to serve God and others, sharing the love of Christ in everyday arenas.

Types of manuscripts: how-to, opinion, personal experience, teaching, testimony

Length: 500–2,500 words

Topics: Christian living/spirituality, church, evangelism, relationships, salvation, service

Rights: electronic, first

Payment: none

Guidelines: *www.newidentitymagazine.com/write/writers-guidelines*

Sample: on the website

Tip: "Articles need creative, well thought-out ideas that offer new insight. We value well researched, factually and biblically supported content."

NOW WHAT?

PO Box 33677, Denver, CO 80233 | 303-452-7973

nowwhat@cog7.org | *nowwhat.cog7.org*

Sherri Langton, associate editor

Denomination: Church of God (Seventh Day)

Type: monthly digital magazine

Audience: seekers

Purpose: to address the felt needs of the unchurched

Submissions: Email complete manuscript or query letter. Unsolicited freelance: 100%. Response in four to ten weeks.

Type of manuscripts: personal experience

Length: 1,000–1,500 words

Topics: issues, salvation

Rights: electronic, first, reprint (with info on where/when previously published)

Payment: on publication, $25–$65

Manuscripts accepted per year: 10–12

Preferred Bible version: NIV

Guidelines: *nowwhat.cog7.org/send_us_your_story*

Sample: on the website

Tip: Avoid unnecessary jargon or technical terms. No Christmas or Easter pieces or fiction. "Think how you can explain your faith, or how you overcame a problem, to a non-Christian. Use storytelling techniques, like dialogue, scenes, etc., with the conflict clearly stated."

OUR SUNDAY VISITOR

200 Noll Plaza, Huntington, IN 46750 | 260-356-8400

oursunvis@osv.com | *www.osvnews.com*

Gretchen R. Crowe, editorial director

Denomination: Catholic

Type: weekly digital and print newspaper

Audience: denomination

Purpose: to examine the news, culture, and trends of the day from a faithful and sound Catholic perspective—to see the world through the eyes of faith

Submissions: Submit complete manuscript or query letter through the website. Response in four to six weeks.

Types of manuscripts: essay, interview, news, profile

Length: 500–1,350 words

Topics: denomination, issues

Payment: on acceptance

Preferred Bible version: RSV

Guidelines: *osv.submittable.com/submit*

Tip: "Especially interested in writers able to do news analysis (with a minimum of three sources) or news features."

OUTREACH

5550 Tech Center, Colorado Springs, CO 80919 | 800-991-6011, x3208

tellus@outreachmagazine.com | *www.outreachmagazine.com*

James P. Long, editor

Type: bimonthly print magazine

Audience: pastors and church leadership, as well as laypeople who are passionate about outreach

Purpose: to further the Kingdom of God by empowering Christian churches to reach their communities for Jesus Christ

Submissions: Email or mail manuscript with cover letter or query letter with clips. Response in two months.

Types of manuscripts: how-to, profile

Length: 200–2,500 words
Topics: church outreach, evangelism, ministry, small groups
Rights: first, reprint (with info on where/when previously published)
Payment: $700–$1,000 for feature articles
Seasonal submissions: six months in advance
Guidelines: *www.outreachmagazine.com/magazine/3160-writers-guidelines.html*
Tip: "While most articles are assigned, we do accept queries and manuscripts on speculation. Please don't query us until you've studied at least one issue of *Outreach*. If you're interested in writing on assignment, submit a cover letter, published writing samples, résumé, and a list of topics you specialize in or are interested in covering. We keep these on file and do not respond to all writing queries or return writing samples."

PARENTING TEENS

1 Lifeway Plaza, Nashville, TN 37234-0172 | 615-251-2196
lwt@lifeway.com | *www.lifeway.com/en/product-family/parenting-teens*
Scott Latta, editor

Denomination: Southern Baptist
Parent company: LifeWay Christian Resources
Type: monthly print magazine
Audience: parents of teens
Purpose: to give parents encouragement and challenge them in their relationship with Christ so that they, in turn, can guide their teens
Submissions: Assignment only. Email résumé, bio, and clips to get assignments.
Type of manuscripts: article
Topics: parenting
Preferred Bible version: CSB
Sample: on the website

PARENTLIFE

1 Lifeway Plaza, Nashville, TN 37234-0172 | 615-251-2196
parentlife@lifeway.com | *www.lifeway.com/en/product-family/parentlife-magazine*
Nancy Cornwell, content editor

Denomination: Southern Baptist
Parent company: LifeWay Christian Resources
Type: monthly print magazine

Audience: parents of children from birth to preteen

Purpose: to encourage and equip parents with biblical solutions that will transform families

Submissions: Email query letter first. Response in six to twelve months.

Type of manuscripts: devotion, how-to, sidebar, teaching

Length: 500–1,500 words

Topics: discipline, education, parenting, spiritual growth

Preferred Bible version: CSB

Sample: order from the website

Guidelines: by email

Tip: "Serves as a springboard for parents who may feel exasperated or overwhelmed with information by offering a biblical approach to raising healthy, productive children. Offers practical ideas and information for individual parents and couples."

PARISH LITURGY

16565 S. State St., South Holland, IL 60473 | 708-331-5485

acp@acpress.org | *www.americancatholicpress.org/parLit.html*

Rev. Michael Gilligan, executive director

Denomination: Catholic

Parent company: American Catholic Press

Type: quarterly print magazine, circulation 1,500

Audience: parish priests, music directors, liturgy planners

Purpose: to provide material for each Sunday: themes, comments, petitions, and music suggestions

Submissions: Only accepts complete manuscript by mail. Unsolicited freelance: 50%. Response in two months.

Types of manuscripts: how-to, teaching

Length: 300 words

Topics: liturgy, music

Rights: all

Payment: on publication, variable

Kill fee: yes

Preferred Bible version: CR

Sample: 9x12" envelope with $2 postage

Tip: "We use articles on the liturgy only—period. Send us well-informed articles on the liturgy."

POINT

11002 Lake Hart Dr., Orlando, FL 32832 | 407-563-6083
mickey.seward@converge.org | *www.converge.org/point-magazine*
Mickey Seward, editor

> **Denomination:** Baptist
> **Parent company:** Converge
> **Type:** triannual digital magazine
> **Audience:** church planters
> **Purpose:** to share captivating stories of God's work through His church and best practices for church planting, strengthening churches and missions
> **Submissions:** Only accepts query letter with clips.
> **Types of manuscripts:** personal experience, profile, report
> **Length:** 300–1,400 words
> **Rights:** electronic, first, reprint
> **Payment:** on publication, $60–$80
> **Sample:** on the website

POWER FOR LIVING

4050 Lee Vance Dr., Colorado Springs, CO 80918 | 719-536-0100
Powerforliving@davidccook.com | *davidccook.org*
Karen Bouchard, managing editor

> **Parent company:** David C. Cook
> **Type:** weekly Sunday school take-home paper
> **Audience:** general, ages 50 and older
> **Purpose:** to connect God's truth to real life
> **Types of manuscripts:** interview, personal experience, poetry, column
> **Length:** features, 1,200–1,500 words; poetry, 20 lines or fewer; columns, 750 words
> **Topics:** holidays, wide variety
> **Rights:** first, onetime, reprint
> **Payment:** on acceptance, $375 for articles, $50 for poems, $150 for columns, $100 for devotions
> **Manuscripts accepted per year:** feature articles, 20; poems, 6–12; columns, 5–8; devotions, rare
> **Seasonal submissions:** 12–18 months in advance
> **Preferred Bible version:** NIV, KJV
> **Guidelines:** *davidccook.org/wp-content/uploads/Power-for-Living-Writers-Guidelines.pdf*

Tip: "Looking for inspiring stories and articles about famous and ordinary people whose experiences and insights show the power of Christ at work in their lives."

PRAYER CONNECT

PO Box 10667, Terre Haute, IN 47801 | 812-238-5504
editor@prayerconnect.net | *prayerleader.com/magazine*
Carol Madison, editor

Parent company: Church Prayer Leaders Network
Type: quarterly digital and print magazine, circulation 3,000, advertising accepted
Audience: pastors and local-church prayer leaders
Purpose: to encourage and equip you in all aspects of prayer, but with the ultimate goal of developing our readers to be intercessors who pray for their friends and families, churches, communities, and the world effectively and with passion
Submissions: Send complete manuscript or query letter. Email as attachment or mail. Unsolicited freelance: 15%. Response in two to three weeks. Usually gives assignments only to regular writers.
Types of manuscripts: column, how-to, news, prayer guide, short idea
Length: 250–1,500 words
Topics: prayer, revival
Rights: first, reprint (with info on where/when previously published)
Payment: on publication, 10¢/word, 5¢/word for reprints
Kill fee: sometimes
Manuscripts accepted per year: 30–40
Preferred Bible version: NIV
Theme list: available via email
Guidelines: *www.prayerleader.com/about-us/write-for-us*
Sample: *www.prayerleader.com/free-issue-pdfs*
Tip: "Short ideas, prayer tips, are the easiest way to break in at *Prayer Connect*."

PRESBYTERIANS TODAY

100 Witherspoon St., Louisville, KY 40202-1396 | 800-728-7228
editor@pcusa.org | *www.presbyterianmission.org/ministries/today*
Donna Frischknecht Jackson, editor

Denomination: Presbyterian Church (USA)
Type: bimonthly digital and print magazine, circulation 56,000
Audience: denomination

Purpose: to explore practical issues of faith and life, tell stories of Presbyterians who are living their faith, and cover a wide range of church news and activities

Submissions: Only accepts query letter. Unsolicited freelance: 25%. Response in two weeks.

Type of manuscripts: articles

Length: 1,500 words

Topics: Bible study, church, denomination, Presbyterians, theology

Payment: on acceptance, $75–300

Seasonal submissions: three months in advance

Preferred Bible version: NRSV

Guidelines: click on Writer's Guidelines

Sample: click on Digital Edition

RELEVANT

55 W. Church St., Ste. 211, Orlando, FL 32801 | 407-660-1411

submissions@relevantmediagroup.com | *relevantmagazine.com*

Emily Brown, associate editor

Type: bimonthly digital and print magazine

Audience: general in 20s and 30s

Purpose: to challenge people to go further in their spiritual journey; live selflessly and intentionally; care about positively impacting the world around them; and find the unexpected places God is speaking in life, music, and culture

Submissions: Email complete manuscript or query letter as attachment. Response in one to two weeks or not interested.

Type of manuscripts: articles

Length: 750–1,000 words

Topics: Christian living/spirituality, culture, faith, justice

Payment: none

Guidelines: *relevantmagazine.com/write*

Sample: on the website

RELIEF: A JOURNAL OF ART & FAITH

8933 Forestview, Evanston, IL 60203

editor@reliefjournal.com | *www.reliefjournal.com*

Daniel Bowman, Jr., editor in chief

Katie Karnehm-Esh, creative nonfiction, katie@reliefjournal.com

Aaron Housholder, fiction, aaron@reliefjournal.com

Julie L. Moore, poetry, julie@reliefjournal.com

Type: biannual print journal

Audience: general

Purpose: to promote full human flourishing in faith and art

Submissions: Only accepts complete manuscript through the website. Simultaneous submissions OK. Submit manuscript through the website only during October 1 to March 31. Costs $2.50 to submit a manuscript.

Types of manuscripts: essay, poetry, short story

Length: stories, 8,000 words maximum; poetry, 1,000 words maximum; creative nonfiction essays, 5,000 words maximum

Rights: first

Payment: none

Guidelines: *www.reliefjournal.com/print-submit*

SACONNECTS

440 W. Nyack Rd., West Nyack, NY 10994-1739 | 845-620-7200

saconnects@use.salvationarmy.org | *saconnects.org*

Robert Mitchell, managing editor

Hugo Bravo, editor, Hispanic correspondent

Denomination: The Salvation Army

Type: monthly digital and print magazine

Audience: denomination in the eastern territory

Submissions: Only accepts email through the website.

Types of manuscripts: how-to, news, personal experience

Topics: denomination

SHARING: A JOURNAL OF CHRISTIAN HEALING

PO Box 780909, San Antonio, TX 78278-0909 | 877-992-5222

sharing@OSLToday.org | *osltoday.org/sharing-magazine*

Jamie Ferger, editor

Parent company: International Order of St. Luke the Physician

Type: bimonthly digital and print magazine, circulation 3,000

Audience: membership

Purpose: to empower God's people throughout the world with Jesus' healing ministry

Submissions: Only accepts email as attachment. Unsolicited freelance: 80%. Response in one week.

Types of manuscripts: poetry, short story

Length: 800–1,500 words

Topics: healing

Rights: all

Payment: none
Manuscripts accepted per year: 40–50
Theme list: available via email
Sample: email
Guidelines: by email

SOJOURNERS

3333 14th St. NW, Ste. 200, Washington, DC 20010 | 202-328-8842

queries@sojo.net | sojo.net/magazine/current

Julie Polter, editor

reviews, reviews@sojo.net
poetry, poetry@sojo.net

Type: bimonthly digital and print magazine
Audience: community influencers
Purpose: to explore the intersections of faith, politics, and culture; uncover in depth the hidden injustices in the world around us; and tell the stories of hope that keep us grounded, inspired, and moving forward
Submissions: Email query letter in body of message. Response in six to eight weeks.
Types of manuscripts: feature, poetry, review
Length: articles, 1,800–2,000 words; poetry, 25 lines maximum
Topics: Christian living/spirituality, culture, faith, justice, politics
Rights: all
Payment: on publication; unspecified, $50 per poem
Guidelines: *sojo.net/magazine/write*
Sample: buy from website

SPORTS SPECTRUM

640 Plaza Dr., Ste. 110, Highlands Ranch, CO 80129 | 866-821-2971

jon@sportsspectrum.com | sportsspectrum.com

Jon Ackerman, managing editor

Parent company: Pro Athletes Outreach
Type: quarterly digital and print magazine, circulation 4,000, advertising accepted
Audience: sports fans
Purpose: to share stories of sports persons displaying an athletic lifestyle pleasing to God
Submissions: Only accepts email as attachment. Gives assignments. Query with clips. Simultaneous OK. Unsolicited freelance: 10%.

Response in one week.
Type of manuscripts: feature
Length: 1,500–2,000 words
Topics: sports
Rights: all
Payment: on acceptance, 15¢/word
Manuscripts accepted per year: two or three
Seasonal submissions: two to three months
Preferred Bible version: NIV
Sample: call the office
Guidelines: not available
Tip: "Come with a story idea and plan for executing it."

ST. ANTHONY MESSENGER

28 W. Liberty St., Cincinnati, OH 45202-6498 | 513-241-5615
MagazineEditors@Franciscanmedia.org | *www.FranciscanMedia.org/st-anthony-messenger*
Christopher Heffron, editorial director

Denomination: Catholic
Type: monthly print magazine
Audience: family-oriented, majority are women ages 40–70
Purpose: to offer readers inspiration from the heart of Catholicism—
the Gospels and the experience of God's people
Submissions: Only accepts email, query letter. Response in eight
weeks.
Types of manuscripts: profile, short story, teaching
Length: feature articles, 2,000–2,500 words; fiction, 2,000–2,500
words
Topics: church, education, family, issues, marriage, sacraments,
spiritual growth
Rights: first
Payment: on acceptance, 20¢/word
Manuscripts accepted per year: short stories, 12
Preferred Bible version: NAB
Guidelines: *www.franciscanmedia.org/writers-guidelines*
Sample: articles are on website

STANDARD

PO Box 843336, Kansas City, MO 4184-3336 | 816-931-1900
standard.foundry@gmail.com | *tinyurl.com/4wmhzumf*

Jeanette Gardner Littleton, editor

Denomination: Nazarene

Parent company: The Foundry Publishing

Type: weekly Sunday school take-home paper, circulation 40,000

Audience: denomination

Purpose: to encourage and inspire our audience and to reinforce curriculum

Submissions: Only accepts email. Primarily assignment only. To get an assignment, send clips of personal-experience articles.

Type of manuscripts: personal experience

Length: 400 and 800–900 words

Topics: theme-related

Rights: all, first, reprint

Payment: on acceptance, $35 and $50

Manuscripts accepted per year: 104

Seasonal submissions: one year

Preferred Bible version: NIV

Theme list: available via email

Sample: email request

Guidelines: by email

Tip: "Writers should know basics of Wesleyan-Arminian theological perspective. Write to the theme list; please indicate which theme you're proposing it for. Nonfiction cannot be preachy. Put full contact information in the body of the manuscript, not only in the email. It helps to know if you're Nazarene or another Wesleyan/holiness denomination."

TEACHERS OF VISION

PO Box 45610, Westlake, OH 44145 | 888-798-1124

tov@ceai.org | ceai.org/teachers-of-vision-magazine

Dawn Molnar, managing editor

Parent company: Christian Educators Association International

Type: triannual digital and print magazine; circulation 4,000 print, 11,750 digital; advertising accepted

Audience: Christian educators in public schools

Purpose: to provide biblically principled resources that encourage, equip, and empower Christian educators

Submissions: Email as attachment complete manuscript or query letter with clips. Simultaneous OK. Unsolicited freelance: 8%. Response in two weeks during school year. Accepts submissions from children and teens. "We, at times, give our regularly published authors assignments. We do not give assignments based on queries."

Types of manuscripts: how-to, personal experience, poetry, trends

Length: features, 600–1,400 words; personal experience, 600–1,200 words; methodology, 600–800 words; inspirational, 600–1200 words

Topics: teaching, theme-related

Rights: electronic, first, reprint

Payment: on publication, $50–$100

Kill fee: yes

Manuscripts accepted per year: 40+

Seasonal submissions: nine months

Preferred Bible version: NIV

Theme list: available on website

Guidelines: *www.ceai.org/wp-content/uploads/2021/10/2022-tov-writers-guidelines.pdf*

Sample: *ceai.org/teachers-of-vision-magazine*

Tip: "Our published writers are: able to integrate secular and spiritual insights; faithful to the teachings of Scripture; mindful of our audience (Christian educators); up-to-date on trends in contemporary education; positive, encouraging, and inspiring; focused on education in general or how the issue's theme relates to education; clear, concise, and creative."

TESTIMONY/ENRICH

2450 Milltower Ct., Mississauga, ON L5N 5Z6, Canada | 905-542-7400

testimony@paoc.org | testimony.paoc.org

Stacey McKenzie, editor

Denomination: Pentecostal Assemblies of Canada

Parent company: Pentecostal Assemblies of Canada

Type: quarterly digital and print magazine

Audience: general and leaders

Purpose: to celebrate what God is doing in and through the Fellowship, while offering encouragement to believers by providing a window into the struggles that everyday Christians often encounter

Submissions: Only accepts email, query letter. Response in six to eight weeks.

Types of manuscripts: interview, personal experience, sidebar

Length: 800–1,000 words

Topics: Christian living/spirituality, denomination

Rights: first
Seasonal submissions: four months in advance
Preferred Bible version: NIV
Guidelines: *testimony.paoc.org/submit*
Tip: "Our readership is 98% Canadian. We prefer Canadian writers or at least writers who understand that Canadians are not Americans in long underwear. We also give preference to members of this denomination, since this is related to issues concerning our fellowship."

TIME OF SINGING: A JOURNAL OF CHRISTIAN POETRY

PO Box 5276, Conneaut Lake, PA 16316 | 814-439-0914

timesing@zoominternet.net | *www.timeofsinging.com*

Lora Zill, editor

Parent company: Wind & Water Press
Type: quarterly print journal, circulation 200
Audience: those who love language and its expression through the art and craft of poetry
Purpose: to provide poets and readers a platform for thought-provoking and reflective work
Submissions: Email or mail complete manuscript. Simultaneous submissions accepted. Unsolicited freelance: 95%. Response in three months. Also accepts submissions from teens. Assigns book reviews of *Time Of Singing* poets; inquire for an assignment.
Types of manuscripts: poetry, review
Length: 40 lines maximum
Rights: first, onetime, reprint (with info on where/when previously published)
Payment: none
Manuscripts accepted per year: 150
Seasonal submissions: six months in advance
Preferred Bible version: any
Guidelines: *www.timeofsinging.com*
Sample: $4 each, including postage (checks, money orders payable to Wind & Water Press)
Tip: "I want poems that aren't afraid to take chances or think outside the theological box. Challenge my assumptions about faith, living the Christian life, and loving God. I prefer poems that don't try to provide answers but fearlessly wrestle with the questions. Trust your reader to 'get it.' It's really best to pick up a back issue to analyze to see what I like. I don't publish greeting-card style poetry or sermons

that rhyme. I love fresh rhyme, free verse, and beg for forms."

TODAY'S CHRISTIAN LIVING

PO Box 5000, Iola, WI 54945 | 715-445-5000
michellea@jpmediallc.com | *www.todayschristianliving.org*
Michelle Adserias, editor

Type: bimonthly digital and print magazine, advertising accepted
Audience: general
Purpose: to challenge Christians in their faith, so they may be
strengthened to fulfill the call of God in their lives
Submissions: Only accepts complete manuscript by email.
Simultaneous submissions OK.
Types of manuscripts: humor, profile, testimony, personal experience
Length: feature testimony, 1,200–1,400 words; "Turning Point," 750–
800 words; "Grace Notes," 750–800 words; humor, 35–50 words
Topics: Christian living/spirituality
Rights: all
Payment: within 60 days of publication; fewer than 750 words: $25;
750–800 words, $75; 801–1,199 words, $100; 1,200–1,800
words, $150
Guidelines: *todayschristianliving.org/writers-guidelines*
Sample: *todayschristianliving.org/free-digital-issue-with-newsletter-signup*
Tip: "Potential articles will be placed in a holding file for possible future
use and will be reviewed each time an issue is being planned and
prepared. An article may be used relatively soon, or after a year
or two, or it may never be used at all. But remember, you're free
to submit an article to other publications unless we purchase and
contract it."

U.S. CATHOLIC

205 W. Monroe St., Chicago, IL 60606 | 312-544-8169
submissions@uscatholic.org | *www.uscatholic.org*
Emily Sanna, managing editor

Denomination: Catholic
Type: monthly digital and print magazine
Audience: denomination
Submissions: Only accepts complete manuscript by email. Response in
six to eight weeks.
Types of manuscripts: essay, feature, opinion, poetry, profile
Length: articles, 800–3,500 words; reviews, 315 words

Rights: first
Topics: denomination
Payment: $75–$500
Seasonal submissions: six months in advance
Guidelines: *uscatholic.org/writers-guide*
Tip: "*U.S. Catholic* does not consider submissions that have simultaneously been sent to any other publication or that have appeared elsewhere in any form, either in print or online. This includes articles published on personal blogs or excerpts from books, published or unpublished."

VIBRANT LIFE

PO Box 5353, Nampa, ID 83653-5353 | 208-465-2584
heather.quintana@pacificpress.com | *www.vibrantlife.com*
Heather Quintana, editor

Denomination: Seventh-day Adventist
Parent company: Pacific Press Publishing Association
Type: bimonthly digital and print magazine
Audience: general
Purpose: to promote physical health, mental clarity, and spiritual balance from a practical, Christian perspective
Submissions: Email as attachment or mail complete manuscript.
Types of manuscripts: how-to, interview, personal experience, profile, teaching
Length: 450–1,000 words plus sidebar if informational
Topics: exercise, family, health, medicine, nutrition, spiritual balance
Rights: first, reprint
Payment: on acceptance, $100–$300
Guidelines: *www.vibrantlife.com/write-for-vibrant-life*
Tip: "Information must be reliable—no faddism. Articles should represent the latest findings on the subject, and if scientific in nature, should be properly documented. (References to other lay journals are generally not acceptable.)"

WAR CRY

615 Slaters Ln., Alexandria, VA 22314 | 703-684-5500
www.thewarcry.org
Lt. Colonel Lesa Davis, editor-in-chief

Denomination: The Salvation Army
Parent company: The Salvation Army

Type: monthly digital and print magazine, circulation 160,000, advertising accepted

Audience: Salvation Army members and associates and general public

Purpose: to represent the mission of The Salvation Army to proclaim the Gospel of Jesus Christ and serve human need in His name without discrimination

Submissions: Simultaneous submissions OK. Submit only through the website. Unsolicited freelance: 50%. Response in three to four weeks.

Types of manuscripts: personal experience, profile

Length: 800–1,250 words

Topics: Christian living/spirituality, culture, discipleship, evangelism, issues, Salvation Army, trends

Rights: first

Payment: on acceptance; 35¢/word, 15¢/word for reprints

Kill fee: sometimes

Manuscripts accepted per year: 40

Seasonal submissions: six months in advance

Preferred Bible version: NLT

Theme list: available on website

Guidelines: *www.thewarcry.org/submission-guidelines*

Sample: on the website

Tip: "Some association/connection/explication of The Salvation Army is helpful when possible."

YOUR BACKYARD

PO Box 127, Cottondale, FL 32431 | 615-613-5040
ybbmedia@gmail.com | *yourbackyard.us/your-backyard-magazine*
shELAH, editor

Parent company: Your Backyard Media

Type: bimonthly digital and print magazine, circulation 500, advertising accepted

Audience: general

Purpose: to encourage writers, artists, musicians, photographers, and brothers and sisters in Jesus Christ

Submissions: Submit complete manuscript by email in body of message, mail, or through the website. Simultaneous submissions OK. Unsolicited freelance: 33%. Response in one month. Also accepts submissions from teens and children.

Types of manuscripts: column, filler, how-to, personal experience, poetry, short story, sidebar

Length: 1,500 words maximum

Topics: arts, inspirational, music

Rights: electronic, first, onetime, reprint (with info on where/when previously published)

Payment: none

Kill fee: none

Manuscripts accepted per year: 25

Seasonal submissions: four months

Preferred Bible version: KJV, open to others

Sample: on the website

Tip: Write about your personal "reason for the hope that is within you." Also looking for original songs, photos, and artwork.

8

TEEN/YOUNG ADULT MARKETS

BOUNDLESS

8605 Explorer Dr., Colorado Springs, CO 80920 | 719-531-3400

editor@boundless.org | *www.boundless.org*

Lisa Anderson, director

Parent company: Focus on the Family

Type: website, 300,000 hits per month

Audience: single young adults in 20s and 30s

Purpose: to help Christian young adults grow up, own their faith, date with purpose, and prepare for marriage and family

Submissions: Only accepts query letter with clips.

Types: articles, blog posts

Length: articles, 1,200–1,800 words; blog posts, 500–800 words

Topics: adulthood, Christian living/spirituality, relationships

Rights: all

Preferred Bible version: ESV

Guidelines: *www.boundless.org/about/write-for-us*

Sample: see the website

Tip: "We don't typically publish unsolicited articles, but we are always open to considering new writers. If you think you've got what it takes to have your work published on *Boundless,* please feel free to send us a sample or two of your writing, a link to your blog, and a proposal of what you're interested in writing about."

THE BRINK

See entry in "Daily Devotional Booklets and Websites."

BRIO

8605 Explorer Dr., Colorado Springs, CO 80920 | 719-531-3400

submissions@briomagazine.com | *focusonthefamily.com/parenting/brio-magazine*
Laura Pottkotter, managing editor

Parent company: Focus on the Family
Type: bimonthly print magazine, circulation 60,000
Audience: teen girls
Purpose: to provide inspiring stories, fashion insights, fun profiles, and practical tips, all from a biblical worldview
Submissions: Only accepts complete manuscript; email as attachment or mail.
Types of manuscripts: articles, profiles, short stories
Length: 200–1,400 words
Topics: entertainment, prayer, relationships, seasonal, social media
Rights: first
Payment: on acceptance, minimum 30¢/word
Guidelines: *media.focusonthefamily.com/brio/pdf/brio-writers-guidelines-2019.pdf*
Sample: on the website
Tip: "We are looking for unique and interesting nonfiction articles, especially stories about real-life teen girls. Every article should have a Christian emphasis, though it shouldn't be preachy or overbearing. The topics, concepts, and vocabulary should be appropriate for our teen audience."

CADET QUEST

See "Children's Markets."

CAFÉ

See "Adult Markets."

GUIDE

See "Children's Markets."

LOVE IS MOVING

9821 Leslie St., Ste. 103, Richmond Hill, ON L4B 3Y4, Canada | 905-479-5885
ilana@loveismoving.ca | *www.loveismoving.ca*
Ilana Reimer, editor

Parent company: The Evangelical Fellowship of Canada
Type: triannual digital and print magazine, circulation 10,100, advertising accepted

Audience: Canadian young adults

Purpose: to reflect a biblical concept of love and challenge readers to live out their faith with passion for Jesus and compassion for others

Submissions: Only accepts email as attachment. Send query letter with clips. Unsolicited freelance: 20%. Response in two to four days.

Types of manuscripts: essays, feature articles, opinion, poetry, reviews, artwork and photography

Length: 600–1,200 words

Topics: Christian living/spirituality, church, culture, ministry

Rights: first, reprint (with info on where/when previously published)

Payment: 15–20¢/word, $50 for poetry

Manuscripts accepted per year: 100

Seasonal submissions: three months in advance

Preferred Bible version: NIV

Theme list: available via email

Guidelines: *loveismoving.ca/about/contribute*

Sample: *www.faithtoday.ca/Subscribe-LIM*

Tip: "We're looking for smart, thoughtful writers who are wrestling with timely topics in the Canadian Church and broader culture through the lens of their faith. Demonstrate your knowledge on the topic you're pitching and don't be afraid to show your enthusiasm!"

NATURE FRIEND

See "Children's Markets."

PEER

615 Sisters Ln., Alexandria, VA 22314 | 703-684-5500

peer@usn.salvationarmy.org | *peermag.org*

Captain Jamie Satterlee, editor

Denomination: Salvation Army

Type: monthly digital and print magazine; circulation: print 30,000, digital 1,400

Audience: 16–22 years old

Purpose: to ignite a faith conversation that will deepen biblical perspective, faith, and holy living by addressing topics related to faith, community, and culture

Submissions: Only accepts complete manuscript through the website. Response in one week. Accepts submissions from teens.

Types of manuscripts: articles, profiles

Length: 800 words

Topics: Christian living/spirituality, culture, current events
Rights: first, onetime
Payment: 35¢/word, 15¢/word for reprints
Preferred Bible version: NLT
Guidelines: *peermag.org/contribute*
Tip: "We are ALWAYS welcoming new submissions from young writers. Do you love to write? Do you consider yourself an expert on a topic that would interest 16- to 22-year-olds? *Peer* is a national publication, and you can most certainly add the experience of writing for us on your résumé!"

TAKE FIVE PLUS
See entry in "Daily Devotional Booklets and Websites."

UNLOCKED
See entry in "Daily Devotional Booklets and Websites."

9

CHILDREN'S MARKETS

CADET QUEST

1333 Alger St. SE, Grand Rapids, MI 49507 | 616-241-5616
submissions@CalvinistCadets.org | *www.calvinistcadets.org/cadet-quest-magazine*
Steve Bootsma, editor

Parent company: Calvinist Cadet Corps
Type: bimonthly print magazine, circulation 5,700
Audience: boys ages 9–14
Purpose: to help boys grow more Christlike in all areas of life
Submissions: Only accepts complete manuscript; email in body of
message or mail. Unsolicited freelance: 5-10%. Response in four
months before publication. Accepts submissions from children and
teens.
Types of manuscripts: profiles, projects, puzzles, short stories
Length: 1,000-1,500 words
Topics: camping, Christian athletes, nature, sports, theme-related
Rights: all, first, reprint
Payment: 8¢/word for first rights, less for reprint rights
Manuscripts accepted per year: 20
Preferred Bible version: NIV
Theme list: available on website
Guidelines: *calvinistcadets.org/wp-content/uploads/Quest-Guidelines.pdf*
Sample: download from website
Tip: "Looking for fun fiction, without being preachy, for preteen boys.
It needs to have some action, and don't be cliché with a Jesus-always-
wins type of ending."

CREATION ILLUSTRATED

PO Box 141103, Spokane Valley, WA 99214 | 530-269-1424
ci@creationillustrated.com | *creationillustrated.com*
Tom and Jennifer Ish, editors/publishers

Parent company: Creation Illustrated Ministries, Inc.

Type: quarterly digital and print magazine, circulation 10,000, advertising accepted

Audience: families, homeschoolers

Purpose: to tell the eternal impact of sharing biblical truth and character-building lessons through the blessings of God's creation

Submissions: Accepts email as attachment, mail, query letter with clips. Unsolicited freelance: 90%. Response in two weeks to two months.

Types of manuscripts: personal experience, short stories

Length: 700–1,500

Topics: nature

Rights: first, reprint (with info on where/when previously published)

Payment: $75–$100; poetry, $15

Kill fee: sometimes

Manuscripts accepted per year: 32

Seasonal submissions: three months

Preferred Bible version: KJV, NKJV, ESV

Theme list: available on website

Guidelines: *www.creationillustrated.com/writer-and-photo-guidelines*

Sample: *www.creationillustrated.com/free-digital-copy*

Tip: "All features are open to freelancers except 'Lens on Creation' and 'Genesis Recipes,' which are assigned. Needing more stories about creatures. Need to query first to be sure we have not written about the creatures recently. Each story needs to lend itself to be illustrated with quality nature photography that our freelance photographers can provide. Don't pick a topic that is difficult to illustrate. Inspire the reader to be in awe of the Creator. Help generate a worshipful spirit. Glorify God the Creator. Make your story uplifting and positive, rather than confrontational, argumentative, or bashing evolution. Do not hide truth, but explain it in a positive way. Inspire the reader to unplug and get outdoors."

DEVOKIDS

See "Daily Devotional Booklets and Websites."

FOCUS ON THE FAMILY CLUBHOUSE

8605 Explorer Dr., Colorado Springs, CO 80920 | 719-531-3400

Rachel.Pfeiffer@fotf.org | *focusonthefamily.com/clubhouse-magazine*

Rachel Pfeiffer, senior associate editor

Parent company: Focus on the Family

Type: monthly print magazine, circulation 80,000+

Audience: ages 8–12

Purpose: to inspire, entertain, and teach Christian values to children

Submissions: Accepts manuscripts only by mail. Unsolicited freelance: 15%. Response in three months. Accepts submissions from children and teens.

Types of manuscripts: articles, crafts, interviews, quizzes, recipes, short stories

Length: 500–2,000 words

Topics: apologetics, Christian living/spirituality

Rights: first

Payment: on acceptance, 15–25¢ per word

Kill fee: sometimes

Manuscripts accepted per year: 80

Seasonal submissions: eight months in advance

Preferred Bible version: HCSB

Guidelines: *focusonthefamily.com/clubhouse-magazine/about/ submission-guidelines*

Sample: $3.99 at *focusonthefamily.com/kidmags*

Tip: "Study the magazine to learn the voice and style. Best way to break in is through nonfiction, especially 'Truth Pursuer' and kid-profile articles. Once an author publishes with us three or more times, we often begin to give assignments. We also give assignments to writers whom we meet at Christian writers conferences."

FOCUS ON THE FAMILY CLUBHOUSE JR.

8605 Explorer Dr., Colorado Springs, CO 80920 | 719-531-3400

Kate.Jameson@fotf.org | *focusonthefamily.com/clubhouse-jr-magazine*

Kate Jameson, associate editor

Parent company: Focus on the Family

Type: monthly print magazine, circulation 60,000

Audience: ages 3–7

Purpose: to inspire, entertain, and teach Christian values to children

Submissions: Only accepts complete manuscript by mail. Unsolicited freelance: 15%. Response in three months. Also accepts submissions from children and teens

Types of manuscripts: activities, Bible stories retold, biography, crafts, interviews, poetry, profiles, rebus stories, recipes, short stories

Length: 400–1,000 words

Topics: animals, Bible stories, Christian living/spirituality, nature, science

Rights: first

Payment: on acceptance, 15–25¢ per word
Manuscripts accepted per year: 50
Seasonal submissions: eight months in advance
Preferred Bible version: NIrV
Guidelines: *focusonthefamily.com/clubhouse-jr-magazine/about/ submission-guidelines*
Sample: $3.99 at *focusonthefamily.com/kidmags*
Tip: "Read the magazine to learn our style and reading level. Aim at early and beginning readers. Rebus and Bible stories are a great way to break in. Once an author publishes with us three or more times, we often begin to give assignments. We also give assignments to writers whom we meet at Christian writers conferences."

GUIDE

PO Box 5353, Nampa, ID 83653-5353
guide.magazine@pacificpress.com | *www.guidemagazine.org*
Randy Fishell, editor

Denomination: Seventh-day Adventist
Parent company: Pacific Press Publishing Association
Type: weekly Sunday school take-home paper, circulation 26,000
Audience: ages 10–14
Purpose: to show readers, through stories that illustrate Bible truth, how to walk with God now and forever
Submissions: Only accepts complete manuscript by mail or through the website; query via email. Unsolicited freelance: 75%, 20% assigned. Response in four to six weeks. Accepts submissions from teens.
Types of manuscripts: biography, humor, personal experience, profile, quiz
Length: 450–1,200 words
Topics: adventure, Christian living/spirituality, missions, nature
Rights: first, reprint (with info on where/when previously published)
Payment: on acceptance, 7–10¢ per word, $25–$40 for games and puzzles
Seasonal submissions: eight months in advance
Preferred Bible version: NKJV
Guidelines: *www.guidemagazine.org/writers-guidelines*
Sample: download from guidelines page
Tip: "Use your best short-story techniques (dialogue, scenes, a sense of plot) to tell a true story starring a kid ages 10–14. Bring out a clear spiritual/biblical message. We publish multipart true stories regularly, two to twelve parts, 1,200 words each. All topics indicated need to be addressed within the context of a true story."

KEYS FOR KIDS

See "Daily Devotional Booklets and Websites."

NATURE FRIEND

4253 Woodcock Ln., Dayton, VA 22821 | 540-867-0764
editor@naturefriendmagazine.com | *www.naturefriendmagazine.com*
Kevin Shank, editor

Parent company: Dogwood Ridge Outdoors
Type: monthly print magazine, circulation 10,000
Audience: ages 6–14, 80% are ages 8–12
Purpose: to increase awareness of God and appreciation for God's works and gifts, to teach accountability toward God's works, and to teach natural truths and facts
Submissions: Only accepts complete manuscript by email as attachment. Simultaneous accepted. Unsolicited freelance: 55%. Accepts submissions from children and teens
Types of manuscripts: articles, crafts, experiments, photo features, profiles, projects, short stories
Length: 500–800 words
Topics: animals, astronomy, first aid, flowers, gardening, marine life, nature, photography, science, weather
Rights: first, reprint
Payment: on publication; 5¢/edited word, 3¢/word for reprints
Manuscripts accepted per year: 40–50
Seasonal submissions: four months in advance
Preferred Bible version: KJV only
Guidelines: *naturefriendmagazine.com/contributors/tips-for-getting-published*
Sample: *naturefriendmagazine.com/sample-issues*
Tip: "While talking animals can be interesting and teach worthwhile lessons, we have chosen to not use them in *Nature Friend*. Excluded are puzzle-type submissions such as 'Who Am I?'"

OUR LITTLE FRIEND

PO Box 5353, Nampa, ID 83653
anita.seymour@pacificpress.com | *primarytreasure.com*
Anita Seymour, managing editor

Denomination: Seventh-day Adventist
Parent company: Pacific Press Publishing Association
Type: weekly Sunday school take-home paper, circulation 16,000
Audience: ages 1–5

Purpose: to teach about Jesus and the Christian life

Submissions: Only accepts complete manuscript; email as attachment. Response in one month.

Types of manuscripts: true stories

Length: one to two double-spaced pages

Topics: Christian living/spirituality, God's love, holidays, nature

Rights: electronic, onetime

Payment: on acceptance, $25–$50

Manuscripts accepted per year: 52

Seasonal submissions: eight to nine months in advance

Preferred Bible version: ICB, NIrV

Theme list: available via mail with SASE

Guidelines: *www.primarytreasure.com/for-writers*

Tip: "We need true, age-appropriate stories that teach about the Christian life." See extensive topic list in the guidelines.

PRIMARY TREASURE

PO Box 5353, Nampa, ID 83653

anita.seymour@pacificpress.com | *www.primarytreasure.com*

Anita Seymour, managing editor

Denomination: Seventh-day Adventist

Parent company: Pacific Press Publishing Association

Type: weekly Sunday school take-home paper, circulation 14,000

Audience: ages 6–9

Purpose: to teach children about the love of God and the Christian life through true stories

Submissions: Only accepts complete manuscript by email as attachment. Unsolicited freelance: 80%. Response in one month.

Types of manuscripts: true stories

Length: three to five double-spaced pages

Topics: Christian living/spirituality, holidays, nature

Rights: electronic, onetime

Payment: on acceptance, $25–$50

Manuscripts accepted per year: 104

Seasonal submissions: eight months in advance

Theme list: available via mail with SASE

Guidelines: *www.primarytreasure.com/for-writers*

Tip: "We need age-appropriate stories that teach about Jesus and the Christian life." See topics list in the guidelines.

10

WRITERS MARKETS

INK & QUILL QUARTERLY

1053 E. 1400 N, Milford, IN 46542 | 574-658-3960

mjhofstetter@hotmail.com

Micah Hofstetter, editor

Rachel Stauffer, prose

Arielle C. Walters, poetry

Denomination: Mennonite

Type: quarterly print magazine, circulation 200, advertising accepted

Audience: Anabaptist writers, but not exclusively

Purpose: to give inspiration to beginning and experienced writers, to provide a safe place for young writers to spread their wings and try their voices, and to help beginning writers learn to use their voices better. We want to use God's gift of language for His glory.

Submissions: Only accepts mail. Unsolicited freelance: 75%. Response in one month.

Types of manuscripts: articles, essays, poetry, writing exercises

Length: maximum of 1,000 words or so

Topics: historical writers, poetry appreciation, writing

Rights: first, reprint (with info on where/when previously published)

Payment: on acceptance; articles, $30; poetry, 50¢ per line

Sample: Write or email us and request a sample copy. Help with postage and shipping is appreciated but not required.

Manuscripts accepted per year: 70

Preferred Bible version: KJV

Guidelines: by email or mail with SASE

Tip: "We are looking for writers with a consistent Christian testimony. We appreciate poetry with traditional forms and meters. Free verse is acceptable, too, provided it employs poetic devices and has a consistent format. We need essays about writing, articles about writers of the past, and poems of all kinds."

INKSPIRATIONS ONLINE
See "Daily Devotional Booklets and Websites."

POETS & WRITERS MAGAZINE
90 Broad St., Ste. 2100, New York, NY 10004-2272 | 212-226-3586
editor@pw.org | *www.pw.org*
Emma Komlos-Hrobsky, senior editor

Parent company: Poets & Writers, Inc.
Type: bimonthly print magazine, circulation 100,000, advertising accepted
Audience: writers of poetry, fiction, and creative nonfiction
Purpose: to provide practical guidance for getting published and pursuing writing careers
Submissions: Email, mail, query letter with clips. Response in four to six weeks.
Types of manuscripts: essay, how-to, interview, news, profile
Length: 500–3,000 words
Topic: writing
Rights: all, reprint
Payment: when scheduled for production, $150–$500
Seasonal submissions: four months in advance
Guidelines: *www.pw.org/about-us/submission_guidelines*
Sample: sold at large bookstores and online
Tip: Most open to "News & Trends," "The Literary Life," and "The Practical Writer."

STORY EMBERS
140 Churchill Ln., Mount Airy, NC 27030
submissions@storyembers.org | *storyembers.org*
Brianna Storm Hilverty, managing editor

Type: biweekly website, 30,000 hits per month
Audience: writers
Purpose: to help Christian writers enthrall readers through honest storytelling that fearlessly grapples with hard issues
Submissions: Only accepts email as attachment. Unsolicited freelance: 40%. Response in two to four weeks.
Type of manuscripts: how-to
Length: 1,000–3,000 words
Topic: writing
Rights: first

Payment: none
Manuscripts accepted per year: 100
Guidelines: *storyembers.org/submissions*
Sample: see the website
Tip: "We're looking for articles that delve into specific writing subjects in-depth in a practical way."

WORDS FOR THE WAY

5042 E. Cherry Hills Blvd., Springfield, MO 65809 | 417-832-8409

ozarksACW@yahoo.com | www.ozarksacw.org

Renee Vajko-Srch, managing editor

Jeanetta Chrystie, acquisitions editor

Parent company: Ozarks Chapter of American Christian Writers
Type: monthly digital newsletter; circulation 55 print, 150 digital; advertising accepted
Audience: writers at all levels
Purpose: to encourage and educate Christians to follow their call to write and learn to write well
Submissions: Email complete manuscript or query letter. Unsolicited freelance: 95%. Response in three weeks. Accepts submissions from teens.
Types of manuscripts: column, filler, how-to, personal experience, poetry, review, sidebar
Length: features, 600–900 words; general writing how-to, 400–600 words; sidebars, 200–400 words; reviews, 200–400 words; devotions, 250–500 words; poetry, 12–40 lines
Topic: writing
Rights: electronic, first, onetime, reprint (with info on where/when previously published)
Payment: none
Manuscripts accepted per year: 45
Seasonal submissions: two months
Preferred Bible version: any
Guidelines: *www.OzarksACW.org/guidelines.php*
Sample: request by email
Tip: "We want content that speaks to our Christian writers by teaching and encouraging them. Specific current needs: How to write in a specific genre (your choice), how to grow spiritually through writing, how to organize a book, how to handle taxes as a freelancer. Also, we need devotions for the website that encourage, inspire, and teach (not preach) Christians to follow their calling to write."

THE WRITER

Editorial, Madavor Media, 25 Braintree Hill Office Park, Ste. 404, Braintree, MA 02184

tweditorial@madavor.com | *www.writermag.com*

Nicki Porter, senior editor

> **Type:** monthly digital and print magazine, circulation 30,000, advertising accepted
>
> **Audience:** writers at all levels
>
> **Purpose:** to expand and support the work of professional and aspiring writers with a straightforward presentation of industry information, writing instruction, and professional and personal motivation
>
> **Submissions:** Only accepts query letter. Simultaneous accepted. Unsolicited freelance: 80%. If no response in two weeks, probably not interested.
>
> **Types of manuscripts:** article, essay, how-to, interview, review, sidebar
>
> **Length:** 300–4,000 words
>
> **Topic:** writing
>
> **Rights:** first
>
> **Payment:** on acceptance, varies by type and department
>
> **Theme list:** available on website
>
> **Guidelines:** *www.writermag.com/the-magazine/submission-guidelines*
>
> **Sample:** sold at large bookstores
>
> **Tip:** "Personal essays must provide takeaway advice and benefits for writers. Include plenty of how-to, advice, and tips on techniques. Be specific. All topics must relate to writing."

THE WRITER'S CHRONICLE

5700 Rivertech Ct., Ste. 225, Riverdale Park, MD 20737-1250 | 240-696-7700

chronicle@awpwriter.org | *www.awpwriter.org/magazine_media/writers_ chronicle_overview*

Supriya Bhatnagar, editor

> **Parent company:** The Association of Writers & Writing Programs
>
> **Type:** bimonthly digital and print magazine, circulation 35,000, advertising accepted
>
> **Audience:** serious writers, writing students and teachers
>
> **Purpose:** to provide diverse insights into the art of writing that are accessible, pragmatic, and idealistic for serious writers; articles are used as teaching tools
>
> **Submissions:** Only accepts query via email through the website. Unsolicited freelance: 90%. Response in three months.

Types of manuscripts: essays, interviews, news, sidebars
Length: 2,000–5,000 words
Topic: writing
Rights: electronic, first
Payment: on publication, $18 per 100 words
Guidelines: *www.awpwriter.org/magazine_media/submission_guidelines*
Tip: "Keep in mind that 18,000 of our 35,000 readers are students or just-emerging writers." The magazine is published only during the academic year. Submit only from February 1 through September 30. Also buys blog posts year round for *The Writer's Notebook,* 1,000–2,000 words, $100 per post.

WRITER'S DIGEST

4665 Malsbary Rd., Blue Ash, OH 45242
wdsubmissions@aimmedia.com | *www.writersdigest.com*
Amy Jones, editor-in-chief

Parent company: Active Interest Media
Type: bimonthly digital and print magazine, circulation 60,000, advertising accepted
Audience: aspiring and professional writers
Purpose: to celebrate the writing life and what it means to be a writer in today's publishing environment
Submissions: Email in body of message; send query letter. Unsolicited freelance: 20%, 60% assigned. Response in two to four months.
Types of manuscripts: essays, how-to, humor, profiles, sidebars
Length: 300–2,400 words
Topic: writing
Rights: electronic, first
Payment: on acceptance, 30–50¢ per word
Kill fee: 25%
Seasonal submissions: eight months in advance
Theme list: available on website
Guidelines: *www.writersdigest.com/resources/submission-guidelines*
Sample: available at newsstands and through *www.writersdigestshop.com*
Tip: "Although we welcome the work of new writers, we believe the established writer can better instruct our readers. Please include your publishing credentials related to your topic with your submission."

WRITERSWEEKLY.COM

12441 N. Main St. #38, Trenton, GA 30752 | 305-768-0261
brian@booklocker.com | *writersweekly.com*

Brian Whiddon, managing editor

> **Parent company:** BookLocker.com
> **Type:** weekly digital newsletter, circulation 100,000
> **Audience:** freelance writers
> **Purpose:** to help freelance writers find writing opportunities and improve their business
> **Submissions:** Only accepts query letter. Unsolicited freelance: 30%. Response in one to two weeks.
> **Types of manuscripts:** features, how-to
> **Length:** 600 words
> **Topics:** marketing, writing
> **Rights:** first, reprint
> **Payment:** on acceptance, $60
> **Manuscripts accepted per year:** 100–200
> **Theme list:** available on website
> **Guidelines:** *writersweekly.com/writersweekly-com-writers-guidelines*
> **Sample:** on the website
> **Tip:** "Understand that we are not a publication about writing but earning income through writing. Proofread your query letter; spelling, capitalization, and punctuation errors leap out at us and tell us what we can expect from you as a writer. *Sell* us your idea—don't just say "I want to write about . . . ."

WRITING CORNER
contests@writingcorner.com | *writingcorner.com*

> **Type:** website
> **Audience:** writers at all levels
> **Purpose:** to provide concrete, useful advice from those who have been in the trenches and made a successful journey with their writing
> **Submissions:** Email complete manuscript or query letter. Response in two days.
> **Type of manuscripts:** how-to
> **Length:** 600–900 words
> **Topic:** writing
> **Rights:** onetime, reprint
> **Payment:** none
> **Guidelines:** *writingcorner.com/main-pages/submission-guidelines*
> **Sample:** on the website
> **Tip:** "Our site visitors are from all areas of writing, so keep that audience in mind when writing for us."

PART 4

SPECIALTY MARKETS

11

DAILY DEVOTIONAL BOOKLETS AND WEBSITES

Note that many of these markets assign all manuscripts. If there is no information listed on getting an assignment, request a sample copy and writers guidelines if they are not on the website. Then write two or three sample devotions to fit that particular format, and send them to the editor with a request for an assignment.

THE BRINK

114 Bush Rd., Nashville, TN 37217 | 800-877-7030
thebrink@randallhouse.com | *www.thebrinkonline.com*
David Jones, senior editor

Denomination: Free Will Baptist
Parent company: Randall House
Audience: young adults
Type: print, quarterly
Submissions: Devotions are by assignment only to coordinate with the curriculum. Length: 200 words. Rights: all. For articles, such as interviews, stories, and opinion pieces, email query with 100- to 200-word excerpt if available. Topics: faith, culture, apologetics, young-adult life, etc. Length: 1,000–1,500 words. Does not respond unless interested. Rights: first, reprint, onetime. Bible: paraphrase.
Guidelines: *thebrinkonline.com/contact*
Payment: varies
Tip: "We do not accept freelance devotions; but on occasion, we do accept freelance articles and interviews. We are looking for articles that connect with a young Christian adult audience."

CHRIST IN OUR HOME

PO Box 1209, Minneapolis, MN 55440-1209 | 800-328-4648

afsubmissions@1517.media | www.augsburgfortress.org

Denomination: Evangelical Lutheran Church in America
Parent company: Augsburg Fortress/1517 Media
Audience: adults
Type: print, quarterly
Submissions: Assignments only. Submit sample devotions as explained in the guidelines. Length: 1190 characters, including spaces, maximum. Rights: all. Bible: NRSV. Also available by email and audio.
Guidelines: download from *tinyurl.com/4ujb7yaw*
Tip: *"Christ in Our Home* is read by people in many nations, so avoid thinking only in terms of those who live in the U.S."

CHRISTIAN DEVOTIONS

PO Box 6494, Kingsport, TN 37663 | 423-384-4821

christiandevotionsministries@gmail.com | www.ChristianDevotions.us

Martin Wiles, managing editor

Cindy Sproles, executive editor

Parent company: Christian Devotions Ministries
Audience: adults, teens
Type: website, daily
Submissions: Accepts freelance submissions. Length: 400 words. Email as attached Word document. Rights: onetime. Bible: any.
Guidelines: *www.christiandevotions.us/writeforus*
Payment: none
Tip: "Follow the guidelines. We mentor if necessary."

DEVOKIDS

PO Box 6494, Kingsport, TN 37663 | 423-384-4821

WritersCoach.us@gmail.com | devokids.com

Eddie Jones, editor

Parent company: Christian Devotions Ministries
Audience: children
Type: website, 3x/week
Submissions: Takes freelance submissions. Length: 75–250 words. Email as an attached Word document. Rights: onetime.
Also accepts: submissions from kids
Guidelines: *devokids.com/write-for-us*
Payment: none

Tip: "We need kid-friendly posts related to crafts, puzzles, coloring pages, games, fun activities, art, and photography. Share an easy and fun recipe for children."

DEVOTIONS
See *The Quiet Hour*.

FORWARD DAY BY DAY
412 Sycamore St., Cincinnati, OH 45202-4110 | 800-543-1813
editorial@forwardmovement.org | *www.forwardmovement.org*
Richelle Thompson, managing editor

Denomination: Episcopal
Parent company: Foreward Movement
Audience: adults
Type: print, website, quarterly
Submissions: Devotions are written on assignment. To get an assignment, send three sample meditations based on three of the following Bible verses: Psalm 139:21; Mark 8:31; Acts 4:12; Revelation 1:10. Responds in six weeks. Authors complete an entire month's worth of devotions. Length: 220 words, including Scripture. Also available as daily podcast and email.
Guidelines: *www.forwardmovement.org/Pages/About/Writers-Guidelines.aspx*
Payment: $300 for a month of devotions
Tip: *"Forward Day by Day* is not the place to score points on controversial topics. Occasionally, when the Scripture passage pertains to it, an author chooses to say something about such a topic. If you write about a hot-button issue, do so with humility and make certain your comment shows respect for persons who hold a different view."

FRUIT OF THE VINE
211 N. Meridian St., Ste. 101, Newberg, OR 97132 | 503-538-9775
fv@barclaypress.com | *www.barclaypress.com*
Cleta Crisman, editor

Denomination: Quaker
Parent company: Barclay Press
Audience: adults
Type: print, website, quarterly
Submissions: Accepts freelance submissions, one week at a time. Length: 250 words. Rights: onetime. Bible: NIV.

Guidelines: *tinyurl.com/y8vwx5gj*
Payment: subscription
Tip: "Writers should be Friends (Quaker) or familiar with the Friends denomination."

GOD'S WORD FOR TODAY

1445 N. Boonville Ave., Springfield, MO 65802 | 417-862-2781
DDawson@ag.org | *ag.org/Resources/Devotionals/Gods-Word-for-Today*
Dilla Dawson, editor

Denomination: Assemblies of God
Parent company: Gospel Publishing House
Audience: adults
Type: print, website, quarterly
Submissions: Request writers guidelines and sample assignment. After samples are approved, writers will be added to the list for assignments. Length: 210 words. Rights: all. Bible: NIV.
Payment: $25/devotion
Tip: "Writers will receive detailed guidelines upon inquiry."

INKSPIRATIONS ONLINE

PO Box 3847, Mooresville, NC 28117
tina@inkspirationsonline.com | *inkspirationsonline.com*
Tina Yeager, publisher

Audience: writers
Type: website, weekly
Submissions: Accepts freelance submissions. Length: 400 words. Payment: none. Rights: reprint, onetime, electronic. Bible: any.
Guidelines: *inkspirationsonline.com/submission-guidelines*
Payment: none
Tip: "Be sure the devotion centers on writing or a writer's life. Please read published content and submission guidelines."

KEYS FOR KIDS DEVOTIONAL

2060 43rd St. SE, Grand Rapids, MI 49508 | 616-647-4500
editorial@keysforkids.org | *www.keysforkids.org*
Courtney Lasater, editor

Parent company: Keys for Kids Ministries
Audience: children
Type: print, website, quarterly
Submissions: Takes only freelance submissions. Rights: all. Length:

375 words, including short fiction story. Buys 30–40 per year. Seasonal four to five months ahead. Bible version: NKJV.

Guidelines: *keysforkids.org/writersguidelines*

Payment: $30 on acceptance

Tip: "Include illustration in devotional story that uses a real-world object/situation to help kids understand a spiritual truth." Also does a phone app.

LIGHT FROM THE WORD

PO Box 50434, Indianapolis, IN 46250-0434 | 317-774-7900

submissions@wesleyan.org | *www.wesleyan.org/communication/dailydevo*

Susan LeBaron, publishing services director

Denomination: Wesleyan

Parent company: Wesleyan Publishing House

Audience: adults

Type: print, website, quarterly

Submissions: Must be affiliated with The Wesleyan Church. Email three sample devotions to fit the format and request an assignment. Write "Devotion Samples" in the subject line. Length: 200–240 words. Rights: all. Bible: NIV.

Guidelines: *www.wesleyan.org/wph/writers-guidelines*

Payment: $200 for seven devotions

Tip: "Writing must lead readers to discover a biblical truth and apply that truth to their lives."

LIVING FAITH

PO Box 292824, Kettering, OH 45429 | 800-246-7390

info@livingfaith.com | *livingfaith.com*

Denomination: Catholic

Parent company: Bayard, Inc.

Audience: adults

Type: print, quarterly

Submissions: Assignments only; email one or two samples and credentials to request an assignment. Bible: NAB.

Tip: "Living Faith provides daily reflections based on a Scripture passage from the daily Mass. With readings for daily Mass listed at the bottom of each devotion, this booklet helps Catholics pray and meditate in spirit with the seasons of the Church Year."

LIVING FAITH FOR KIDS

PO Box 292824, Kettering, OH 45429 | 800-246-7390
editor@livingfaithkids.com | www.livingfaith.com/kids
Connie Clark, editor

> **Denomination:** Catholic
> **Parent company:** Bayard, Inc.
> **Audience:** children
> **Type:** print, quarterly
> **Submissions:** Assignments only; email samples and credentials to request an assignment.
> **Tip:** *"Living Faith for Kids* features daily devotions based on the daily Scripture readings from the Catholic Mass. Each quarterly issue helps children 8–12 develop the habit of daily prayer and build their relationship with Jesus and the Church."

LOVE LINES FROM GOD

128 Leyland Ct., Greenwood, SC 29649 | 864-554-3204
mandmwiles@gmail.com | lovelinesfromgod.blogspot.com
Martin Wiles, managing editor

> **Audience:** adults
> **Type:** website, daily
> **Submissions:** Accepts freelance submissions. Length: 400 words. Rights: first. Bible version: NIV.
> **Guidelines:** *lovelinesfromgod.blogspot.com/p/write-for-us_3.html*
> **Payment:** none
> **Tip:** "We are looking for devotions that encourage, not preach. Following the submission guidelines will result in a better chance of having the submission accepted."

THE QUIET HOUR and DEVOTIONS

4050 Lee Vance, Colorado Springs, CO 80919
thequiethour@davidccook.com | davidccook.org
Scott Stewart, editor

> **Parent company:** David C Cook
> **Audience:** adults
> **Type:** print, quarterly
> **Submissions:** *Devotions* and *The Quiet Hour* jointly publish new devotionals. By assignment only. Must have North American postal address for contract and payment. Length: 200 words. Rights: all. Bible version: NIV, KJV.

Guidelines: *tinyurl.com/yc5pes8m*
Payment: $140 for seven
Tip: "Submit spec devotional on a key verse you select in a Scripture passage of your choice. Begin with anecdotal opening then transition to relevant biblical insight and encouragement for a life of faith rooted in the key verse."

REFLECTING GOD

PO Box 419427, Kansas City, MO 64141 | 816-931-1900
dcbrush@wordaction.com | *reflectinggod.com*
Duane Brush, editor

Denomination: Nazarene
Parent company: The Foundry Publishing
Audience: adults
Type: website, daily
Submissions: Send a couple of sample devotions to fit the format and request an assignment. Length: 180–200 words.
Payment: $115 for seven
Tip: "Our purpose is the pursuit to embrace holy living. We want to foster discussion about what it means to live a holy life in the 21st century."

REJOICE!

35094 Laburnum Ave., Abbotsford, BC V2S 8K3, Canada | 540-434-6701
DorothyH@mennomedia.org | *www.mennomedia.org/rejoice*
Dorothy Hartman, editor

Denomination: Mennonite
Parent company: MennoMedia
Audience: adults
Type: print, quarterly
Submissions: Prefers that you send a couple of sample devotions and inquire about assignment procedures. Length: 250–300 words. Rights: first. Bible version: prefers NRSV. Also accepts testimonies: 500–600 words, eight per year. Poems: free verse, light verse, 60 characters, eight per year. Submit maximum of three poems.
Payment: devotions, $100–$125 for seven; poems, $25; on publication
Tip: "Don't apply for assignment unless you are familiar with the publication and Anabaptist theology."

THE SECRET PLACE

1075 First Ave., King of Prussia, PA 19406 | 610-768-2084

thesecretplace@judsonpress.com | *www.judsonpress.com*

Katelyn Morgan, administrator

Denomination: American Baptist
Parent company: Judson Press
Audience: adults
Type: print, quarterly
Submissions: Accepts freelance submissions; does not give assignments. Length: 250 words. Rights: first. Bible: NRSV updated.
Guidelines: *tinyurl.com/ynf6zhfu*
Payment: $20 each
Tip: "Write for comfort, inspiration, and hope in people's everyday lives."

TAKE FIVE PLUS

1445 N. Boonville Ave., Springfield, MO 65802 | 417-862-2781

rl-take5plus@ag.org | *myhealthychurch.com*

Wade Quick, team leader

Denomination: Assemblies of God
Parent company: Gospel Publishing House
Audience: teens
Type: print, quarterly
Submissions: Assignment only. Request writers guidelines and sample assignment via email. After samples are approved, writers will be added to the list for assignments. Length: 210–235 words. Rights: all. Bible version: NIV.
Payment: $25 each, on acceptance
Tip: "Study the publication before attempting the sample assignment."

THESE DAYS: Daily Devotions for Living by Faith

100 Witherspoon St., Louisville, KY 40202 | 800-624-2412

mlindberg@presbypub.com | *www.thethoughtfulchristian.com/Pages/Item/59264/These-Days.aspx*

Denomination: Presbyterian
Parent company: Presbyterian Publishing Corporation
Audience: adults
Type: print, quarterly
Submissions: Accepts freelance submissions. Length: 190 words. Rights: first. Bible version: NRSV.

Payment: $100 or $150 worth of books for seven

Tip: "Write thoughtful entries based on a Scripture passage, use gender-inclusive language for God and humanity, and include a brief closing prayer."

UNLOCKED

2060 43rd St. SE, Grand Rapids, MI 49508 | 616-647-4500

editorial@unlocked.org | *unlocked.org*

Hannah Howe, editor

Parent company: Keys for Kids Ministries

Audience: teens

Type: print, website, quarterly

Submissions: Accepts only freelance submissions. Rights: all. Length: devotion and personal story, 200–315 words; fiction, 200–350 words; poetry, 16–23 lines. Takes teen writers. Bible version: CSB, NIV, NLT, WEB.

Guidelines: *unlocked.org/writers-guidelines*

Payment: $30 on acceptance

Tip: "We are open to styles and genres not typically seen in teen devotionals as long as they fit the overall purpose outlined in our guidelines. We want our devotional pieces to challenge teens and help them wrestle with things they're dealing with, not talk down to them or shy away from deep topics."

THE UPPER ROOM

1908 Grand Ave., Nashville, TN 37212 | 615-340-7252

ureditorial@upperroom.org | *upperroom.org*

Amy Densk, assistant editor

Parent company: The Upper Room

Audience: adults

Type: print, website, bimonthly

Submissions: Accepts freelance submissions. Length: 300 words that include everything on the printed page. Rights: first, exclusive for one year. Bible versions: NIV, NRSV, CEB, KJV. Submit through the website form (preferred), by mail, or by email.

Guidelines: *submissions.upperroom.org/en/guidelines*

Payment: $30, on publication

Tip: "A strong devotional will include three main elements: 1. A personal story or experience. 2. A connection to Scripture. 3. A way for the reader to apply the message to his or her own life."

THE WORD IN SEASON

PO Box 1209, Minneapolis, MN 55440 | 414-963-1222

rochelle@writenowcoach.com | *www.augsburgfortress.org*

Rochelle Melander. managing editor

Denomination: Evangelical Lutheran Church in America

Parent company: Augsburg Fortress/1517 Media

Audience: adults

Type: print, quarterly

Submissions: Gives assignments based on samples. Request guidelines, and write trial devotions. Length: 200 words. Rights: all. Bible: NRSV. Also available as an Amazon ebook.

Guidelines: download from *tinyurl.com/4ujb7yaw*

Payment: $40

Tip: "We prefer writers with a background in Lutheran theology and who have used the historical critical method to study the Bible."

12

DRAMA

CHRISTIAN PUBLISHERS, LLC

PO Box 248, Cedar Rapids, IA 52406 | 844-841-6387

editor@christianpub.com | *www.christianpub.com*

Parent Company: Brooklyn Publishers

Audiences: adult, children, teens

Types: children's Christmas and Easter pageants, full-length musicals, full-length plays, one-act musicals, one-act plays

Submissions: Publishes plays for the Christian market, including but not limited to elementary through high school, adults, and youth groups. Submit complete script through the website form or by mail. Response time varies according to the time of the year.

Payment: 10% royalty, often to a fixed amount, no advance

Guidelines: *www.christianpub.com/default.aspx?pg=ag*

Tip: "Be sure your play builds. People have short attention spans, and if the story is too bogged down in excessive dialogue, or if the play wonders aimlessly, they will simply tune out. If the comedy or suspense doesn't build from scene to scene, if we're not involved with the main character(s) or the dramatic question, then the play isn't going anywhere."

CSS PUBLISHING COMPANY, INC.

5450 N. Dixie Hwy., Lima, OH 45807 | 419-227-1818

editor@csspub.com | *www.csspub.com*

Audiences: adult, children, teens

Types: monologues, one-act plays, reader's theatre, short skits, skit compilations

Submissions: Publishes five to ten books per year. Receives 20–30 submissions per year. Length: 15 minutes. Contact: email or mail query letter or complete script. Responds in six months. Simultaneous submissions OK.

Payment: negotiated, no advance

Guidelines: *store.csspub.com/page.php?Custom%20Pages=10*

Tip: "Content needs to be fresh and imaginative."

DRAMA MINISTRY

2814 Azalea Pl., Nashville, TN 37204 | 866-859-7622

service@dramaministry.com | www.dramaministry.com

Vince Wilcox, general manager

> **Audiences:** adult, children, teens
>
> **Types:** monologues, reader's theatre, short skits
>
> **Submissions:** Open to all topics, including seasonal/holidays. Email or mail script. Buys all rights.
>
> **Guidelines:** *www.dramaministry.com/faq*

ELDRIDGE CHRISTIAN PLAYS AND MUSICALS

PO Box 4904, Lancaster, PA 17804 | 850-385-2463

newworks@histage.com | www.95church.com

Susan Shore, editor

> **Audiences:** adult, children, teens
>
> **Types:** full-length musicals, full-length plays, monologues, one-act plays, reader's theatre, skit compilations
>
> **Submissions:** Publishes 15–20 scripts per year; receives hundreds of submissions annually. Length: plays and musicals, minimum 30 minutes. Submit complete script via email attachment with cover letter in the body of the message. Simultaneous OK. Responds in eight weeks.
>
> **Payment:** 50% royalty plus 10% copy sales, no advance
>
> **Guidelines:** *95church.com/submission-guidelines*
>
> **Tip:** "We like all kinds of plays and are always open to new ideas. Generally speaking, our customers like plays with more female than male roles or flexible casting in which roles can be played by either men or women. This is not a hard-and-fast rule, however. We like easy costuming and scenery, if possible, as many church budgets are limited."

13

GREETING CARDS
AND **GIFTS**

BLUE MOUNTAIN ARTS

PO Box 1007, Boulder, CO 80306 | 303-449-0536

editorial@sps.com | *www.sps.com*

Audience: adult

Product: greeting cards

Submissions: General card publisher with some inspirational cards. Not looking for rhymed poetry, religious verse, or one-liners. Length: 50–300 words. Buys all rights. Accepts freelance submissions by email, website form, or mail. Responds in two months or not interested. Holiday deadlines: Christmas and general holidays, July 15; Valentine's Day, September 12; Easter, November 8; Mother's Day and graduation, December 13; Father's Day, February 7.

Guidelines: *www.sps.com/greeting-card-guidelines-submissions*

Tip: "Because our cards capture genuine emotions on topics such as love, friendship, family, missing you, and other real-life subjects, we suggest that you have a friend, relative, or someone else in your life in mind as you write. Writings on special occasions (birthday, anniversary, congratulations, etc.) as well as the challenges, difficulties, and aspirations of life are also considered."

DICKSONS, INC.

709 B Ave. E, Seymour, IN 47274 | 812-522-1308

submissions@dicksonsgifts.com | *www.dicksonsgifts.com*

Audience: adults

Products: figurines, crosses, wall decor, mugs, flags

Submissions: Two to eight lines, maximum sixteen, suitable for plaques, bookmarks, etc. Email submission. Responds in three months. Subjects can cover any gift-giving occasion and Christian, inspirational, and everyday social-expression topics. Phrases or acrostics of one or two lines for bumper stickers are also considered.

Payment: royalty, negotiable

Tip: Looking for religious verses.

ELLIE CLAIRE

6100 Tower Cir., Ste. 210, Franklin, TN 37013 | 615-932-7600

ellieclaire.com

Jeana Ledbetter, acquisitions editor

> **Parent company:** Worthy Publishing/Hachette Book Group
> **Audience:** adults
> **Products:** journals, devotionals, gift books
> **Submissions:** Submit through agents only. Buys all rights.
> **Payment:** flat fee, royalty
> **Tip:** "We operate in the gift market, and the writing will need to reflect that. We are not interested in Bible studies but in inspirational and encouraging devotions, funny stories with a spiritual component, and compilations from a Christian worldview."

INK & WILLOW

10807 New Allegiance Dr., Ste. 500, Colorado Springs, CO 80921 | 719-590-4999

info@waterbrookmultnomah.com | *waterbrookmultnomah.com/ink-and-willow*

Jamie Lapeyrolerie, senior marketing manager and acquisitions

> **Parent company:** WaterBrook & Multnomah
> **Audience:** adults
> **Products:** journals, adult coloring books
> **Submissions:** Submit through agents only.
> **Tip:** "Ink & Willow encompasses a line of interactive products that infuse contemplation and inspiration into the regular spiritual practice of creative-minded Christians, wherever they are in their faith journey. Each thoughtfully curated gift product is based in biblical truth and sparks a reminder of how God reveals beauty in the midst of our ordinary."

WARNER CHRISTIAN RESOURCES

2902 Enterprise Dr., Anderson, IN 46013 | 800-741-7721

rloisch@warnerpress.org | *www.warnerpress.org*

Robin Fogle, kids & family ministry editor

> **Audience:** adult

Product: greeting cards

Submissions: Themes include birthday, anniversary, baby congratulations, sympathy, get well, kid's birthday and get well, thinking of you, friendship, Christmas, praying for you, encouragement. Use a conversational tone with no lofty poetic language, such as *thee, thou, art.* Don't preach or use a negative tone. Strive to share God's love and provide a Christian witness. Length: average of four lines. Responds in six to eight weeks. Email as attachment. Buys all rights. Deadlines: everyday, July 31; Christmas, October 1.

Payment: $25

Guidelines: *www.warnerpress.org/submission-guidelines*

Tip: "Visit our website and view the greeting cards we currently offer before submitting. We publish material for boxed cards, not counter-line cards."

14

TRACTS

The following companies publish gospel tracts but do not have writers guidelines. If you are interested in writing for them, email or phone to find out if they currently are looking for submissions. Also check your denominational publishing house to see if it publishes tracts.

FELLOWSHIP TRACT LEAGUE
PO Box 164, Lebanon, OH 45036 | 513-494-1075
mail@fellowshiptractleague.org | *www.fellowshiptractleague.org*

GOOD NEWS PUBLISHERS
1300 Crescent St., Wheaton, IL 60187 | 630-682-4300
info@crossway.org | *www.crossway.org/tracts*

GOSPEL TRACT SOCIETY
PO Box 1118, Independence, MO 64051 | 816-461-6086
gospeltractsociety@gmail.com | *gospeltractsociety.org*

GRACE VISION PUBLISHERS
321-745-9966 (text only)
www.gracevision.com

MOMENTS WITH THE BOOK
PO Box 322, Bedford, PA 15522 | 814-623-8737
email through the website | *mwtb.org*

TRACT ASSOCIATION OF FRIENDS
1501 Cherry St., Philadelphia, PA 19102
info@tractassociation.org | *www.tractassociation.org*

15

BIBLE CURRICULUM

This list includes only the major, nondenominational curriculum publishers. If you are in a denominational church, also check its publishing house for curriculum products. Plus some organizations, like Awana and Pioneer Clubs, produce curriculum for their programs.

Since Bible curriculum is written on assignment only, you'll need to get samples for age groups you want to write for (from the company's website, large Christian bookstores, or your church) and study the formats and pieces. Look for editors' names on the copyright pages of teachers manuals, or call the publishing house for this information.

Then write query letters to specific editors. Tell why you're qualified to write curriculum for them, include a sample of curriculum you've written or other sample of your writing, and ask for a trial assignment. Since the need for writers varies widely, you may not get an assignment for a year or more.

Some of these companies also publish undated, elective curriculum books that are used in a variety of ministries. Plus some book publishers publish lines of Bible-study guides. (See "Traditional Book Publishers.") These are contracted like other books with a proposal and sample chapters.

DAVID C. COOK

4050 Lee Vance Dr., Colorado Springs, CO 80918 | 800-323-7543
davidccook.org/curriculum

Type: Sunday school
Imprints: Bible-in-Life, Echoes, Gospel Light, HeartShaper, Scripture Press, SEEN Youth, Standard Lesson, Tru

GROUP PUBLISHING

1515 Cascade Ave., Loveland, CO 80538 | 800-447-1070
submissions@group.com | *www.group.com*

Types: Sunday school, vacation Bible school, children's worship
Imprints: Be Bold, Dig In, FaithWeaver NOW, Fearless Conversation, Hands-On Bible, LIVE, Simply Loved, KidsOwn Worship, Play-n-Worship

PENSACOLA CHRISTIAN COLLEGE

PO Box 17900, Pensacola, FL 32522-7900 | 877-356-9385
www.joyfullifesundayschool.com

Type: Sunday school
Imprint: Joyful Life

UNION GOSPEL PRESS

PO Box 301055, Cleveland, OH 44130 | 800-638-9988
editorial@uniongospelpress.com | *uniongospelpress.com*

Type: Sunday school

URBAN MINISTRIES, INC.

1551 Regency Ct., Calumet City, IL 60409-5448 | 800-860-8642
urbanministries.com

Types: Sunday school, vacation Bible school

16

MISCELLANEOUS

These companies publish a variety of books and other products that fall into the specialty-markets category, such as puzzle books, game books, children's activity books, craft books, charts, church bulletins, and coloring books.

BARBOUR PUBLISHING
See entry in "Traditional Book Publishers."

BEAMING BOOKS
See entry in "Traditional Book Publishers."

BROADSTREET PUBLISHING
See entry in "Traditional Book Publishers."

CHRISTIAN FOCUS PUBLICATIONS
See entry in "Traditional Book Publishers."

CSS PUBLISHING GROUP, INC.
See entry in "Traditional Book Publishers."

DAVID C. COOK
See entry in "Traditional Book Publishers."

GROUP PUBLISHING
See entry in "Traditional Book Publishers."

JUST FOR KIDS

2 Overlea Blvd., Toronto, ON M4H 1P4, Canada

justforkids@can.salvationarmy.org | salvationist.ca/editorial/just-for-kids/2022-back-issues

Kristin Ostensen, editor

Parent company: The Salvation Army in Canada and Bermuda

Audience: ages 5-12

Type: activity page published weekly

Submissions: Short stories: True-to-life situations of children living as young followers of Jesus Christ. An effort is made to ensure children from as many cultures and ethnic backgrounds as possible are highlighted in our stories. Maximum of 175 words. Bible lessons: Maximum of 175 words. Puzzles: Prefers puzzles that relate to a biblical story or concept. Also looking for puzzles that touch on seasons, holidays, and activities (e.g., sports, traveling, animals).

Payment: none

Guidelines: *salvationist.ca/files/salvationarmy/Magazines/Just-for-Kids-Guidelines.pdf*

PAULINE BOOKS AND MEDIA

See entry in "Traditional Book Publishers."

ROSE PUBLISHING

See entry in "Traditional Book Publishers."

ROSEKIDZ

See entry in "Traditional Book Publishers."

WARNER CHRISTIAN RESOURCES

2902 Enterprise Dr., Anderson, IN 46013 | 800-741-7721

editors@warnerpress.org | www.warnerpress.org

Church bulletins: Short devotions that tie into a visual image and incorporate a Bible verse. Especially interested in material for holidays and special Sundays, such as Christmas, New Year's Day, Palm Sunday, Easter, Pentecost, and Communion. General themes are also welcome. Length: 250 words maximum. Submission period: January 1–March 15 annually. Buys all rights. Payment varies.

Children's coloring and activity books: Most activity books focus on a Bible story or biblical theme, such as love and forgiveness. Ages range from preschool (ages 2-5) to upper elementary (ages 8-10). Include activities and puzzles in every upper-elementary book. Coloring-book manuscripts should present a picture idea and a portion of the story for each page. Deadlines: May 1 and October 1. Payment varies.

Children's teaching resources: Books with skits, science experiments, and crafts. Length: 48-144 pages. Activities must be interesting for kids, teach important biblical lessons, and be easy to use in a class. Payment varies.

Guidelines: *www.warnerpress.org/submission-guidelines*

PART 5

SUPPORT
FOR
WRITERS

17

LITERARY AGENTS

Asking editors and other writers is a great way to find a reliable agent. You may also want to visit *www.sfwa.org/other-resources/for-authors/writer-beware/agents* for tips on avoiding questionable agents and choosing reputable ones.

The general market has an Association of American Literary Agents (*www.aalitagents.org*), also known as AALA. To be a member, the agent must agree to a code of ethics. The website has a searchable list of agents. Some listings below indicate at least one agent belongs to the AALA. Lack of such a designation, however, does not indicate the agent is unethical; most Christian agents are not members.

A DROP OF INK LITERARY AGENCY

8587 Green Valley Rd. SE, Caledonia, MI 49316 | 616-443-1993
tomdean@adropofink.pub | *www.adropofink.pub*

Agent: Tom Dean
Agency: Established in 2020. Represents 20 clients. Also does publishing consulting, marketing consulting.
Types of books: adult nonfiction
New clients: Open to well-established book authors and writers met at conferences. First contact: phone, website form, referral from current client. Responds in five to seven business days.
Commission: 15%
Tip: "Be as thorough as possible in your initial proposal draft."

AKA LITERARY MANAGEMENT

11445 Dallas Rd., Peyton, CO 80831 | 719-339-0077
terrie@akaliterary.com | *akalm.net*

Agent: Terrie Wolf
Agency: Established in 2009. Represents 35+ clients. Member of Association of American Literary Agents. Responds in six to

eight weeks; feel free to nudge after eight weeks. Specializes in manuscript to film/TV/media adaptation, but does not take scripts or screenplays.

Types of books: adult fiction, adult nonfiction, children's fiction, children's nonfiction, general market children's, general market fiction, general market nonfiction

New clients: Open to all writers except self-published. First contact: website form, referral from current client. Query first via the instructions on the website through Submittable or Query Manager, then full proposal. Simultaneous OK.

Commission: 15%

Fees: none

Tip: "Visit our website, then make sure to carefully follow instructions for how to submit your project. Please provide concise and applicable information regarding your manuscript, and show us nothing short of your very best work."

ALIVE LITERARY AGENCY

5001 Centennial Blvd. #50742, Colorado Springs, CO 80908

admin@aliveliterary.com | www.aliveliterary.com

Agents: Bryan Norman, Lisa Jackson, Rachel Jacobson, Kathleen Kerr

Agency: Established in 1989.

Types of books: adult nonfiction

New clients: Open only to well-established book writers. Contact through the website. Response time varies.

Commission: 15%

Fees: none

AMBASSADOR LITERARY AGENCY

PO Box 50358, Nashville, TN 37205 | 615-370-4700

info@AmbassadorAgency.com | www.AmbassadorAgency.com

Agent: Wes Yoder

Agency: Established in 1997. Represents 25–30 clients.

Types of books: adult fiction, adult nonfiction, crossover

New clients: Open to unpublished book authors. Contact by email with a short description of the manuscript and a request to submit for review. Responds in four to six weeks.

Commission: 15%

Fees: none

APOKEDAK LITERARY AGENCY

113 Winn Ct., Waleska, GA 30183

submissions@sally-apokedak.com | *sally-apokedak.com*

Agent: Sally Apokedak

Agency: Established in 2018. Represents almost 15 clients. Specialty: picture books, middle grade, YA fiction.

Types of books: Christian living, devotionals, middle grade, picture books, teen/YA fiction, teen/YA nonfiction

New clients: Open to writers met at conferences and online and who know authors currently represented. Initial contact: email with full proposal and full manuscript, referral from current client. Accepts simultaneous submissions. Responds in three months. Other services: freelance editing.

Commission: 15%

Fees: none

Tip: "Before you send me anything, read all the bestsellers in your category. Then send work that is ready to publish, that fits into a known category, and that has a fresh concept or a fresh twist on an old concept."

AUTHORIZEME LITERARY FIRM, LLC

PO Box 1816, South Gate, CA 90280 | 310-508-9860

AuthorizeMeNow@gmail.com | *www.AuthorizeMe.net*

Agent: Dr. Sharon Norris Elliott

Agency: Established in 2019. Represents 55 clients. Other services: coaching, editorial work, and consulting; see listing in "Editorial Services."

Types of books: adult fiction, Bible study, board books, Christian living, devotionals, early readers, picture books, women's issues

New clients: Open to all writers, including self-published. Represents clients of all ethnicities. Welcoming and sensitive to people of color, African American pastors, and all authors, new and seasoned, who are teachable and excited about sharing God's truth that will change lives by ushering readers into God's presence. Contact: email, website form, referral from current client. Query first. Simultaneous OK. Responds in three months.

Commission: 15%

Fees: none

Tip: "Love Jesus, be teachable, be patient, desire and reach for excellence, remain humble, smile a lot."

BANNER LITERARY

PO Box 1828, Winter Park, CO 80482

mike@mikeloomis.co | www.mikeloomis.co

Agent: Mike Loomis

Agency: Established in 2004. Represents 48 clients. Other services: See listings in "Editorial Services" and "Publicity and Marketing Services."

Types of books: adult nonfiction, business, inspiration, politics, self-help

New clients: Open to writers who have not published a book and self-published writers. Contact through email or website form. Responds in two weeks.

Commission: 15%

Fees: none

Tip: "Send your web address with query."

BBH LITERARY

david@bbhliterary.com | www.bbhliterary.com

Agents: David Bratt; Laura Bardolph, *laura@bbhliterary.com*

Agency: Established in 2021. Represents 30 clients. Other services: publicity and developmental editing; see listings in "Editorial Services" and "Publicity and Marketing Services."

Types of books: adult nonfiction

New clients: Open to all book writers. Contact: email, website form, referral from current client. Accepts simultaneous submissions. Responds in one week.

Commission: 15%

Tip: "Please tell us why your book has some urgency to its message. We are most interested in books that speak to real life in a complicated world with nuance and wisdom."

THE BINDERY AGENCY

2727 N. Cascade Ave., Ste. 170, Colorado Springs, CO 80207

info@thebinderyagency.com | www.thebinderyagency.com

Agents: Alex Field, Andrea Heinecke, Trinity McFadden, Ingrid Beck, John Blase

Agency: Established in 2017. Represents 200 clients. Member of Association of American Literary Agents. In addition to nonfiction, accepting queries for select fiction in the following genres: science fiction, mystery and suspense, literary and upmarket fiction, romance.

Types of books: adult fiction, adult nonfiction, Christian living, culture, memoir, mental health, self-help, social issues

New clients: Open to all book writers, including self-published. Initial contact: email, referral from current client, website form. Query first or send full proposal. Accepts simultaneous submissions. Responds in 8–12 weeks.

Commission: 15%

Fees: none

Tip: "We're looking for compelling book ideas, quality proposals, and authors who are doing the work to build a platform for a future book."

THE BLYTHE DANIEL AGENCY, INC.

PO Box 64197, Colorado Springs, CO 80962-4197 | 719-213-3427

blythe@theblythedanielagency.com | *www.theblythedanielagency.com*

Agents: Blythe Daniel; Stephanie Alton, *stephanie@ theblythedanielagency.com*

Agency: Established in 2005. Represents 100 clients. Sells to general market too. Other services: traditional publicity (media-driven); blog campaigns, launch teams, podcast interviews; writing, branding, social media, and email coaching. See listing in "Publicity and Marketing Services."

Types of books: adult nonfiction, Bible studies, business, Christian living, current events, general-market nonfiction, gift books, leadership, marriage, parenting, social issues, spiritual growth, women's issues

New clients: Open to writers who have not published a book. Contact: email with full proposal, referral from current client. Accepts simultaneous submissions. Responds in eight weeks.

Commission: 15% of standard book royalties, other formats vary

Fees: none

Tip: "Visit our website to see the types of projects we represent and services we offer. We are happy to consider your project, coaching needs, or marketing you want to pursue. We have a projects manager who assists us with these (*rebecca@theblythedanielagency.com*)."

BOOKS & SUCH LITERARY MANAGEMENT

representation@booksandsuch.com | *www.booksandsuch.com*

Agents: Janet Kobobel Grant, *janet@booksandsuch.com;* Wendy Lawton, *wendy@booksandsuch.com;* Rachel Kent, *rachel@*

booksandsuch.com; Cynthia Ruchti, *cynthia@booksandsuch.com;* Barb Roose, *barb@booksandsuch.com;* Debbie Alsdorf, *debbie@ booksandsuch.com*

Agency: Established in 1996. Represents 275 clients.

Types of books: adult fiction, adult nonfiction, children's fiction, children's nonfiction, middle grade, teen/YA fiction, teen/YA nonfiction

New clients: Open to writers who have not published a book. Contact by email with query first. Responds in one month.

Commission: 15%

Fees: none

Tip: "We're especially interested in writers who have developed a social-media presence and have a website."

CHRISTIAN LITERARY AGENT

PO Box 428, Newburg, PA 17257 | 717-423-6621

keith@christianliteraryagent.com | www.christianliteraryagent.com

Agent: Keith Carroll

Agency: Established in 2010. Represents 10–15 new clients annually. Other service: writer coach.

Types of books: adult nonfiction

New clients: Open to first-time book authors and self-published writers. Initial contact: email, phone, website form. Responds in two to four weeks.

Commission: 10%

Fees: $90 application fee

Tip: "I try to help you make your material more of an effective read."

THE CHRISTOPHER FEREBEE AGENCY

submissions@christopherferebee.com | christopherferebee.com

Agents: Christopher Ferebee, Angela Scheff, Jana Burson, Jonathan Merritt

Agency: Established in 2011.

Types of books: adult fiction, adult nonfiction

New clients: Submit query letter and proposal as email attachment. Responds in four weeks.

Tip: "As a small agency, we focus our efforts on a very select group of authors. Our primary focus and attention is always on existing client relationships. But we are looking for the right authors with important ideas."

CREATIVE MEDIA AGENCY, INC.
query@cmalit.com | cmalit.com

Agent: Paige Wheeler, *paige@cmalit.com*

Agency: Established in 1997. Represents 20 clients. Member of Association of American Literary Agents. Specializes in women's fiction, romance, crime fiction, book-club fiction, and commercial nonfiction.

Types of books: adult fiction, adult nonfiction

New clients: Open to writers at all levels, except self-published. Query by email. Responds in six to eight weeks.

Commission: standard

Fees: none

Tip: "We are very specific on our website; check it out."

CURTIS BROWN, LTD.
10 Astor Pl., New York, NY 10003-6935 | 212-473-5400

lbp@cbltd.com | www.curtisbrown.com

Agent: Laura Blake Peterson

Agency: Member of Association of American Literary Agents. General agency that handles some religious/inspirational books.

Types of books: adult fiction, adult nonfiction, children's fiction, children's nonfiction

New clients: Email query, and attach the first 50 pages of your manuscript. Include "lbpquery" in the subject line of your email. Responds in three to four weeks only if interested in your book.

Commission: 15%

CYLE YOUNG LITERARY ELITE, LLC
PO Box 1, Clarklake, MI 49230 | 330-651-1604

submissions@cyleyoung.com | cyleyoung.com

Agents: Cyle Young, Tessa Emily Hall, Del Duduit, Megan Burkhart, Bethany Jett, Antwan Houser, Andy Clapp

Agency: Established in 2018. Represents 80 clients. Specialty: children's and nonfiction

Types of books: adult fiction, adult nonfiction, children's fiction, children's nonfiction, middle grade, teen/YA fiction, teen/YA nonfiction

New clients: Currently closed to queries and proposals except when meeting one of the agents at a writers conference or an online writing event. Check the website for changes in this policy.

Simultaneous submissions OK. Responds in three months or longer.

Commission: 15%

Tip: "We look for projects with great writing, big ideas, and great platform."

DUNAMIS WORDS

www.cherylricker.com/dunamis-words

Agent: Cheryl Ricker

Agency: Established in 2015. Represents 15 clients.

Types of books: adult fiction, business, Charismatic, Christian living, current events, devotionals, gift books, leadership, marriage, memoir, ministry, parenting, social issues, women's issues

New clients: Accepts queries—maximum of six pages—only through the website. If interested, will ask for more information and sample chapters.

Tip: "One's heart matters as much as one's calling and ability to write. These authors work diligently at growing their craft and tuning their antennae to the Creator and wellspring of life. From a deep abiding relationship with Christ flows the richest substance and wisdom."

EMBOLDEN MEDIA GROUP

PO Box 953607, Lake Mary, FL 32795

submissions@emboldenmediagroup.com | *emboldenmediagroup.com*

Agents: Jevon Bolden, Quantrilla Ard, Cynthia Crawford

Agency: Established in 2017. Represents 42 clients. Also offers content development, editorial, writing coaching.

Types of books: adult fiction, adult nonfiction, children's fiction, children's nonfiction

New clients: Open to writers at every level, including self-published. Email a query, use the website form, or current client referral. Accepts simultaneous submissions. Responds in 8–12 weeks.

Commission: 15%

Fees: none

Tip: "Follow us and our agents on social media, keep up with the kind of authors we represent and themes that catch our hearts and eyes."

GARDNER LITERARY, LLC

gardnerliterary@gmail.com | *rachellegardner.com*

Agents: Rachelle Gardner, Kristy Cambron

Agency: Established in 2021. Represents 50 clients. Represents some general-market books.

Types of books: adult fiction, adult nonfiction

New clients: Open to writers who have not published a book and writers met at conferences. First contact by email query. Simultaneous OK. Responds in about a week.

Commission: 15%

Tip: "Please visit the Submissions page of our website for complete information on what we represent and how to submit."

THE GATES GROUP

don@the-gates-group.com | *www.the-gates-group.com*

Agent: Don Gates

Agency: Established in 2013. Represents more than 50 authors. Member of Association of American Literary Agents.

Types of books: adult nonfiction, Bible studies, children's fiction, children's nonfiction, curriculum, devotionals, gift books, leadership

New clients: Open to writers who have not published a book and well-established book writers. Initial contact: email, referral from current client. Responds quickly.

Commission: 15%

Fees: none

Tip: "Have a good attitude."

GOLDEN WHEAT LITERARY

goldenwheatliterary.com

Agents: Jessica Schmeidler, *jessica@goldenwheatliterary.com;* Nicole Payne, *submissions@goldenwheatliterary.com*

Agency: Established in 2015. Also sells to the general market.

Types of books: adult fiction, devotionals, general-market fiction, memoir, middle grade, picture books, teen/YA nonfiction

New clients: Email query letter and first three chapters, all in body of message; no attachments. If no response in six months, assume the agent is not interested.

ILLUMINATE LITERARY AGENCY

support@illuminateliterary.com | *illuminateliterary.com*

Agents: Jenni Burke, Tawny Johnson

Agency: Established in 2006. Represents 50 clients. Specialty: adult nonfiction.

Types of books: adult nonfiction, Bible studies, business, children's fiction, children's nonfiction, church and ministry, culture, devotionals, family, gift books, leadership, lifestyle, memoir, personal development, relationships, spiritual growth, women's issues

New clients: Open to writers who are well-established or have not published a book and have a significant platform. Initial contact: website form, referral from current client, full proposal. Responds in four weeks if proposal catches their interest.

Commission: 15%

Fees: none

Tip: "Please thoroughly review our website before submitting."

KIRKLAND MEDIA MANAGEMENT

PO Box 1539, Liberty, TX 77575 | 936-581-3944

jessica@kirklandmediamanagement.com | *jessiekirkland.com*

Agent: Jessica Kirkland

Agency: Established in 2015. Sells to general market too.

Types of books: adult fiction, Christian living, general-market fiction, general-market nonfiction, TV/movie scripts

New clients: For fiction: Email a one-sheet first. If she likes the story, she will request a proposal and sample chapters at that time. For nonfiction: Email a full proposal plus three sample chapters. If no response in three months, not interested.

Commission: 15%

Tip: "She is searching for powerful stories that encourage, equip, challenge, and change, but is most enthusiastic about inspirational true stories."

THE KNIGHT AGENCY

232 W. Washington St., Madison, GA 30650 | 706 473-0994

pamela.harty@knightagency.net | *knightagency.net*

Agent: Pamela Harty

Agency: General agency established in 1996. Member of Association of American Literary Agents.

Types of books: adult fiction, children's fiction, children's nonfiction, Christian living

New clients: Open to writers who have not published a book and self-published writers. Initial contact by query via Query Manager on the website. All other queries will not be reviewed or returned. Responds in six weeks. Currently closed to submissions, but check her wish list for changes.

Commission: 15%

Fees: none

Tip: "Please visit our website for submission guidelines."

LINDA S. GLAZ LITERARY AGENCY, LLC

51670 Washington St., New Baltimore, MI 48047 | 586-822-1061
linda@lindasglaz.com | *lindasglaz.com*

Agent: Linda S. Glaz

Agency: Established in 2022. Represents 32 clients. Fiction wish list: historic, historic romance, suspense, romantic suspense, contemporary romance; no profanity or graphic sexuality, but clean reads are fine. "My heart is definitely in the fiction market, but I do love an amazing nonfiction work from an author who understands the need for platform."

Types of books: adult fiction, adult nonfiction

New clients: Open to all book writers, including self-published. Has met most clients through conferences. First contact: email with full proposal, referral through current client. Accepts simultaneous submissions. Responds in two to six weeks; after that feel free to nudge. "I'm very hands on, so if you work with me, we'll polish until it shines."

Commission: 15%

Fees: none

Tip: "Send me clean proposals that have been read aloud to remove any typos and errors. I love to pick up a proposal with no mistakes. That makes me realize you've done your work. Also, a *first page that pops!* Draw me in right away. Don't give me a chapter or two of backstory first. Your story starts on *page one!*"

LITERARY MANAGEMENT GROUP

1020 San Antonio Ln., Lady Lake, FL 32159 | 615-812-4445
brucebarbour@literarymanagementgroup.com | *www.literarymanagement-group.com*

Agent: Bruce R. Barbour

Agency: Established in 1995. Represents 100 clients. Specialty: general-interest Christian books for men and women. Does not represent fiction, children's books, gift or poetry books, biblical reference or commentaries. Also does: author coaching, self-publishing services, and consulting for all book-publishing disciplines.

Types of books: adult nonfiction

New clients: Open only to well-established book writers. Represents a few hundred clients. Contact: email query. Accepts simultaneous submissions. Immediately acknowledges receipt of a query and either declines or expresses interest in reviewing the material. Makes every effort to review and reply with a decision within three weeks.

Commission: 15%

Fees: none

Tip: "Query letter should not include pasted proposal. Prefer authors use the proposal template on the website or cover all elements of our proposal form on their own form. Proposals and sample chapters should not be formatted or sent as PDF. Simple Word or Google documents allow me to reply with comments."

MACGREGOR AND LEUDEKE

PO Box 1316, Manzanita, OR 97124 | 503-389-4803

submissions@macgregorliterary.com | *www.MacGregorLiterary.com*

Agents: Amanda Luedeke, *amanda@macgregorliterary.com;* Chip MacGregor, *chip@macgregorliterary.com;* Alina Mitchell, *alina@ macgregorliterary.com*

Agency: Established in 2006. Member of Association of American Literary Agents. Represents 75 clients.

Types of books: adult fiction, Christian living, deeper life, marriage, parenting, prescriptive, self-help

New clients: Open to published writers, including self-published, with a platform. Initial contact: website form, referral from a current client. No simultaneous submissions. Responds in one to two months.

Commission: 15%

Fees: none

Tip: "Take the time to finish your work. Most rejected projects are rejected because they are not really complete—they are 60% complete. As a writer, you'll find you have more success if you polish, listen to experienced advice, revise, rework, go back and look again, then finish the manuscript to the best of your abilities. A rough draft rarely sells. A polished work of a salable idea, presented by an author with a platform to help market and sell copies, is a winning combination."

MARK SWEENEY & ASSOCIATES

302 Sherwood Dr., Carol Stream, IL 60188 | 615-403-1937

sweeney2@comcast.net

Agents: Mark Sweeney, Janet Sweeney

Agency: Established in 2003. Represents more than 75 clients.

Specialty: popular apologetics.

Types of books: adult nonfiction, apologetics, Bible study, Christian living, memoir

New clients: Looking for authors with a great book idea who have both the skill to communicate in writing and a platform from which to write. Open to well-established book writers, as well as those who have not published a book. Initial contact: email, referral from current client. Query first. Responds in one week.

Commission: 15%

Fees: none

Tip: "Check with the agency's current author clients for a referral."

MARY DEMUTH LITERARY

2150 Heather Glen Dr., Rockwall, TX 75087 | 214-475-9083

mary@marydemuthliterary.com | marydemuthliterary.com

Agent: Mary DeMuth

Agency: Established in 2022; former agent with Books & Such Literary Management. Represents 20 clients. Other services: platform, media, and marketing coaching

Types of books: accessible theology, Christian living, cookbook, design, gift books, global church

New clients: Open to writers met at conferences. First contact: website form, referral from current client. Query first. Simultaneous OK. Responds in one week.

Commission: 15%

Fees: none

Tip: "Know the industry. Know what I'm looking for. Be an amazing writer. Don't be shy about platform."

NATASHA KERN LITERARY AGENCY, INC.

PO Box 1069, White Salmon, WA 98672

agent@natashakern.com | natashakernliterary.com

Agent: Natasha Kern

Agency: Established in 1987. Represents 36 religious clients.

Types of books: adult fiction

New clients: Closed to queries from unpublished writers. Open to meeting with writers at conferences and accepting referrals from current clients and editors. Cannot read unsolicited queries or proposals.

PAPE COMMONS

11327 Rill Pt., Colorado Springs, CO 80921

don@papecommons.com | papecommons.com

Agent: Don Pape

Agency: Established in 2021. Represents 50 clients. Responds in one week.

Types of books: adult fiction, adult nonfiction, children's fiction, children's nonfiction

New clients: Open to unpublished book authors. Contact: email, website form, referral from a current client. Also does publishing-industry consulting.

Commission: 15%

Fees: $500 fee for publishing-industry consulting beyond representation

Tip: "Not looking at science fiction or alternative fiction."

THE SEYMOUR AGENCY

475 Miner Street Rd., Canton, NY 13617 | 239-398-8209

nicole@theseymouragency.com | www.theseymouragency.com

Agents: Nichole Resciniti; Julie Gwinn, *querymanager.com/JulieGwinn*

Agency: Established in 1992. Member of Association of American Literary Agents.

Types of books: adult fiction, adult nonfiction, middle grade, teen/YA fiction, teen/YA nonfiction

New clients: Open to writers who have not published a book and self-published writers. First contact: email with one-page query, Query Manager, or referral from current client. Responds in two weeks to queries, three months to proposals.

Commission: 15%

Fees: none

Tip: "Hone your craft. Take advantage of writers groups, critique partners, etc., to polish your manuscript into the best shape it can be."

SPENCERHILL ASSOCIATES

1767 Lakewood Ranch Blvd. #268, Bradenton, FL 34211

submissions@spencerhillassociates.com | www.spencerhillassociates.com

Agent: Ali Herring

Agency: General agency established in 2001. Represents 25 clients with Christian books.

Types of books: adult fiction

New clients: Open to all book writers except self-published. Query first on the website form. Accepts simultaneous queries. Responds in 16 weeks.

Commission: 15%

Tip: "Follow the submission guidelines on the website."

THE STEVE LAUBE AGENCY

24 W. Camelback Rd. A-635, Phoenix, AZ 85013 | 602-336-8910

info@stevelaube.com | *www.stevelaube.com*

Agents: Steve Laube, *krichards@stevelaube.com;* Tamela Hancock Murray, *ewilson@stevelaube.com;* Bob Hostetler, *rgwright@ stevelaube.com;* Dan Balow, *vseem@stevelaube.com*

Agency: Established in 2004. Represents more than 300 clients. See website blog post by each agent for what he or she is looking for. Not actively pursuing children's picture book projects at this time.

Types of books: adult fiction, adult nonfiction

New clients: Open to unpublished authors. Email proposal as attachment according to the guidelines on the website. Steve Laube also will take proposals by mail. Accepts simultaneous submissions. Responds in 8–12 weeks.

Commission: 15%; foreign, 20%

Fees: none

Tip: "Please follow the guidelines! Since your book proposal is like a job application, you want to present yourself in the most professional manner possible. Your proposal will be a simple vehicle to convey your idea to us and, ultimately, to a publisher. Don't call the office to pitch your book idea. We'd rather read the proposal."

WILLIAM K. JENSEN LITERARY AGENCY

119 Bampton Ct., Eugene, OR 97404 | 541-688-1612

queries@wkjagency.com | *www.wkjagency.com*

Agents: William K. Jensen, Rachel McMillan, Teresa Evenson

Agency: Established in 2005. Represents more than 50 clients.

Types of books: adult nonfiction

New clients: Open to unpublished authors. Contact by email only; no attachments. See the website for complete query details. Accepts simultaneous submissions. Responds in one month or not interested.

Commission: 15%

Fees: none

Tip: "Due to the changes in book retailing over the last ten years, publishers will only accept authors with a robust social media and/ or speaking platforms. That being the case we can only consider queries by writers with at least 20,000 online followers and/or a dynamic speaking ministry."

WINTERS & KING, INC.

2448 E. 81st St., Ste. 5900, Tulsa, OK 74137-4259 | 918-494-6868
dboyd@wintersking.com | *wintersking.com/practice-areas/publishing-agent-services*

Agent: Thomas J. Winters

Agency: Established in 1983. Represents 150 clients. Part of a law firm. Other services: legal review of publishing contracts, drafting of work-for-hire agreements to contract writer/editor services, copyright/trademark filing

Types of books: adult fiction, adult nonfiction

New clients: Open to writers with a story to tell. Contact by email or website form. Responds in two weeks.

Commission: 15%

Fees: none

Tip: "Submissions should be carefully edited and free of typos. Accompanying manuscripts or sample chapters for presentation to publishers should be edited, typo-free, and basically print-ready."

WOLGEMUTH & ASSOCIATES

info@wolgemuthandassociates.com | *www.wolgemuthandassociates.com*

Agents: Robert Wolgemuth, Andrew Wolgemuth, Erik Wolgemuth, Austin Wilson

Agency: Established in 1992. Represents 150 clients. Responds in two weeks if interested.

Types of books: adult nonfiction, Bible studies, children's fiction, children's nonfiction

New clients: Works only with established book writers or references from a current client or close contact. Contact: email.

Commission: 15%

Fees: none

WORDSERVE LITERARY GROUP

7500 E. Arapahoe Rd., Ste. 285, Centennial, CO 80112 | 303-471-6675
admin@wordserveliterary.com | *www.wordserveliterary.com*

Agents: Greg Johnson, Sarah Freese, Nick Harrison, Keely Boeving

Agency: Established in 2003. Represents 175 clients. In addition to Christian books, has a strong footprint in history/military nonfiction projects in the general market, as well as recent sales in the general market in business, health/wellness, humor, sports, memoir, graphic novels, YA/children's. Does a limited amount of publishing on books they can't sell or books where the author needs a faster turnaround.

Types of books: adult fiction, adult nonfiction, children's fiction, children's nonfiction, general-market fiction, general-market nonfiction

New clients: Open to writers who have not published a book yet and writers met at conferences. Referrals from agency clients get immediate attention. Email query first. Accepts simultaneous submissions. Responds in two to four weeks.

Commission: 15%

Fees: none

Tip: "Read the submissions info on our website."

WORDWISE MEDIA SERVICES

4083 Avenue L, Ste. 255, Lancaster, CA 93536

submit@wordwisemedia.com | www.wordwisemedia.com/agency

Agents: Steven Hutson, David Fessenden, Michelle S. Lazurek

Agency: Established in 2011. Member of Association of American Literary Agents. Represents 70 clients.

Types of books: adult fiction, adult nonfiction, apologetics, children's fiction, children's nonfiction, Christian living, culture, devotionals, picture books, social issues, theology

New clients: Open to unpublished book authors and writers met at conferences. Contact: Submit query form as email attachment. Accepts simultaneous submissions. Responds in one month; OK to nudge after then.

Commission: 15%

Fees: none

Tip: "Follow instructions carefully. Meet us at a conference. Specify the agent's name in the email subject line if you have a preference."

YATES & YATES

1551 N. Tustin Ave., Ste. 710, Santa Ana, CA 92705 | 714-480-4000

email@yates2.com | www.yates2.com

Agents: Sealy Yates, Matt Yates, Curtis Yates, Mike Salisbury, Karen Yates

Agency: Established in 1989. Represents fewer than 50 clients.

Types of books: adult nonfiction

New clients: No unpublished authors. Contact by email with full proposal. Responds in one to two months. Other services: author coaching and ecourses available at *authorcoaching.com*.

Commission: negotiable

Tip: "We serve passionate, articulate, gifted Christian communicators, using our strengths to guide, counsel, and protect them, fiercely advocate for them, and help them advance life- and culture-transforming messages for the sake of the Kingdom."

18

WRITERS CONFERENCES AND SEMINARS

This chapter is divided by states in alphabetical order, various locations, international in alphabetical order, and online. Many directors had not set dates for 2023 when this book went to print.

ALABAMA

SOUTHERN CHRISTIAN WRITERS CONFERENCE

Tuscaloosa, AL | June | *scwritersconferenc.wixsite.com/website*

Director: Cheryl Wray, 4195 Waldort Dr., Northport, AL 35473; 205-534-0595; *scwritersconference@gmail.com*

Description: The SCWC is a two-day conference for beginners or experienced writers that focuses on several genres: nonfiction books, magazines, fiction, grammar, business aspects, legal aspects, etc.

Faculty: agents, editors, publishers

Attendance: 160–200

CALIFORNIA

CHRISTIAN WRITERS RETREAT AT MOUNT HERMON

Mount Hermon, CA (near Santa Cruz) | early November | *www.ChristianWritersRetreat.com/mount-hermon*

Director: Kathy Ide, *KathyIde@ChristianWritersRetreats.com*

Description: Get away for a few days of refreshment and

rejuvenation; powerful connections with God; and meeting kindred spirits who will understand, encourage, support, and pray for you at the Holy Spirit-infused Mount Hermon Christian Conference Center. And carve out some uninterrupted writing time in this inspiring setting surrounded by stunning coastal redwoods, streams, and waterfalls.

Scholarships: full, partial
Attendance: 40–50

VISION CHRISTIAN WRITERS CONFERENCE AT MT. HERMON

Mt. Hermon, CA (near Santa Cruz) | March 31–April 4 | *vcwconf.com*

Director: Robynne Elizabeth Miller, 530-217-8233, *director@vcwconf.com*

Description: Vision is a full-service premier conference, featuring top agents, editors, and publishers from across the country, as well as more than 50 workshops, tracks, and speakers. One-on-one appointments with agents, editors, publishers, and industry experts are free (as are the gorgeous redwoods!).

Special track: advanced writers
Faculty: agents, editors, publishers
Speakers: David A.R. White, James Rubart, Robynne Elizabeth Miller, Mary DeMuth
Scholarships: full, partial
Attendance: 200
Contest: Most Promising Writer, Most Encouraging, and more

WEST COAST CHRISTIAN WRITERS CONFERENCE

Roseville, CA (Sacramento area) | October | *www.westcoastchristianwriters.com*

Director: Susy Flory, 1750 Prairie City Rd., Ste. 130, #689, Folsom, CA 95630; 800-660-0747; *president@westcoastchristianwriters.com*

Description: West Coast Christian Writers (WCCW) is a strong community of writers with writing events known for high value, expert speakers and teachers, along with hands-on help and innovation. A legacy conference of nearly 30 years, WCCW is a place where writers thrive.

Special tracks: advanced writers, speaking
Faculty: agents, editors, publishers
Scholarships: full, partial
Attendance: 225
Contest: Goldie Awards recognize excellence in different genres and include a fun "Bad Writing" contest.

COLORADO

COLORADO CHRISTIAN WRITERS CONFERENCE

Estes Park, CO | May 17–20 | *colorado.writehisanswer.com*

Director: Marlene Bagnull, 951 Anders Rd., Lansdale, PA 19446; 484-991-8581; *mbagnull@aol.com*

Description: We plan to be back in person at the YMCA of the Rockies for our 26th conference. Six powerful keynotes, eight continuing sessions, approximately 50 workshops, panels, one-on-one appointments, and more in a magnificent retreat setting.

Special track: teens

Faculty: agents, editors, publishers

Scholarships: partial, full

Attendance: 200

Contest: Poetry (12–30 lines) or prose (500–800 words) on our conference theme, "Write His Answer"—not only how He is calling you to "write His answer" but also what you have found to be His answer in the struggles you have faced as you have sought to "live His answer." Published and not-yet published writers are judged in separate categories. The four first-place winners receive $50 off next year's registration fee.

DELAWARE

DELMARVA CHRISTIAN WRITERS CONFERENCE

Georgetown, DE | October 21 | *delmarvawriters.com/conference*

Director: Elizabeth Boerner, 107 Elizabeth St., Georgetown, DE 19947; 302-542-8510; *info@delmarvawriters.com*

Description: The Delmarva Christian Writers Conference is for writers who want to be obedient to God's call to write. It is your opportunity to be encouraged, equipped, and inspired.

Faculty: editors, publishers

Attendance: 60–80

FLORIDA

FLORIDA CHRISTIAN WRITERS CONFERENCE

Leesburg, FL | October 18–22 | *Word-Weavers.com/FloridaEvents*

Director: Eva Marie Everson, PO Box 520224, Longwood, FL 32752; 407-414-8188; *FloridaCWC@aol.com*

Description: We offer 10 continuing classes, dozens of one-hour workshops, meetings with professionals and mentors, and a yearly keynote speaker and one-day genre intensive (2023: nonfiction). Writers of all levels welcome.

Special tracks: advanced writers, speaking

Faculty: agents, editors, publishers

Scholarships: full, partial

Attendance: 200

Contest: See website for details.

GEORGIA

SHE WRITES & SPEAKS PROCLAIM!

Columbus, GA | February 2–4 | *www.shewritesandspeaks.com*

Director: Carol Tetzlaff, 1602 Cole St., Enumclaw, WA 98022; 360-226-3488; *carol@redemption-press.com*

Description: A different kind of conference with small-group interaction that nourishes your soul while preparing you to engage in your calling. Held in conjunction with Christian Product Expo Winter Show.

Special tracks: advanced writers, speaking

Faculty: agents, editors, publishers

Speakers: Erica Wiggenhorn, Shannon Popkin, Mary R. Snyder

Scholarships: partial

Attendance: 100+

ILLINOIS

WRITE-TO-PUBLISH CONFERENCE

Wheaton, IL (Chicago area) | June 13–16 | *writetopublish.com*

Director: Dan Balow, 24 W. Camelback Rd. A635, Phoenix, AZ 85013; 630-464-1377; *dan@christianwritersinstitute.com*

Description: For more than 50 years, Write-to-Publish has been training writers and connecting them with editors who want to publish their work and with agents who want to represent them. Owned by the Christian Writers Institute.

Faculty: agents, editors, publishers

Scholarships: partial
Attendance: 150

INDIANA

TAYLOR UNIVERSITY'S PROFESSIONAL WRITERS' CONFERENCE

Upland, IN | July | *taylorprofessionalwritersconference.weebly.com*

Director: Linda K. Taylor, 236 W. Reade Ave., Upland, IN 46989; 765-998-5591; *taylorPRWConference@gmail.com*

Description: Hear from agents, editors, and authors who will inspire and encourage you.

Special track: teens

Faculty: agents, editors, publishers

Attendance: 100

KENTUCKY

KENTUCKY CHRISTIAN WRITERS CONFERENCE

Elizabethtown, KY | June | *www.kychristianwriters.com*

Director: Jean Matthew Hall, 704-578-0858, *jean@jeanmatthewhall.com*

Description: Our purpose is to provide an annual, interdenominational event to equip and encourage writers in their quest for publication. The conference provides a safe environment where writers can discover their gifts and share their work.

Faculty: agents, editors, publishers

Attendance: 75

MICHIGAN

MARANATHA CHRISTIAN WRITERS' CONFERENCE

Muskegon, MI | September | *www.maranathachristianwriters.com*

Director: Sherry Hoppen, 4759 Lake Harbor Rd., Norton Shores, MI 49441; 231-798-2161; *info@maranathachristianwriters.com*

Description: A broad variety of publishers, agents, and editors. Up to five one-to-one appointments with the experts at no additional charge.

Faculty: agents, editors, publishers

Scholarships: partial

Attendance: 80

Contest: Leona Hertel Awards Contests; details on the website.

SPEAK UP CONFERENCE

Grand Rapids, MI, and online | July 13–15 | *speakupconference.com*

Director: Bonnie Emmorey, *eventsupport@speakupconference.com*

Description: We are training the next generation of Christian communicators: writers, speakers, and leaders. Our speaking and writing sessions are designed to take your ministry to the next level and are presented by globally recognized authors and speakers.

Special tracks: advanced writers, speaking

Faculty: agents, editors, publishers

Speaker: Carol Kent

Scholarships: partial

Attendance: 300+

MISSOURI

AMERICAN CHRISTIAN FICTION WRITERS (ACFW)

St. Louis, MO | August 24–27 | *www.acfw.com-conference*

Director: Robin Miller, PO Box 101066, Palm Bay, FL 32910-1066; *director@acfw.com*

Description: Continuing education sessions and workshop electives specifically geared for five levels of fiction-writing experience from beginner to advanced. Track for readers: ACFW Storyfest. Note: This conference changes locations every year.

Special track: advanced writers

Faculty: agents, editors

Scholarships: full

Attendance: 500

Contest: The Genesis Contest is for unpublished writers whose Christian fiction manuscript is completed. The Carol Awards honor the best of Christian fiction from the previous calendar year.

HEART OF AMERICA CHRISTIAN WRITERS FALL CONFERENCE

Kansas City, MO | October | *www.hacwn.org*

Director: Jeanette Littleton, 3706 N.E. Shady Lane Dr., Gladstone, MO 64119; 816-459-8016; *hacwnkc@gmail.com*

Description: We specialize in having faculty who are looking for new writers.

Faculty: agents, editors, publishers

Attendance: 100

Contest: In eight categories. Prizes include critiques and consultations.

REALM MAKERS WRITERS CONFERENCE

St. Louis, MO | July 13–15 | *www.realmmakers.com*

Director: Becky Minor, *becky@realmmakers.com*

Description: Are you a creative person who loves science fiction and fantasy, but also makes your spiritual growth a high priority? Have you found that you're a little too weird for the usual church crowd, but don't exactly fit in with the sci-fi convention set either? Now there's a place for you to learn, share your talents, and commune with people a lot like yourself. Find your tribe at Realm Makers.

Special tracks: advanced writers, teens

Faculty: agents, editors, publishers

Scholarships: full, partial

Attendance: 400

Contest: The Realm Awards is open to all Christian authors of speculative fiction with a book published the previous calendar year. Not limited to attendees of the conference. Submissions open January 1–21 each year.

NEW YORK

RENEW – spiritual retreat for writers & speakers

Speculator, NY | April 27–30 | *reNEWwriting.com*

Director: Lucinda Secrest McDowell, 232 Clearfield Rd., Wethersfield, CT 06129; 860-402-9551; *info@reNEWwriting.com*

Description: How do you fill up, so you can pour out to others with words of life, hope, and courage? reNEW spiritual retreat for writers & speakers is not a large, busy conference, but a retreat where a community gathers in nature and beauty, at desks to write, in workshops to learn, and in worship to pray and draw closer to God. We want to help fill up your body, soul, and spirit, so you can powerfully respond to God's call on your life.

Special track: speaking

Attendance: 100

NORTH CAROLINA

ASHEVILLE CHRISTIAN WRITERS CONFERENCE

Asheville, NC | February 24–26 | *www.ashevillechristianwritersconference. com*

Director: Cindy Sproles, PO Box 6494, Kingsport, TN 37663; 423-384-4821; *cindybootcamp@gmail.com*

Description: Training writers one writer at a time to follow their call from God to write.

Special track: advanced writers

Faculty: agents, editors, publishers

Speakers: Bob Hostetler, Eva Marie Everson

Scholarships: partial

Attendance: 119

Contest: Sparrow Award Book Contest judged according to appeal, content, flow, and writing

BLUE RIDGE MOUNTAINS CHRISTIAN WRITERS CONFERENCE

Black Mountain, NC | May 28–June 1 | *www.BlueRidgeConference.com*

Director: Edie Melson, 604 S. Almond Dr., Simpsonville, SC 29681; 864-373-4232; *ediegmelson@gmail.com*

Description: This is a multidiscipline conference that caters to writers of all levels. In addition to outstanding craft/industry instruction, there is a strong focus on preparing spiritually to follow God as He directs our words for His glory.

Special tracks: advanced writers, speaking, teens

Faculty: agents, editors, publishers

Scholarships: partial

Attendance: 550

Contest: Selah Awards (industry-wide published books), Directors' Choice Awards (for former attendees and those in attendance at the 2023 event), Foundation Awards (restricted to unpublished writers who are attending the 2023 event)

MOUNTAINSIDE NOVELIST RETREAT

Black Mountain, NC | October 1–4 | *www.BlueRidgeConference.com/ mountainside-retreats*

Director: Edie Melson, 604 S. Almond Dr., Simpsonville, SC 29681; 864-373-4232; *ediegmelson@gmail.com*

Description: Through small-group instruction and hands-on exercises from bestselling writers, the craftsman is able to focus on building strengths from challenges. Writers developing all levels of their careers will benefit from one-on-one consultations, brainstorming, and instruction. This event will be a guided intensive where all participants have the opportunity to practice what they're learning under experienced team leaders.

Attendance: 40

SHE SPEAKS CONFERENCE

Concord, NC | July | *shespeaksconference.com*

> **Director:** Lisa Allen, 630 Team Rd. #100, Matthews, NC 28105; 704-849-2270; *shespeaks@Proverbs31.org*
> **Description:** Speaking and writing tracks.
> **Special track:** speaking
> **Faculty:** agents, editors
> **Attendance:** 700

OREGON

CASCADE CHRISTIAN WRITERS CONFERENCE (hosted by Oregon Christian Writers)

Canby, OR (Portland area) | June 25–28 | *oregonchristianwriters.org*

> **Contact:** Sue Miholer, PO Box 20214, Kelzer, OR 97307; *contact@oregonchristianwriters.org*
> **Description:** A conference for all levels of writers with publishers, editors, agents, and published authors on the faculty. Outstanding classes and workshops on all facets of writing and publishing, mentoring opportunities, and time to network in a lovely and relaxed setting.
> **Faculty:** agents, editors, publishers
> **Speaker:** Amanda Dykes
> **Attendance:** 120

OREGON CHRISTIAN WRITERS ONE-DAY CONFERENCE

Salem, OR | March 11 | *www.oregonchristianwriters.org*

> **Contact:** Sue Miholer, *contact@oregonchristianwriters.org*
> **Description:** Two morning keynote addresses and two one-hour workshop sessions in the afternoon with four choices in each session, a great time to further the craft of writing.
> **Speaker:** Patricia Raybon
> **Attendance:** 120

PENNSYLVANIA

EVANGELICAL PRESS ASSOCIATION ANNUAL CONVENTION

Lancaster, PA | April 12–14 | *www.epaconvention.com*

Director: Lamar Keener, PO Box 1787, Queen Creek, AZ 85142; 480-868-2466; *director@evangelicalpress.com*

Description: The annual EPA convention is a source of new ideas and creative innovations. It provides an intense time of professional learning, networking and inspiration for those in the periodical publishing industry, both print and digital. Focused for periodical editors, but writers are welcome and can meet the editors. Note: This conference changes locations every year.

Faculty: editors, publishers

Attendance: 200

Contest: Freelance writers may submit articles and/or blog entries into contest, which requires EPA membership.

MONTROSE CHRISTIAN WRITERS CONFERENCE

Montrose, PA | July | *www.montrosebible.org*

Director: Marsha Hubler, 1833 Dock Hill Rd., Middleburg, PA 17842; 570-837-0002; *marshahubler@outlook.com*

Description: In a family atmosphere at the restored home and conference center of evangelist R.A. Torrey, the conference always offers a faculty of best-selling authors, agents, editors, and publishers who present classes for beginners as well as published authors, teaching fiction, nonfiction, children's fiction and nonfiction, marketing, poetry, music, drama, and numerous subgenres. Private critiques are always offered, as well as works-in-progress sessions.

Special tracks: advanced writers, teens

Faculty: agents, editors, publishers

Scholarships: partial

Attendance: 70

Contest: The Shirley Brinkerhoff Scholarship Fund offers $200 to the best entry of a 300-piece submission based on the year's theme.

ST. DAVIDS CHRISTIAN WRITERS' CONFERENCE

Meadville, PA | June | *www.stdavidswriters.com/conference*

Director: Sue Boltz, *treasurer@stdavidswriters.com*

Faculty: agents, editors

Scholarships: full, partial
Attendance: 45
Contest: See detailed list on the website.

SUPER SATURDAY

Lancaster, PA | April | *lancasterchristianwriters.com*

Director: JP Robinson, *lancasterwrites@gmail.com*
Description: One-day conference with fiction and nonfiction tracks, keynote, bookstore, and individual consultations with faculty.
Attendance: 80

SOUTH CAROLINA

CAROLINA CHRISTIAN WRITERS CONFERENCE

Spartanburg, SC | March 9–11; 9th is for pastors and ministry leaders only | *www.fbs.org/writers*

Director: Linda Gilden, 250 E. Main St., Spartanburg, SC 29306; 864-706-5250; *linda@lindagilden.com*
Description: Carolina Christian Writers Conference exists to help writers grow and move to the next step in their Christian writing careers.
Special track: pastors
Faculty: agents, editors, publishers
Scholarships: full
Attendance: 125
Contest: Kudos contest for book and article writers, published and unpublished

TENNESSEE

THE ART OF WRITING

Nashville, TN | November | *thechristyaward.com*

Director: Cindy Carter, ECPA, 5801 S. McClintock Dr., Ste. 104, Mesa, AZ 85283; 480-966-3998; *TheChristyAward@ecpa.org*
Description: The Art of Writing is a conference for writers, storytellers and publishing curators that is run in conjunction with The Christy Award® program. It features four timely sessions for authors and publishing professionals. Networking and learning from featured authors and high-level publishing professionals sets

this conference apart. The Christy Award® Gala celebrating excellence in Christian fiction by naming the year's best in nine categories follows the conference. Bundle pricing is available.
Faculty: agents, editors, publishers
Attendance: 200

MID-SOUTH CHRISTIAN WRITERS CONFERENCE

Collierville, TN (Memphis area) | March 17–18 | *midsouthconferenceonline.com*

Director: Beth Gooch, PO Box 823, Byhalia, MS 38611; 901-277-5525; *midsouthchristianwriters@gmail.com*

Description: This conference, started in 2014, offers a broad range of speakers for fiction and nonfiction, as well as the business aspects of writing. The Saturday lineup features a morning keynote, followed by a selection of breakout sessions, and concludes with an afternoon keynote. We typically include at least one session on poetry and/or songwriting. Optional Friday afternoon workshops are also available. Registration covers one-on-one appointments with agents, editors, and published authors, as well as a Friday evening meet-and-greet and Saturday lunch.

Special track: advanced writers
Faculty: agents, editors, publishers
Speaker: Cynthia Ruchti
Scholarships: full
Attendance: 100

TEXAS

TEXAS CHRISTIAN WRITERS CONFERENCE

Houston, TX | August | *www.centralhoustoniwa.com*

Director: Martha Rogers, 6038 Greenmont, Houston, TX 77092; 713-686-7209; *marthalrogers@sbcglobal.net*
Faculty: editors
Attendance: 60
Contest: Inspirational Writers Alive! Open Writing Competition

WASHINGTON

NORTHWEST CHRISTIAN WRITERS RENEWAL

Bellevue, WA | May 19–20 | *nwchristianwriters.org*

Director: Charles Harris, PO Box 2706, Woodinville, WA 98072; 206-

250-6885; *renewal@nwchristianwriters.org*

Description: This conference is where writers, editors, and publishers can connect, network, and collaborate. Conferees will sharpen their skills, learn strategies, and form connections to boost their success on the writing journey.

Faculty: agents, editors, publishers

Scholarships: full

Attendance: 130

SHE WRITES FOR HIM RETREAT

Enumclaw, WA | November 13–18 | *www.shewritesforhimretreat.com*

Director: Carol Tetzlaff, 1602 Cole St., Enumclaw, WA 98022; 360-226-3488; *carol@redemption-press.com*

Description: An intensive writing retreat where you will gain all the insight you need to organize the content of your manuscript. It is intimate, exclusive, relaxed, fun, transforming, and productive.

Faculty: editors, publishers

Speaker: Janet McHenry

Attendance: 12

VARIOUS LOCATIONS

REALM MAKERS WINTER RETREAT

varies + virtual | February | *www.realmmakers.com*

Director: Rebecca Minor, *becky@realmmakers.com*

Description: The Realm Makers Winter Retreat seeks to gather writers of all experience levels in an encouraging, intimate setting where they can learn from a master writer and experience fellowship along the way. Writers will enjoy time gaining new skills, as well as opportunities to focus on the manuscript of their choosing.

Attendance: 40

CANADA

INSCRIBE CHRISTIAN WRITERS' FELLOWSHIP CONFERENCE

Edmonton, AB, Canada | September | *inscribe.org/fall-conference*

Director: Box 68025, Edmonton, AB T6C 4N6, Canada; *president@ inscribe.org*

Description: InScribe's Fall Conference features a seasoned author, publisher, or other expert as the keynote speaker; plus we offer a variety of workshop topics and presenters. It's a weekend where writers—whether they are seasoned or beginning—can connect for fellowship, encouragement, and support.

Scholarships: partial

Contest: See *www.inscribe.org/contests*.

WRITE! CANADA

Canada | September | *writecanada.org*

Director: Box 77001, Markham, ON L3P 0C8; *director@ thewordguild.com*

Description: Write! Canada is an annual writers conference hosted by The Word Guild. Seasoned writers host workshops where writers of all experience levels and genres can meet and hone their skills.

NEW ZEALAND

NZ CHRISTIAN WRITERS RETREAT

Whitianga, New Zealand | April 27–30 | *www.nzchristianwriters.org*

Director: Justin St. Vincent, 179B St. Johns Rd., St. Johns, Auckland, North Island, New Zealand 1072; *editor@xtrememusic.org*

Description: Our seminar speakers will inspire, refresh, and upskill each of us on our writing journey.

Faculty: editors, publishers

Attendance: 40

ONLINE

GREATER PHILLY CHRISTIAN WRITERS CONFERENCE

August 2–5 | *writehisanswer.com/conferences*

Director: Marlene Bagnull, 951 Anders Rd., Lansdale, PA 19446; 484-991-8581; *mbagnull@aol.com*

Description: Approximately 100 hours of live video content (available to view through the end of the year), plus small-group breakouts, round tables, critique sessions, live chats, appointments with editors and agents, and preconference webinars.

Special track: teens
Faculty: agents, editors
Scholarships: partial
Attendance: 200
Contest: Poetry (12–30 lines) or prose (500–800 words) on our conference theme, "Write His Answer"—not only how He is calling you to "write His answer" but also what you have found to be His answer in the struggles you have faced as you have sought to "live His answer." Published and not-yet published writers are judged in separate categories. The four first-place winners receive $50 off next year's registration fee.

MT ZION RIDGE PRESS CHRISTIAN WRITER'S CONFERENCE

May 4–6 | *www.mtzionridgepress.com/writing-off-the-beaten-path-confere*

Director: Tamera Lynn Kraft, *mtzionridgepress@gmail.com*
Description: Christian writer's conference online.
Faculty: editors, publishers
Attendance: 100

OMEGA CHRISTIAN WRITERS CONFERENCE

October 7–8 | *www.omegawriters.org/conference*

Director: Penny Reeve, *president@aomegawriters.org*
Description: The Omega Writers Conference supports and networks writers in Australia and beyond with quality speakers and workshops designed to encourage, resource, and inspire you on your writing journey. Whether you are a new Christian writer or an established author, a nonfiction writer or a creator of kids lit, the opportunities to network with other likeminded and supportive writers means you will leave with new ideas, new connections, and a renewed excitement for your writing project.
Faculty: editors, publishers
Scholarships: partial
Attendance: 100

PENCON EDITORS' CONFERENCE

May 3–5 | *PENCONeditors.com*

Director: *director@PENCONeditors.com*
Description: PENCON is the only annual conference for Christian editors and proofreaders. Our goal is to provide networking,

education, and inspiration for Christians in the publishing industry.
Faculty: editors, publishers
Scholarships: full, partial
Attendance: 75

PUBLISHING IN COLOR

March 9–10 | *publishingincolor.com*

> **Director:** Brian Allain, *brian@publishingincolor.com*
> **Description:** Publishing in Color has only one objective: Increase the number of books published by spiritual writers of color. This includes such groups as African Americans, Asian Americans, Latinx Americans, and Native Americans, who have been under-represented in terms of the number of published books.
> **Faculty:** agents, editors
> **Scholarships:** full
> **Attendance:** 70

ROAR MARKETING CONFERENCE

October 13–14 | *www.roarmarketingconference.com*

> **Director:** Carol Tetzlaff, 1602 Cole St., Enumclaw, WA 98022; 360-226-3488; *carol@redemption-press.com*
> **Description:** Roar has broken the conference mold. Join us for an interactive, hands-on, apply-what-you've-learned experience. Equipping you with priceless tips, tricks, and tools to build your platform and expand your reach.
> **Attendance:** 200+

SHE WRITES FOR HIM BOOTCAMP

May 10–24, September 13–27 | *www.shewritesforhimbootcamp.com*

> **Director:** Carol Tetzlaff, 1602 Cole St., Enumclaw, WA 98022; 360-226-3488; *carol@redemption-press.com*
> **Description:** Fourteen-day virtual bootcamp to take you step by step through completing an annotated table of contents for the book you plan to write.
> **Speakers:** Dori Harrell, Allie Pleiter, Athena Dean Holtz
> **Attendance:** 40

SHE WRITES FOR HIM GREATER THINGS

April 14–15 | *www.shewritesforhimconference.com*

> **Director:** Carol Tetzlaff, 1602 Cole St., Enumclaw, WA 98022; 360-226-3488; *carol@redemption-press.com*

Description: Two days of a power-packed, live, online event with 20+ publishing-industry professionals to help you strengthen, sharpen, write, and market your message.
Faculty: agents, editors, publishers
Attendance: 300

WE WRITE FOR HIM 5-DAY CHALLENGE SERIES

January 3–7, March 7–11, May 2–6, September 5–9, November 7–11 | *www.wewriteforhimchallenge.com*

Director: Carol Tetzlaff, 1602 Cole St., Enumclaw, WA 98022; 360-226-3488; *carol@redemption-press.com*
Description: Join us to jumpstart your writing path with tried and true techniques to write your book, tell your hard story, and nourish your soul.
Attendance: 200+

WRITING FOR YOUR LIFE

March 6–7 | *writingforyourlife.com/conferences*

Director: Brian Allain, *info@writingforyourlife.com*
Description: If you write or read books that matter—books with substance and soul—then this is the place for you. Writing for Your Life produces writing conferences featuring leading authors and industry experts presenting on various topics in the areas of how to write, how to get published, and how to market.
Faculty: agents, editors
Speaker: Barbara Brown Taylor
Attendance: 70

19

WRITERS GROUPS

In addition to the groups listed here, check the writers organizations for new groups in your area and information about starting a group.

WRITERS ORGANIZATIONS

AMERICAN CHRISTIAN FICTION WRITERS
acfw.com

> **Contact:** Robin Miller, PO Box 101066, Palm Bay, FL 32910-1066; *director@acfw.com*
>
> **Services:** Email loop, genre Facebook pages, online courses, critique groups, and local and regional chapters. Sponsors contests for published and unpublished writers and conducts the largest Christian fiction writers conference annually.
>
> **Members:** 2600+
>
> **Membership fee:** $75 to join, $49/year to renew

CHRISTIAN AUTHORS NETWORK
ChristianAuthorsNetwork.com

> **Contact:** Susan U. Neal, *contact@christianauthorsnetwork.com*
>
> **Services:** "CAN is a group of traditionally published Christian authors who have joined together in a supportive association to spread the news about books to book lovers everywhere. We operate as a cooperative, Christ-centered marketing organization, to encourage and teach one another, and get the word out about CAN authors' books to readers, retailers, and librarians." Membership open to authors with two or more published books. One must be a Christian book published by a traditional royalty-paying publisher (with no financial input by

the author) and are currently available in publication (in any and all formats) at the date of the membership application.

Members: 140
Membership fee: $90/year

CHRISTIAN INDIE AUTHOR NETWORK

www.christianindieauthors.com

    Contact: Mary C. Findley, 918-805-0669, *mjmcfindley@gmail.com*
    Services: Provides a readers site to connect independently published books to readers, several Facebook groups for both authors and readers, and book promotion opportunities.
    Members: 400+
    Membership fee: none

THE CHRISTIAN PEN: PROOFREADERS AND EDITORS NETWORK

www.TheChristianPEN.com

    Contact: *Director@TheChristianPEN.com*
    Services: "The Christian PEN: Proofreaders and Editors Network provides aspiring, beginning, established, and professional editors and proofreaders with networking, community, and industry discounts. If you are an editor or proofreader, or are thinking about becoming one, join this community of like-minded professionals who share our knowledge and experience with one another."
    Members: 200
    Membership fee: $25–$90/year

CHRISTIAN WOMEN WRITERS

cwwriters.com

    Contact: Jen Gentry, 918-724-3996, *jennyokiern37@gmail.com*
    Services: "A professional organization of women Christian writers working toward a common goal, shining a light into a dark place. Our mission is to pool our resources and collective wisdom to help each other grow in our craft, build/expand our readership, and glorify Him in all that we do." Offers critique groups, marketing help, and promotion events.
    Members: 100+
    Membership fee: none
    Affiliation: Christian Indie Author Network

INSPIRE CHRISTIAN WRITERS

www.inspirewriters.com

Contact: Robynne Miller, 530-217-8233, *inspiredirectors@gmail.com*

Services: "Through Inspire you'll find a community of writers working together to achieve writing and publication goals. By taking advantage of our online and in-person critique groups, you'll give and receive feedback and grow in your craft. We offer web-based and local training through workshops and conferences to help you navigate publishing decisions, create your online presence and polish your writing until it shines. You'll have opportunities to network with other writers—multi-published as well as those just starting out." Sponsors the Vision Christian Writers Conference at Mt. Hermon.

Members: 150

Membership fee: $50/year

REALM MAKERS

www.realmmakers.com

Contact: Scott Minor, scott@realmmakers.com

Services: "Realm Makers supports writers and artists who create science fiction and fantasy in their journeys from idea to marketplace. Whether participating artists wish to gear their content for inspirational or mainstream audiences, Realm Makers seeks to encourage them from a faith-friendly perspective." Offers a membership program, where authors can connect throughout the year, critique one another's work, and participate in periodic webinars to keep their writing and marketing toolkits sharp. Sponsors the Realm Makers conference.

Members: 100

Membership fee: ranges from $4.99 to $24.99/month

WORD WEAVERS INTERNATIONAL, INC.

www.Word-Weavers.com

Contact: Eva Marie Everson, president, PO Box 520224, Longwood, FL 32752; 407-615-4112, *WordWeaversInternational@aol.com*

Services: Local traditional chapters and online pages (Zoom) for manuscript critiquing. Sponsors Florida Christian Writers Conference.

Members: 1,000

Membership fee: $50/year, traditional and online; $65/year, traditional + online

NATIONAL ONLINE GROUPS

ACFW QIP AUTHORS
www.facebook.com/groups/ACFWQIPAuthors
> **Meetings:** online
> **Contact:** Hallee Bridgeman
> **Membership fee:** national fee
> **Affiliation:** American Christian Fiction Writers

WORD WEAVERS ONLINE GROUPS
www.Word-Weavers.com
> **Meetings:** online via Zoom, times vary, two hours
> **Contact:** Eva Marie Everson, 407-615-4112,
>   *WordWeaversInternational@aol.com*
> **Membership fee:** $50/year
> **Affiliation:** Word Weavers

ALABAMA

WORD WEAVERS NORTH ALABAMA
www.facebook.com/groups/936711453176211
> **Meetings:** 105 Village Dr. NE, Hartselle; third Thursday of each
>   month, 10:00 a.m.–noon
> **Contact:** Lisa Worthey Smith, 256-612-7404, *lisawsmith57@gmail.com*
> **Members:** 7
> **Membership fee:** $50/year
> **Affiliation:** Word Weavers

ARIZONA

ACFW ARIZONA
www.christianwritersofthewest.com
> **Meetings:** Denny's Restaurant, 3315 N. Scottsdale Rd., Scottsdale;
>   third Saturday of the month, 11:00 a.m.–1:00 p.m.
> **Contact:** Pamela Tracy, *arizona@acfwchapter.com*
> **Members:** 30
> **Membership fee:** $10/year plus national fee
> **Affiliation:** American Christian Fiction Writers

CHANDLER WRITERS' GROUP

chandlerwriters.wordpress.com

> **Meetings:** member's home, Ocotillo Rd., Chandler; first Friday of the month, 9:00–11:30 a.m.
> **Contact:** Jenne Acevedo, 480-510-0419, *jenneacevedo@gmail.com*
> **Members:** 12
> **Membership fee:** none

FOUNTAIN HILLS CHRISTIAN WRITERS' GROUP

> **Meetings:** Fountain Hills Presbyterian Church, 13001 N. Fountain Hills Blvd., Fountain Hills; second Friday of the month, 9:00 a.m.–noon
> **Contact:** Jewell Johnson, 480-836-8968, *tykeJ@juno.com*
> **Members:** 12
> **Membership fee:** $10/year
> **Affiliation:** American Christian Writers

WORD WEAVERS NORTHERN ARIZONA

> **Meetings:** Verde Community Church, 102 S. Willard, Cottonwood; second Saturday of the month, 9:30–11:30 a.m.
> **Contact:** Alice Klies, *Alice.Klies@Gmail.com*
> **Membership fee:** $50/year
> **Affiliation:** Word Weavers

ARKANSAS

ACFW NW ARKANSAS

www.facebook.com/groups/127662834752320

> **Meetings:** Springdale; first Monday of the month, 5:30 p.m.
> **Contact:** Robyn Hook, *NWArkansas@acfwchapter.com*
> **Members:** 20
> **Membership fee:** national fee
> **Affiliation:** American Christian Fiction Writers

CALIFORNIA

ACFW ORANGE COUNTY

www.acfwoc.com

> **Meetings:** Mimi's Cafe, 17231 E. 17th St., Tustin; second Thursday of each month, 6:30 p.m.

Contact: Susan K. Beatty, *orangecounty@acfwchapter.com*
Members: 20
Membership fee: $10/year plus national fee
Affiliation: American Christian Fiction Writers

ACFW SAN FRANCISCO BAY AREA

www.acfwsfba.wordpress.com

Meetings: Sunnyvale; third Saturday of odd months, 10 a.m.–noon
Contact: Katie Vorreiter, *acfwsfbayarea@gmail.com*
Members: 30
Membership fee: national fee
Affiliation: American Christian Fiction Writers

WORD WARRIORS

www.facebook.com/wordwarriorswriters

Meetings: 3 Crosses Church, 20600 John Dr., Castro Valley; first
  Monday of the month September–June, 7:00 p.m.
Contact: Debbie Jones Warren, 510-329-4141, *debbiencj@aim.com*
Members: 15
Membership fee: none

COLORADO

ACFW COLORADO SPRINGS

acfwcosprings.net

Meetings: Living Hope Church, 640 Manitou Blvd., Colorado Springs;
  first Saturday of the month, 10:00 a.m.–noon
Contact: Susan G. Mathis, *info@acfwcosprings.com*
Members: 45
Membership fee: $25/year plus national fee
Affiliation: American Christian Fiction Writers

SPRINGS WRITERS

springswriters.wordpress.com

Meetings: Woodmen Valley Chapel, 250 E. Woodmen Rd., Colorado
  Springs; second Tuesday of each month except July, August,
  December, 6:00–8:00 p.m.
Contact: Scoti Springfield Domeij, 719-209-9066, *springswriters@gmail.com*
Members: 350
Membership fee: none

WOLF CREEK CHRISTIAN WRITERS NETWORK
wolfcreekwriters.com
> **Meetings:** CrossRoad Christian Fellowship and online, 1044 Park Ave., Pagosa Springs; every Monday except holidays, 9:00–11:00 a.m.
> **Contact:** Betty J. Slade, 970-264-2824, *bettyslade@centurytel.net*
> **Members:** 35
> **Membership fee:** $30

WORD WEAVERS PIKES PEAK
> **Meetings:** 2650 Leoti Dr., Colorado Springs; third Saturday of each month, 9:30–11:30 a.m.
> **Contact:** Tez Brooks, 407-797-4408, *tezwrites@gmail.com*
> **Members:** 10
> **Membership fee:** $50/year
> **Affiliation:** Word Weavers

WORD WEAVERS WESTERN SLOPE
www.facebook.com/groups/568085077249557
> **Meetings:** The Rock Church, 2170 Broadway Ave., Grand Junction; fourth Saturday of each month, 9:30 a.m.–noon
> **Contact:** Templa Melnick, 970-261-7230, *templa.melnick@gmail.com*
> **Members:** 10
> **Membership fee:** $50/year
> **Affiliation:** Word Weavers

WRITERS ON THE ROCK
www.writersontherock.com
> **Meetings:** various places around Denver and Colorado Springs; monthly
> **Contact:** David Rupert, 720-237-7487, *info@writersontherock.com*
> **Members:** 170
> **Membership fee:** none

DELAWARE

CWF EAGLES NEST
www.delmarvawriters.com/meetings/word-weavers-international/
eagles-nest-christian-writers-fellowship
> **Meetings:** 18939 Shore Pointe Ct., Unit 2301 (Bldg. 23 in Woods Cove), Rehoboth; second Thursday of the month, 11:00 a.m.–1:00 p.m.

Contact: Donna Carver, 302-547-8121, *dcarver189@comcast.net*
Membership fee: none
Affiliation: Delmarva Christian Writers' Fellowship

DELMARVA CHRISTIAN WRITERS' ASSOCIATION

www.delmarvawriters.com
>   **Meetings:** Abundant Life Church, 20488 Donovan's Rd., Georgetown;
>   third Saturday of the month, 9:00 a.m.–noon
>   **Contact:** Candy Abbott, 302-856-6649, *cfa@candyabbott.com*
>   **Members:** 20
>   **Membership fee:** none

KINGDOM WRITERS FELLOWSHIP

www.delmarvawriters.com/meetings/word-weavers-international/
kingdom-writers-fellowship
>   **Meetings:** Atlanta Road Alliance Church, 22625 Atlanta Rd., Seaford;
>   second Tuesday of the month, 6:00–9:00 p.m.
>   **Contact:** Teresa Marine, 302-841-2432, *tdm4Him@yahoo.com*
>   **Members:** 10
>   **Membership fee:** none
>   **Affiliation:** Delmarva Christian Writers' Fellowship

WORD WEAVERS DELMARVA

>   **Meetings:** Laurel Wesleyan Church, 30186 Seaford Rd. #3836, Laurel;
>   fourth Saturday of each month, 9:00–11:00 a.m.
>   **Contact:** Andrew Jackson, *info@aejackson.com*
>   **Membership fee:** $50/year
>   **Affiliation:** Word Weavers

FLORIDA

ACFW CENTRAL FLORIDA

www.cfacfw.org
>   **Meetings:** online by Zoom, third Saturday of the month; in-person,
>   November/December
>   **Contact:** Dorothy Mays, *centralflorida@acfwchapter.com*
>   **Membership fee:** national fee
>   **Affiliation:** American Christian Fiction Writers

WORD WEAVERS CLAY COUNTY
www.facebook.com/groups/WordWeaversClayCounty
> **Meetings:** Panera Bread, 1510 County Rd. 220, Fleming Island;
> second Saturday of every month, 9:00–11:00 a.m.
> **Contact:** Victoria Roberts, 904-505-5693, *carpediem4christ@gmail.com*
> **Members:** 12
> **Membership fee:** $50/year
> **Affiliation:** Word Weavers

WORD WEAVERS DESTIN
> **Meetings:** Crosspoint Church, 4400 Highway 20 E, Ste. 600,
> Niceville; second Saturday of the month, 9:30 a.m.
> **Contact:** Felicia Ferguson, *fergufl@yahoo.com*
> **Members:** 20
> **Membership fee:** $50/year
> **Affiliation:** Word Weavers

WORD WEAVERS GAINESVILLE
> **Meetings:** 5003 N.W. 13th Ave., Gainesville; second Sunday of the
> month, 2:00–4:30 p.m.
> **Contact:** June F. Carlson, 352-548-4846, *jfcarlson@bellsouth.net*
> **Members:** 6
> **Membership fee:** $50/year
> **Affiliation:** Word Weavers

WORD WEAVERS JENSEN BEACH
> **Meetings:** First Baptist Jensen Beach, 1400 N.E. Jensen Beach Blvd.,
> Jensen Beach; fourth Saturday of the month, 10:00 a.m.–noon
> **Contact:** Penny Cooke, *LifeCoachPenny@yahoo.com*
> **Membership fee:** $50/year
> **Affiliation:** Word Weavers

WORD WEAVERS LAKE COUNTY
www.facebook.com/groups/1790245144535020
> **Meetings:** Leesburg Public Library, 100 E. Main, Leesburg; third
> Saturday of the month, 9:30 a.m.
> **Contact:** Michael Anderson, 678-477-3649, *andersonwriter@gmail.com*
> **Members:** 15
> **Membership fee:** $50/year
> **Affiliation:** Word Weavers

WORD WEAVERS MERRITT ISLAND

www.facebook.com/groups/1187819688313104

Meetings: Lighthouse Church, 1250 N. Banana River Dr., Merritt Island; first Saturday of the month, 10:00 a.m.–noon
Contact: Irene Wintermyer, 248-962-5528, *iwintermyer@yahoo.com*
Members: 5
Membership fee: $50/year
Affiliation: Word Weavers

WORD WEAVERS OCALA CHAPTER

Meetings: Belleview Public Library, 13145 S.E. County Highway 484, Belleview; second Friday of the month, 10:00 a.m.–12:30 p.m.
Contact: Jennifer Odom, *odomj@live.com*
Members: 10+
Membership fee: $50/year
Affiliation: Word Weavers

WORD WEAVERS ORLANDO

www.facebook.com/groups/216603998394619

Meetings: Calvary Chapel, 5015 Goddard Ave., Orlando; second Saturday of the month, 10:00 a.m.–12:30 p.m.
Contact: Julie Payne, 407-376-6581, *info@juliamargaretauthor.com*
Members: 60
Membership fee: $50/year
Affiliation: Word Weavers

WORD WEAVERS PENSACOLA

Meetings: Hillcrest Baptist Church, 800 E. Nine Mile Rd., Pensacola; second Tuesday of the month, 5:30–8:00 p.m.
Contact: Ginny Cruz, *ginnycruzwriting@gmail.com*
Members: 5
Membership fee: $50/year
Affiliation: Word Weavers

WORD WEAVERS SARASOTA

Meetings: First United Methodist Church, 104 S. Pineapple Ave., Sarasota; fourth Sunday of the month, 2:00–4:00 p.m.
Contact: Sam Wright, *drsamwright@comcast.net*
Members: 10
Membership fee: $50/year
Affiliation: Word Weavers

WORD WEAVERS SOUTH FLORIDA
www.facebook.com/groups/132148070172748
> **Meetings:** Gracepoint Church, 5590 N.E. 6th Ave., Fort Lauderdale; second Saturday of the month, 9:00 a.m.
> **Contact:** Patricia Hartman, 954-295-1103, *Patricia@PatriciaHartman. net*
> **Members:** 12
> **Membership fee:** $50/year
> **Affiliation:** Word Weavers

WORD WEAVERS TAMPA
> **Meetings:** 1901 S. Village Ave., Tampa; first Saturday of the month, 9:30 a.m.–12:30 p.m.
> **Contact:** Donna Mumma, *writemore30@gmail.com*
> **Members:** 25
> **Membership fee:** $50/year
> **Affiliation:** Word Weavers

WORD WEAVERS TREASURE COAST
www.facebook.com/groups/480150568723000
> **Meetings:** First Church of God Vero Beach, 1105 58th Ave., Vero Beach; first Saturday of each month, 9:30 a.m.–noon
> **Contact:** Del Bates, *hands2blessu_@hotmail.com*
> **Members:** 10
> **Membership fee:** $50/year
> **Affiliation:** Word Weavers

WORD WEAVERS VOLUSIA COUNTY
www.facebook.com/groups/227447203952675
> **Meetings:** Faith Church, 4700 S. Clyde Morris Blvd., Port Orange; first Monday of each month, 7:00 p.m.
> **Contact:** Renee Hanson, *rlhhh2@gmail.com*
> **Members:** 18
> **Membership fee:** $50/year
> **Affiliation:** Word Weavers

GEORGIA

ACFW NORTH GEORGIA

www.acfwnga.wix.com/home

> **Meetings:** Buford First United Methodist, 285 E. Main St. NE, Buford; fourth Tuesday of each month, 7:00 p.m.
> **Contact:** Hope Welborn, *acfwnga@gmail.com*
> **Members:** 25
> **Membership fee:** $15/year plus national fee
> **Affiliation:** American Christian Fiction Writers

ACFW NORTHWEST GEORGIA

acfwnorthwestga.blogspot.com

> **Meetings:** Zoom; second Tuesday of the month except July and December, 6:30–8:30 p.m.
> **Contact:** Cindy Stewart, *nwgeorgia@acfwchapter.com*
> **Members:** 27
> **Membership fee:** $15/year plus national fee
> **Affiliation:** American Christian Fiction Writers

CHRISTIAN AUTHORS GUILD

www.christianauthorsguild.org

> **Meetings:** Sojourn Woodstock, 8816 Main St., Woodstock; first Monday of the month, 7:00 p.m.
> **Contact:** Deborah Crawford, *deborahrdcrawford@gmail.com*
> **Members:** 30
> **Membership fee:** $30/year

WORD WEAVERS BROOKHAVEN

www.facebook.com/groups/200656040663612

> **Meetings:** call for location in Brookhaven; second Saturday each month, 10:00 a.m.–12:30 p.m.
> **Contact:** Debra Bryant, *dbryant2941@gmail.com*
> **Members:** 8
> **Membership fee:** $50/year
> **Affiliation:** Word Weavers

WORD WEAVERS COLUMBUS, GA

www.facebook.com/groups/541016626433688

> **Meetings:** Cornerstone Church of God, 7701 Lloyd Rd., Columbus;

third Monday of every month, 6:30 p.m.
Contact: Terri Miller, *wordweaverscolumbus@gmail.com*
Members: 9
Membership fee: $50/year
Affiliation: Word Weavers

WORD WEAVERS CONYERS
www.facebook.com/groups/638509006538934

Meetings: Bethel Christian Church, 1930 Bethel Rd. NE, Conyers; second Saturday of each month, 10:00 a.m.–noon
Contact: Leigh DeLozier, *LeighDeLozier@Bellsouth.net*
Members: 6
Membership fee: $50/year
Affiliation: Word Weavers

WORD WEAVERS GREATER ATLANTA

Meetings: 4541 Vendome Pl. NE, Roswell; first Saturday of the month, 9:30 a.m.–noon
Contact: Barbara Fox, *barb@barbjfox.com*
Membership fee: $50/year
Affiliation: Word Weavers

WORD WEAVERS MACON-BIBB
www.facebook.com/groups/173188826644758

Meetings: Central City Church, 621 Foster Rd., Macon; second Sunday of every month, 3:00–5:30 p.m.
Contact: Robin Dance, *RobinDance.me@gmail.com*
Members: 45
Membership fee: $50/year
Affiliation: Word Weavers

WORD WEAVERS VALDOSTA

Meetings: Corinth Baptist Church, 4089 Corinth Church Rd., Lake Park; third Saturday of the month, 2:00–4:00 p.m.
Contact: Christy Adams, *ChristyAdams008@gmail.com*
Membership fee: $50/year
Affiliation: Word Weavers

WORD WEAVERS WOODSTOCK

Meetings: Prayer & Praise Christian Fellowship, 6409 Bells Ferry Rd., Woodstock; third Monday of the month, 6:30–9:00 p.m.

Contact: Frieda Dixon, *friedas@bellsouth.net*
Members: 15
Membership fee: $50/year
Affiliation: Word Weavers

ILLINOIS

ACFW CHICAGO
www.facebook.com/acfwchicago
Meetings: email for location in Schaumburg; second Friday of every month, 6:30–8:30 p.m.
Contact: Candace Yamnitz, *chicago@acfwchapter.com*
Members: 20
Membership fee: national fee
Affiliation: American Christian Fiction Writers

WORD WEAVERS AURORA
Meetings: Colonial Cafe, 1961 W. Galena Blvd., Aurora; second Saturday of the month, 1:00–3:00 p.m.
Contact: JoDee Starrick, *jodee.starrick@gmail.com*
Members: 10
Membership fee: $50/year
Affiliation: Word Weavers

WORD WEAVERS LAND OF LINCOLN
Meetings: email for location in Pekin; second Saturday of every month, 10:00 a.m.–noon
Contact: Robin McClallen, *ramtwm@msn.com*
Members: 10
Membership fee: $50/year
Affiliation: Word Weavers

WORD WEAVERS ON THE BORDER
Meetings: email for location; fourth Thursday of the month, 7:00–8:30 p.m.
Contact: Jim Pas, *drallih@gmail.com*
Members: 10
Membership fee: $50/year
Affiliation: Word Weavers

INDIANA

ACFW INDIANA
www.hoosierink.blogspot.com
> **Meetings:** various places in Indiana and Zoom; four to six times per year
> **Contact:** Linda Samaritoni, 317-691-4115, *acfwindianachapter@gmail.com*
> **Members:** 40
> **Membership fee:** $15/year plus national fee
> **Affiliation:** American Christian Fiction Writers

BLUFFTON CHRISTIAN WRITING CLUB
www.facebook.com/groups/137239503139200
> **Meetings:** Wells County Public Library, 200 W. Washington St.,
>   Bluffton; third Monday of each month, 6:00 p.m.
> **Contact:** Beth Steury, *Mbsteury@embarqmail.com*
> **Members:** 10
> **Membership fee:** none

HEARTLAND CHRISTIAN WRITERS
www.heartlandchristianwriters.com
> **Meetings:** Mount Pleasant Christian Church, 381 N. Bluff Rd.,
>   Greenwood; third Monday of every month, 9:30 a.m. and 6:30 p.m.
> **Contact:** John Matthew Walker, *admin@heartlandchristianwriters.com*
> **Members:** 10
> **Membership fee:** none

IOWA

WORD WEAVERS DES MOINES
www.facebook.com/groups/495808943830132
> **Meetings:** The Church at Union Park, 821 Arthur Ave., Des Moines;
>   last Monday of each month, 6:30–8:00 p.m.
> **Contact:** Susan R. Lawrence, 515-238-6675, *srlauthor@mchsi.com*
> **Members:** 12
> **Membership fee:** $50/year
> **Affiliation:** Word Weavers

KANSAS

HEART OF AMERICA CHRISTIAN WRITERS NETWORK

www.hacwn.org

> **Meetings:** Colonial Presbyterian Church (Quivira Campus), 12501 W. 137th St., Overland Park; second Thursday of every month, 7:00 p.m.
> **Contact:** Jeanette Littleton, 816-459-8016, *HACWN@earthlink.net*
> **Members:** 150
> **Membership fee:** $3/meeting, members; $5/meeting, nonmembers

KENTUCKY

ACFW LOUISVILLE

acfwlouisville.com

> **Meetings:** Southeast Christian Church, room WC 448, 920 Blankenbaker Pkwy., Louisville; fourth Saturday of the month, 10:30 a.m.–12:30 p.m.
> **Contact:** Karen Richardson
> **Members:** 30
> **Membership fee:** national fee
> **Affiliation:** American Christian Fiction Writers

WORD WEAVERS BOONE COUNTY

www.facebook.com/groups/349709925923088

> **Meetings:** email for location in Union; first Saturday of every month, 10:30 a.m.–12:30 p.m.
> **Contact:** Karisa Moore, 859-380-3449, *karisam660@gmail.com*
> **Members:** 10
> **Membership fee:** $50/year
> **Affiliation:** Word Weavers

LOUISIANA

ACFW LOUISIANA

www.facebook.com/pages/ACFW-Louisiana/1525862364304046

> **Meetings:** email for location in Bossier City; last Saturday of each month

Contact: Carole Lehr Johnson, *louisiana@acfwchapter.com*
Membership fee: national fee
Affiliation: American Christian Fiction Writers

SOUTHERN CHRISTIAN WRITERS

scwguild.com
Meetings: Gospel Bookstore, 91 Westbank Expressway, Gretna; third
Saturday of each month, 10:30 a.m.
Contact: Teena Myers, *teena@scwguild.com*
Members: 20
Membership fee: $50/year

MARYLAND

MOUNTAIN CHRISTIAN WRITER'S GROUP

Meetings: New Life Center, room 26, 1824 Mountain Rd., Bel Air;
Sundays, 2:30–4:30 p.m.
Contact: Christy Struben, 410-259-3673, *cstruben711@gmail.com*
Members: 20–30
Membership fee: none

MICHIGAN

ACFW GREAT LAKES

greatlakeschapter.blogspot.com
Meetings: first Saturday of various months
Contact: Greta Picklesimer, *greatlakes@acfwchapter.com*
Membership fee: $10/year plus national fee
Affiliation: American Christian Fiction Writers

WORD WEAVERS MIDDLE OF THE MITTEN

Meetings: Rusty Nail, 10002 E. Carson City Rd., Carson City; fourth
Tuesday of each month, 6:30–8:30 p.m.
Contact: Mindy Buffman, 989-261-6024, *mittenwriters@gmail.com*
Membership fee: $50/year
Affiliation: Word Weavers

WORD WEAVERS WEST MICHIGAN—HOLLAND ZEELAND

Meetings: City on a Hill, 100 Pine St., Zeeland; first and third Tuesdays

of the month, 12:00–2:00 p.m.
Contact: Kathy Bruins, *Kbruins77@gmail.com*
Members: 10
Membership fee: $50/year
Affiliation: Word Weavers

WORD WEAVERS WEST MICHIGAN—MUSKEGON/ NORTON SHORES

Meetings: Hendrick Meijer Library, Muskegon Community College, 221 S. Quarterline Rd., Muskegon; first and third Tuesdays, 6:00– 8:00 p.m.
Contact: Kathy Bruins, *Kbruins77@gmail.com*
Members: 10
Membership fee: $50/year
Affiliation: Word Weavers

WORD WEAVERS WEST MICHIGAN—NORTH GRAND RAPIDS

Meetings: Russ' Restaurant, 3531 Alpine Ave. NW, Walker; first and third Tuesdays of the month, 6:00–8:00 p.m.
Contact: Kathy Bruins, *Kbruins77@gmail.com*
Members: 12
Membership fee: $50/year
Affiliation: Word Weavers

MINNESOTA

ACFW MINNESOTA N.I.C.E.

www.acfwmnnice.com

Meetings: Life Point Church, 2220 Edgerton St., Maplewood; fourth Sunday of the month, 6:00–8:00 p.m.
Contact: Michelle Aleckson, *minnesota@acfwchapter.com*
Members: 25
Membership fee: $25/year plus national fee
Affiliation: American Christian Fiction Writers

MINNESOTA CHRISTIAN WRITERS GUILD

www.mnchristianwriters.com

Meetings: Oak Knoll Lutheran Church, 600 Hopkins Crossroad,

Minnetonka; second Monday of the month, September–May, 7:00–8:30 p.m.
Contact: Jason Sisam, *info@mnchristianwriters.com*
Members: 50
Membership fee: $70/year

MISSISSIPPI

BYHALIA CHRISTIAN WRITERS
www.facebook.com/groups/129990696510
> **Meetings:** First United Methodist Church, 2511 Church St., Byhalia; first Saturday of the month, 9:00–11:00 a.m.
> **Contact:** Beth Gooch, 901-277-5525, *gooch.beth@gmail.com*
> **Members:** 20
> **Membership fee:** none
> **Affiliation:** American Christian Writers

MISSOURI

ACFW MOZARKS
www.facebook.com/MozArksACFW
> **Meetings:** The Library Center, 4653 S. Campbell Ave., Springfield; third Saturday of the month, 2:00 p.m.
> **Contact:** Erin Miffin, *mozarks@acfwchapter.com*
> **Members:** 10
> **Membership fee:** national fee
> **Affiliation:** American Christian Fiction Writers

OZARKS CHAPTER OF AMERICAN CHRISTIAN WRITERS
www.OzarksACW.org
> **Meetings:** University Heights Baptist Church, 1010 S. National, Springfield; second Saturday, September–May, 10:00 a.m.–noon
> **Contact:** Dr. Jeanetta Chrystie, 417-832-8409, *OzarksACW@yahoo.com*
> **Members:** 50
> **Membership fee:** $20/year; family, $30; newsletter only, $10
> **Affiliation:** American Christian Writers

NEBRASKA

MY THOUGHTS EXACTLY WRITING WORKSHOP

mythoughtsexactlywriters.wordpress.com

Meetings: Keene Memorial Library, 1030 N. Broad St., Fremont; third
Monday of the month, 6:30–8:00 p.m.
Contact: Cheryl, *mythoughtse@gmail.com*
Membership fee: none

NEW JERSEY

ACFW NY/NJ

www.facebook.com/groups/955365637934907

Meetings: online; first Saturday of each month (October-June), 10
a.m.–noon; critique groups at other times
Contact: Olivia Ciotta, *nynj@acfwchapter.com*
Members: 50
Membership fee: $20/year plus national fee

NORTH JERSEY CHRISTIAN WRITERS GROUP

www.njcwg.blogspot.com

Meetings: Cornerstone Christian Church (in the Barn, second building
on the right), 495 Wyckoff Ave., Wyckoff; first Saturday of the
month, 10:00 a.m.–noon
Contact: Barbara Higby, 551-804-1014, *bhigby9323@gmail.com*
Members: 12
Membership fee: none

NEW YORK

SOUTHERN TIER CHRISTIAN WRITERS

Meetings: Olean First Baptist Church, 133 S. Union St., Olean;
monthly
Contact: Deb Wuethrich, 716-379-8702, *deborahmarcein@gmail.com*
Members: 8
Membership fee: none
Affiliation: American Christian Writers

WORD WEAVERS NEW HAVEN

Meetings: 245 Sundown Rd., Fulton; fourth Saturday of the month, 10:00 a.m.–noon
Contact: Mary Curcio, *mathmary56@gmail.com*
Membership fee: $50/year
Affiliation: Word Weavers

WORD WEAVERS WESTERN NEW YORK

Meetings: 2458 Rush Mendon Rd., Honeoye Falls; third Thursday of the month, 5:30 p.m.
Contact: Karen Rode, 585-571-7124, *karen.a.rode@gmail.com*
Members: 5
Membership fee: $50/year
Affiliation: Word Weavers

NORTH CAROLINA

ACFW NORTH CAROLINA

www.facebook.com/groups/336801510020700

Meetings: Raleigh; email contact person
Contact: Kyle Beale, *northcarolina@acfwchapter.com*
Membership fee: national fee
Affiliation: American Christian Fiction Writers

WORD WEAVERS CHARLOTTE

Meetings: email for location; first Saturday of the month, 10:00 a.m.–noon
Contact: Kim Dent, *cltwordweavers@yahoo.com*
Members: 15
Membership fee: $50/year
Affiliation: Word Weavers

WORD WEAVERS HICKORY-NEWTON

www.facebook.com/groups/2328785447421711

Meetings: Vertical Life Church, 111 W. 8th St., Newton; first Saturday of each month, 9:30–11:30 a.m.
Contact: Shannon Ratcliffe, *Shannonparkerratcliffe@gmail.com*
Members: 9
Membership fee: $50/year
Affiliation: Word Weavers

WORD WEAVERS PIEDMONT TRIAD

Meetings: Emmaus Road Farm, 5925 Davis Mill Rd, Greensboro; third
   Saturday of the month, 9:30 a.m.
Contact: Renee Leonard Kennedy, 336-491-2040,
   Reneeleonardkennedy@gmail.com
Members: 10
Membership fee: $50/year
Affiliation: Word Weavers

WORD WEAVERS WILMINGTON

Meetings: Calvary Baptist Church, 423 23rd St., Wilmington; second
   Monday of the month, 6:30–8:30 p.m.
Contact: Laurel Senick, *lsenick6@gmail.com*
Membership fee: $50/year
Affiliation: Word Weavers

WORD WEAVERS WINSTON-SALEM

Meetings: 1038 Pine Place Dr., Germanton; second Saturday of each
   month, 9:30–11:30 a.m.
Contact: Diane Virginia Cunio, *Diane@dianevirginia.com*
Membership fee: $50/year
Affiliation: Word Weavers

NORTH AND SOUTH DAKOTA

ACFW DAKOTAS
www.facebook.com/groups/ACFWDakotas

Meetings: varies by region
Contact: Jan Drexler, *Dakotas@acfwchapter.com*
Members: 25
Membership fee: national fee
Affiliation: American Christian Fiction Writers

OHIO

ACFW OHIO
www.facebook.com/groups/220166801456380

Meetings: Etna United Methodist Church, 500 Pike St., Etna; first
   Saturday of the month

Contact: Betty Boswell, *ohio@acfwchapter.com*
Members: 65
Membership fee: national fee
Affiliation: American Christian Fiction Writers

COLUMBUS CHRISTIAN WRITERS ASSOCIATION

www.facebook.com/profile.php?id=100057586834554

Meetings: Zoom; second Sunday of each month, 3:00–5:00 p.m.
Contact: Mina R. Raulston, 614-507-7893, *m_raulston@hotmail.com*
Members: 5
Membership fee: none
Affiliation: American Christian Writers

DAYTON CHRISTIAN SCRIBES

www.facebook.com/DaytonChristianScribes

Meetings: Kettering Seventh-Day Adventist Church, 3939 Stonebridge
Rd., Kettering; second Thursday of the month, 7:00–9:00 p.m.
Contact: Kim D. Villalva, 512-680-8729, *Kdanisk@yahoo.com*
Members: 20
Membership fee: $15/year

DAYTON CHRISTIAN WRITERS GUILD

www.facebook.com/ChristianAuthorToles

Meetings: Corinthian Baptist Church, 700 S. James McGhee Blvd.,
Dayton; second Saturday of the month, 2:00 p.m.
Contact: Tina Tole, *tinatoles@yahoo.com*
Membership fee: none

MIDDLETOWN AREA CHRISTIAN WRITERS (M.A.C. WRITERS)

middletownwriters.blogspot.com

Meetings: Healing Word Assembly of God, 5303 S. Dixie Hwy.,
Franklin; second Tuesday of each month, 7:00–8:30 p.m.
Contact: Donna J. Shepherd, 513-373-5671, *donna.shepherd@gmail.com*
Members: 25
Membership fee: $30/year or $5/meeting

WORD WEAVERS NORTHEAST OHIO

Meetings: Good Shepherd Villa, 726 Center St., Ashland; first
Thursday of each month, 6:30–8:30 p.m.
Contact: Cherie Martin, *kitties395@yahoo.com*

Members: 10
Membership fee: $50/year
Affiliation: Word Weavers

OKLAHOMA

ACFW OKLAHOMA CITY

www.okchristianfictionwriters.com
> **Meetings:** New Hope Church of Christ, 700 W. 2nd St., Edmond; third
> Saturday of each month, 1:00–3:00 p.m.
> **Contact:** Chris Tarpley, *OCFWchapter@gmail.com*
> **Members:** 35
> **Membership fee:** $20/year plus national fee
> **Affiliation:** American Christian Fiction Writers

FELLOWSHIP OF CHRISTIAN WRITERS

fellowshipofchristianwriters.org
> **Meetings:** Kirk of the Hills Presbyterian Church and Zoom, 4102 E.
> 61st St., Tulsa; second Tuesday of each month, 6:30–8:00 p.m.
> **Contact:** Mike Moguin, 918-704-1244, *mwmog68@gmail.com*
> **Members:** 40
> **Membership fee:** $35

WORDWRIGHTS (OK)

www.wordwrights-ok.com
> **Meetings:** The Last Drop Coffee Shop, 5425 N. Lincoln Blvd.,
> Oklahoma City; second Saturday of the month, 10:00 a.m.
> **Contact:** *info@wordwrightsok.com*
> **Members:** 30
> **Membership fee:** $20/year

OREGON

OREGON CHRISTIAN WRITERS

www.oregonchristianwriters.org
> **Meetings:** Portland metro area; two or three all-day Saturday
> conferences, summer coaching conference
> **Contact:** president, 503-393-3356, *president@oregonchristianwriters.com*
> **Membership fee:** $60/year; couples, $75; students and seniors (62+), $35

WORDWRIGHTS (OR)

Meetings: Gresham/east Multnomah County; two times a month,
Thursday afternoons
Contact: Susan Thogerson Maas, 503-663-7834, *maas.susan@gmail.com*
Members: 5
Membership fee: none
Affiliation: Oregon Christian Writers

PENNSYLVANIA

CHRISTIAN WRITERS GUILD

Meetings: Perkin's Restaurant, 505 Galleria Dr., Johnstown; last
Tuesday of each month, 1:00 p.m.
Contact: Betty Rosian, 814-255-4351, *wordsforall@hotmail.com*
Members: 12
Membership fee: $1/meeting

LANCASTER CHRISTIAN WRITERS

lancasterchristianwriters.com

Contact: JP Robinson, 717-341-8457, *lancasterwrites@gmail.com*
Members: 450
Membership fee: none

WRITE HIS ANSWER CRITIQUE GROUPS

writehisanswer.com/critiquegroups

Meetings: online; every other Thursday, 10:30 a.m.–noon or
alternating Thursdays, 8:30–10:00 p.m.
Contact: Marlene Bagnull, 484-991-8581, *mbagnull@aol.com*
Members: 15 each group
Membership fee: none

SOUTH CAROLINA

ACFW SOUTH CAROLINA LOWCOUNTRY

www.facebook.com/groups/ACFWSCLowCountry

Meetings: Seacoast Church, 750 Long Point Rd., Mt. Pleasant; fourth
Saturday of each month, 10:00 a.m.–noon
Contact: Laurie Larsen, 309-212-4157, *sclowcountry@acfwchapter.com*

Members: 18
Membership fee: national fee
Affiliation: American Christian Fiction Writers

ACFW UPSTATE SOUTH CAROLINA
acfwupstatesc.wordpress.com

Meetings: Cross Roads Baptist Church, 705 Anderson Ridge Rd., Greer; fourth Saturday of the month, 10:00 a.m.–1:00 p.m.
Contact: Christine Boatwright, *upstatesc@acfwchapter.com*
Membership fee: national fee
Affiliation: American Christian Fiction Writers

WORD WEAVERS AIKEN
www.AikenWordWeavers.com

Meetings: Trinity United Methodist Church, 2724 Whiskey Rd., Aiken; second Tuesday of the month, 7:00–9:00 p.m.
Contact: Lee-Allen Russ, 864-608-5530, *AikenWordWeavers@gmail.com*
Members: 5
Membership fee: $50/year
Affiliation: Word Weavers

WORD WEAVERS CHARLESTON
www.facebook.com/groups/2112701302307131

Meetings: email for location; third Saturday of the month, 10:00 a.m.–noon
Contact: Timothy Griggs, 843-224-3159, *timothygriggs@gmail.com*
Members: 15
Membership fee: $50/year
Affiliation: Word Weavers

WORD WEAVERS LEXINGTON, SC
LexingtonWordWeavers.com

Meetings: Trinity Baptist Church, 2003 Charleston Hwy., Cayce; second Monday of each month, 6:45–9:00 p.m.
Contact: Jean Wilund, *Jwilund@icloud.com*
Members: 40
Membership fee: $50/year
Affiliation: Word Weavers

WORD WEAVERS UPSTATE SC

Meetings: Renovation Church, 611 Richardson St., Simpsonville; second Thursday of each month, 9:30 a.m.–noon
Contact: Jason Thompson, 864-881-7801, *Jason@therenovation.church*
Members: 15
Membership fee: $50/year
Affiliation: Word Weavers

WRITING 4 HIM

Meetings: First Baptist Church, 250 E. Main St., Spartanburg; second Thursday of the month, 9:45 a.m.
Contact: Linda Gilden, *linda@lindagilden.com*
Members: 50
Membership fee: none

TENNESSEE

ACFW KNOXVILLE

www.facebook.com/groups/341397182924371

Meetings: Parkway Baptist Church, 401 S. Peters Rd., Knoxville; second Tuesday of the month
Contact: Jenny Lynn Keller, *knoxville@acfwchapter.com*
Members: 20
Membership fee: national fee
Affiliation: American Christian Fiction Writers

ACFW MEMPHIS

facebook.com/groups/699561666820044

Meetings: M.R. Davis Library, 8554 Northwest Dr., Southaven; third Saturday of the month except December, 10:15 a.m.–noon
Contact: Jessica Patch, *jrpatch@yahoo.com*
Members: 20
Membership fee: $20/year plus national fee
Affiliation: American Christian Fiction Writers

ACFW MID-TENNESSEE

acfwmidtn.org

Meetings: email for location in Nashville; first Saturday of the month, 10:00 a.m.–noon
Contact: Suzie Waltner, *midtennessee@acfwchapter.com*

Members: 25
Membership fee: $24/year plus national fee
Affiliation: American Christian Fiction Writers

WORD WEAVERS KNOXVILLE
www.facebook.com/groups/336414403544597
> **Meetings:** Rio Revolution Church, 3419 E. Lamar Alexander Pkwy.,
> Maryville; third Saturday of the month, 9:30 a.m.– noon
> **Contact:** Beth Boring, 865-679-3370, *boringb@bellsouth.net*
> **Members:** 12
> **Membership fee:** $50/year
> **Affiliation:** Word Weavers

WORD WEAVERS NASHVILLE
> **Meetings:** Goodletsville Public Library, 205 Rivergate Pkwy.,
> Goodlettsville; second Saturday of each month, 10:00 a.m.–noon
> **Contact:** Kim Aulich, *KAAfterGodsOwnHeart@gmail.com*
> **Members:** 10
> **Membership fee:** $50/year
> **Affiliation:** Word Weavers

WORD WEAVERS SOUTH MIDDLE TENNESSEE
www.facebook.com/groups/323376445183667
> **Meetings:** Edgemont Baptist Church, 150 Fairfield Pike, Shelbyville;
> third Saturday of the month, 10:00 a.m.
> **Contact:** Amanda West, 931-808-8054, *awestwrites@outlook.com*
> **Members:** 8
> **Membership fee:** $50/year
> **Affiliation:** Word Weavers

TEXAS

ACFW ALAMO CITY
www.facebook.com/groups/243114107289
> **Meetings:** email for location in San Antonio; second Saturday of the
> month, 10 a.m. –noon
> **Contact:** Allison Pittman, *alamocity@acfwchapter.com*
> **Members:** 15
> **Membership fee:** national fee
> **Affiliation:** American Christian Fiction Writers

ACFW DFW

acfwdfwtx.com

> **Meetings:** Dallas/Fort Worth; second Saturday of every month, 10:00 a.m.
> **Contact:** Paula Peckham, *acfwdfw@gmail.com*
> **Members:** 40
> **Membership fee:** national fee
> **Affiliation:** American Christian Fiction Writers

ACFW THE WOODLANDS

wotsacfw.blogspot.com

> **Meetings:** email for location in The Woodlands; third or fourth Saturday of each month
> **Contact:** Linda Kozar, *wotsacfw@gmail.com*
> **Members:** 40
> **Membership fee:** $20/year plus national fee
> **Affiliation:** American Christian Fiction Writers

CHRISTIAN WRITERS WORKSHOP

www.facebook.com/groups/374145049720167

> **Meetings:** First Woodway Baptist Church, 101 Ritchie Rd., Woodway; Sundays, 5:30–7:00 p.m., September 11–October 30
> **Contact:** Linda Hammond, 254-498-4619, *lyhammond86@gmail.com*
> **Members:** 50
> **Membership fee:** none

CROSS REFERENCE WRITERS

sites.google.com/site/crossreferencewriters

> **Meetings:** email for location; first Thursday of the month, 7:00–8:30 p.m.
> **Contact:** Tammy Hensel, 979-204-0674, *CrossRefWriters@yahoo.com*
> **Members:** 10
> **Membership fee:** none

INSPIRATIONAL WRITERS ALIVE! CENTRAL HOUSTON

www.centralhoustoniwa.com

> **Meetings:** Houston's First Baptist Church, 7474 Katy Fwy., Houston; second Thursday of most months, 7:00 p.m.
> **Contact:** Diana Battista, *centralhoustoniwaweb@gmail.com*
> **Members:** 15
> **Membership fee:** none

ROARING WRITERS

roaringwriters.org

Meetings: various locations in Dallas/Fort Worth area; check the website
Contact: Jan Johnson
Members: 250
Membership fee: none

ROCKWALL CHRISTIAN WRITERS GROUP

www.facebook.com/groups/rockwallchristianwritersgroup

Meetings: Lake Pointe Church, room 212, 701 E. Interstate 30, Rockwall; second Wednesday of each month except December, 7:00–9:30 p.m.
Contact: Leslie Wilson, 214-505-5336, *leslieporterwilson@gmail.com*
Members: 15–20 in person, 300 on Facebook page
Membership fee: none

VIRGINIA

ACFW VIRGINIA

acfwvirginia.com

Meetings: online and Leesburg and Virginia Beach; first Saturday of each month
Contact: Kelly Goshorn, *acfwvirginia@gmail.com*
Membership fee: $15/year plus national fee
Affiliation: American Christian Fiction Writers

CAPITAL CHRISTIAN WRITERS FELLOWSHIP

ccwritersfellowship.org

Meetings: Centreville Presbyterian Church and virtual, 15450 Lee Hwy., Centreville; quarterly in-person meetings Saturday morning; off-months virtual, Wednesdays, 8:00 p.m.
Contact: Sarah Hamaker, *president@ccwritersfellowship.org*
Members: 60
Membership fee: $40

WORD WEAVERS HAMPTON ROADS

www.facebook.com/groups/244135990554237

Meetings: Great Bridge Baptist Church, 604 S. Battlefield Blvd.,

Chesapeake; first Tuesday of every month, 6:30-8:30 p.m.
Contact: Amy L. Harden, 757-699-1118, *amylharden@gmail.com*
Members: 12+
Membership fee: $50/year
Affiliation: Word Weavers

WORD WEAVERS RICHMOND

Meetings: West End Assembly of God, South Hall (come in through the south entrance), 401 N. Parham Rd., Henrico; first Monday of each month, 6:45-9:00 p.m.
Contact: Sue Schlesman, *sueschlesman@gmail.com*
Members: 20
Membership fee: $50/year
Affiliation: Word Weavers

WORD WEAVERS WOODBRIDGE

Meetings: Chinn Library Community Room, 13065 Chinn Park Dr., Woodbridge; last Saturday of the month, 10:00 a.m.–noon
Contact: Lauren Craft, *laurenchristianauthor@gmail.com*
Membership fee: $50/year
Affiliation: Word Weavers

WASHINGTON

VANCOUVER CHRISTIAN WRITERS

Meetings: email for address in Vancouver; first Monday of the month, 9:00 a.m.
Contact: Jon Drury, 510-909-0848, *jondrury2@yahoo.com*
Members: 8–10
Membership fee: none
Affiliation: Oregon Christian Writers

WISCONSIN

ACFW WI SOUTHEAST

www.facebook.com/wiseacfw

Meetings: email for location; first Thursday of the month, 6:30–8:30 p.m.
Contact: Laura DeNooyer Moore, *wisconsinSE@acfwchapter.com*
Members: 25

Membership fee: $25/year plus national fee
Affiliation: American Christian Fiction Writers

PENS OF PRAISE CHRISTIAN WRITERS

www.susanmarlene.com/writers–pens

Meetings: Manitowoc Public Library and online, 707 Quay St., Manitowoc; third Tuesday of each month except December and holidays, 6:00–7:30 p.m.
Contact: Susan Marlene Kinney, 920-242-3631, *susanmarlenewrites@gmail.com*
Members: 10
Membership fee: none

WORD AND PEN CHRISTIAN WRITERS

wordandpenchristianwriters.com

Meetings: St. Thomas Episcopal Church, 226 Washington St., Menasha; second Monday each month April–November, 7:00–9:00 p.m.; Zoom January–March
Contact: Chris Stratton, 920-739-0752, *gcefsi@new.rr.com*
Members: 15
Membership fee: $10/year

AUSTRALIA AND NEW ZEALAND

ACFW BEYOND THE BORDERS

www.facebook.com/groups/ACFWBeyondtheBorders

Meetings: online
Contact: Iola Goulton, *BeyondBorders@acfwchapter.com*
Members: 100
Membership fee: national fee
Affiliation: American Christian Fiction Writers

AUSTRALASIAN CHRISTIAN WRITERS

australasianchristianwriters.com

Services: Online group of writers in Australia, New Zealand, and region. Weekly Tuesday book chats.
Members: 700
Membership fee: none

CHRISTIAN WRITERS DOWNUNDER

christianwritersdownunder.blogspot.com

Meetings: Facebook
Contact: Jeanette O'Hagan, *CWDBloggers@gmail.com*
Members: 1,300
Affiliation: Omega Writers

NEW ZEALAND CHRISTIAN WRITERS

www.nzchristianwriters.org

Meetings: various places; see website
Contact: Justin St. Vincent, *president@nzchristianwriters.org*
Members: 210+
Membership fee: none

OMEGA WRITERS

www.omegawriters.org

Contact: *membership@omegawriters.org*
Services: Australian group with local and online chapters across
the country and New Zealand. See the website for locations.
Also sponsors an annual conference and the CALEB Award to
recognize the best in Australasian Christian writing, published and
unpublished.
Members: 125
Membership fee: $60/year

CANADA

INSCRIBE CHRISTIAN WRITERS' FELLOWSHIP

inscribe.org

Contact: *president@inscribe.org*
Services: Canadian group with chapters across the country. See the
website for locations. Also sponsors workshops, a fall conference,
and contests and produces the quarterly magazine *FellowScript* that
is included with membership.
Members: 160
Membership fee: varies, see website

MANITOBA CHRISTIAN WRITERS ASSOCIATION

Meetings: Bleak House, 1637 Main St., Winnipeg; first Saturday of

the month except July and August, 1:00 p.m.
Contact: Frieda Martens, 204-770-8023, *friedamartens1910@gmail.com*
Members: 23
Membership fee: $30
Affiliation: InScribe Christian Writers' Fellowship

THE WORD GUILD
www.thewordguild.com

Contact: Box 77001, Markham ON L3P 0C8, Canada; 800-969-9010, *info@thewordguild.com*
Services: Regional chapters across Canada. Sponsors contests and awards for Canadian Christian writers and the Write! Canada conference.
Members: 325
Membership fee: $65/year; professional, $105; student, $30

SOUTH SUDAN

WORD WEAVERS CENTRAL EQUATORIA SOUTH SUDAN
Meetings: ACROSS Compound, Buluk off Ministries Rd., Juba; third Saturday of the month, 2:00–4:00 p.m.
Contact: Teresa Janzen, WhatsApp: +6162325480, *teresajanzen@gmail.com*
Membership fee: $50/year
Affiliation: Word Weavers

20

EDITORIAL SERVICES

Entries in this chapter are for information only, not an endorsement of editing skills. Before hiring a freelance editor, ask for references if they are not posted on the website; and contact two or three to help determine if this editor is a good fit for you. You may also want to pay for an edit of a few pages or one chapter before hiring someone to edit your complete manuscript.

A LITTLE RED INK | BETHANY KACZMAREK
115 1st St., Somerset, WI 54025 | 715-907-5144
contact@bethanykaczmarek.com | *www.bethanykaczmarek.com/little-red-ink2*
> **Contact:** website
> **Services:** copyediting, manuscript evaluation, substantive/ developmental editing
> **Types of manuscripts:** adult, middle grade, novels, teen/YA
> **Charges:** hourly rate
> **Credentials/experience:** "An ACFW Editor of the Year finalist (2015), Bethany enjoys working with both traditional and indie authors. Several of her clients are award-winning and best-selling authors, though she does work with aspiring authors as well. She has edited speculative fiction for Enclave Fiction and Gilead, and general fiction for Sunrise Publishing."

A LITTLE RED INK | ERYNN NEWMAN
1 Fairway One, Taylors, SC 29687 | 919-229-1357
ErynnNewman@gmail.com | *www.ALittleRedInk.com*
> **Contact:** email, website
> **Services:** copyediting, proofreading, substantive/developmental editing
> **Types of manuscripts:** adult, novels, teen/YA
> **Charges:** hourly rate

Credentials/experience: "I specialize in helping authors find their unique voice, deepening point of view, and bringing characters to life. I'm an unapologetic grammar nerd, but I don't take anything (except the Oxford Comma) too seriously. I have edited over 100 published novels including several *NYT* and *USA Today* best sellers, have authored two award-winning novels of my own, and won the National Readers' Choice Award and the Rita Award for editing."

A WAY WITH WORDS WRITING AND EDITORIAL SERVICES | RENEE GRAY-WILBURN
waywords@earthlink.net | *awaywithwordswriting.wordpress.com*

Contact: email

Services: back-cover copy, coauthoring, copyediting, discussion questions for books, ghostwriting, proofreading, résumés, substantive/developmental editing, transcription, write children's manuscripts

Types of manuscripts: adult, articles, Bible studies, curriculum, devotionals, easy readers, gift books, middle grade, nonfiction books, novels, picture books, query letters, short stories, technical material, teen/YA

Charges: custom, hourly rate

Credentials/experience: "More than twenty years of freelance writing and editing. Wrote five children's books for Capstone Press; extensive curriculum writing for David C. Cook and Group Publishing; wrote children's articles/activities and parenting articles for Focus on the Family; developed online study guides for Wallbuilders; extensive copyediting and proofreading for NavPress (including the Remix Message Bible), David C. Cook, WaterBrook, and major international ministries, as well as numerous independent authors. Coauthored nonfiction book and wrote dozens of articles and devotionals. Writing and editing experience for both fiction and nonfiction manuscripts in children, YA, and adult markets."

A WORD IN SEASON | SAMANTHA HANNI
3400 Windsor Ter., Oklahoma City, OK 73122 | 405-642-7855
samantha.hanni@mrshanni.com | *mrshanni.com/work-with-me*

Contact: email, website

Services: copyediting, manuscript evaluation, substantive/developmental editing

Types of manuscripts: adult, articles, Bible studies, curriculum, devotionals, nonfiction books, teen/YA

Charges: flat fee, word rate

Credentials/experience: "I am passionate about wielding words for good, whether it be writing my own or refining the words of others. For the past decade, I've had the privilege of writing and editing, helping individuals and businesses share the content that's most important to them. As a freelance writer and editor, I have self-published four books for Christian teens and edited dozens of manuscripts for Christian authors, many of them debut authors. I have provided copy editing services for two Christian publishing houses and for The Odyssey Online. Specialty: non-fiction."

AB WRITING SERVICES, LLC | ANN BYLE

annbyle@gmail.com | *www.annbylewriter.com*

Contact: email

Services: articles, back-cover copy, consulting, copyediting, discussion questions for books, ghostwriting, manuscript evaluation, press releases

Types of manuscripts: adult, articles, book proposals, devotionals, nonfiction books, novels, query letters

Charges: hourly rate

Credentials/experience: "Ann's experience includes years as a newspaper copy editor, freelance journalist for newspapers and magazines including *Publishers Weekly*, writing her own books including *Christian Publishing 101*, and co- and ghost-writing book projects."

ABOVE THE PAGES EDITORIAL SERVICES | PAM LAGORMARSINO

1123 Cherry Tree Rd., Burkesville, KY 42717 | 270-433-7053

abovethepages@gmail.com | *www.abovethepages.com*

Contact: email

Services: back-cover copy, copyediting, discussion questions for books, ghostwriting, manuscript evaluation, proofreading, substantive/developmental editing

Types of manuscripts: adult, articles, Bible studies, curriculum, devotionals, easy readers, gift books, middle grade, nonfiction books, novels, picture books, short stories, teen/YA

Charges: word rate

Credentials/experience: "Editor with over seven years of experience in Christian nonfiction, fiction, devotionals, Bible studies, ministry materials, articles, blogs, and more. I work with children's and adult materials. No job too small or too large! Email today about package discounts for your editing needs. I am comfortable working with new and experienced authors. I can come alongside you to make your book the best it can be."

ACEVEDO WORD SOLUTIONS, LLC | JENNE ACEVEDO
editor@jenneacevedo.com | www.jenneacevedo.com

Contact: email

Services: back-cover copy, coauthoring, copyediting, discussion questions for books, project management, proofreading, substantive/developmental editing, writing coach

Types of manuscripts: adult, articles, Bible studies, book proposals, curriculum, devotionals, easy readers, gift books, middle grade, nonfiction books, query letters, teen/YA

Charges: hourly rate, word rate

Credentials/experience: "Consultant for private and corporate clients, cofounder of Christian Editor Network LLC, former director of The Christian PEN, former director of PENCON, member of Christian Editor Connection, editing/proofreading instructor for The PEN Institute, founder and director of Chandler Writers' Group."

AM EDITING AND FREELANCE WRITING | ANGELA McCLAIN
amediting35@gmail.com | www.amediting.webs.com

Contact: email, website

Services: back-cover copy, coauthoring, copyediting, discussion questions for books, ghostwriting, manuscript evaluation, proofreading, writing coach

Types of manuscripts: adult, articles, Bible studies, devotionals, easy readers, gift books, middle grade, nonfiction books, novels, picture books, poetry, short stories, teen/YA

Charges: page rate

Credentials/experience: "As an editor, Angela is a communications professional who assists writers with writing tasks. Angela is an experienced editor and writer with thorough knowledge of grammar, composition, and other fields relating to the written word. Angela works as a freelance contractor who assists writers with the creation and presentation of written material. Angela works on written material in various capacities, from simple proofreading of internal documents to the creation, presentation, and sometimes even publication of mass-printed material. In addition to the general requirements of written language, she ensures the material conforms to the needs of the author. Angela pays close attention to detail. Angela possesses these traits as well as an overall talent for written communication."

AMBASSADOR COMMUNICATIONS | CLAIRE HUTCHINSON

13733 West Gunsight Dr., Sun City West, AZ 85375 | 812-390-7907
clairescreenwriter@gmail.com | *www.clairehutchinson.net*

Contact: email
Services: coauthoring, copyediting, proofreading, screenwriting, substantive/developmental editing, writing coach
Types of manuscripts: scripts
Charges: flat fee
Credentials/experience: "M.A. English, Professional Program in Screenwriting UCLA, produced and award-winning screenwriter and producer and script analyst."

AMERICAN CHRISTIAN WRITERS | REG A. FORDER

4854 Aster Dr., Nashville, TN 37211 | 615-498-8630
ACWriters@aol.com | *www.ACWriters.com*

Contact: email
Services: copyediting, manuscript evaluation, proofreading, substantive/developmental editing
Types of manuscripts: adult, devotionals, gift books, nonfiction books, novels, poetry, short stories, teen/YA
Charges: word rate
Credentials/experience: "Over 40 years' experience in Christian book publishing. Staff of experienced editors."

AMI EDITING | ANNETTE IRBY

editor@AMIediting.com | *www.AMIediting.com*

Contact: email
Services: copyediting, critiquing, manuscript evaluation, proofreading, substantive/developmental editing
Types of manuscripts: novels, short stories
Charges: hourly rate
Credentials/experience: "Annette spent five years working in acquisitions with a CBA publisher. She has almost twenty years

of experience editing in the CBA marketplace and has worked with several well-known authors and publishers. She's an award-winning author and book reviewer. See her website for testimonials."

ANDREA MERRELL

60 McKinney Rd., Travelers Rest, SC 29690 | 864-616-5889
AndreaMerrell7@gmail.com | www.AndreaMerrell.com

> **Contact:** email, website
> **Services:** back-cover copy, copyediting, proofreading
> **Types of manuscripts:** adult, articles, devotionals, nonfiction books, novels, short stories
> **Charges:** hourly rate
> **Credentials/experience:** "Professional freelance editor. Associate editor for LPC Books and Christian Devotionals Ministries. Member of The Christian PEN: Proofreaders and Editors Network."

ANN KROEKER, WRITING COACH

ann@annkroeker.com | annkroeker.com/writing-coach

> **Contact:** email, website
> **Services:** writing coach
> **Types of manuscripts:** adult, articles, blog posts, book proposals, nonfiction books, query letters, social-media content
> **Charges:** flat fee, hourly rate, word rate
> **Credentials/experience:** "A writing coach, author, speaker, and host of the *Ann Kroeker, Writing Coach* podcast, Ann works with clients one-to-one, through programs and courses like The Art & Craft of Writing, and through Your Platform Matters (YPM), her platform membership program. Her website has landed on *The Write Life*'s annual "100 Best Websites for Writers" list six years in a row thanks to years of valuable writing-related content. She leverages over three decades of experience in the writing and publishing world to support writers looking for input and confidence to advance their careers. Ann's clients have achieved personal goals, landed contracts, hit bestseller lists, and won awards. She's presented at conferences, retreats, and summits; coauthored *On Being a Writer: 12 Simple Habits for a Writing Life that Lasts*; and authored *Not So Fast: Slow-Down Solutions for Frenzied Families and The Contemplative Mom*."

ARMOR OF HOPE WRITING & PUBLISHING SERVICES |
DENISE M. WALKER

info@armorofhopewritingservices.com | www.armorofhopewritingservices.com

Contact: email

Services: copyediting, proofreading, writing coach

Types of manuscripts: Bible studies, board/picture books, devotionals, easy readers, nonfiction books

Charges: flat fee, word rate

Credentials/experience: "I have been in business for over five years and have copyedited and/or proofread 100+ nonfiction, children's picture books, and easy readers. In addition, I serve as a writing coach, assisting nonfiction authors with organizing and developing their thoughts. I am also a full-service nonfiction self-publishing coach and an author of middle grades/YA fiction, women's Christian fiction, and Bible literacy journals. I have attended several book writing and editing workshops. I am also certified in middle grades English language arts and have taught English for over 20 years."

AUTHOR GATEWAY | CALEB BREAKEY
424 W. Bakerview Rd., Ste. 105, Bellingham, WA 98226

team@authorgateway.com | www.authorgateway.com

Contact: email

Services: book proposals, writing coach

Types of manuscripts: books of all kinds and all ages

Charges: $3,500–$5,500

Credentials/experience: "Backed by more than 200 years of experience, HarperCollins Christian Publishing's Author Gateway provides the best team in the country dedicated to helping men and women of faith land a prominent literary agent and sign with a major Christian publisher. We serve authors who are looking to up their game when it comes to pitching to literary agents and acquisition editors."

AUTHORIZEME® LITERARY FIRM, LLC | SHARON
NORRIS ELLIOTT

PO Box 1816, South Gate, CA 90280 | 310-508-9860

AuthorizeMeNow@gmail.com | www.AuthorizeMe.net

Contact: email, website

Services: back-cover copy, book-contract evaluation, copyediting, discussion questions for books, ghostwriting, manuscript evaluation, proofreading, substantive/developmental editing, writing coach

Types of manuscripts: adult, articles, Bible studies, board/picture books, book proposals, devotionals, easy readers, gift books, nonfiction books, novels, poetry, short stories

Charges: hourly rate, page rate, word rate

Credentials/experience: "I am a 36-year veteran English and writing instructor with over 20 years of experience as a professional editor for publishing companies and private clients. I now work full time as a book developer, writing coach, ghostwriter, and editor hired by royalty publishing houses and private clients." Also offers AuthorizeMe Academy Masterclass Series.

AUTHORS WHO SERVE | RACHEL HILLS

1290 Crafton Ct., Mooresville, IN 46158 | 317-443-0019

rachel@authorswhoserve.com | authorswhoserve.com

Contact: website

Services: coauthoring, copyediting, ghostwriting, manuscript evaluation, substantive/developmental editing, writing coach

Types of manuscripts: academic, adult, book proposals, nonfiction books, novels, query letters

Charges: flat fee

Credentials/experience: "I love to help authors write their best books to serve in the Kingdom. I began editing over 20 years ago for a professor. I liked it so much I pursued training to go freelance, including a certificate in book coaching. I also have a certificate in ghostwriting. How can I help you?"

AVODAH EDITORIAL SERVICES | CHRISTY DISTLER

www.avodaheditorialservices.com

Contact: website

Services: copyediting, manuscript evaluation, proofreading, substantive/developmental editing

Types of manuscripts: adult, devotionals, easy readers, nonfiction books, novels, picture books, poetry, short stories

Charges: word rate

Credentials/experience: "Educated at Temple University and University of California–Berkeley. Thirteen years of editorial experience, both as an employee and a freelancer. Currently works mostly for publishing houses but accepts freelance work as scheduling allows."

BANNER LITERARY | MIKE LOOMIS

mike@mikeloomis.co | www.MikeLoomis.co

Contact: email, website

Services: back-cover copy, book-contract evaluation, coauthoring, copyediting, discussion questions for books, ghostwriting, manuscript evaluation, proofreading, substantive/developmental editing, writing coach

Types of manuscripts: articles, book proposals, devotionals, nonfiction books, query letters

Charges: custom, flat fee

Credentials/experience: "I'm a book developer, ghostwriter, and editor. I also coach authors on planning the best book for their goals. Because of my twenty years of experience in publishing, I help authors refine their idea, polish their work, and reach their audience. I've worked with *New York Times* bestselling authors and publishers (Simon & Schuster, Multnomah, Zondervan, Random House, Nelson, NavPress, and Penguin) but am most energized by helping first-time authors."

BARBARA KOIS

7135 W. Amber Burst Ct., Tucson, AZ 85743 | 630-532-2941

barbara.kois@gmail.com

Contact: email

Services: coauthoring, copyediting, ghostwriting, manuscript evaluation, proofreading, substantive/developmental editing, writing coach

Types of manuscripts: adult, Bible studies, devotionals, easy readers, gift books, middle grade, nonfiction books, novels, teen/YA

Charges: word rate

Credentials/experience: "As a writer, ghostwriter, editor, teacher, coach, corporate communication consultant and journalist, Barbara has written or co-written ten books, published more than 600 articles in the *Chicago Tribune*, and edited more than 200 books for various publishers and authors. Barbara has helped dozens of writers prepare for the publication of their books, including both those who have published with traditional publishers and those who have chosen to self-publish. She aims for clear and memorable writing that makes what's complicated easily understandable."

BBH LITERARY | DAVID BRATT
david@bbhliterary.com | bbhliterary.com
- **Contact:** email, website
- **Services:** manuscript evaluation, substantive/developmental editing
- **Types of manuscripts:** academic, articles, book proposals, nonfiction books, query letters
- **Charges:** hourly rate
- **Credentials/experience:** "Twenty-one years editing for Eerdmans Publishing; Ph.D. in American religion (Yale University, 1999)."

BECCA WIERWILLE EDITORIAL SERVICES
becca@beccawierwille.com | beccawierwille.com/editing-services
- **Contact:** email, website
- **Services:** copyediting, manuscript evaluation, proofreading, substantive/developmental editing, writing coach
- **Types of manuscripts:** adult, articles, board/picture books, book proposals, devotionals, easy readers, middle grade, novels, query letters, short stories, teen/YA
- **Charges:** word rate
- **Credentials/experience:** "Becca Wierwille is a freelance editor and writing coach who has worked with writers of various genres and experience levels. As a former newspaper reporter and avid critique group member, she has years of experience doing edits at every level. She loves partnering with authors to help make their stories shine and focuses on editing clean fiction, with a specialization in middle grade and YA. Her editing portfolio and testimonials are available upon request."

BESTSELLING BOOK SHEPHERD | PAMELA GOSSIAUX
15011 Reiman Rd., Grass Lake, MI 49240 | 734-846-0112
pam@pamelagossiaux.com | BestsellingBookShepherd.com
- **Contact:** email
- **Services:** back-cover copy, coauthoring, copyediting, discussion questions for books, ghostwriting, manuscript evaluation, proofreading, substantive/developmental editing, writing coach
- **Types of manuscripts:** adult, articles, Bible studies, board/picture books, book proposals, devotionals, easy readers, gift books, middle grade, nonfiction books, novels, query letters, short stories, teen/YA
- **Charges:** custom, flat fee, hourly rate, packages

Credentials/experience: "30 years experience writing, editing, journalism, book PR. Dual degree in Creative Writing & English Language and Literature from University of Michigan. International bestselling author. Have coached and promoted authors to Amazon, *USA Today* and *Wall Street Journal* bestsellers."

BOOKHOUND EDITING | KATY SCHLOMACH
katy@bookhoundediting.com | *www.bookhoundediting.com*

Contact: email, website
Services: copyediting, manuscript evaluation, proofreading
Types of manuscripts: adult, novels, short stories
Charges: word rate
Credentials/experience: "Katy Schlomach specializes in proofreading, copyediting, and line editing for fiction, particularly the romance, speculative, historical, and suspense genres. Her goal is to refine and polish while carefully preserving the author's voice. She is a freelance editor with a background in education, a BA in communication, and a passion for the craft of writing fiction that is clear, correct, consistent, and compelling for readers. She is certified through Edit Republic and The PEN Institute and a member of the Christian Editor Connection. Her love of language has turned into a career that allows her to help writers communicate their ideas and stories clearly."

BOOKOX | THOMAS WOMACK
165 S. Timber Creek Dr., Sisters, OR 97759 | 541-788-6503
Thomas@BookOx.com | *www.BookOx.com*

Contact: email
Services: copyediting, discussion questions for books, manuscript evaluation, substantive/developmental editing
Types of manuscripts: Bible studies, devotionals, nonfiction books, novels, short stories
Charges: word rate
Credentials/experience: "My decades of editing experience have centered on Christian books published by Crossway, Zondervan, Multnomah, WaterBrook, NavPress, Harvest House, David C. Cook, and other publishing houses. I've had the great privilege of working on projects by gifted and godly authors such as Jerry Bridges, J. I. Packer, Henry Blackaby, Randy Alcorn, Os Guinness, Louie Giglio, Tony Evans, Larry Osborne, Christopher Yuan, Bob

Kauflin, Kay Arthur, Larry Crabb, Jeramy Clark, Dave Harvey, Greg Laurie, Richard Blackaby, Ruth Myers, C. J. Mahaney, Andy Stanley, Thelma Wells, David Jeremiah, Norm Wright, James Kennedy, Richard Halverson, Carolyn Castleberry, and a great many others. These have included numerous titles in the categories of spiritual nurture and care, spiritual disciplines and devotion, Bible study and theology, and marriage and family, as well as memoirs, fiction, and business and leadership books."

BREAKOUT EDITING | DORI HARRELL
doriharrell@gmail.com | *www.doriharrell.wix.com/breakoutediting*

Contact: email

Services: copyediting, proofreading, substantive/developmental editing, website text

Types of manuscripts: adult, articles, devotionals, middle grade, nonfiction books, novels, picture books, query letters, short stories, teen/YA

Charges: word rate

Credentials/experience: "Dori is a multiple-award-winning writer and a highly experienced editor who freelance edits full time and has edited more than 300 novels and nonfiction books. Breakout authors final in awards or win awards almost every year! She edits for publishers, including Gemma Halliday Publishing and Kregel Publications, and as an editor, she releases more than twenty books annually."

BROOKSTONE CREATIVE GROUP | JOHN HERRING
100 Missionary Ridge, Birmingham, AL 35242 | 302-514-7899
www.brookstonecreativegroup.com

Contact: website

Services: book proposals, copyediting, ghostwriting, one-sheets, proofreading, substantive/developmental editing, writing coach

Types of manuscripts: books of all kinds and all ages

Charges: flat fee

Credentials/experience: "Brookstone Creative Group is changing the landscape for how writers, authors, speakers, pastors, musicians, and other creatives navigate the ever-changing landscape of platform development. Through true and tested solutions, training, and community-building, Brookstone Creative Group guides their clients in the who, where, when, and how to inspirational success."

BUTTERFIELD EDITORIAL SERVICES | DEBRA L. BUTTERFIELD

4810 Gene Field Rd., Saint Joseph, MO 64506 | 816-752-2171

deb@debralbutterfield.com | *themotivationaleditor.com*

> **Contact:** email
> **Services:** copyediting, substantive/developmental editing
> **Types of manuscripts:** adult, book proposals, nonfiction books, novels
> **Charges:** word rate
> **Credentials/experience:** "Debra began her writing career as a copywriter for Focus on the Family. She has been editing manuscripts since 2010."

byBRENDA | BRENDA WILBEE

4631 Quinn Ct. #202, Bellingham, WA 98226 | 360-389-6895

Brenda@BrendaWilbee.com | *www.BrendaWilbee.com*

> **Contact:** email
> **Services:** substantive/developmental editing, writing coach
> **Types of manuscripts:** adult, devotionals, nonfiction books, novels
> **Charges:** hourly rate
> **Credentials/experience:** "I hold an MA in English/Professional Writing and have taught Composition at the university and college level for seven years. I was a frequent teacher at writers conferences, Elder Hostels, and community organizations, and have been editing for 30 years. I'm not just an editor; I am, more importantly, a writer. I've written hundreds of articles and my ten books have sold over 700,000 copies. I understand the art and craft of writing and offer the nitty gritty as to what is working and what is not—and why."

C. S. LAKIN, COPYEDITOR AND WRITING COACH

20406 Tiger Tail Rd., Grass Valley, CA 95949 | 530-200-5466

cslakin@gmail.com | *www.livewritethrive.com*

> **Contact:** website
> **Services:** back-cover copy, copyediting, manuscript evaluation, proofreading, substantive/developmental editing, writing coach
> **Types of manuscripts:** adult, articles, Bible studies, board/picture books, book proposals, devotionals, easy readers, gift books, middle grade, nonfiction books, novels, poetry, query letters, short stories, teen/YA
> **Charges:** flat fee, hourly rate
> **Credentials/experience:** "I have 17 years editing and critiquing

thousands of manuscripts for writers, agents, and publishers in 6 continents. I teach workshops and master classes in person and online at *cslakin.teachable.com* and am the author of more than 30 published books, fiction and nonfiction. My award-winning blog has more than 1 million words of instruction for writers."

CATHY STREINER

South Carolina

Cathy@thecorporatepen.com | thecorporatepen.com

Contact: email

Services: back-cover copy, coauthoring, copyediting, discussion questions for books, proofreading, substantive/developmental editing, writing coach

Types of manuscripts: academic, adult, articles, Bible studies, devotionals, easy readers, gift books, middle grade, nonfiction books, novels, scripts, short stories, technical material, teen/YA

Charges: custom, flat fee, hourly rate, word rate

Credentials/experience: "Author of a Christian novel, I have experience with the start-to-finish self-publishing process. I also have extensive experience working with writers who need editing and proofreading services as well as limited coaching with constructive feedback."

CELTICFROG EDITING | ALEX MCGILVERY

Canada

thecelticfrog@gmail.com | celticfrogediting.com

Contact: email, website

Services: manuscript evaluation, writing coach

Types of manuscripts: adult, articles, devotionals, middle grade, nonfiction books, novels, short stories, teen/YA

Charges: word rate

Credentials/experience: "I have been reviewing and critiquing books for more than three decades, and editing since 2014. One client compared my work favourably with the editors at a traditional publisher."

CHERI FIELDS EDITING

1232 Garfield Ave. NW, Grand Rapids, MI 49504 | 269-953-4271

Cherifieldsediting@gmail.com | Cherifields.com

Contact: email

Services: copyediting, manuscript evaluation, substantive/ developmental editing, writing coach

Types of manuscripts: academic, articles, Bible studies, board/ picture books, book proposals, curriculum, devotionals, easy readers, middle grade, nonfiction books, teen/YA

Charges: word rate

Credentials/experience: "Gold member of the Christian PEN for nonfiction and children's editing."

CHRISTIAN COMMUNICATOR MANUSCRIPT CRITIQUE SERVICE | SUSAN TITUS OSBORN

3133 Puente St., Fullerton, CA 92835 | 714-313-8651

susanosb@aol.com | *www.christiancommunicator.com*

Contact: email, phone, website

Services: back-cover copy, book-contract evaluation, coauthoring, copyediting, discussion questions for books, ghostwriting, manuscript evaluation, proofreading, writing coach

Types of manuscripts: academic, adult, articles, Bible studies, book proposals, curriculum, devotionals, easy readers, gift books, middle grade, nonfiction books, novels, picture books, poetry, query letters, scripts, short stories, technical material, teen/YA

Charges: hourly rate, page rate

Credentials/experience: "Our critique service, comprised of 14 professional editors, has been in business for almost 40 years. We are recommended by ECPA, the Billy Graham Association, and a number of publishing houses and agents."

CHRISTIAN EDITING SERVICES | IOLA GOULTON

New Zealand

igoulton@christianediting.co.nz | *www.christianediting.co.nz*

Contact: website

Services: copyediting, manuscript evaluation, writing coach

Types of manuscripts: adult, novels, teen/YA

Charges: custom

Credentials/experience: "Iola is a member of The Christian PEN: Proofreaders and Editors Network, American Christian Fiction Writers, Romance Writers of New Zealand, and Omega Writers. She has completed fiction editing courses with The Christian PEN and Lawson Writers Academy, and won the 2016 ACFW Genesis Award (Novella), and edited the 2018 RITA Award winner (Romance with Religious or Spiritual Elements)."

CHRISTIAN EDITOR CONNECTION | CHRISTY DISTLER

PO Box 9243, Brea, CA 92822

director@ChristianEditor.com | www.ChristianEditor.com

Contact: website

Services: copyediting, ghostwriting, indexing, manuscript evaluation, proofreading, substantive/developmental editing, writing coach

Types of manuscripts: academic, adult, articles, Bible studies, board/picture books, book proposals, curriculum, devotionals, easy readers, gift books, middle grade, nonfiction books, novels, poetry, query letters, short stories, technical material, teen/YA

Charges: hourly rate, page rate, word rate

Credentials/experience: "Christian Editor Connection is a matchmaking service that connects Christian authors, project managers, agents, and publishers with vetted, professional Christian editors."

CHRISTIANBOOKPROPOSALS.COM | CINDY CARTER

ccarter@ecpa.org | ChristianBookProposals.com

Contact: website

Services: online proposal-submission service

Types of manuscripts: books of all kinds and all ages

Charges: $98 for six months

Credentials/experience: "Operated by the Evangelical Christian Publishers Association (ECPA), it is the only manuscript service created by the top Christian publishers looking for unsolicited manuscripts in a traditional, royalty-based relationship. It allows authors to submit their manuscript proposals in a secure, online format for review by editors from publishing houses that are members of ECPA."

COLLABORATIVE EDITORIAL SOLUTIONS | ANDREW BUSS

info@collaborativeeditorial.com | collaborativeeditorial.com

Contact: email

Services: copyediting, proofreading

Types of manuscripts: academic, adult, articles, Bible studies, devotionals, nonfiction books, technical material

Charges: hourly rate, page rate

Credentials/experience: "I'm a professional editor with more than five years of full-time experience working with authors and scholarly publishers such as InterVarsity Press, Reformation Heritage, P&R Publishing, Georgetown University Press, and Baylor University Press.

Although I primarily work in the genre of scholarly nonfiction, I'm always keen to work with creative and thoughtful authors, whatever the topic or genre. I'm a member of the Editorial Freelancers Association and the Society of Biblical Literature."

COMMUNICATION ASSOCIATES | KEN WALKER

729 Ninth Ave. #331, Huntington, WV 25701 | 304-525-3343
kenwalker33@gmail.com | *www.KenWalkerWriter.com*

Contact: email
Services: back-cover copy, coauthoring, copyediting, discussion questions for books, ghostwriting
Types of manuscripts: adult, articles, Bible studies, devotionals, nonfiction books
Charges: flat fee, hourly rate
Credentials/experience: "Started freelancing in 1983 and fulltime in 1990. Experienced in ghostwriting, substantive editing, and book editing. Written or edited more than 85 books."

CORNERSTONE-INK EDITING | VIE HERLOCK

vherlock@yahoo.com | *www.cornerstone-ink.com*

Contact: email, website
Services: copyediting, manuscript evaluation, substantive/developmental editing
Types of manuscripts: adult, articles, book proposals, devotionals, gift books, middle grade, nonfiction books, novels, query letters, short stories, teen/YA
Charges: word rate
Credentials/experience: "Vie Herlocker provides 'Tough-Love Editing with a Tender Touch.' She is a member of Christian Editor Connection, Christian Proofreaders and Editors Network, ACFW, and Word Weavers, Int. Her experience includes: editing for a small Christian publisher (10 years), editing for a regional magazine, judging a national writing contest, and freelance editing. She uses *The Chicago Manual of Style, Christian Writers' Manual of Style,* and *Merriam-Webster* 11th."

CREATIVE EDITORIAL SOLUTIONS | CLAUDIA VOLKMAN

cvolkman@mac.com

Contact: email, phone
Services: back-cover copy, copyediting, discussion questions for books, proofreading, substantive/developmental editing, writing coach

Types of manuscripts: adult, Bible studies, devotionals, gift books, nonfiction books, novels

Charges: flat fee, hourly rate, page rate, word rate

Credentials/experience: "I have more than thirty-five years of experience in acquisitions, product development, editing, and typesetting and have worked full-time for several trade publishing houses, including Tyndale House. Now, as the owner of Creative Editorial Solutions, I assist publishers, authors, entrepreneurs, and speakers with their editorial needs. Services include book coaching, developmental editing, book doctoring, copyediting, proofreading, and creating book interiors."

CREATIVE ENTERPRISES STUDIO | MARY HOLLINGSWORTH

1507 Shirley Way, Ste. A, Bedford, TX 76022-6737 | 817-312-7393

ACreativeShop@aol.com | *CreativeEnterprisesStudio.com*

Contact: email

Services: coauthoring, copyediting, discussion questions for books, ghostwriting, manuscript evaluation, proofreading, substantive/developmental editing

Types of manuscripts: adult, book proposals, curriculum, devotionals, easy readers, gift books, middle grade, nonfiction books, novels, picture books, short stories, teen/YA

Charges: custom

Credentials/experience: "CES is a publishing services company, hosting more than 150 top Christian publishing freelancers. We work with large, traditional Christian publishers on books by best-selling authors. We also produce custom, first-class books on a turnkey basis for independent authors, ministries, churches, and companies."

CROSS & DOT EDITORIAL SERVICES | KATIE VORREITER

Katie@CrossAndDot.net | *www.CrossAndDot.net*

Contact: email, website

Services: copyediting, proofreading

Types of manuscripts: adult, articles, curriculum, devotionals, gift books, middle grade, nonfiction books, novels, short stories, technical material, teen/YA

Charges: flat fee

Credentials/experience: "Certificate in professional sequence in editing, U.C. Berkeley; MA in international management; BA in English and Spanish."

DILLER DESIGNS | LILA DILLER
128 Teak Dr., Statesville, NC 28625
liladiller78@gmail.com | *www.liladiller.com/editingservices*

    Contact: email
    Services: copyediting, proofreading
    Types of manuscripts: adult, Bible studies, devotionals, middle
      grade, nonfiction books, novels
    Charges: word rate
    Credentials/experience: "As a life-long reader and lover of grammar,
      I love to help new authors turn their book babies into professional
      and gripping prose."

DONE WRITE EDITORIAL SERVICES | MARILYN A.
ANDERSON
127 Sycamore Dr., Louisville, KY 40223 | 502-244-0751
shelle12@aol.com

    Contact: email, phone
    Services: copyediting, proofreading, substantive/developmental
      editing, writing coach
    Types of manuscripts: academic, adult, articles, Bible studies, book
      proposals, children, curriculum, devotionals, gift books, nonfiction
      books, novels, poetry, query letters, short stories, technical material
    Charges: hourly rate
    Credentials/experience: "I am qualified by both bachelor's and
      master's degrees in English. I am also qualified because I have
      tutored more than thirty English/writing students since 2004.
      Most of them have been English-language learners. Also, I have
      taught English/writing as a classroom teacher. I have additionally
      conducted business-project editing for several corporations
      over the years. I currently copyedit for nonfiction and fiction
      independent writers, as well as for publishers and a few Christian
      ministries and am in the process of mentoring several other
      writers/editors. I copyedit both books (such as memoirs) and
      doctoral dissertations, theses, and other academic journal articles
      and papers.
        "I offer a free sample edit, and my rates are both reasonable and
      competitive. I am a Gold charter member of The Christian PEN
      proofreaders and editors' network, along with a tested member of
      the Christian Editor Connection."

ECHO CREATIVE MEDIA | BRENDA NOEL
bnoel@thewordeditor.com | *echocreativemedia.weebly.com*

Contact: email

Services: copyediting, discussion questions for books, ghostwriting, proofreading, substantive/developmental editing

Types of manuscripts: adult, articles, book proposals, curriculum, devotionals, easy readers, gift books, nonfiction books, picture books, short stories, teen/YA

Charges: flat fee, hourly rate

Credentials/experience: "Sixteen years of experience in the Christian publishing industry."

EDIT RESOURCE, LLC | ERIC STANFORD
19265 Lincoln Green Ln., Monument, CO 80132 | 719-290-0757

info@editresource.com | *www.editresource.com*

Contact: email

Services: back-cover copy, book proposals, coauthoring, copyediting, discussion questions for books, ghostwriting, indexing, manuscript evaluation, proofreading, substantive/developmental editing, writing coach

Types of manuscripts: adult, Bible studies, book proposals, curriculum, devotionals, middle grade, nonfiction books, novels, query letters, teen/YA

Charges: depends on the service

Credentials/experience: "Owners Eric and Elisa have a combined 40 years of experience and have worked with numerous bestselling authors and books. They also represent a team of other top writing and editing professionals."

EDIT WITH CLAIRE | CLAIRE TUCKER
editor@editwithclaire.com | *www.editwithclaire.com*

Contact: email

Services: copyediting, manuscript evaluation, proofreading

Types of manuscripts: adult, articles, novels, short stories

Charges: word rate

Credentials/experience: "I have worked with authors seeking publication and have prepared a manuscript for publication. Other experience includes editing advertising copy, articles, and short stories. My passion is to work with authors and help them polish their manuscripts to the highest standard, thereby showing the glory of God."

EDITING BY LUCY | LUCY CRABTREE
editingbylucy@gmail.com | editingbylucy.com

> **Contact:** email, website
> **Services:** copyediting, discussion questions for books, manuscript evaluation, proofreading, substantive/developmental editing
> **Types of manuscripts:** academic, adult, articles, Bible studies, devotionals, gift books, nonfiction books, novels, teen/YA
> **Charges:** word rate
> **Credentials/experience:** "I have been a communications professional since 2007—at a national syndicate, a public university, and even an art museum. So when I say I've edited a little bit of everything ... I do mean everything! Crossword puzzles, faculty manuscripts, advice columns, political commentaries, comic strips, university websites, grant proposals, promotional copy—you name it, I've (probably) read it."

EDITING GALLERY, LLC | CAROL CRAIG
2622 Willona Dr., Eugene, OR 97408 | 541-735-1834
kf7orchid@gmail.com | www.editinggallery.com

> **Contact:** email
> **Services:** back-cover copy, coauthoring, copyediting, manuscript evaluation, proofreading, substantive/developmental editing, writing coach
> **Types of manuscripts:** adult, board/picture books, book proposals, easy readers, middle grade, nonfiction books, novels, query letters, teen/YA
> **Charges:** hourly rate
> **Credentials/experience:** "University of Oregon/English Major—I have edited for many well-known fiction authors and have over thirty years of experience as an editor."

eDITMORE EDITORIAL SERVICES | TAMMY DITMORE
501-I S. Reino Rd. #194, Newbury Park, CA 91320 | 805-630-6809
tammy@editmore.com | www.editmore.com

> **Contact:** email
> **Services:** copyediting, discussion questions for books, manuscript evaluation, proofreading, substantive/developmental editing
> **Types of manuscripts:** academic, articles, Bible studies, devotionals, nonfiction books
> **Charges:** flat fee, hourly rate

Credentials/experience: "An editor for award-winning nonfiction clients, Tammy Ditmore offers writing, editing, and consulting services to publishers, authors, businesses, organizations, and scholars. Tammy has worked as an editor and writer for daily newspapers, academic journals, books, magazines, and individual authors. Her published writing includes interview-based features, research-driven reports, and first-person essays. As a specialist in nonfiction, she offers critiques, consultations, developmental editing, copyediting, and proofreading services."

EDITOR FOR YOU | MELANIE RIGNEY

4201 Wilson Blvd. #110328, Arlington, VA 22203 | 703-863-3940
editor@editorforyou.com | *www.editorforyou.com*

Contact: email
Services: manuscript evaluation
Types of manuscripts: adult, book proposals, devotionals, nonfiction books, novels
Charges: flat fee
Credentials/experience: "Melanie has decades of professional editing experience, including time as editor of *Writer's Digest* magazine and a publishing manager for what was Hayden Books. Since 2003, her consultancy, Editor for You, has helped hundreds of publishers, agents, and authors. Melanie knows what it's like on the other side of the desk; she's authored several books for Catholic publishers."

EDITOR WORLD: EDITING AND PROOFREADING SERVICES | PATTI FISHER

11815 Fountain Way, Ste. 300, Newport News, VA 23606 | 614-500-3348
info@editorworld.com | *www.editorworld.com*

Contact: website
Services: copyediting, proofreading
Types of manuscripts: academic, adult, articles, Bible studies, board/picture books, book proposals, curriculum, devotionals, easy readers, gift books, middle grade, nonfiction books, novels, poetry, query letters, scripts, short stories, technical material, teen/YA
Charges: word rate
Credentials/experience: "We are a U.S.-based editing and proofreading services company. All editors at Editor World are native English speakers who have passed a stringent test of their editing and proofreading skills. We have expert editors available 24/7 to help you improve your writing."

EDITORIAL SERVICES | KIM PETERSON

1114 Buxton Dr., Knoxville, KY 37922

petersk.ktp@gmail.com | *naturewalkwithgod.wordpress.com/about-kim*

Contact: email

Services: back-cover copy, copyediting, discussion questions for books, manuscript evaluation, proofreading, writing coach

Types of manuscripts: academic, adult, articles, blog posts, book proposals, curriculum, devotionals, easy readers, gift books, middle grade, nonfiction books, novels, picture books, poetry, query letters, short stories, technical material, teen/YA

Charges: hourly rate

Credentials/experience: "Freelance writer; college writing instructor; conference speaker. MA in print communication from Wheaton College."

ELOQUENT EDITS | DENISE ROEPER

1025 Third St., Port Orange, FL 32129 | 386-290-4117

denise.eloquentedits@gmail.com | *www.eloquentedits.com*

Contact: email, website

Services: copyediting, proofreading

Types of manuscripts: board/picture books, easy readers, gift books, middle grade, nonfiction books, novels, short stories, teen/YA

Charges: word rate

Credentials/experience: "I have edited manuscripts for independent authors and publishing companies. You've worked hard on your manuscript. I'll work hard with you on that final step so that it's ready and polished."

EMH INDEXING SERVICES | ELISE HESS

emhess5@gmail.com

Contact: email

Services: indexing

Charges: page rate

Credentials/experience: "I have experience in subject, Scripture, and name indexes, as well as index updates. I have written indexes for Moody Publishers, Wiley Publishers, and many more. My husband and I are pastors, and I have a Biblical Studies degree so I am very familiar with Christian materials."

EXEGETICA PUBLISHING | CATHY CONE

312 Greenwich #112, Lee's Summit, MO 64082

editor@exegeticapublishing.com | *exegeticapublishing.com/editing*

Contact: website

Services: copyediting, manuscript evaluation, proofreading, substantive/developmental editing

Types of manuscripts: academic, articles, Bible studies, curriculum, devotionals, nonfiction books

Charges: page rate

Credentials/experience: "Exegetica editorial staff have more than 30 years editing experience with diverse media and publishers."

EXTRA INK EDITS | MEGAN EASLEY-WALSH

Ireland

Megan@ExtraInkEdits.com | *www.ExtraInkEdits.com*

Contact: email

Services: back-cover copy, discussion questions for books, manuscript evaluation, proofreading, writing coach

Types of manuscripts: adult, articles, devotionals, easy readers, middle grade, nonfiction books, novels, picture books, poetry, query letters, short stories, teen/YA

Charges: flat fee, word rate

Credentials/experience: "Megan Easley-Walsh is an Amazon international multi-bestselling author of historical fiction, a researcher, and a writing consultant and editor at Extra Ink Edits. She is an award-winning writer and has taught college writing in the UNESCO literature city of Dublin, Ireland. Her degrees are in history-focused International Relations. Megan is a professional member of the Irish Writers Centre and a member of the Historical Novel Society. She has over 10 years of experience with Extra Ink Edits, helping writers with everything from query critiques to full manuscript critiques."

FAITH EDITORIAL SERVICES | REBECCA FAITH

PO Box 184, Novelty, OH 44072 | 216-906-0205

rebecca@faitheditorial.com | *www.faitheditorial.com*

Contact: email, website

Services: copyediting, manuscript evaluation, proofreading

Types of manuscripts: academic, adult, articles, Bible studies, book proposals, curriculum, devotionals, medical, nonfiction books, technical material

Charges: hourly rate

Credentials/experience: "My experience editing in the Christian market includes six years as managing editor for a Christian nonprofit, another eight years editing/transcribing content for a global Christian ministry, and copyediting nonfiction Christian books and devotionals. In addition I have eleven years experience editing technical, engineering, medical, and educational material for university presses, journal publishers, and independent clients. I hold membership in the EFA, the Christian PEN (Gold), and the Christian Editor Connection."

FAITHWORKS EDITORIAL & WRITING, INC. | NANETTE THORSEN SNIPES

PO Box 1596, Buford, GA 30518 | 770-945-3093

nsnipes@bellsouth.net | www.faithworkseditorial.com

Contact: email, website

Services: copyediting, manuscript evaluation, proofreading, work-for-hire projects

Types of manuscripts: adult, articles, business materials, devotionals, easy readers, gift books, memoir, middle grade, nonfiction books, picture books, poetry, query letters, short stories

Charges: hourly rate, page rate

Credentials/experience: "Member: The Christian PEN (Proofreaders & Editors Network), Christian Editor Connection, Christian Editor Network. Proofreader for corporate newsletters, thirteen years. Published writer for more than twenty-five years. Published hundreds of articles in magazines and stories in more than sixty compilation books, including Guideposts, B&H, Regal, and Integrity. Twelve years of editorial experience in both adult and children's short fiction and books, memoirs, short stories, devotionals, articles, business. Rates are generally by page but, under specific circumstances, by the hour. Editorial clients have published with such houses as Zondervan, Tyndale, and Revell."

FINAL TOUCH PROOFREADING & EDITING | HEIDI MANN

www.FinalTouchProofreadingAndEditing.com

Contact: website

Services: copyediting, proofreading

Types of manuscripts: adult, articles, Bible studies, board/picture books, devotionals, nonfiction books, teen/YA

Charges: hourly rate

Credentials/experience: "Along with my expertise in writing and editing, I bring my experience as a former pastor in the Evangelical Lutheran Church in America (mainline/progressive), which includes strong knowledge of the Bible and Christian theology, as well as deep understanding of church leadership, congregational life, and Christian faith."

THE FOREWORD COLLECTIVE | MOLLY HODGIN

1726 Charity Dr., Brentwood, TN 37027 | 615-497-4322

molly.hodgin@theforewordcollective.com | *www.theforewordcollective.com*

Contact: email, website

Services: back-cover copy, book-contract evaluation, coauthoring, discussion questions for books, ghostwriting, manuscript evaluation, substantive/developmental editing, writing coach

Types of manuscripts: adult, apps, board/picture books, book proposals, cookbooks, devotionals, easy readers, gift books, middle grade, nonfiction books, novels, query letters, style books, teen/YA

Charges: flat fee, hourly rate

Credentials/experience: "Molly Hodgin, founder and CEO of The Foreword Collective, has over twenty years of publishing experience. She served as the Associate Publisher for the Specialty Division of HarperCollins Christian Publishing, the Editorial Director for Zondervan Gift, Thomas Nelson Gift Books, Tommy Nelson Kids Books, and The Thomas Nelson New Media Division, a Senior Editor for Scholastic Inc. and an editor for Penguin Young Readers Group. Molly has extensive experience in acquiring and editing gift books, cookbooks, style books, devotionals, trade nonfiction books, YA and middle grade fiction, and children's picture books and board books. Her specialty is helping authors craft a book proposal that will stand out to land them an agent or publishing deal. She has also written, ghost written, and co-authored over seventy-five books.

"If Molly isn't the right fit for your book, well, The Foreword Collective also employs a number of highly experienced industry professionals from all areas of Christian publishing. Whether you are an experienced author looking for editorial help or brand building or a new author who wants to make the leap into traditional publishing, The Foreword Collective is here to help!"

FRENCH AND ENGLISH COMMUNICATION SERVICES |
DIANE GOULLARD

3104 E. Camelback Rd., PMB 124, Phoenix, AZ 85016-4502 | 602-870-1000

RequestFAECS2008@cox.net | frenchandenglish.com

Contact: email, phone, website

Services: copyediting, English to French translation, French to English translation, proofreading, voiceovers/narration

Types of manuscripts: academic, adult, articles, back-cover copy, Bible studies, board/picture books, book proposals, curriculum, devotionals, easy readers, gift books, legal documents, memoir, middle grade, nonfiction books, novels, poetry, query letters, scripts, short stories, technical material, teen/YA

Charges: custom, flat fee, hourly rate, page rate, word rate

Credentials/experience: "Diane is experienced and loves what she does."

GINA KAMMER, THE INKY BOOKWYRM

1054 Deer Ridge Ct. NW, Lonsdale, MN 55046 | 507-381-1887

ginalkammer@gmail.com | ginakammer.com

Contact: website

Services: copyediting, manuscript evaluation, proofreading, substantive/developmental editing, writing coach

Types of manuscripts: adult, easy readers, middle grade, novels, picture books, teen/YA

Charges: word rate

Credentials/experience: "Gina Kammer specializes in editing and book coaching for science fiction and fantasy. She is a former Capstone editor and Bethany Lutheran College writing/journalism instructor with 10+ years of experience in fiction and children's nonfiction. Using brain science hacks, hoarded craft knowledge, and solution-based direction, this book dragon helps science-fiction and fantasy authors get their stories—whether on the page or still in their heads—ready to enchant their readers."

GRACE BRIDGES

4/11 Hall Rd., Glenfield, Auckland 0629, New Zealand | 64224722301

www.gracebridges.kiwi/hire-me

Contact: website

Services: copyediting, proofreading, substantive/developmental editing, writing coach

Types of manuscripts: middle grade, nonfiction books, novels, short stories, teen/YA

Charges: word rate

Credentials/experience: Listed at *gracebridges.kiwi/hire-me/experience.html*.

GRACE NOTES, LLC | GALADRIEL GRACE

1289 Marseille Dr. #149, Miami Beach, FL 33141 | 918-268-9808

galadrielgrace.com

Contact: website

Services: back-cover copy, copyediting, proofreading, self-publishing book formatting package, writing coach

Types of manuscripts: adult, articles, Bible studies, board/picture books, book proposals, curriculum, devotionals, easy readers, gift books, middle grade, nonfiction books, novels, poetry, query letters, short stories, social-media content, teen/YA, websites

Charges: flat fee, word rate

Credentials/experience: "Over eighteen years' experience online—editing, marketing, cover design, and helping authors publish their books. All genres from children's and homeschool to novels. Free to ask questions for marketing tips, ideas, suggestions with social media, websites, etc."

HANEMANN EDITORIAL | NATALIE HANEMANN

nathanemann@gmail.com | *www.nataliehanemannediting.com*

Contact: email, website

Services: copyediting, manuscript evaluation, substantive/developmental editing

Types of manuscripts: adult, book proposals, middle grade, nonfiction books, novels, teen/YA

Charges: flat fee

Credentials/experience: "Eleven years in-house at publishing houses, eight of those at Thomas Nelson in the fiction division under the tutelage of Allen Arnold. Since 2012, I've been freelance editing fiction and nonfiction (substantive and line), as well as helping authors get their synopses ready to submit to agents. I've edited more than three hundred manuscripts and particularly love working with newer authors or authors who are unsure if they should publish traditionally or indie. Certified by the Christian Editors Connection."

HEATHER PUBOLS

heather.pubols@gmail.com | heatherpubols.com/editing-services

Contact: email, website

Services: copyediting, substantive/developmental editing

Types of manuscripts: academic, articles, Bible studies, nonfiction books, technical material

Charges: hourly rate

Credentials/experience: "More than 20 years of editorial experience working in corporate communications for Christian missions organizations. Freelance editor since 2018."

HENRY MCLAUGHLIN

henry@henrymclaughlin.org | www.henrymclaughlin.org

Contact: email

Services: coauthoring, copyediting, ghostwriting, manuscript evaluation, substantive/developmental editing, writing coach

Types of manuscripts: adult, nonfiction books, novels, short stories

Charges: custom

Credentials/experience: "Award winning author, teacher at conferences, editing, coaching, mentoring for several years."

HONEST EDITING | BILL LELAND

PO Box 310, Sisters, OR 97759

bill@writersedgeservice.com | www.honestediting.com

Contact: email, website

Services: book proposals, copyediting, substantive/developmental editing

Types of manuscripts: academic, adult, Bible studies, book proposals, devotionals, gift books, middle grade, nonfiction books, novels, teen/YA

Charges: flat fee

Credentials/experience: "Work done by professional freelance editors with years of experience who have worked with or been employed by major Christian Publishers."

IMMORTALISE | BEN MORTON

PO Box 656, Noarlunga Centre, SA 5168, Australia | +611410240513

info@immortalise.com.au | www.immortalise.com.au

Contact: email, website

Services: back-cover copy, copyediting, ghostwriting, proofreading, writing coach

Types of manuscripts: academic, Bible studies, devotionals, middle grade, nonfiction books, novels, poetry, scripts, short stories, teen/YA

Charges: custom, flat fee, hourly rate, page rate, word rate

Credentials/experience: "Following several years as an adjunct tertiary creative writing lecturer, I went on to assist with writing, editing and publishing a large number of books over the last decade or so as an author, and as an editor for another company as well as with my own assisted publication business."

INKSMITH EDITORIAL SERVICES | LIZ SMITH

liz@inksmithediting.com | www.inksmithediting.com

Contact: email

Services: copyediting, indexing, proofreading, sermon transcription

Types of manuscripts: academic, adult, articles, Bible studies, devotionals, nonfiction books

Charges: page rate, word rate

Credentials/experience: "Liz edits primarily Christian nonfiction. She works with self-publishing authors as well as writers preparing a manuscript for submission to traditional publishers. Her other services include general and Scripture indexes, sermon transcription, typesetting (interior design), and e-book formatting."

INKSNATCHER | SALLY HANAN

429 S. Avenue C, Elgin, TX 78621 | 512-265-6403

inksnatcher.com

Contact: text, website

Services: back-cover copy, coauthoring, copyediting, discussion questions for books, ghostwriting, manuscript evaluation, proofreading, substantive/developmental editing

Types of manuscripts: adult, Bible studies, devotionals, gift books, nonfiction books, novels, short stories, teen/YA

Charges: custom, flat fee, hourly rate, word rate

Credentials/experience: "Inksnatcher has helped hundreds of authors through the process of self-publishing their books since 2007. Her own books are self-published under the imprint Fire Drinkers Publishing."

INSPIRATION FOR WRITERS, INC. | SANDY TRITT

1527 18th St., Parkersburg, WV 26101 | 304-428-1218

IFWeditors@gmail.com | www.InspirationForWriters.com

Contact: email

Services: copyediting, ghostwriting, manuscript evaluation, proofreading, substantive/developmental editing, writing coach

Types of manuscripts: academic, adult, articles, Bible studies, book proposals, curriculum, devotionals, easy readers, gift books, middle grade, nonfiction books, novels, query letters, scripts, short stories, technical material, teen/YA

Charges: word rate

Credentials/experience: "More than 75 percent of Inspiration for Writers, Inc.'s business is repeat business, and we relish establishing long-term relationships with our writers. As per our mission statement, we believe in treating our writers exactly as we would want to be treated—with respect and compassion. Yet, we also believe in being honest. We want our writers to be happy with us ten years from now, so we tell you the truth about your writing. We just make sure all our criticism is of the constructive sort. After all, our purpose is to improve your writing, not destroy your confidence. The best way to get started is to request a no obligation, free sample edit. That allows us to see the level of your writing and recommend a service to you, as well as match you up with the editor who is best suited to your specific genre, writing level and personality. It also allows you to see what to expect from us before any money changes hands."

JAMI'S WORDS | JAMI BENNINGTON

jami@jamiswords.com | *jamiswords.com*

Contact: email

Services: copyediting, manuscript evaluation, proofreading

Types of manuscripts: adult, articles, Bible studies, curriculum, devotionals, nonfiction books, novels, short stories, teen/YA

Charges: word rate

Credentials/experience: "After spending over twenty years as a teacher of language arts, Jami launched her editing business in 2017. She is a graduate of UC San Diego's copyediting certificate program, is a fan of continuing education, and is a member of The Christian PEN."

JAMIE CHAVEZ, EDITOR

3035 Argyle Ave., Murfreesboro, TN 37127 | 615-948-4430

jamie.chavez@gmail.com | *www.jamiechavez.com*

Contact: email

Services: copyediting, manuscript evaluation, substantive/ developmental editing

Types of manuscripts: adult, devotionals, easy readers, gift books, middle grade, nonfiction books, novels, picture books, teen/YA

Charges: flat fee

Credentials/experience: "Jamie Chavez worked for more than ten years in the Christian publishing industry and twenty as a professional copywriter before becoming a freelance editor in 2004. Books she's edited have become *New York Times* best sellers, won Christy and Carol Awards, and been finalists for many other awards and honors. She enjoys the collaborative nature of editing and finds long-term relationships especially rewarding—bring on the second, third, fourth book in the series! Jamie counts many national publishing houses as clients, many authors as friends, and spends her days making good books better."

JAY K. PAYLEITNER & ASSOCIATES

629 N. Tyler Rd., Saint Charles, IL 60174 | 630-377-7899

jaypayleitner@gmail.com | *www.jaypayleitner.com*

Contact: email, phone, website

Services: back-cover copy, coauthoring, ghostwriting

Types of manuscripts: adult, devotionals, gift books, nonfiction books

Charges: flat fee

Credentials/experience: "Author of 30 books with Harvest House, Broadstreet, DaySpring, Tyndale, Multnomah, Bethany House, and Worthy."

JEANETTE GARDNER LITTLETON, PUBLICATION SERVICES

3706 NE Shady Lane Dr., Gladstone, MO 64119-1958 | 816-459-8016

jeanettedl@earthlink.net | *www.linkedin.com/in/jeanette-littleton-b1b790101*

Contact: email

Services: back-cover copy, book-contract evaluation, copyediting, discussion questions for books, indexing, manuscript evaluation, proofreading, substantive/developmental editing

Types of manuscripts: adult, articles, Bible studies, book proposals, curriculum, devotionals, gift books, nonfiction books, novels, query letters, short stories, technical material, teen/YA

Charges: flat fee, hourly rate, page rate

Credentials/experience: "I've been a full-time editor and writer for more than thirty years for a variety of publishers. I've written five thousand articles and edited thousands of articles and dozens of books. Please see my profile at LinkedIn."

JEANETTE HANSCOME
jeanettehanscome@gmail.com | jeanettehanscome.com/services-for-writers

Contact: email

Services: back-cover copy, coauthoring, discussion questions for books, ghostwriting, manuscript evaluation, substantive/developmental editing, writing coach

Types of manuscripts: adult, articles, book proposals, devotionals, gift books, middle grade, nonfiction books, novels, query letters, short stories, teen/YA

Charges: flat fee, hourly rate

Credentials/experience: "Jeanette Hanscome has written five books and hundreds of articles, devotionals and stories, as well as contributing to over a dozen devotionals and story collections. As a freelance editor and coach, Jeanette has experience in a variety of genres including devotionals, women's contemporary fiction, historical romance, YA, memoirs, and general non-fiction. She is also a speaker and regularly teaches workshops at writers conferences. She is currently on the board of the West Coast Christian Writers Conference."

JENNIFER EDWARDS COMMUNICATIONS
mail.jennifer.edwards@gmail.com | www.jedwardsediting.net

Contact: email, website

Services: back-cover copy, copyediting, discussion questions for books, manuscript evaluation, proofreading, writing coach

Types of manuscripts: academic, adult, Bible studies, book proposals, curriculum, nonfiction books, query letters

Charges: hourly rate

Credentials/experience: "Jennifer Edwards is an established professional nonfiction editor, writer, and publishing coach serving Christian authors and publishers. She has worked with 40+ authors and numerous Christian publishers and ministries, including Penguin Random House, Faithlife (Lexham Press), Principles to Live By Publishing, BMH Books, Compel/She Speaks, FDM.World, Redemption Press, Gospel Advocate, The Sophos Group, and more. Her master's degree in Biblical and Theological Studies from Western Seminary has proven invaluable in helping Christian authors with their manuscripts by providing a critical eye for content, a thorough understanding of Scripture, and insightful theological thinking."

JENWESTWRITING | JENNIFER WESTBROOK

14030 Connecticut Ave. #6813, Silver Spring, MD 20916

support@jenwestwriting.com | *www.jenwestwriting.com*

Contact: email, website

Services: back-cover copy, copyediting, ghostwriting, manuscript evaluation, substantive/developmental editing

Types of manuscripts: Bible studies, devotionals, nonfiction books, novels

Charges: custom

Credentials/experience: "I've been editing books for over 20 years and have worked with over 40 authors. My clients' books run the gamut of genres, including non-fiction, novels, self-help, devotionals, Bible studies, and children's books. My approach to editing is goal-oriented, keeping my clients' desires in mind so I can help them create a book that meets their needs."

JHWRITING+ | NICOLE HAYES

jhwritingplus@yahoo.com | *www.jhwritingplus.com*

Contact: email, website

Services: coauthoring, copyediting, discussion questions for books, ghostwriting, manuscript evaluation, proofreading, substantive/developmental editing, writing coach

Types of manuscripts: adult, articles, curriculum, devotionals, gift books, nonfiction books, novels, poetry, short stories, technical material, teen/YA

Charges: flat fee, word rate

Credentials/experience: "Bachelor's degree in English; PhD in education. Although I do most writing, editing, and proofreading projects, my niche is creative nonfiction (engaging, dramatic, factual prose). I have been writing and editing for more than twenty-five years."

JLC SERVICES | JODY L. COLLINS

1403 Newport Ct. SE, Renton, WA 98058 | 425-260-0948

jodyleecollins.com/coach-and-editor

Contact: email

Services: back-cover copy, copyediting, proofreading, substantive/developmental editing, writing coach

Types of manuscripts: academic, Bible studies, book proposals, curriculum, easy readers, middle grade, nonfiction books, poetry, teen/YA

Charges: flat fee

Credentials/experience: "B.A. Liberal Studies, English Major. Member, EFA (Editorial Freelancers Association). Ten years' experience with WordPress and Blogger websites. Create/design/ maintain 25 years' writing online and in print. Author of *Living the Season Well—Reclaiming Christmas* (2017, rev. 2018), *Hearts on Pilgrimage—Poems & Prayers* (2021), ebook *Emmanuel Poems— Verses for the Holidays*."

JOHN D. LOEWEN EDITING SERVICE

12720 Robindale Dr., Rockville, MD 20853 | 202-536-7688
authorjohndloewen@gmail.com

Contact: email, phone

Services: back-cover copy, book-contract evaluation, coauthoring, copyediting, discussion questions for books, ghostwriting, manuscript evaluation, proofreading, substantive/developmental editing, writing coach

Types of manuscripts: academic, adult, articles, Bible studies, book proposals, curriculum, devotionals, easy readers, gift books, middle grade, nonfiction books, novels, poetry, scripts, short stories, technical material, teen/YA

Charges: custom, flat fee, hourly rate, word rate

Credentials/experience: "As a *Cum Laude* graduate in both Geography and Civil Engineering and with a nomination to the Phi Beta Kappa Honor Society, John cut his teeth writing in the upper echelons of academia. Later on, after being born-again, God gave John an anointing to write a wide variety of genres, which he has since used to transition into the world of editing. As the editor of more than twenty published books, including the award winning, *Be Made Whole* (Kathy Armstrong, Xulon Press, 2007), John has also authored two of his own published books (*Breakthrough and Breakout!* and *The Battle*)."

JOHN SLOAN, LLC

830 Grey Eagle Cir. N, Colorado Spring, CO 80919 | 719-888-0365
jsjohnsloan@gmail.com | *sloanhinds.com*

Contact: email

Services: coauthoring, substantive/developmental editing, writing coach

Types of manuscripts: academic, adult, Bible studies, devotionals, easy readers, gift books, nonfiction books, short stories, teen/YA

Charges: flat fee, hourly rate, word rate

Credentials/experience: "I have worked in publishing and editorial roles for 40 years, with Multnomah Press and HarperCollins Christian Publishing, Zondervan. I am offering my services for freelance work in the areas of book development, collaboration, writer coaching, book doctoring, macro editing, content editing. I have worked with a broad spectrum of book and author types: I have edited the literary and general market works of authors like Philip Yancey and Frederick Buechner; the popular issues volumes of writers like Chuck Colson; the high visibility authors like Lee Strobel and Ben Carson; the broader market authors and pastors like John Ortberg and Mark Batterson; and I've worked in the area of the popular academic works. For 3 years my partner Meredith Hinds and I have operated a successful freelance business."

JOT OR TITTLE EDITORIAL SERVICES | SAMUEL RYAN KELLY

sam@jotortittle.com | *jotortittle.com*

Contact: email

Services: copyediting, manuscript evaluation, proofreading, substantive/developmental editing, writing coach

Types of manuscripts: academic, adult, articles, Bible studies, devotionals, nonfiction books, novels, short stories

Charges: hourly rate

Credentials/experience: "Sam has a double BA in English and biblical and religious studies and an MA in theology. He specializes in academic writing and has a background in biblical languages, but he likes to bring his expertise to a variety of projects. In addition to his freelance work, Sam does research for pastors and churches at Docent Research Group and serves as an associate editor with Wordsmith Writing Coaches."

JOY MEDIA | JULIE-ALLYSON IERON

PO Box 413, Mt. Prospect, IL 60056

j-a@joymediaservices.com | *www.joymediaservices.com*

Contact: email

Services: back-cover copy, coauthoring, copyediting, discussion questions for books, ghostwriting, manuscript evaluation, substantive/developmental editing, writing coach

Types of manuscripts: adult, articles, Bible studies, book proposals, devotionals, gift books, nonfiction books, novels, query letters, teen/YA

Charges: hourly rate

Credentials/experience: "Julie was a mentor/master craftsman with the Jerry B. Jenkins Christian Writers Guild. She mentored more than 100 professional writers through Guild studies. Her students reached their writing goals of signing publishing contracts and seeing articles published. Julie was lead writer for the Guild's Writing Essentials and Apprentice curriculum in 2010. She works with late-teen through senior-adult writers of Christ-centered materials."

JR'S RED QUILL EDITING | JUDITH ROBL

PO Box 802, Lyons, KS 67554 | 620-257-3143

jrlight620@yahoo.com | www.judithrobl.com/editing-2

Contact: email, website

Services: back-cover copy, copyediting, discussion questions for books, manuscript evaluation, proofreading, writing coach

Types of manuscripts: adult, Bible studies, devotionals, gift books, novels, query letters, short stories

Charges: custom

Credentials/experience: "Educated as a secondary English teacher decades ago, I've edited for people for many years. My first major accomplishment in editing was published in 2010. I use *The Chicago Manual of Style* unless another style guide is provided. No project is undertaken without a sample edit to see if we are a good fit. I believe the relationship between author and editor is second only to competence."

KAREN APPOLD

kappold@msn.com

Contact: email

Services: copyediting, proofreading

Types of manuscripts: academic, articles, curriculum

Charges: flat fee, hourly rate, word rate

Credentials/experience: "I am an award-winning journalist with a BA from Penn State University in English (Writing). I have more than 25 years of professional editorial experience. I mainly write on healthcare/medical and retail, but welcome Christian-themed work."

KATHY IDE WRITER SERVICES

Kathy@KathyIde.com | www.KathyIde.com

Contact: email

Services: coauthoring, copyediting, ghostwriting, manuscript evaluation, proofreading, substantive/developmental editing, writing coach

Types of manuscripts: adult, articles, Bible studies, book proposals, curriculum, devotionals, gift books, nonfiction books, novels, query letters, screenplays, scripts, short stories, technical material, teen/YA

Charges: hourly rate

Credentials/experience: "Kathy Ide is the author of *Proofreading Secrets of Best-Selling Authors* and *Editing Secrets of Best-Selling Authors* and the editor/compiler of the Fiction Lover's Devotional series. She's been a professional freelance editor for 20+ years, and in 2022 started proofreading screenplays for Pinnacle Peak/PureFlix. Kathy owns Christian Editor Network, parent organization to the four divisions she founded: The Christian PEN: Proofreaders and Editors Network, The PEN Institute, PENCON, and Christian Editor Connection. CEN sponsors the Editors' Choice Award. After speaking at numerous writers' conferences for over ten years and directing three of them for six years, she now puts on Christian Writers Retreats."

KATIE PHILLIPS CREATIVE SERVICES

1500 E. Tall Tree Rd. #6206, Derby, KS 67037-6033 | 316-293-9202

katie@katiephillipscreative.com | www.katiephillipscreative.com

Contact: email

Services: back-cover copy, branding, copyediting, substantive/developmental editing, writing coach

Types of manuscripts: adult, book proposals, middle grade, novels, query letters, short stories, teen/YA

Charges: hourly rate, word rate

Credentials/experience: "Edited six award-finalist novels in multiple categories, including the winners of the Realm Award for Book of the Year, Reader's Choice, and Fantasy. Instructor for The Author Conservatory, run by bestselling and award-winning authors Brett Harris and Kara Swanson. Over ten years industry experience writing and editing both fiction and non-fiction. Bachelor of Arts in Journalism."

KEELY BOEVING EDITORIAL

keely.boeving@gmail.com | *www.keelyboeving.com*

Contact: website

Services: coauthoring, copyediting, ghostwriting, manuscript evaluation, substantive/developmental editing

Types of manuscripts: adult, book proposals, middle grade, nonfiction books, novels, query letters, teen/YA

Charges: hourly rate

Credentials/experience: "Experienced editor and copy editor, formerly worked in editorial for Oxford University Press. Have worked with independent clients, literary agencies, and publishers as a freelancer for the past several years."

KRISTEN STIEFFEL

kristen@kristenstieffel.com | *www.kristenstieffel.com*

Contact: email

Services: copyediting, manuscript evaluation, proofreading, substantive/developmental editing, writing coach

Types of manuscripts: middle grade, novels, short stories, teen/YA

Charges: word rate

Credentials/experience: "Kristen Stieffel is a published novelist and freelance editor specializing in speculative fiction for the Christian submarket. She has been a full-time freelance editor since 2011 and before that had ten years of experience in a newsroom. Kristen is trained in developmental editing and copyediting by the Editorial Freelancers Association and in the specific requirements of fiction by The Christian PEN: Proofreaders and Editors Network."

LEE WARREN COMMUNICATIONS

leewarrenjr@outlook.com | *www.leewarren.info/editing*

Contact: email

Services: copyediting, proofreading

Types of manuscripts: adult, articles, devotionals, gift books, nonfiction books, novels, short stories

Charges: word rate

Credentials/experience: "Lee Warren has twenty-plus years of experience in the Christian publishing industry (both traditional and indie publishing) and has been a contract editor for various publishers. He's also written 19 books (a mixture of nonfiction and fiction), as well as worked as a freelance journalist."

LESLIE L. MCKEE EDITING

lmckeeediting@gmail.com | *lmckeeediting.wixsite.com/lmckeeediting*

Contact: email

Services: back-cover copy, copyediting, discussion questions for books, proofreading, substantive/developmental editing

Types of manuscripts: adult, articles, devotionals, easy readers, middle grade, nonfiction books, novels, picture books, poetry, short stories, teen/YA

Charges: flat fee, page rate, word rate

Credentials/experience: "Freelance editor and proofreader with various publishing houses (large and small) since 2012, working with traditionally published and self-published authors. Also an editor with Havok Publishing. Member of The Christian PEN and American Christian Fiction Writers. See website for details on services offered, as well as testimonials and a portfolio."

LESLIE SANTAMARIA

PO Box 195861, Winter Springs, FL 32719

leslie@lesliesantamaria.com | *lesliesantamaria.com*

Contact: email

Services: back-cover copy, copyediting, manuscript evaluation, proofreading, writing coach

Types of manuscripts: board/picture books, easy readers, middle grade, teen/YA, short stories for children, book proposals for children's books

Charges: flat fee, page rate

Credentials/experience: "With over 200 pieces published in periodicals, including *Highlights for Children, Pockets*, and *Spider* and a picture book, Leslie Santamaria is a candidate for Master of Fine Arts in Creative Writing for Children at Spalding University. A longtime freelance editor for publishers, businesses, ministries, and individuals, she has coached many writers to publication. A frequent contest judge and workshop presenter, Leslie specializes in children's literature and would love to help you, too."

LESLIE STOBBE WRITING COACH

201 E. Howard St. #E46, Tryon, NC 28782 | 828-808-7127

lhstobbe123@gmail.com | *stobbeliterary.com*

Contact: email

Services: back-cover copy, book-contract evaluation, coauthoring, discussion questions for books, ghostwriting, manuscript evaluation, substantive/developmental editing, writing coach

Types of manuscripts: adult, Bible studies, book proposals, curriculum, devotionals, nonfiction books, query letters

Charges: hourly rate

Credentials/experience: "Sixty-five years in Christian publishing, many ghostwritten books, curriculum writer, 25 years as literary agent, hundreds of book proposals evaluated, many authors coached. Also acquisitions editor for Elk Lake Publishing."

LIBBY GONTARZ

libbygontarz@gmail.com | libbygontarz.com

Contact: email, phone

Services: copyediting, substantive/developmental editing

Types of manuscripts: adult, articles, Bible studies, curriculum, devotionals, nonfiction books

Charges: custom, page rate, word rate

Credentials/experience: "After a career of teaching and nationwide educational training, I accepted a curriculum development position at an educational publishing company. Writing lessons and assessments gradually led into editing. Since 2015, I have focused on Christian nonfiction, editing for various publishers and individuals. Earned 2022 Excellence in Editing award for copyediting winning book, *On Wings Like Eagles*. Worked on editing team for two other award-winning books—a devotional and a business book. Your project deserves professional editing!"

LIFE LAUNCH ME | JANE RUBIETTA

9030 Federal Ct., Des Plaines, IL 60016 | 847-363-6364

jane@lifelaunchme.com | www.LifeLaunchMe.com

Contact: email, phone

Services: coauthoring, copyediting, discussion questions for books, ghostwriting, manuscript evaluation, proofreading, substantive/developmental editing, writing coach

Types of manuscripts: adult, articles, book proposals, devotionals, nonfiction books, novels, query letters

Charges: hourly rate

Credentials/experience: "The author of 21 books and hundreds of articles and devotionals, Jane has helped launch many writing careers as a writing coach and editor. Her writing savvy and marketing background help writers find their own voices and progress in their callings. She can turn one idea into 100 articles and numerous books."

LIGHTHOUSE EDITING | DR. LON ACKELSON
13326 Community Rd. #11, Poway, CA 92064 | 858-748-9258
Isaiah68la@sbcglobal.net | *lighthouseedit.com*

Contact: website

Services: back-cover copy, book-contract evaluation, coauthoring, copyediting, ghostwriting, manuscript evaluation, substantive/ developmental editing

Types of manuscripts: adult, Bible studies, book proposals, curriculum, devotionals, nonfiction books, query letters

Charges: flat fee, hourly rate, page rate

Credentials/experience: "A professional editor for thirty-four years and a published writer for forty years."

LIGHTNING EDITING SERVICES | DENISE LOOCK
699 Golf Course Rd., Waynesville, NC |28786 | 908-868-5854
denise@lightningeditingservices.com | *www.lightningeditingservices.com*

Contact: email

Services: coauthoring, copyediting, discussion questions for books, ghostwriting, manuscript evaluation, proofreading, substantive/ developmental editing

Types of manuscripts: adult, articles, Bible studies, book proposals, devotionals, nonfiction books, teen/YA

Charges: flat fee, hourly rate

Credentials/experience: "Former high school English teacher and college instructor Denise Loock is a general editor for Iron Stream Media and also accepts freelance projects. With thirty years' experience in the academic world coupled with ten years in the publishing industry, she helps writers produce books that attract publishers and engage readers."

LISA BARTELT
lmbartelt@gmail.com | *lisabartelt.com*

Contact: website

Services: back-cover copy, coauthoring, copyediting, manuscript evaluation, proofreading

Types of manuscripts: nonfiction books, novels

Charges: hourly rate

Credentials/experience: "20 years of experience including 8 years as a newspaper editor/reporter, 4 years as a contest judge for a well-known writing organization, ACFW contest judging, 2 co-authored books, avid reader of all kinds of books, middle school reading teacher's aide."

LISSA HALLS JOHNSON EDITORIAL

13926 Double Girth Ct., Matthews, NC 28105 | 479-220-8662
lissahallsjohnson@gmail.com | *lissahallsjohnson.com*

Contact: email, website
Services: manuscript evaluation, substantive/developmental editing, writing coach
Types of manuscripts: memoir, novels, teen/YA
Charges: hourly rate
Credentials/experience: "Editor for fiction, nonfiction narrative, memoir for 20+ years. Some writers have received Christy Award finalist awards or nominations, on bestselling lists, *Publishers Weekly* starred reviews."

LOGOS WORD DESIGNS, LLC | LINDA NATHAN

PO Box 735, Maple Falls, WA 98266-0735 | 360-599-3429
editor@logosword.com | *www.logosword.com*

Contact: email
Services: back-cover copy, copyediting, discussion questions for books, ghostwriting, manuscript evaluation, proofreading, substantive/developmental editing
Types of manuscripts: academic, adult, articles, Bible studies, book proposals, devotionals, gift books, nonfiction books, novels, query letters, short stories, technical material, teen/YA
Charges: custom, flat fee, hourly rate, page rate, word rate
Credentials/experience: "Linda Nathan has over 30 years of experience as a professional independent freelance writer, editor, and publishing consultant, working with authors and institutions on a wide range of projects. She is a published author with 10 years of experience in the legal field and has spoken on the radio and at conferences and seminars. Since 1992 she has run her own company, Logos Word Designs, LLC. Linda has a B.A. in Psychology from the University of Oregon and master's level work. She is a freelance staff editor with Redemption Press, a Gold member of the Christian Editor Connection, and a member of four other professional writers' and editors' associations."

LOUISE M. GOUGE, COPYEDITOR

900 Jamison Loop #105, Kissimmee, FL 34744 | 407-694-5765

Louisemgouge@aol.com | *louisemgougeauthor.blogspot.com*

> **Contact:** email
> **Services:** copyediting, substantive/developmental editing
> **Types of manuscripts:** novels
> **Charges:** word rate
> **Credentials/experience:** "Louise M. Gouge is a retired college English professor and the author of twenty-eight novels. For editing, she utilizes *CMOS* and *CWMoS*. Copyediting includes checking grammar, punctuation, spelling, and phrasing. Substantive editing includes making sure character arcs are balanced, the story is well-paced, and the conclusion is satisfying. Checking a client's research will raise the cost, the amount depending upon how much research is required. Novel editing $2000–$3000, depending on word count and services required."

LUCIE WINBORNE

116 Hickory Rd., Longwood, FL 2750-2708 | 321-439-7743

lwinborne704@gmail.com | *www.bluetypewriter.com*

> **Contact:** email
> **Services:** copyediting, proofreading
> **Types of manuscripts:** adult, devotionals, middle grade, nonfiction books, novels, poetry, short stories, teen/YA
> **Charges:** hourly rate
> **Credentials/experience:** "Conversant with *Chicago Manual of Style, Merriam-Webster Collegiate Dictionary*, Google Docs and Microsoft Word, with experience in fiction, nonfiction, educational, and business documents. Demonstrated adherence to deadlines and excellent communication and organizational skills."

LYNNE TAGAWA

5606 Onyx Way, San Antonio, TX 78222 | 210-544-4397

lbtagawa@gmail.com | *www.lynnetagawa.com/editing*

> **Contact:** email
> **Services:** back-cover copy, copyediting
> **Types of manuscripts:** adult, articles, novels, short stories, teen/YA
> **Charges:** word rate
> **Credentials/experience:** "I am an author, educator, and editor. Experienced with ministry materials as well as Christian fiction. I

use the *Chicago Manual of Style* and Hudson's *The Christian Writer's Manual of Style*. My specialty is historical fiction."

MARTI PIEPER, COLLABORATIVE WRITER AND EDITOR

246 Maple Grove Rd., Seneca, SC 29678 | 352-409-3136

marti@martipieper.com | *www.martipieper.com*

Contact: email, website

Services: coauthoring, copyediting, discussion questions for books, ghostwriting, manuscript evaluation, proofreading, writing coach

Types of manuscripts: adult, articles, Bible studies, book proposals, curriculum, devotionals, gift books, nonfiction books, query letters, teen/YA

Charges: custom

Credentials/experience: "Marti Pieper's eclectic publishing career includes ghostwriting a young adult memoir that made the ECPA bestseller list and traveling to six Latin American countries to share stories of teen mission trips and an award-winning missionary memoir. She has written seven traditionally published nonfiction books and edited several more, written and edited for both print and digital publications, and taught at multiple writers conferences."

MEGHAN STOLL EDITING

meghanstollediting.com

Contact: website

Services: copyediting, manuscript evaluation, substantive/ developmental editing

Types of manuscripts: devotionals, nonfiction books, novels

Charges: hourly rate, word rate

Credentials/experience: "For the past six years, I've been helping independent authors bring their books to a high level of excellence. It's a great joy to aid them in producing works that are true to their vision and valuable and enjoyable to their audience. Please see my website for more information."

MG LITERARY SERVICES | MEGAN GERIG

mgliteraryservices@gmail.com | *mgliteraryservices.com*

Contact: website

Services: copyediting, proofreading, substantive/developmental editing

Types of manuscripts: middle grade, teen/YA

Charges: word rate

Credentials/experience: "I am a proofreader for Enclave Publishing and have also performed several developmental edits for a Penguin Random House imprint. I've also worked with several incredible self-published and aspiring authors to bring their manuscripts to the next level. Client testimonials are available on my website."

MIDWEST PROOFREADING SERVICES | TRACY ADAMS
12101 E. 211th St., Peculiar, MO 64078 | 618-709-1827
tracy.adams@midwest-proofreading-services.com | *midwest-proofreading-services.com*
   Contact: website
   Services: proofreading
   Types of manuscripts: academic, adult, articles, Bible studies, curriculum, devotionals, nonfiction books, novels, short stories
   Charges: word rate
   Credentials/experience: "I have done a variety of proofreading from business documents and grad papers to an 87,000 word manuscript. I have a love for Jesus and a desire to be used by Him in spreading the gospel in whatever way He wants to use me."

MISSION AND MEDIA | MICHELLE RAYBURN
info@missionandmedia.com | *www.missionandmedia.com*
   Contact: email
   Services: copyediting, discussion questions for books, ghostwriting, proofreading, substantive/developmental editing
   Types of manuscripts: Bible studies, nonfiction books
   Charges: flat fee, hourly rate, word rate
   Credentials/experience: "Michelle Rayburn has been a freelance writer for more than 20 years and has edited for Christian publishers as well as for indie authors. Has also worked in the marketing and public relations industry. Michelle has an MA in ministry leadership and has published hundreds of articles and Bible studies as well as five books. She specializes in Christian living, Bible study, humor, and self-help."

NEXT INDEX SERVICES | JESSICA MCCURDY CROOKS
jessica@JessicaCrooks.com | *www.next-index.com*
   Contact: email, website
   Services: indexing, proofreading, website text
   Types of manuscripts: adult, articles, devotionals, middle grade, nonfiction books, novels, teen/YA
   Charges: flat fee, hourly rate, page rate, word rate
   Credentials/experience: "My training as a librarian and records manager gives me an eye for detail and finding information. I also know how

readers tend to search for information, a skill that helps me arrive at keywords and phrases for the indexes I write. I have more than twenty years of indexing experience."

NOBLE CREATIVE, LLC | SCOTT NOBLE

PO Box 131402, St. Paul, MN 55113 | 651-494-4169

snoble@noblecreative.com | *www.noblecreative.com*

Contact: email

Services: copyediting, ghostwriting, manuscript evaluation, proofreading, substantive/developmental editing, writing coach

Types of manuscripts: adult, articles, book proposals, curriculum, devotionals, nonfiction books, query letters

Charges: flat fee

Credentials/experience: "Nearly twenty years of experience as an award-winning journalist, writer, editor, and proofreader. More than 1,000 published articles, many of them prompting radio and television appearances. Won several awards from Evangelical Press Association. Worked with dozens of published authors and other public figures, as well as first-time authors and small businesses. Have a BA and MS from St. Cloud State University and an MA from Bethel Seminary."

NOVEL IMPROVEMENT EDITING SERVICES | JEANNE MARIE LEACH

PO Box 552, Hudson, CO 80642

jeanne@novelimprovement.com | *novelimprovement.com*

Contact: website

Services: substantive/developmental editing, writing coach

Types of manuscripts: book proposals, novels, query letters

Charges: flat fee

Credentials/experience: "Jeanne Marie Leach is a multi-published Christian fiction author, freelance editor, and a writing and editing coach. She is also a staff editor at Elk Lake Publishing, Inc. She has edited over 150 books in fifteen years, and many of her clients have gone on to win Christian writer's awards and make bestseller's lists. She is a Gold member of The Christian PEN: Proofreaders and Editors Network and is an editor with the Christian Editor Connection."

OASHEIM EDITING SERVICES, LLC | CATHY OASHEIM

Central Florida | 202-389-8207

cathy@cathyoasheim.com | *www.cathyoasheim.com*

Contact: email, website

Services: copyediting, discussion questions for books, manuscript evaluation, proofreading, substantive/developmental editing, writing coach

Types of manuscripts: academic, articles, Bible studies, curriculum, devotionals, devotionals, doctoral dissertations/theses, nonfiction books, novels, query letters, short stories, technical material

Charges: custom, flat fee, hourly rate, page rate, word rate

Credentials/experience: "Cathy is a professional freelance editor since 2012, blogger, and writing coach who specializes in nonfiction, true fiction, and fiction for Indy authors. She has judged over 1,000 Indie books for the Next Generation Indie Book Awards since 2016. Her services also include academic editing and fact checking for doctoral candidates, and blogs. A BS degree in Applied Psychology from Regis University allows Cathy to 'Refine Your Masterpiece.' Earlier engineering and military experiences support highly technical work and complex storytelling to get the rough draft manuscript out of the head, to the heart, and out of the plume to a polished product for the readers.

"Organizations: Author Alliance of Independent Authors, Journal Storage, National Association of Independent Writers & Editors, Nonfiction Authors Association, Toastmasters International—Distinguished Toastmaster, and The Christian PEN Proofreaders and Editors Network—Silver Member."

ODD SOCK PROOFREADING & COPYEDITING | STEVE MATHISEN

807 Maple St., Hoquiam, WA 98550 | 425-741-8392

scmathisen98037@hotmail.com | *oddsock.me*

Contact: email, website

Services: copyediting, proofreading, substantive/developmental editing

Types of manuscripts: adult, devotionals, nonfiction books, novels, scripts, short stories, teen/YA

Charges: page rate, word rate

Credentials/experience: "Thoughtful editing at reasonable prices. Join my award-winning clients and allow me to help you put your best foot forward."

PAGE & PIXEL PUBLICATIONS | SUSAN MOORE

pageandpixelpublications@gmail.com | pageandpixelpublications.com

Contact: email

Services: back-cover copy, coauthoring, copyediting, ghostwriting, manuscript evaluation, proofreading, substantive/developmental editing

Types of manuscripts: academic, adult, articles, Bible studies, book proposals, devotionals, nonfiction books, novels, query letters, short stories, technical material, teen/YA

Charges: hourly rate

Credentials/experience: "Over thirty-five years experience editing for Christian publishers and independent authors. Offering individual attention, taking into consideration the client's preferences. Familiar with *Chicago Manual of Style*. Attention to detail. Satisfaction guaranteed. Also offer interior design service, e-book formatting, cover design. Your one-stop shop for the independent author."

PERFECT WORD EDITING SERVICES | LINDA HARRIS

lharris@perfectwordediting.com | www.perfectwordediting.com

Contact: email

Services: copyediting

Types of manuscripts: board/picture books

Charges: flat fee

Credentials/experience: "Experienced editor for 40 years. Gold Member of the Christian PEN, Instructor of Editing Children's Books at the PEN Institute, Intake Coordinator for the Christian Editor Connection."

PERPEDIT PUBLISHING INK | BECKY LYLES

PO Box 190246, Boise, ID 83719 | 208-562-1592

beckylyles@beckylyles.com | www.beckylyles.com

Contact: email

Services: copyediting, ghostwriting, manuscript evaluation, proofreading, writing coach

Types of manuscripts: adult, articles, Bible studies, book proposals, devotionals, nonfiction books, novels, query letters, short stories, teen/YA

Charges: flat fee, hourly rate, word rate

Credentials/experience: "15 years creating/proofing/editing articles, newsletters and magazines for government and corporate entities and 15 years freelance-editing fiction and nonfiction, including Bible studies, white papers, résumés, novels and short stories."

PICKY, PICKY INK | SUE MIHOLER
suemiholer@comcast.net

>**Contact:** email
>**Services:** copyediting
>**Types of manuscripts:** Bible studies, devotionals, nonfiction books
>**Charges:** hourly rate
>**Credentials/experience:** "Freelance editing for publishers, ministries, individuals since 1998. References available on request."

PRAIRIE FALLS BOOKS | DEBRA L. BUTTERFIELD and TAMARA CLYMER
4810 Gene Field Rd. #2, St. Joseph, MO 64506 | 816-752-2171
prairiefallsbooks.com

>**Contact:** website
>**Services:** back-cover copy, copyediting, proofreading, substantive/developmental editing
>**Types of manuscripts:** adult, articles, board/picture books, book proposals, devotionals, easy readers, gift books, middle grade, nonfiction books, novels, short stories, teen/YA
>**Charges:** word rate
>**Credentials/experience:** "An award-winning editorial team with decades of experience in Christian writing, editing, and publishing."

PRATHERINK LITERARY SERVICES | VICKI PRATHER
20 Parkview Rd., Clinton, MS 39056 | 601-573-4295
pratherINK@gmail.com | pratherink.wordpress.com

>**Contact:** email
>**Services:** copyediting, discussion questions for books, proofreading, substantive/developmental editing
>**Types of manuscripts:** academic, articles, Bible studies, curriculum, devotionals, gift books, nonfiction books, novels, short stories, teen/YA
>**Charges:** custom, flat fee, word rate
>**Credentials/experience:** "I'm the friend who people call to look over their words. I've written procedure manuals, speeches, poetry, & taught writing skills to middle schoolers. I've been editing fiction & nonfiction for over 8 years."

PROFESSIONAL PUBLISHING SERVICES | CHRISTY CALLAHAN
PO Box 1164, Frankston, TX 75763 | 912-388-1898
professionalpublishingservices@gmail.com | professionalpublishingservices.us

Contact: email, website

Services: copyediting, discussion questions for books, French to English translation, French-language editing, manuscript evaluation, proofreading, substantive/developmental editing, writing coach

Types of manuscripts: academic, adult, articles, Bible studies, curriculum, devotionals, easy readers, gift books, nonfiction books, novels, picture books, poetry, short stories, technical material, teen/YA

Charges: flat fee, hourly rate, word rate

Credentials/experience: "Christy graduated Phi Beta Kappa from Carnegie Mellon University and then earned her MA in Intercultural Studies from Fuller Seminary. A gold member of The Christian PEN: Proofreaders and Editors Network and certified by the Christian Editor Connection and Reedsy, she also completed the 40-hour Foundational Course (Christian track) with the Institute for Life Coach Training."

PROVISION EDITING | NINA HUNDLEY

mrshundley14@gmail.com | *ninahundley.com*

Contact: email, website

Services: copyediting, manuscript evaluation, substantive/developmental editing

Types of manuscripts: adult, articles, Bible studies, book proposals, devotionals, middle grade, nonfiction books, novels, query letters, teen/YA

Charges: flat fee, word rate

Credentials/experience: "Freelance editor with a focus on fiction manuscripts. Member of the Editorial Freelancers Association and silver member of The Christian Pen: Proofreaders and Editors Network."

PURPOSEFUL AUTHOR SUPPORT | MARSHA MALCOLM

Savanna-la-mar, Westmoreland, Jamaica

purposefulnitpicker@gmail.com | *www.purposefulauthorsupport.com*

Contact: email

Services: copyediting, proofreading

Types of manuscripts: adult, Bible studies, devotionals, gift books, nonfiction books, novels, short stories

Charges: word rate

Credentials/experience: "I've been doing freelance for over 20 years. In addition to having an inborn gift, I am certified by ExpertRating (USA) and Centre of Excellence (UK). My clients have been located all over the world, including the USA, Canada, the United Kingdom, Australia, my native Jamaica, and other territories. I edit various dialects of English but the large majority of my projects have been written in American English. I have a very flexible schedule and welcome new clients with interesting books written to glorify God. As an award-winning author myself, I understand the importance of finding an editor with the same Christian mission as my own: to know Christ and make Him known."

PWC EDITING | PAUL W. CONANT

527 Bayshore Pl., Dallas, TX 75217-7755 | 214-289-3397
pwcediting@gmail.com | *PWC-editing.com*

> **Contact:** email
> **Services:** copyediting, proofreading
> **Types of manuscripts:** academic, adult, articles, Bible studies, business materials, devotionals, nonfiction books, novels, poetry, short stories, technical material, textbooks
> **Charges:** hourly rate, word rate
> **Credentials/experience:** "Book editor since '94; textbook editor for 1.5 years; academic editor since 2001; Silver member of The Christian PEN (Proofreaders and Editors Network); contract editor for Holy Fire Publishing; copyeditor for Christian Editing & Design, Redemption Press, and Creative Enterprises Studio."

REBECCA LUELLA MILLER'S EDITORIAL SERVICES

rluellam@yahoo.com | *rewriterewordrework.wordpress.com*

> **Contact:** email, website
> **Services:** back-cover copy, copyediting, manuscript evaluation, proofreading, substantive/developmental editing, writing coach
> **Types of manuscripts:** academic, adult, articles, devotionals, middle grade, nonfiction books, novels, query letters, short stories, teen/YA
> **Charges:** page rate, word rate
> **Credentials/experience:** "I became an editor as a direct result of my work as a critique partner. Behind that were the thirty years I spent as an English teacher evaluating student writing. Since 2004 I have had the privilege of working with numerous traditionally published authors, self-published authors, and aspiring authors alike."

REDEMPTION PRESS | ATHENA DEAN HOLTZ

1602 Cole St., Enumclaw, WA 98022 | 360-226-3488

www.redemption-press.com

> **Contact:** website
> **Services:** back-cover copy, book-contract evaluation, coauthoring, copyediting, discussion questions for books, ghostwriting, indexing, manuscript evaluation, proofreading, substantive/developmental editing, writing coach
> **Types of manuscripts:** adult, Bible studies, board/picture books, curriculum, devotionals, easy readers, gift books, middle grade, nonfiction books, novels, short stories, teen/YA
> **Charges:** flat fee, word rate
> **Credentials/experience:** "Redemption Press offers editing services outside of a publishing contract. Our Managing Editor, Dori Harrell of Breakout Editing, oversees a team of professional editors and coaches. Many of our books developed and edited by her team have won Selah awards, Golden Scroll awards, and Excellence in Editing Awards from PENCON."

REFINE SERVICES, LLC | KATE MOTAUNG

kate@refineservices.com | *www.refineservices.com*

> **Contact:** email
> **Services:** copyediting, proofreading
> **Types of manuscripts:** adult, articles, Bible studies, board/picture books, book proposals, devotionals, easy readers, gift books, middle grade, nonfiction books, novels, poetry, query letters, scripts, short stories, teen/YA
> **Charges:** word rate
> **Credentials/experience:** "I have over seven years of experience copy editing a wide range of written materials, from articles to book proposals to full-length manuscripts."

REVISIONS BY RACHEL, LLC | RACHEL E. BRADLEY

1512 Lynhaven Ave., Richmond, VA 23224 | 918-207-2833
editor@RevisionsbyRachel.com | *www.RevisionsbyRachel.com*

> **Contact:** email
> **Services:** back-cover copy, coauthoring, copyediting, ghostwriting, indexing, manuscript evaluation, proofreading, substantive/developmental editing
> **Types of manuscripts:** adult, Bible studies, curriculum, nonfiction books, novels, teen/YA
> **Charges:** custom, flat fee, hourly rate, word rate
> **Credentials/experience:** "Rachel holds a BS degree in Paralegal

Studies from Northeastern State University in Oklahoma. She graduated *summa cum laude* in 2006 and has been awarded the Advanced Certified Paralegal designation by the National Association of Legal Assistants. She is a gold member of the Christian PEN: Proofreaders and Editors Network, is an established freelance editor with the Christian Editor Connection, is an instructor with the PEN Institute, and has served as a judge for the Excellence in Editing Award and as faculty for PENCON, the only conference for editors in the Christian market."

RICK STEELE EDITORIAL SERVICES

26 Dean Rd., Ringgold, GA 30736 | 706-937-8121

rsteelecam@gmail.com | *steeleeditorialservices.myportfolio.com*

Contact: website

Services: back-cover copy, book-contract evaluation, copyediting, manuscript evaluation, proofreading, substantive/developmental editing, writing coach

Types of manuscripts: academic, adult, articles, Bible studies, book proposals, curriculum, devotionals, middle grade, nonfiction books, novels, query letters, short stories, teen/YA

Charges: flat fee

Credentials/experience: "To fulfill your dream to be that great author, you may find you need some professional publishing help. Rick Steele Editorial Services has the experience and know-how to provide the attention you need, whether it involves coaching or more hands-on editing. Can help with all aspects of both traditional and custom publishing, including editorial critiques, query letter and proposal coaching services, developmental editing, and copyediting."

ROBIN L. REED

1857 Alcan Dr., Medford, OR 97504 | 541-301-0869

robin@robinlreed.com | *robinlreed.com*

Contact: email

Services: copyediting, proofreading

Types of manuscripts: academic, adult, articles, Bible studies, curriculum, devotionals, nonfiction books, novels, short stories, teen/YA

Charges: word rate

Credentials/experience: "I'm an experienced editor who specializes in helping independent authors get their books into print with the highest possible quality. My priority is to preserve and strengthen my clients' original writing voice and support them through the editing process. I've received training through the PEN Institute and Proofread Anywhere as well as earning a master's degree in history."

SARA LAWSON

423 N. Monterey St., Alhambra, CA 91801 | 530-933-9838

sarareneelawson@gmail.com | *www.sarasbooks.com*

Contact: email, website

Services: back-cover copy, copyediting, discussion questions for books, proofreading, substantive/developmental editing

Types of manuscripts: academic, adult, articles, Bible studies, devotionals, middle grade, nonfiction books, novels, scripts, short stories, teen/YA

Charges: custom

Credentials/experience: "Sara Lawson has over 10 years of freelance editing experience working with fiction and nonfiction books, magazine articles, television scripts, and academic papers of all lengths. She has also served at both predominantly white and Asian American churches, so she understands a variety of ministry contexts. She loves to help writers because she believes that everyone has a story to tell and no one should have to let technical writing abilities get in the way of telling that story."

SARAH HAYHURST EDITORIAL, LLC

1441 Haynescrest Ct., Grayson, GA 30017 | 470-825-2905

sarah@sarahhayhurst.com | *www.sarahhayhurst.com*

Contact: email, website

Services: copyediting, proofreading, substantive/developmental editing

Types of manuscripts: articles, Bible studies, curriculum, devotionals, nonfiction books, short stories

Charges: word rate

Credentials/experience: "Sarah is a gold-level member of The Christian PEN and Christian Editor Network with whom she passed extensive testing and demonstrated expertise in the substantive editing, copyediting, and proofreading of both fiction and nonfiction manuscripts. Sarah has over ten years of editing experience and started her editorial company in 2014."

SCRIPTS4C.COM | DAVID M. HYDE

2245 Q St., Rio Linda, CA 95673 | 916-261-1816

scripts4c@icloud.com | *Scripts4c.com*

Contact: email, website

Services: copyediting, manuscript evaluation, novel adaptation, substantive/developmental editing

Types of manuscripts: scripts

Charges: flat fee

Credentials/experience: "All Scripts4c analysts are experienced multi-award winning screenwriters in the Family & Faith-based film market."

SETTINGS CHRISTIAN PUBLISHING, LLC | REBEKAH MCKAMIE

editor@settingschristian.com | *www.settingschristian.com*

Contact: website

Services: book-contract evaluation, copyediting, manuscript evaluation, substantive/developmental editing, writing coach

Types of manuscripts: adult, articles, Bible studies, book proposals, curriculum, devotionals, nonfiction books, novels, poetry, query letters, short stories, teen/YA

Charges: custom

Credentials/experience: "I hold a Master of Arts in English Composition, have edited dozens of works, and have published works of my own."

SHARMAN EDITS | SHARMAN J. MONROE

3431 S. Dakota Ave. NE, Washington, DC 20018 | 240-353-8000

myjourneytome@gmail.com | *www.sharmansedits.com*

Contact: website

Services: book coach, copyediting, proofreading, substantive/developmental editing

Types of manuscripts: adult, devotionals, nonfiction books, novels, teen/YA

Charges: flat fee, hourly rate

Credentials/experience: "I have over 25 years of experience writing, editing and proofreading. Since starting my business in 2011, I have edited and proofed over 50 manuscripts, fiction and non-fiction, and of different genres ranging from Christian to devotionals, entrepreneurship, motivational, mystery, self-help/personal development, urban to young adult to name a few. The majority of my clients are first-time authors and their books can be found on Amazon, and Barnes and Noble."

STICKS AND STONES | JAMIE CALLOWAY-HANAUER
snsedits@gmail.com | *www.snsedits.com*

Contact: email

Services: book-contract evaluation, coauthoring, copyediting, discussion questions for books, ghostwriting, manuscript evaluation, proofreading, substantive/developmental editing, writing coach

Types of manuscripts: adult, articles, book proposals, curriculum, devotionals, easy readers, middle grade, nonfiction books, novels, poetry, query letters, short stories, teen/YA

Charges: flat fee

Credentials/experience: "Jamie has eighteen years of experience in the editing field. Previously a full-time public interest attorney who also edited part-time, she is now the owner/operator of Sticks and Stones, where she specializes in academic, legal, and faith-based fiction and nonfiction for adults and teens; ghostwriting; and proposal and query review and development."

SUE A. FAIRCHILD, EDITOR
512 Elm St., Watsontown, PA 17777 | 570-939-0318
sueafairchild74@gmail.com | *www.sueafairchild.wordpress.com*

Contact: email

Services: back-cover copy, copyediting, manuscript evaluation, proofreading, substantive/developmental editing, writing coach

Types of manuscripts: adult, Bible studies, devotionals, gift books, middle grade, nonfiction books, novels, teen/YA

Charges: word rate

Credentials/experience: "Editor for Elk Lake Publishing Inc.; writing coach, content/copy editor, and proofreader for Iron Stream Media; writing coach for Redemption Press; proofreader for Zeitgeist a division of Penguin Random House."

SUSAN KING EDITORIAL SERVICES
1113 Brookside Dr., Nashville, TN 37069 | 615-202-6019
susankingedits.com

Contact: website

Services: coauthoring, copyediting, discussion questions for books, ghostwriting, manuscript evaluation, proofreading, substantive/developmental editing, writing coach

Types of manuscripts: academic, adult, articles, Bible studies, book proposals, devotionals, gift books, nonfiction books, novels, poetry, query letters, short stories, teen/YA

Charges: hourly rate

Credentials/experience: "Of my more than 30 years in the industry, I served 24 years as an editor for *The Upper Room,* the world's premier daily devotional guide reaching 3 million subscribers in 100 countries and 35 languages. For the past 20 years, I have trained writers at over one hundred Christian writers' conferences in the U.S. and Canada. My professional life has also included teaching freshman English, American literature, and feature-writing classes at Lipscomb University, Biola University, and Abilene Christian University for a total of 27 years. Currently, I am the compiler and editor of the Short and Sweet anthology series."

SUSAN R. EDITORIAL | SUSAN RESCIGNO

PO Box 939, South Orleans, MA 02662 | 914-844-5217

SusanR.Edit@gmail.com | *srescigno7.wixsite.com/mysite*

Contact: website

Services: copyediting, indexing, proofreading

Types of manuscripts: academic, adult, nonfiction books, teen/YA

Charges: flat fee

Credentials/experience: "I have 25+ years of publishing experience. I have worked as a journals production editor, a book production editor, and a reference book editor at several small academic publishing houses. I have also been copyediting, proofreading, and indexing manuscripts during that time. I copyedit manuscripts electronically and proofread on typeset page proofs. I specialized in Christian book publishing for many years, but I also enjoy working on nonfiction books in history and politics, as well as all areas of wellness."

TANDEM SERVICES | JENNIFER CROSSWHITE

PO Box 220, Yucaipa, CA 92399 | 414-465-2567

www.tandemservicesink.com

Contact: website

Services: back-cover copy, copyediting, copywriting, manuscript evaluation, proofreading, substantive/developmental editing, writing coach

Types of manuscripts: adult, devotionals, middle grade, nonfiction books, novels, teen/YA

Charges: custom, flat fee

Credentials/experience: "Jennifer Crosswhite is owner and CEO of Tandem Services. Her experience spans both sides of the publishing desk, from author to former managing editor of a Big 5 publisher for over 20 years. She and her team have worked with hundreds of authors at every stage to help them tell the story of their heart."

THREE FATES EDITING | SARAH GRACE LIU

28 Close Hollow Dr., Hamlin, NY 14464

sarah.grace@threefatesediting.com | www.threefatesediting.com

Contact: email, website

Services: copyediting, ghostwriting, manuscript evaluation, proofreading, substantive/developmental editing

Types of manuscripts: academic, adult, Bible studies, middle grade, nonfiction books, novels, poetry, short stories, teen/YA

Charges: word rate

Credentials/experience: "I have an MA in Creative Writing and have run my own editing business since 2012. My true specialization is speculative fiction. For nonfiction, I am more comfortable with progressive texts."

TISHA MARTIN EDITORIAL, LLC

tisha@tishamartin.com | www.tishamartin.com

Contact: website

Services: back-cover copy, book idea and social-media brainstorming, copyediting, discussion questions for books, manuscript evaluation, manuscript evaluations for contests, proofreading, substantive/developmental editing, writing coach

Types of manuscripts: adult, book proposals, devotionals, memoir, nonfiction books, novels, teen/YA

Charges: flat fee, hourly rate, word rate

Credentials/experience: "Tisha Martin empowers authors to write their best, life-giving story. She has seen over 250 projects (for individuals and publishers) and is a former contest judge for Writer's Digest and other premier writing contests, as well as assistant director for an editing conference. Tisha works with motivated authors who write redemptive or resilient themes. She enjoys connecting and speaking at conferences. Editing is a gift to your readers. Visit her website today for more information about working with her."

TRAILBLAZE EDITORIAL | SARAH BARNUM
sarah@trail-blazes.com | trail-blazes.com

>**Contact:** email, website
>**Services:** back-cover copy, copyediting, substantive/developmental editing, writing coach
>**Types of manuscripts:** adult, articles, devotionals, gift books, nonfiction books, short stories
>**Charges:** flat fee, word rate
>**Credentials/experience:** "Sarah discovered her passion for writing and editing after earning a bachelor's degree with highest honors. She is a recipient of the 2022 Excellence in Editing Award and serves on the leadership team for the West Coast Christian Writers Conference."

TUPPANCE ENTERPRISES | JAMES PENCE
PO Box 99, Greenville, TX 75403 | 469-730-6478
james@pence.com | jamespence.com

>**Contact:** email, phone, website
>**Services:** coauthoring, copyediting, ghostwriting, manuscript evaluation, proofreading, substantive/developmental editing, writing coach
>**Types of manuscripts:** adult, articles, Bible studies, book proposals, devotionals, middle grade, nonfiction books, novels, query letters, short stories, technical material, teen/YA
>**Charges:** flat fee, hourly rate, word rate
>**Credentials/experience:** "James has been writing and editing professionally since 2000, and is a traditionally published author of ten books. Publishers include Osborne/McGraw-Hill, Tyndale, Kregel, Baker (co-author), Thomas Nelson (ghostwriter), and Mountainview Books. Published works include textbooks, how-to, novels (adult and YA), Christian living, and memoir."

TURN THE PAGE CRITIQUES | CINDY THOMSON
PO Box 298, Pataskala, OH 43062 | 614-354-3904
cindyswriting@gmail.com | cindyswriting.com/index.php/critique-service

>**Contact:** email
>**Services:** critiquing, manuscript evaluation, proofreading
>**Types of manuscripts:** articles, book proposals, novels, query letters
>**Charges:** flat fee
>**Credentials/experience:** "Published author both traditionally

and independently of fiction and non-fiction, author of numerous magazine articles, and a former mentor with the Jerry B. Jenkins Christian Writers Guild, I can help you get a solid footing as you prepare to publish."

VQ SUCCESS | SETH CZEREPAK
PO Box 15892, Tampa, FL 33614 | 813-563-9630
sethczerepak.com

Contact: website
Services: ghostwriting, substantive/developmental editing, writing coach
Types of manuscripts: articles, Bible studies, nonfiction books, short stories
Charges: flat fee
Credentials/experience: "Since 2009, I have ghostwritten and edited hundreds of books on the topics of leadership, cognitive behavior therapy, entrepreneurship, spiritual growth, and critical thinking. I have 15,000 hours of direct response copywriting experience and 10,000 hours of one-on-one counseling experience and degrees and certifications in philosophy, music theory, and developmental psychology."

WHALIN & ASSOCIATES | W. TERRY WHALIN
9457 S. University Blvd., Ste. 621, Highlands Ranch, CO 80129 | 720-708-4953
terry@terrywhalin.com | *terrywhalin.blogspot.com*

Contact: email
Services: coauthoring, discussion questions for books, ghostwriting, substantive/developmental editing
Types of manuscripts: adult, book proposals, devotionals, gift books, nonfiction books
Charges: flat fee
Credentials/experience: "Terry has written more than sixty books for traditional publishers, including one book that has sold more than 100,000 copies. He has written for more than fifty publications and worked in acquisitions at three publishing houses."

WORDMELON | MARGOT STARBUCK
308-B Northwood Cir., Durham, NC 27701 | 919-321-5440
wordmelon@gmail.com | *www.wordmelon.com*

Contact: website
Services: book proposals, coauthoring, ghostwriting, manuscript

evaluation, substantive/developmental editing, writing coach

Types of manuscripts: book proposals, nonfiction books

Charges: flat fee, word rate

Credentials/experience: "Margot, a graduate of Westmont College and Princeton Seminary, is the award-winning writer of more than thirty books. She's touched over 200 major publishing projects as author, writer, coach, and editor."

WORDPRO COMMUNICATION SERVICES | LIN JOHNSON

9118 W. Elmwood Dr., Ste. 1G, Niles, IL 60714-5820 | 847-296-3964

ljohnson@wordprocommunications.com | *wordprocommunications.com*

Contact: email

Services: back-cover copy, book-contract evaluation, copyediting, discussion questions for books, proofreading, small-group Bible study guides

Types of manuscripts: adult, Bible studies, Bible curriculum, devotionals, nonfiction books

Charges: flat fee, hourly rate

Credentials/experience: "I've worked in Christian publishing for more than four decades as an in-house and freelance Bible curriculum editor and writer; award-winning writer of more than 70 books and hundreds of articles, devotions, and reviews; former managing editor of *Christian Communicator, Advanced Christian Writer,* and *Church Libraries;* and freelance editor and proofreader for traditional and independent publishing houses, organizations, and authors. Clients have praised me for being accurate, detailed, thorough, and deadline oriented. In addition, I've trained thousands of writers at conferences, as an adjunct writing instructor at Taylor University, and in international settings. I have an English minor from Adrian College, a BA in Christian education from Cedarville University, a BA in Bible-theology from Moody Bible Institute, and an MS in adult and continuing education from National-Louis University."

WORDPOLISH EDITORIAL SERVICES | YVONNE KANU

yvonne@wordpolish.net | *www.wordpolish.net*

Contact: email, website

Services: copyediting, discussion questions for books, manuscript evaluation, proofreading, writing coach

Types of manuscripts: academic, Bible studies, devotionals, easy readers, nonfiction books, novels, short stories, teen/YA

Charges: word rate

Credentials/experience: "Over 10 years of experience in publishing, business communication, and technical writing. BA degree in English, and certificates in Editing, Publishing, and Technical Writing."

WORDS FOR WRITERS | GINNY L. YTTRUP

PO Box 1651, Lincoln, CA 95648

ginny@wordsforwriters.net | wordsforwriters.net

Contact: email, website

Services: manuscript evaluation, substantive/developmental editing, writing coach

Types of manuscripts: adult, book proposals, devotionals, novels, query letters, teen/YA

Charges: hourly rate, word rate

Credentials/experience: "Ginny is an award-winning author, a writing coach who received a certificate in coaching through Western Seminary, and a developmental editor who has trained under other editors, taken courses through UC Berkeley's Extension program in editing, and has had the honor of editing several award-winning or bestselling manuscripts."

WRITE BY LISA | ELIZABETH (LISA) R. THOMPSON

200 Laguna Dr. S, Litchfield Park, AZ 85340 | 623-258-5258

writebylisa@gmail.com | www.writebylisa.com

Contact: email

Services: back-cover copy, citations, coauthoring, copyediting, discussion questions for books, ghostwriting, manuscript evaluation, proofreading, substantive/developmental editing, writing coach

Types of manuscripts: adult, Bible studies, board/picture books, curriculum, devotionals, easy readers, gift books, middle grade, nonfiction books, novels, short stories, teen/YA

Charges: flat fee, hourly rate, word rate

Credentials/experience: "I have been writing and editing full-time since May 2009. I have a BA in elementary education with a minor in English. I have edited about 300 books to date. On Facebook, I also admin an editing group and a Christian writing group and am the mod for a proofreading group and a second Christian writing group."

WRITE CONCEPTS, LLC | ALICE CRIDER

590 Highway 105 #107, Monument, CO 80132 | 719-651-0160
editoralicecrider@gmail.com | *www.alicecrider.com*

> **Contact:** email
> **Services:** back-cover copy, coauthoring, ghostwriting, manuscript evaluation, substantive/developmental editing, writing coach
> **Types of manuscripts:** adult, book proposals, nonfiction books, query letters
> **Charges:** custom
> **Credentials/experience:** "I am a certified life coach and author coach with more than ten years of experience in helping individuals and authors achieve their dreams and goals. I am also a non-fiction editor with 20+ years of experience in book publishing, including eight years in a division of Random House. I specialize in developmental, content, and line editing. I am skilled at analyzing a manuscript's strengths and weaknesses, and at suggesting improvements and revisions. I love strategizing and brainstorming ideas with writers. Most recently, I have been a collaborative writer for authors who don't have the time or talent to write their own books."

THE WRITE EDITOR | ERIN K. BROWN

595 Farm Way, Corvallis, MT 59828 | 406-239-5590
thewriteeditor@gmail.com | *www.writeeditor.net*

> **Contact:** email
> **Services:** copyediting, manuscript evaluation, proofreading, substantive/developmental editing
> **Types of manuscripts:** adult, articles, Bible studies, book proposals, curriculum, devotionals, nonfiction books
> **Charges:** flat fee
> **Credentials/experience:** "Erin K. Brown, aka The Write Editor, is a full-time, professional freelance editor, proofreader, and writer. Erin's formal training in editorial practices and procedures, ten years in Christian retailing, twenty-six years in education, and over ten years as a Christy Award judge affords her a wide knowledge and experience base. She combines her love of editing and teaching by mentoring new writers and teaching nonfiction editing skills to other professional editors. Visit her website to view a selected client list, and read what editors and authors say about Erin and her work. The Write Editor . . . is the right editor!"

THE WRITE FLOURISH | TIM and NOLA PASSMORE

nola@thewriteflourish.com.au | *www.thewriteflourish.com.au*

Contact: email

Services: copyediting, manuscript evaluation, mentoring, proofreading, substantive/developmental editing

Types of manuscripts: academic, adult, articles, book proposals, devotionals, memoir, nonfiction books, novels, poetry, short stories, teen/YA

Charges: hourly rate

Credentials/experience: "Tim and Nola Passmore each have more than 20 years' experience as university academics. Nola also has a degree in creative writing. They founded The Write Flourish in 2014 and have edited a wide range of manuscripts across a variety of styles and genres. They have also had many of their own short pieces published including fiction, poetry, devotionals, memoir, nonfiction and academic articles. They would love to help you add the right flourish to your manuscript."

WRITE HIS ANSWER MINISTRIES | MARLENE BAGNULL

951 Anders Rd., Lansdale, PA 19446 | 484-991-8581

mbagnull@aol.com | *writehisanswer.com/editingmentoring*

Contact: email

Services: copyediting, manuscript evaluation, proofreading, substantive/developmental editing

Types of manuscripts: adult, articles, devotionals, nonfiction books, novels

Charges: flat fee, hourly rate

Credentials/experience: "More than thirty-five years of experience in publishing, leading critique groups, and directing writers conferences; author of twelve books and more than a thousand sales to Christian periodicals; editor, typesetter, and publisher of eleven Ampelos Press books."

WRITE NOW EDITING | KARIN BEERY

PO Box 31, Elk Rapids, MI 49629

karin@karinbeery.com | *writenowedits.com*

Contact: email

Services: back-cover copy, copyediting, ghostwriting, manuscript evaluation, substantive/developmental editing, writing coach

Types of manuscripts: adult, novels, teen/YA

Charges: page rate, word rate

Credentials/experience: "Member of The Christian Proofreaders and Editors Network and the Christian Editor Network; PEN Institute instructor."

WRITE PATHWAY EDITORIAL SERVICES | ANN KNOWLES

annknowles03@aol.com | write-pathway.blogspot.com

Contact: email

Services: coauthoring, copyediting, ghostwriting, proofreading, Spanish translation, transcription, writing coach

Types of manuscripts: adult, articles, book proposals, curriculum, devotionals, easy readers, gift books, middle grade, nonfiction books, novels, picture books, poetry, query letters, short stories, teen/YA

Charges: custom

Credentials/experience: "Retired educator, MA in education, certified ESL and Spanish; ESL training consultant for public schools and community colleges. I joined The Christian PEN: Proofreaders and Editors Network in 2005 and started Write Pathway in 2007. I have taken numerous courses from The Christian PEN, American Christian Fiction Writers, Write Integrity Press, and Christian Writers International."

THE WRITE STAGE | RONNELL GIBSON and KENZI NEVINS

info@thewritestage.com | TheWriteStage.com

Contact: website

Services: consulting, manuscript evaluation, story coaching

Types of manuscripts: adult, book proposals, devotionals, easy readers, middle grade, novels, picture books, query letters, short stories, teen/YA

Charges: flat fee, word rate

Credentials/experience: "Editor and former literary agent turned social media manager, Ronnell and Kenzi have published hundreds of articles, devotionals, stories, and won multiple awards. They both teach at various conferences, writers groups, and classrooms and are members of The Christian PEN, SCBWI, and Realm Makers. They specialize in story coaching and social media branding."

WRITE WAY | PEGGYSUE WELLS

3419 E 1000 North, Roanoke, IN 46783 | 260-433-2817

peggysuewells@gmail.com | www.PeggySueWells.com

Contact: email, website

Services: back-cover copy, coauthoring, copyediting, discussion questions for books, ghostwriting, manuscript evaluation, substantive/developmental editing, writing coach

Types of manuscripts: adult, articles, Bible studies, board/picture books, book proposals, curriculum, easy readers, gift books, middle grade, nonfiction books, novels, query letters, scripts, short stories, teen/YA

Charges: flat fee, hourly rate

Credentials/experience: "Bestselling author of 32 books and ghostwriter for many more, PeggySue Wells collaborates with authors to tell their story. She coaches writers, and polishes fiction and nonfiction manuscripts to be publish ready."

WRITE WAY COPYEDITING, LLC | DIANA SCHRAMER

diana@writewaycopyediting.com | *www.writewaycopyediting.com*

Contact: email

Services: copyediting, manuscript evaluation

Types of manuscripts: Bible studies, devotionals, gift books, memoir, nonfiction books, novels

Charges: hourly rate

Credentials/experience: "I started my business in 2010 and have copyedited 100+ book-length manuscripts and have reviewed 200+ manuscripts. In addition, I have copyedited and reviewed front- and back-cover copy as well as business-related documents and blogs."

WRITER JUSTIFIED | JUDY HAGEY

judy.hagey@gmail.com | *judyhagey.com*

Contact: email, website

Services: back-cover copy, copyediting, proofreading, substantive/ developmental editing

Types of manuscripts: academic, adult, articles, devotionals, nonfiction books, novels

Charges: word rate

Credentials/experience: "I have filled various roles in Christian higher education and the nonprofit world, including ten years as the writing director of a ministry producing small-group discipleship materials. Editing credits include theological dissertations, fiction, and nonfiction manuscripts. I currently freelance for traditional publishers as well as individual clients. I have a BA degree in education from Dordt University and am a (certified) Gold Member of the Christian Professional Editors Network."

THE WRITER'S EDGE | BILLCARMICHAEL

info@writersedgeservice.com | *www.writersedgeservice.com*

Contact: website

Services: manuscript evaluation

Types of manuscripts: books of all kinds and all ages

Charges: $99

Credentials/experience: "Professional editors with many years of experience in working with major Christian publishers evaluate, screen, and expose potential books to traditional Christian publishing companies."

WRITER'S TABLET, LLC | TERRI WHITMIRE

3155 Hembree Trace Dr., Marietta, GA 30062 | 770-331-4326

Twhitmire@writerstablet.org | *www.Writerstablet.org*

Contact: email

Services: back-cover copy, copyediting, discussion questions for books, ghostwriting, indexing, manuscript evaluation, proofreading, substantive/developmental editing, writing coach

Types of manuscripts: academic, adult, articles, Bible studies, curriculum, devotionals, easy readers, middle grade, nonfiction books, novels, picture books, poetry, scripts, short stories, teen/YA

Charges: page rate

Credentials/experience: "Writers Tablet, LLC has been helping aspiring writers become authors for over seven years, including three bestselling authors. With well over 60 years of combined experience, the Writers Tablet Team consists of highly sought-after editors, publishers, poets, illustrators, and graphic artists who are industry experts. As a Christian assisted self-publishing agency, we pray with and for your project and attribute all of our success to our Father in heaven. With certifications in literature, editing, and graphic artists, the Writers Tablet team has received numerous awards, accolades, and recognition for its service to the writing community."

WRITERS COACH SARAH HAMAKER

4207 Collier Rd., Fairfax, VA 22030 | 703-691-1676

sarah@sarahhamaker.com | *www.sarahhamaker.com/editorial-services*

Contact: email, website

Services: copyediting, ghostwriting, proofreading, substantive/developmental editing, writing coach

Types of manuscripts: articles, book proposals, nonfiction books, novels

Charges: flat fee, hourly rate

Credentials/experience: "Sarah is an experienced editor with both nonfiction and fiction books under her belt. She's been published traditionally and indie. She's also an AWSA certified writers and speakers coach."

WRITING PURSUITS | KATHRESE MCKEE

27708 Tomball Pkwy., PMB 107, Tomball, TX 77375

kmckee@writingpursuits.com | *www.writingpursuits.com*

Contact: website

Services: copyediting, manuscript evaluation, substantive/developmental editing

Types of manuscripts: adult, middle grade, novels, short stories, teen/YA

Charges: flat fee, hourly rate

Credentials/experience: "Kathrese McKee has edited fiction professionally since 2014 in the following genres: urban and paranormal fantasy, fairytale retellings, dystopian and military science fiction, women's fiction, and contemporary and historical romance. She hosts the *Writing Pursuits* podcast and writes and produces a weekly newsletter, *Writing Pursuits Tips for Authors*."

YO PRODUCTIONS, LLC | YOLANDA SANDERS

1543 Reynoldsburg, Columbus, OH 43068 | 614-452-4920

info_4u@yoproductions.net | *www.yoproductions.net*

Contact: email, phone, website

Services: back-cover copy, coauthoring, copyediting, discussion questions for books, ghostwriting, manuscript evaluation, proofreading, substantive/developmental editing, writing coach

Types of manuscripts: academic, adult, articles, Bible studies, book proposals, curriculum, devotionals, nonfiction books, novels, poetry, query letters, scripts, style books, technical material, teen/YA

Charges: custom, flat fee, hourly rate, word rate

Credentials/experience: "More than thirteen years of professional editing and writing experience, editor and writer for a national publication."

21

PUBLICITY AND MARKETING SERVICES

THE ADAMS GROUP PUBLIC RELATIONS | GINA ADAMS

6688 Nolensville Rd. 108-149, Brentwood, TN 37027 | 888-253-3622

gina@adamsprgroup.com | *www.adamsprgroup.com*

Contact: email, phone, website form

Services: public relations, publicity campaigns, press releases, press-release distribution, press-kit creation, contributed content, video production

Books: all genres

Charges: flat fee

Credentials/experience: "Honored by the prestigious Communicator Awards in 2019, 2020, and 2022, The Adams Group has represented faith-based artists, authors, films, speakers, comedians, pastors, and major conference events for over three decades. Gina received her B.S. degree in business and marketing from Murray State University. She is a member of the National Religious Broadcasters and the Evangelical Press Association. She serves on the Gospel Music Association Hall of Fame committee, as well as the Publicity Committee for the Arts of Southern Kentucky. Gina has also earned a certificate of apologetics from Biola University, has an Expert Rating Certification in Social Media Marketing and is a Hootsuite Certified Professional in Social Marketing."

AUDRA JENNINGS PR

2609 Sandy Ln., Corsicana, TX 75110 | 903-874-8363

ajenningspr@gmail.com | *www.audrajennings.com*

Contact: email

Services: publicity, blog tours, social-media management, graphics packages

Specialty: Christian books to Christian media

Books: nonfiction, fiction, children's

Charges: flat fee, hourly rate

Credentials/experience: "I have worked as a publicist in the Christian market since 2002. For 16 years, I worked for two different agencies before going freelance on my own and have worked with every major Christian publisher over the years."

AUTHOR MEDIA | THOMAS UMSTATTD JR.

PO Box 5690, Austin, TX 78763 | 512-582-7290

thomas@authormedia.com | *authormedia.com*

Contact: website form

Services: marketing consulting, web development, branding, web design

Books: fiction, nonfiction, children's

Charges: flat fee, hourly rate

Credentials/experience: More than ten years of experience. Included in "101 Best Websites for Authors" by *Writer's Digest*.

BANNER CONSULTING | MIKE LOOMIS

mike@mikeloomis.co | *www.mikeloomis.co*

Contact: email, website form

Services: book-launch planning, branding, article curation and placement, web development, PR

Specialty: branding and marketing strategy

Books: nonfiction

Charges: custom

Credentials/experience: "I've worked with internationally known brands and *New York Times* bestsellers. I've helped clients get breakthrough PR, speaking engagements, and bestseller lists."

BBH LITERARY | LAURA BARDOLPH

616-319-1641

laura@bbhliterary.com | *bbhliterary.com*

David Bratt, david@bbhliterary.com

Contact: email, website form

Services: book publicity

Books: nonfiction

Charges: flat fee

Credentials/experience: "Nine years on staff in the marketing department at Eerdmans Publishing, with roles that included publicist, publicity manager, and director of marketing and publicity."

BLUE RIDGE READER CONNECTION | EDIE MELSON

604 S. Almond Dr., Simpsonville, SC 29681 | 864-373-4232

ediegmelson@gmail.com | *www.blueridgereaderconnections.com*

Debb Hackett, brreaderconnection@gmail.com

Darlene Franklin, brreaderconnection@gmail.com

Heather Kreke, brreaderconnection@gmail.com

> **Contact:** email, website form
> **Services:** connecting authors to readers
> **Books:** all clean reads in all genres
> **Charges:** flat fee
> **Credentials/experience:** "Our aim is to create a place for readers and book clubs to take their reading experience deeper. This is more than opening a new book. This is where you can find new authors or rediscover old favorites and interact with them, check out new writers, and hear about upcoming releases." BRRC falls under the Blue Ridge Mountains Christian Writers Conference.

THE BLYTHE DANIEL AGENCY, INC. | BLYTHE DANIEL

www.theblythedanielagency.com

Blythe Daniel, publicist

Stephanie Alton, marketing manager

> **Contact:** website form
> **Services:** range of publicity campaigns utilizing broadcast and print media and the Internet, including blogs, podcasts, articles, TV and radio interviews, book reviews, and book launches
> **Books:** primarily adult and young-adult nonfiction
> **Charges:** custom
> **Credentials/experience:** "We have personal relationships with hundreds of media outlets that we have developed over the past twenty years in the business. Through our relationships, understanding of the changing media landscape, and careful selection of content we promote, we are able to provide our clients more opportunities to bring recognition to their books." Blythe worked five years as the publicity director and two years as the marketing director for Thomas Nelson.

BROOKSTONE CREATIVE GROUP | JOHN HERRING

100 Missionary Ridge, Birmingham, AL 35242 | 302-514-7899

www.brookstonecreativegroup.com

> **Contact:** website form

Services: Amazon optimization, social-media assessment and consulting, video interviews, email and digital marketing, search-engine optimization, Facebook and Google ad management
Books: all
Charges: custom, flat fee
Credentials/experience: "Brookstone Creative Group is changing the landscape for how writers, authors, speakers, pastors, musicians, and other creatives navigate the ever-changing landscape of platform development. Through true and tested solutions, training, and community-building, Brookstone Creative Group guides their clients in the who, where, when, and how to inspirational success."

CHOICE MEDIA & COMMUNICATIONS | HEATHER ADAMS
404-423-8411

hello@choicemediacommunications.com | www.choicemediacommunications.com
Allie Ellis, senior publicist, Allie@ChoiceMediaCommunications.com
Brittany Battista, associate publicist, Brittany@ChoiceMediaCommunications.com
Hannah Harter, associate publicist, Hannah@ChoiceMediaCommunications.com
Devon Brown, senior publicist, Devon@ChoiceMediaCommunications.com
Abbie Holcombe, publicist, Abbie@ChoiceMediaCommunications.com
Emily Taylor, associate publicist, Emily@ChoiceMediaCommunications.com

Contact: website form
Services: media relations, branding and strategy, social media, events
Books: nonfiction
Charges: flat fee, retainer-based partnership
Credentials/experience: "Choice Media & Communications is a boutique media and communications business dedicated to providing clients with quality public relations. Choice helps authors create a clear communications plan, gain media coverage, and receive guidance they won't get anywhere else. With more than two decades of high-level professional communications experience across varying industries and with many of today's tastemakers and thought leaders, Choice founder Heather Adams created a public relations business marked with warmth and enthusiasm, strategic development, clear communication, detailed execution, and thorough reporting."

CHRISTIAN INDIE PUBLISHING ASSOCIATION | SUSAN NEAL
PO Box 481022, Charlotte, NC 28269 | 704-277-7194
cipa@christianpublishers.net | www.christianpublishers.net
Contact: email

Services: resources and tools for publishing and marketing for independent authors
Specialty: marketing services
Books: all genres
Credentials/experience: "Our mission is to support, strengthen, and promote independent authors and small publishers in the Christian marketplace. We have been doing this since 2004."

EABOOKS PUBLISHING | CHERI COWELL
1136 W. Winged Foot Cir., Winter Springs, FL 32708 | 407-712-3431
Cheri@eabookspublishing.com | *www.eabookspublishing.com*
Rhonda Robinson, Rhonda@eabookspublishing.com

Contact: email, website form
Services: helps authors reach the world with the messages God's given them
Specialty: websites, social media, e-newsletters, and marketing plan
Books: fiction, nonfiction, devotionals, memoirs, children's, Bible study
Charges: flat fee
Credentials/experience: "Serving Christian authors with integrity since 2010."

EPIC—A RESULTS AGENCY
Murfreesboro, TN | 615-829-6441
hello@epic.inc | *epic.inc*
Jennifer Willingham, CEO

Contact: email, phone, website form
Services: social-media management, email marketing, publicity campaigns, press materials, media training, platform development
Credentials/experience: Group of PR and marketing specialists with years of experience.

JONES LITERARY | JASON JONES
2233 Surrey Dr., Murfreesboro, TN 37129-1043 | 512-720-2996
jason@jonesliterary.com | *jonesliterary.com*
Mark Breta, publicist, mark@jonesliterary.com
Marianna Gibson, publicist, marianna@jonesliterary.com
Alex May, publicist, alex@jonesliterary.com

Contact: email
Services: publicity, digital marketing strategy, podcast production
Specialty: areas of Christian faith, apologetics, persecution of the

church, religious liberty, American history, conservative politics, culture, marriage/family

Books: nonfiction

Charges: custom

Credentials/experience: "Jason led campaigns for HarperCollins Christian/Thomas Nelson's top nonfiction books, brands, and authors between 2007 and 2013. For many years since he has run one of the nation's most successful literary publicity agencies, having directed PR campaigns for over 400 books and 12 *New York Times* bestsellers. He is also host of *The Book Publicist Podcast* and an author."

McCLURE MUNTSINGER PUBLIC RELATIONS | PAMELA McCLURE and JANA MUNTSINGER

PO Box 804, Franklin, TN 37065 | 615-595-8321

info@mmpublicrelations.com | *www.mmpublicrelations.com*

Contact: email

Services: customized publicity campaigns, including radio, TV, Internet, and social media

Books: any book they like

Charges: custom

Credentials/experience: "After more than 40 combined years of book publicity, we have long and strong relationships with dozens of editors, writers, and producers. We specialize in knowing how to place religious books in Christian and general-market media, traditional outlets, and online."

McWRITING SERVICES | SHARON CARTER JENKINS

2162 Spring Stuebner Rd., Ste. 140-1018, Spring, TX 77389 | 832-930-0604

sharon@mcwritingservices.com | *www.mcwritingservices.com*

Contact: email, phone, website form

Services: digital marketing services and public relations support

Specialty: helping aspiring authors develop a marketing plan and strategy that fits their specific Kingdom calling

Books: fiction, nonfiction, children, inspirational

Charges: custom

Credentials/experience: "Sharon C. Jenkins is the Inspirational Principal for The Master Communicator's Writing Services. Her business provides writing and coaching services to small businesses, nonprofits, and authors. Her professional experience ranges from working as an editor for a major minority communications and marketing company to being an author's virtual coach. She is also a certified authors assistant and life coach. She's hosted events, such as the Authors Networking Summit, America's Favorite Author, Write Your Book in 90 Days at Alpine Resort, and is the founder of the Authorpreneur Coach Certification Program."

MEDIA CONNECT | SHARON FARNELL

301 E. 57th St., New York City, NY 10022 | 212-593-6337
sharon.farnell@finnpartners.com | www.media-connect.com

Contact: email
Services: full-service book publicity firm with TV and radio campaigns, print, online, book tours, etc.
Books: primarily nonfiction but also children's and some fiction
Charges: flat fee
Credentials/experience: "Since joining the company in 1997, Sharon has been instrumental in helping faith-based authors and publishers reach both the Christian and mainstream audience. She has successfully placed her clients in a variety of top media outlets."

REDEMPTION PRESS | ATHENA DEAN HOLTZ

1602 Cole St., Enumclaw, WA 98022 | 360-226-3488
athena@redemption-press.com | www.redemption-press.com
Micah Juntunen, director of marketing & acquisitions,
  micah@redemption-press.com
Christina Custodio, author platform coach, christina@redemption-press.com
Shelly Brown, Amazon marketing and book launch/relaunch strategist,
  shellyb@redemption-press.com

Contact: email, website
Services: custom-designed book launch/relaunch, development of companion products to increase exposure, author-platform coaching, multiauthor virtual events, book launch/speaking tour coaching, website design, branding, lead magnet development, one-sheets and other marketing materials, She Writes for Him tribe and community
Specialty: helping newer authors build their platforms and gain exposure with excellence
Books: nonfiction, fiction, children's
Charges: custom
Credentials/experience: "Redemption Press serves authors by promoting their message using both traditional and unique methods. From the first virtual conference launched in May 2020 to meet

the needs of writers during the worldwide shutdown to the expanding of our marketing strategies, we aim to meet the needs in an ever-changing world. Our online and offline approach offers opportunities for everyone regardless of their expertise. From best sellers on Amazon and social-media training to community relations and national publicity, we have seen our authors reach their audience in extraordinary ways beyond what they could accomplish on their own. Our services have expanded to include authors not published with us who are in need of quality marketing to bring their message to the world."

SIDE DOOR COMMUNICATIONS | DEBBIE LYKINS
224-234-6699

deb@sidedoorcom.net | *www.sidedoorcom.net*

Contact: website form

Services: media relations, press-kit creation, consulting, publicity-plan development

Books: primarily nonfiction, also children's and fiction but highly selective, no self-published novels, not much self-published nonfiction

Charges: custom

Credentials/experience: "Side Door Communications is a national publicity agency that connects faith-based publishers and personalities with national and local media outlets as well as bloggers, with the goal of obtaining coverage in newspapers and magazines, and on radio, television, and the Internet. Based in the Milwaukee area, founder Debbie Lykins has more than two decades of experience in marketing, publicity, and communications."

VERITAS COMMUNICATIONS | DON S. OTIS
318 Huppert Ln., Sandpoint, ID 83864 | 719-275-7775

don@veritasincorporated.com | *www.veritasincorporated.com*

Contact: email

Services: author and ministry publicity and promotion

Specialty: interviews, writing media materials

Books: nonfiction, issues-driven Christian and conservative

Charges: flat fee

Credentials/experience: "More than 30 years of experience in publicity and promotion, author of five books."

WILDFIRE MARKETING | ROB EAGAR

3625 Chartwell Dr., Suwanee, GA 30024 | 770-887-1462

Rob@StartaWildfire.com | *www.StartaWildfire.com*

Contact: phone, website form

Services: all facets of book marketing, including book launches, author websites, email marketing, social media, public speaking, and author-revenue growth

Specialty: book marketing

Books: all genres

Charges: flat fee

Credentials/experience: "Rob Eagar is the founder of Wildfire Marketing, a consulting practice that has coached more than 1,000 authors and helped books hit *The New York Times* best-seller list in three different categories: new fiction, new nonfiction, and backlist nonfiction. His company has attracted numerous best-selling authors, including Dr. Gary Chapman, Lysa TerKeurst, DeVon Franklin, Wanda Brunstetter, and Dr. John Townsend."

22

LEGAL AND ACCOUNTING SERVICES

CAROL TOPP CPA

10288 Amberwood Ct., Cincinnati, OH 45241 | 513-290-4730
Carol@TaxesforWriters.com | TaxesForWriters.com

> **Contact:** email, phone
> **Services:** consultations, tax questions
> **Charges:** hourly rate
> **Credentials/experience:** "I am a CPA (Certified Public Accountant) and author of 15 books both self-published and small publishers. I am the author of *Business Tips and Taxes for Writers*. I do one-on-one consultations via phone or email with writers to discuss their business set-up, operation, and taxes. I am no longer accepting clients for individual tax preparation."

CHRIS MORRIS CPA, LLC

11209 N. 161st Ln., Surprise, AZ 85379 | 623-451-8182
cmorris@chrismorriscpa.com | chrismorriscpa.com/cwmg

> **Contact:** website form
> **Services:** accounting, contract review, taxes
> **Charges:** custom, flat fee
> **Credentials/experience:** "Chris Morris CPA is a firm that has focused its resources on developing a deep understanding of the creative entrepreneur space. We have the privilege of counting photographers, authors, publishing presses, editors, virtual assistants, and bloggers among our clients. In other words, we live and breathe the world of the creative entrepreneur."

TOM UMSTATTD CPA

13276 Research Blvd., Austin, TX 78750 | 512-250-1090

tom@taxmantom.com | www.taxmantom.com

Contact: email, phone
Services: accounting, taxes
Charges: hourly rate
Credentials/experience: More than 35 years of experience.

WINTERS & KING

2448 E. 81st St., Ste. 5900, Tulsa, OK 74137 | 918-494-6868

wintersking.com/attorneys/thomas-j-winters

Thomas J. Winters, attorney

Contact: phone, website form
Service: contract negotiation
Credentials/experience: "We understand that negotiating with major publishers can feel like a lopsided process, and we work hard to level the playing field. Our experience in the publishing industry allows us to negotiate comprehensive and ironclad publishing contracts based on the realities of the industry. Our goal is to help our clients tell their stories on their own terms and receive the rightful benefits of their hard work through royalties and advances."

23

SPEAKING SERVICES

ADVANCED WRITERS AND SPEAKERS ASSOCIATION (AWSA)

PO Box 6421, Longmont, CO 80501

ReachOut2Linda@gmail.com | awsa.com

Director: Linda Evans Shepherd

Contact: email

Services: website directory, online prayer group, coaching, online training and community, annual conference prior to the opening of Christian Product Expo, fall retreat at the Christian Booksellers Expo at Munce, awards

Membership: Main membership qualifications: two major forms of communication from this list: national media (column, blog, podcast, radio or TV show), published book, speaking more than twice a year outside your community, making movies, acting; protégé membership for beginning to intermediate communicators

Fee: women only, $45/year

CHRISTIAN COMMUNICATORS

contact@christiancommunicators.com | www.ChristianCommunicators.com

Directors: Tammy Whitehurst, Lori Boruff

Contact: website form

Services: annual conference to educate, validate, and launch speakers to the next level for beginning or seasoned speakers; speaker directory listing on website

CHRISTIAN SPEAKER NETWORK

christianspeaker.net

Contact: website form

Services: web page that is listed in the online database

Fee: $39.95/year

CHRISTIAN WOMEN SPEAKERS

womenspeakers.com

Director: Marnie Swedberg
Contact: website form
Services: web page that is listed in the online database
Fees: free; $29.99/month or $499/year for higher ranking, extra features and benefits; $897/lifetime for highest level of promotion

DECLARE

info@wearedeclare.com | wearedeclare.com

Directors: Eryn Hall, Megan Fish
Contact: email, website form
Services: annual conference to equip women to be effective communicators, blog, podcasts, community, webinars

NEXT STEP COACHING SERVICES

info@nextstepcoachingservices.com | nextstepcoachingservices.com

Director: Amy Carroll
Contact: website form
Services: coaching for women speakers to sharpen messages, develop marketing, and gain organizational tools; monthly newsletter

NORTHWEST CHRISTIAN SPEAKERS

Bellingham, WA | 360-966-0203
Coordinator@NWSpeakers.com | www.christianspeakersnw.com

Director: Christie Miller
Contact: website form
Services: speakers bureau, not limited to the Northwest; speaker training
Qualifications/requirements: attend training workshops/evaluation session

SHE SPEAKS CONFERENCE

See entry in "Writers Conferences and Seminars."

SPEAK UP SPEAKER SERVICES
3141 Winged Foot Dr., Lakeland, FL 33803 | 586-481-7661
gene4speakup@aol.com | *speakupspeakerservices.com*

> **Director:** Carol Kent
> **Contact:** mail
> **Services:** speakers bureau, fee negotiation, contracts for services, speech and TV-interview coaching, SpeakUp Conference (see listing in "Writers Conferences and Seminars")
> **Qualifications/requirements:** at least two books or CDs currently available in the Christian market and regularly speaking nationally; see list of application details to mail
> **Representation:** exclusive, nonexclusive

24

WRITING EDUCATION RESOURCES

A WRITER'S DAY

podcasts.apple.com/us/podcast/a-writers-day/id1472104073

Type: podcast

Host: R. A. Douthitt

Description: "A helpful podcast to help writers learn more about the craft, talk with published authors, and learn more about the publishing industry in order to have a competitive edge. Today, it takes more than just a good story to become a successful writer. You must know about marketing strategies, publishing options, and platforms that will help you stand out from the millions of writers out there. This podcast will help you."

ANN KROEKER, WRITING COACH

annkroeker.com/podcasts

Type: podcast

Host: Ann Kroeker

Description: "These writing podcast episodes offer practical tips and motivation for writers at all stages. . . . Tune in for solutions addressing anything from self-editing and goal-setting . . . to administrative and scheduling challenges."

AUTHOR SCHOOL

authorschool.com

Type: courses

Director: Rachelle Gardner

Description: Pen to Published: Giving you the tools you need while pursuing publishing. Every week, you will receive a new lesson jam-packed with information and resources to help you take the next step toward publishing. Live online sessions with replays.

THE BOOK PUBLICIST PODCAST

podcasts.apple.com/us/podcast/the-book-publicist-podcast/id1503562889

Type: podcast
Host: Jason Jones
Description: "Helping authors become their own publicist. Join long-time literary agent/publicist/host Jason Jones as he asks authors, publicists, and media the key questions." No new episodes.

CHRISTIAN EDITING SERVICES

christianediting.co.nz

Type: courses
Director: Iola Goulton
Description: "Free and paid email courses on novel revision and platform building."

CHRISTIAN EDITOR NETWORK, LLC

www.ChristianEditorNetwork.com

Type: organization
Director: Kathy Ide
Description: "Our goal is to equip, empower, and encourage editors in the Christian market. Join our community of like-minded professionals in The Christian PEN. Advance your knowledge and skills through The PEN Institute. Attend the PENCON editors conference. Once you're established, apply to join Christian Editor Connection to get more job leads."

CHRISTIAN PUBLISHING SHOW

christianpublishingshow.com

Type: podcast
Host: Thomas Umstattd Jr.
Description: *"The Christian Publishing Show* is a podcast to help Christian authors change the world. We talk about how to improve in the craft of writing, how to get published, and how to market effectively. Get expert advice from industry insiders."

CHRISTIAN WRITERS INSTITUTE

christianwritersinstitute.com

Type: organization, courses
Director: Steve Laube
Description: "The Christian Writers Institute was created to help

Christians become proficient in the skills, craft, and business of writing. To build the Kingdom of God word-by-word. It does so by providing audio and video courses taught by some of the industry's best teachers. In addition, the Institute publishes a number of books on writing for writers, including *The Christian Writers Market Guide*. Originally founded in 1945, it is estimated that over 30,000 students have been trained by the Christian Writers Institute. It also runs the Write-to-Publish Conference held in Wheaton, IL."

CREATE IF WRITING

createifwriting.com/podcast-and-show-notes

Type: podcast

Host: Kirsten Oliphant

Description: *"Create If Writing* is a podcast for writers and bloggers dealing with authentic platform building online. You will hear from experts on list-building, connecting through Twitter, and how to utilize Facebook. But tools for building an audience would feel empty without a little inspiration, so these training episodes are balanced with inspirational interviews with writers who share their creative process, ups and downs, and how they have dealt with success or failure." Currently on haitus.

DECLARE PODCAST

podcasts.apple.com/us/podcast/declare/id867933809

Type: podcast

Host: Anne Watson

Description: "The mission of Declare is to equip women to walk in their callings as Christian communicators." No new episodes.

FIGHTWRITE PODCAST

www.fightwrite.net/podcast

Type: podcast

Host: Carla Hoch

Description: "A writer's resource for writing action and fight scenes." No new episodes.

THE GATECRASHERS PODCAST

www.stitcher.com/show/the-gatecrashers-podcast

Type: podcast

Hosts: Amanda Luedeke, Charis Crowe

Description: "Teaming up to talk about both sides of publishing (self-publishing and traditional), Amanda and Charis share their combined twenty years of experience in the industry from both sides of the desk. They offer a glimpse behind the 'gates' as they share the realities, opportunities, and difficulties of the publishing world."

GLOBAL PUBLISHING PODCAST

globalpublishingpodcast.buzzsprout.com

Type: podcast
Host: Laurie Nichols
Description: "The *Global Publishing Podcast* gives you an inside look into writing and publishing around the world. We look at what it means to create excellent content that enriches the Church and influences society by having one-on-one conversations with some of the world's leading creatives and influencers seeking to use words to change the world. GPP is a media initiative of Media Associates International."

THE HABIT

thehabit.co/the-habit-podcast

Type: podcast
Host: Jonathan Rogers
Description: "Conversations about writing with writers."

HOME ROW: JUST KEEP WRITING

homerowpod.com

Type: podcast
Host: J. A. Medders
Description: "Get inspired to write from some of today's best writers. Listen. Learn. Just keep writing. You might learn how to get a book deal, write a best-seller, or quit your day job. Maybe you'll get that nudge you need to . . . write the blog, article, or book you've been thinking on for far too long. As Christians, our aim is to write in such a way that Jesus is made much of and the Church is encouraged to follow our risen Lord." No new episodes.

THE JERRY JENKINS WRITERS GUILD

JerrysGuild.com

Type: organization, courses
Director: Jerry Jenkins
Description: "The Writers Guild is like a writing conference you can

access from anywhere 24/7. Instant access to video training on any writing topic. Additionally, several times each month Jerry answers your questions live, hosts new writing workshops, interviews industry experts, and so much more." Membership is open only periodically; email *wecare@jerryjenkins.com* for the next open period. Jerry also offers individual online courses at *jerryjenkins.com*.

KINGDOM WRITERS
authors.libsyn.com/podcast

> **Type:** podcast
> **Hosts:** CJ and Shelley Hitz
> **Description:** "CJ and Shelley Hitz are passionate about equipping and empowering Christian writers of all genres to share their unique gifts with the world. This podcast is filled with spiritual encouragement as well as prayers to help you overcome the resistance you face as a writer. Your story matters! We believe that you have a specific role to play in the kingdom of heaven to impact lives for eternity. And because of this, we will pour out our lives encouraging writers like you to not only tell your stories but to take the courageous step of self-publishing your stories in books that will outlive you and leave behind a powerful legacy."

NOVEL MARKETING PODCAST
authormedia.com/novel-marketing

> **Type:** podcast
> **Host:** Thomas Umstattd Jr.
> **Description:** "This is the show for writers who want to build their platform, sell more books, and change the world with writing worth talking about. Whether you self-publish or are with a traditional house, this podcast will make book promotion fun and easy. Thomas Umstattd Jr. interviews publishers, indie authors and best-selling traditional authors about how to get published and sell more books."

PASTOR WRITER
pastorwriter.com/episodes

> **Type:** podcast
> **Host:** Chase Replogle
> **Description:** "Join me as I interview pastors, authors, and writing experts in my journey to better understand the calling and the craft of writing, reading, and living the Christian life."

THE PEN INSTITUTE

PENInstitute.com

Type: organization, courses
Director: *Director@PENinstitute.com*
Description: "Whether you are just beginning your editing career or are looking for an advanced class to update your skills, The PEN Institute has training opportunities for you. We offer group courses, one-on-one instruction, webinars, videos, lesson packs, and individual mentoring for aspiring and established freelance and in-house editors. Instructors are all experienced industry professionals."

THE PORTFOLIO LIFE WITH JEFF GOINS

podcasts.apple.com/us/podcast/the-portfolio-life-with-jeff-goins/ id844091351

Type: podcast
Host: Jeff Goins
Description: "Jeff Goins shares thoughts & ideas that will help you to pursue work that matters, make a difference with your art & discover your true voice!" No longer recorded.

THE PROLIFIC CREATOR

www.ryanjpelton.com/podcast

Type: podcast
Host: Ryan Pelton
Description: "*The Prolific Creator* is about life, art, and doing the generous thing. Follow writer, artist, and publisher Ryan J. Pelton as he discusses processes and strategies for writing lots of words, creating lots of art, and the motivation driving the whole thing. TPC podcast also interviews fellow prolific creators, writers, artists, and entrepreneurs as they discuss tips, tricks, and motivation for making art, and doing the generous thing in the world."

SERIOUS WRITER, INC.

seriouswriter.com

Type: organization, courses
Directors: Cyle Young, Bethany Jett
Description: "Serious Writer's mission is to set the industry standard for excellence for the clean and Christian writing markets through online courses, intensive events, and writers conferences. The

Serious Writer Academy offers recorded classes and workshops. The Serious Writer Club offers various levels of membership, so you can take your writing journey to the next level with hundreds of hours of training, live calls, networking opportunities, and more."

SERIOUS WRITER PODCAST

seriouswriterpodcast.buzzsprout.com

Type: podcast
Host: Cyle Young, Bethany Jett
Description: "No matter where you are in your writing journey— just starting out, working on proposals, looking for an agent, or marketing your book—happy you're here and we're happy to help."

THE STORY BLENDER PODCAST

www.thestoryblender.com

Type: podcast
Host: Steven James
Description: "We are passionate about well-told, impactful stories. We love to listen to them. Watch them. Create them. So, we decided to talk with premier storytellers from around the country. Hear their stories and get their insights. From novelists to comedians to film makers to artists. Stories are told through a variety of people in a variety of ways. And here they are. The secrets of great storytelling from great storytellers."

THE STORY EMBERS PODCAST

storyembers.org/podcast

Type: podcast
Host: James Noller
Description: "A discussion-based podcast where Story Embers staff members explore how to glorify God through storytelling. New episodes are released every third Monday of the month and cover all areas of story craft, including plot, theme, characters, and more."

THE STORYTELLER'S MISSION

www.buzzsprout.com/872170

Type: podcast
Host: Zena Dell Lowe
Description: "Zena Dell Lowe is a seasoned and engaging teacher with a passion for writers and storytellers. Her focused, concise,

and practical episodes (all under 20 minutes) not only explore the nuts and bolts of the craft, but also dive deep into the inner life of the artist and the 'why' behind creativity. If you believe that story matters, you'll want to give this podcast a listen."

WRITE FROM THE DEEP
writefromthedeep.com/write-from-the-deep-podcast

Type: podcast
Hosts: Karen Ball, Erin Taylor Young
Description: "Encouragement, refreshment, and truth from writers, for writers. Every writer, at some point, faces the deep places of crushing trials and struggles. But the deep is also a place where we can learn to abide in God as never before. This podcast reminds writers they're not alone, and equips and helps them to embrace the deep, to discover their truest voice and message, and to share it with refined craft and renewed passion."

WRITE2IGNITE MASTER CLASSSES FOR CHRISTIAN WRITERS OF CHILDREN AND YOUNG ADULT LITERATURE
write2ignite.com

Type: courses
Director: Jean Matthew Hall
Description: Write2Ignite offers two Master Classes a year to target specific skills and genres to help Christians who write for children and young adults to master those skills.

THE WRITE HOUR
thewritecoach.biz/the-write-hour-podcast

Type: podcast
Host: Joyce Glass
Description: "How do I start writing a book? Why do I need to write a book? What is the process to write a book? What is next after I have written my book? Are you a personal development leader ready to expand your business with a book? Have your questions answered by Joyce Glass, The Write Coach For Personal Development Leaders. Learn from leaders in the publishing world and begin your writing journey or take your writing career to the next level. Dig deeper with step-by-step instructions and miniworkshops. Joyce's strong point is breaking down the overwhelm and guides you to the next step in your journey. In

every episode, she gives practical advice you can implement immediately. Join *The Write Hour* each week for your dose of writing motivation!" No new episodes.

THE WRITERLY LIFE

podcasts.apple.com/us/podcast/the-writerly-life/id914574328

Type: podcast

Host: hope*writers

Description: "Are you ready to take the next step in your writing life? Whether you're a beginner stumped about what to do first or an experienced writer who's ready for new growth, you'll find what you're looking for here at *The Writerly Life*, brought to you by hope*writers, the most encouraging place on the internet for writers to make progress.

"Each episode of *The Writerly Life* offers you practical tips and interviews with publishing pros to help you skip the long learning curve and put you ahead of the game. *The Writerly Life* is all about balancing the art of writing with the business of publishing so that you can hustle without losing heart. Listen in and be inspired to keep putting your pen to the page. We'll help you find clarity to take the next step in your writing journey. 'You have words, and your words matter. Let's get them out into the world!'"

WRITING AT THE RED HOUSE

www.writingattheredhouse.com/podcast-2

Type: podcast

Host: Kathi Lipp

Description: "The podcast is for those who love God and want to share His story through writing, speaking, social media—and yes—even marketing. . . . The refreshing and honest take on the 'industry' do's and don'ts, as well as insight on what makes you stand out from the rest, will not only entertain, but will serve in helping you propel your career to the next level."

WRITING FOR YOUR LIFE

writingforyourlife.com

Type: organization

Director: Brian Allain

Description: "Writing for Your Life is committed to offering a wide variety of useful resources and services to support spiritual writers. We offer online and in-person conferences featuring leading spiritual writers and publishing industry experts. We also provide a host of services and free resources to support your spiritual writing. We cannot guarantee that you will become a best-selling author, but we will help you take your best shot. Learn to tell your own story; write for your life!"

WRITING FOR YOUR LIFE PODCAST

writingforyourlife.com/writing-for-your-life-podcast

Type: podcast
Host: Brian Allain
Description: "If you write, or read, books that matter—books with substance and soul—then this is the place for you. We are here to help you gain inspiration and knowledge to empower your writing. Join us weekly for interviews and presentations from our author partners and industry professionals."

WRITING PURSUITS

www.writingpursuits.com/podcast

Type: podcast
Host: Kathrese McKee
Description: "Writing Pursuits with Kathrese McKee is a weekly podcast for authors who drink too much coffee, endure judgmental looks from their furry writing companions, and struggle for words. If you are a writer seeking encouragement, information, and inspiration, this podcast is for you."

YOUR BEST WRITING LIFE

www.buzzsprout.com/1127762

Type: podcast
Host: Linda Goldfarb
Description: "Christian writing industry experts share weekly content for all levels of Christian writers. Whether you're a beginner or bestseller, you receive practical information and how-to application you can use to grow your writing career as a faith-based author. Each week, Linda Goldfarb and her guests cover various topics, including the craft of writing, fiction topics, nonfiction topics, self-care for writers, and the business of writing to name a few. If you're an aspiring Christian writer, we have content to help you grow. Published writers, we have current content to make your next book proposal, manuscript editing, speaking event, and writer's conference worth your time and energy."

25

CONTESTS

A listing here does not guarantee endorsement of the contest. For guidelines on evaluating contests, go to *www.sfwa.org/other-resources/for-authors/writer-beware/contests*.

> **Note:** Dates may not be accurate since many sponsors had not posted their 2023 dates before press time.

CHILDREN AND TEENS

CORETTA SCOTT KING BOOK AWARD
www.ala.org/awardsgrants/awards/24/apply
> **Description:** Sponsored by Coretta Scott King Task Force, American Library Association. Annual award for children's books published the previous year by African-American authors and/or illustrators. Books must promote an understanding and appreciation of the "American Dream" and fit one of these categories: preschool to grade 4, grades 5–8, grades 9–12.
> **Deadline:** December 9
> **Entry fee:** none
> **Prizes:** $1,000 and plaque

SOCIETY OF CHILDREN'S BOOK WRITERS AND ILLUSTRATORS
www.scbwi.org/awards/grants/for-authors
> **Description:** Sponsors a variety of contests, scholarships, and grants.
> **Deadline:** varies
> **Entry fee:** none
> **Prizes:** ten awards for published authors and five for unpublished authors plus grants for emerging voices and student writers

WORDS AND MUSIC WRITING COMPETITION
wordsandmusic.org/contest

Description: Sponsored by The Pirate's Alley Faulkner Society, Inc. Seven categories: novel, novella, book-length narrative fiction, novel-in-progress, short story, essay, poetry, and short story by a high-school student. For previously unpublished work only.
Deadline: August 1
Entry fee: varies by category
Prizes: $250–$7,500, depending on category

FICTION

AMERICAN CHRISTIAN FICTION WRITERS CONTESTS
acfw.com/acfw-contests

Description: Genesis Contest for unpublished Christian fiction writers in a number of categories/genres. First Impressions award for unpublished writers. Carol Awards for best Christian fiction published the previous year.
Deadline: varies by contest
Entry fee: varies by category and membership

AWP PRIZE FOR THE NOVEL
www.awpwriter.org/contests/awp_award_series_overview

Description: Sponsored by Association of Writers and Writing Programs. Open to published and unpublished authors. Length: at least 60,000 words.
Deadline: submit between January 1 and February 28
Entry fee: $15 for members, $30 for nonmembers
Prize: $2,500 and publication by the University of Nebraska Press

BARD FICTION PRIZE
www.bard.edu/bfp

Description: Sponsored by Bard College. Awarded to a promising, emerging young writer of fiction, 39 years or younger and an American citizen. Entries must be previously published.
Deadline: June 15
Entry fee: none
Prize: $30,000 and appointment as writer-in-residence for one semester at Bard College, Annandale-on-Hudson, New York

BOSTON REVIEW AURA ESTRADA SHORT STORY CONTEST
www.bostonreview.net/contests

> **Description:** Previously unpublished short stories no longer than
> 5,000 words.
> **Deadline:** June 30
> **Entry fee:** $20
> **Prize:** $1,000 plus publication

BULWER-LYTTON FICTION CONTEST
www.bulwer-lytton.com

> **Description:** Sponsored by San Jose State University English
> Department. For the worst opening line to a novel. Each submission
> must be a single sentence; multiple entries allowed. Entries will be
> judged by categories: general, detective, western, science fiction,
> romance, etc. Overall winners, as well as category winners.
> **Deadline:** June 30
> **Entry fee:** none
> **Prize:** publication on the website

FLANNERY O'CONNOR AWARD FOR SHORT FICTION
www.ugapress.org/index.php/series/FOC

> **Description:** Sponsored by University of Georgia Press. For collections
> of short fiction. Length: 40,000–75,000 words. Contestants must be
> residents of North America.
> **Deadline:** submit between April 1 and May 31
> **Entry fee:** not stated
> **Prize:** $1,000 plus publication under royalty book contract

GET PUBBED
scriveningspress.com/get-pubbed

> **Description:** Sponsored by Scrivenings Press. Entries will be divided
> among four broad categories: speculative, historical, contemporary,
> and mystery/suspense. Submit the first ten pages.
> **Deadline:** Submit between May 1 and June 30
> **Entry fee:** $25
> **Prizes:** grand prize: publishing contract, paid registration for annual
> author retreat, thorough critique of up to 25 pages of your
> manuscript, and $75 Amazon gift card; entry with the highest score
> in each genre: critique of up to 25 pages of your manuscript and
> $25 Amazon gift card

GRACE PALEY PRIZE FOR SHORT FICTION

www.awpwriter.org/contests/awp_award_series_overview

Description: Sponsored by Association of Writers and Writing
Programs. Short-story collections. May contain stories previously
published in periodicals. Length: 150–300 pages.
Deadline: submit between January 1 and February 28
Entry fee: $25
Prize: $5,500 and publication

HAVOK

gohavok.com/submission-guidelines

Description: Sponsored by Havok Publishing. For flash fiction 300–
1,000 words. Havok operates as an ongoing publishing contest, with
monthly themes and deadlines, seasonal awards, and smaller prizes
randomly throughout the year ("Best Story Title," "Most Prolific
Author," etc.). Publishes stories in five major genres (mashups
allowed): science fiction, fantasy, mystery, thriller, and comedy. Each
month, 20 stories win the website publication round. Then each six-
month season, 30 of those published stories win their way into print
and ebook anthologies (with payment varying by season as company
grows; we paid $30 to each anthology winner in 2020). Top two
stories in each six-month season are awarded $100 each.
Deadline: monthly
Entry fee: free
Prizes: $100 Readers' Choice Award, $100 Editors' Choice Award,
and more

JAMES JONES FIRST NOVEL CONTEST

tinyurl.com/v8ee2t8v

Description: Sponsored by Wilkes University. For a first novel or novel-
in-progress by a US writer who has not published a novel. Submit a
two-page outline and the first fifty pages of an unpublished novel.
Deadline: March 15
Entry fee: $30 plus $3 processing fee
Prizes: first place, $10,000; two runners-up, $1,000 each; a selection
from the winning work is published in *Provincetown Arts*

KATHERINE ANNE PORTER PRIZE FOR FICTION

untpress.unt.edu/authors/porter-prize-submissions

Description: Sponsored by University of North Texas Press. Quality
unpublished fiction by emerging writers of contemporary literature.

Can be a combination of short-shorts, short stories, and novellas from 100 to 200 pages (27,500–50,000 words). Material should be previously unpublished in book form.

Deadline: submit between May 1 and June 30

Entry fee: $25

Prize: $1,000 and publication by UNT Press

NATIONAL WRITERS ASSOCIATION NOVEL-WRITING CONTEST

www.nationalwriters.shoppingcartsplus.com/f/Novel_Form4.pdf

Description: To encourage development of creative skills and recognize and reward outstanding ability in the area of novel writing. Any genre or category of novel manuscript may be entered. Only unpublished works in the English language. Maximum length: 100,000 words. Must be submitted via USPS.

Deadline: postmarked by April 1

Entry fee: $35

Prizes: first place, $500 and possible representation; second place, $250; third place, $150; fourth through tenth places, book of the winner's choice; honorable mentions, certificate

NATIONAL WRITERS ASSOCIATION SHORT-STORY CONTEST

www.nationalwriters.shoppingcartsplus.com/f/Short_Story_Contest1.pdf

Description: Any genre of story. Length: 5,000 words maximum. Submit only unpublished works in the English language via mail.

Deadline: postmarked by July 1

Entry fee: $15

Prizes: first place, $250; second place, $100; third place, $50; fourth through tenth places: recognition

NOVEL STARTS

scriveningspress.com/novel-starts

Description: Sponsored by Scrivenings Press. For an unfinished novel in four genres: speculative, historical, contemporary, and mystery/suspense. Submit the first five pages.

Deadline: submit between May 1 and June 30

Entry fee: $25

Prizes: grand prize: author retreat, invitation to submit novel for consideration by Scrivenings Press once it is finished, thorough critique of up to 25 pages of your manuscript, and $75 Amazon gift card; entry with the highest score in each genre: critique of up to 25 pages of your manuscript and $25 Amazon gift card

REALM AWARD: READER'S CHOICE

www.realmmakers.com/realm-award-readers-choice-alliance-award

> **Description:** Sponsored by The Faith and Fantasy Alliance to give readers their say in what speculative fiction novels they enjoyed most in the preceding year. Only readers may nominate books in this contest. Books may be traditionally published or self- published.
> **Deadline:** submit between April 2 and 23
> **Entry fee:** none
> **Prize:** certificate of recognition

REALM MAKERS AWARDS

www.realmmakers.com/enter-the-awards

> **Description:** Sponsored by The Faith and Fantasy Alliance. Realm Makers Genre Awards in these categories: debut, science fiction, fantasy, young adult, supernatural/horror, and other (for those who don't feel other categories accurately characterize their speculative work). Realm Award recognizes the most excellent speculative novel written by a Christian author in the previous calendar year. Length: 60,000 words minimum; 50,000 words minimum for young adult. Parable Award for Excellence in Cover Design is awarded to the best overall cover for a speculative novel written by a Christian author.
> **Deadline:** submit between January 1 and 20
> **Entry fee:** $35
> **Prizes:** cash

SERENA MCDONALD KENNEDY AWARD

www.snakenationpress.org/snakenation

> **Description:** Sponsored by Snake Nation Press. Novellas up to 50,000 words or short-story collections up to 200 pages, published or unpublished.
> **Deadline:** August 31
> **Entry fee:** $25
> **Prize:** $1,000 and publication

TOBIAS WOLFF AWARD FOR FICTION

www.bhreview.org/contest-submissions-guidelines

> **Description:** Sponsored by Western Washington University's *Bellingham Review*. Length: 5,000 words maximum.

Deadline: submit between December 1 and March 15
Entry fee: $20
Prize: $1,000 plus publication

ZOETROPE: ALL-STORY SHORT FICTION COMPETITION
www.zoetrope.com/contests

Description: For all genres of literary fiction. Entries must be unpublished and strictly 5,000 words or fewer. More than one entry allowed.
Deadline: October 1
Entry fee: $30
Prizes: first place, $1,000; second place, $500; third place, $250; plus publication of winning story and consideration for agency representation

MULTIPLE GENRES

BLUE RIDGE MOUNTAINS CHRISTIAN WRITERS CONFERENCE CONTESTS
www.blueridgeconference.com/contest-info

Description: Sponsors three book contests for fiction or nonfiction: Foundation Awards, Directors' Choice, and The Selahs. Look for details about guidelines, deadlines, and entry fees on the website after January 1.
Deadline: varies by contest
Entry fee: $35–$40

THE BRAUN BOOK AWARDS
wordalivepress.ca/pages/the-braun-book-awards

Description: Sponsored by Word Alive Press. For unpublished Christian books written by Canadian citizens and permanent residents in Canada. Categories: nonfiction and fiction.
Deadline: March 15
Entry fee: none
Prizes: One fiction and one nonfiction manuscript will each receive a royalty-based book publishing contract. A select number of secondary winners will also receive prizes, including credit towards publishing.

CALEB AWARD

www.omegawriters.org/caleb-award

> **Description:** Sponsored by Omega Writers. CALEB stands for Christian Authors Lifting Each other's Books and recognizes the best in Australasian Christian writing, published and unpublished.
> **Deadline:** April 30
> **Entry fee:** AUD $40
> **Prize:** AUD $400 (services in kind)

CASCADE WRITING CONTEST

www.oregonchristianwriters.org

> **Description:** Sponsored by Oregon Christian Writers. Open to anyone, with emphasis on unpublished works. All contestants receive three score sheets from the judges reviewing their work, and finalists receive an additional two score sheets.
> **Deadline:** submit between January 15 and February 15
> **Entry fee:** $40
> **Prizes:** certificates to all finalists; in addition, pins to the winners

CHRISTIAN INDIE AWARDS

www.christianaward.com

> **Description:** Sponsored by Christian Indie Publishing Association. This award is designed to promote and bring recognition to quality Christian books by small publishers and independently published authors. Books must be printed in English, for sale in the United States, and promote the Christian faith. Awards are offered in eighteen categories. Publishers and authors may nominate titles, and Christian readers vote to determine the winners.
> **Deadline:** November 15
> **Entry fee:** $77–$97, depending on submission date
> **Prize:** promotion

COLUMBIA JOURNAL CONTESTS

columbiajournal.org/submit/winter-contest

> **Description:** Fiction and nonfiction, 7,500 words maximum; poetry, five pages maximum.
> **Deadline:** submit between March 7 and December 15
> **Entry fee:** $10 and $15
> **Prizes:** $250 and $400 in each category plus publication

EDITORS' CHOICE AWARD
www.ChristianEditorNetwork.com/eca

Description: This award (which ran for seven years as Excellence in Editing Award) celebrates the authors, editors, and publishers behind books that are superbly written, well edited, and published by a Christian publisher or self-published by a Christian author. Each year's contest is open to books published the previous calendar year. Winners announced at PENCON.

Deadline: December 31

Entry Fee: $50 before November 15, $60 after; discounts for members

Prizes: Promotion of finalist and winning books on websites and social media, digital emblems, printed stickers, certificates, blog and newsletter interviews. Winning authors and editors receive select benefits from divisions of Christian Editor Network. Judges' notes provided on request.

ERIC HOFFER BOOK AWARD
www.hofferaward.com

Description: Eighteen categories for books from small, academic, and micro presses, including self-published, ebooks, and older books. The prose category is for creative fiction and nonfiction fewer than 10,000 words.

Deadline: January 21

Entry fee: varies by category

Prizes: $2,500 grand prize, other prizes awarded in categories

EVANGELICAL PRESS ASSOCIATION CONTEST
www.evangelicalpress.com/contest

Description: Higher Goals awards in a variety of categories for periodical manuscripts published in the previous year. Although most submissions are made by publication staff members, associate EPA members may also submit their articles.

Deadline: January 14

Entry fee: $27

Prizes: certificates

INSCRIBE CHRISTIAN WRITERS' FELLOWSHIP CONTEST
inscribe.org/contests

Description: Sponsors contests for InScribe members: Fall Contest,

Winter Contest, Word Challenge, FellowScript Contests, Barnabas Award, Janette Oke Award.
Deadline: varies with each contest
Entry fee: varies with each contest
Prizes: vary by category

NARRATIVE MAGAZINE CONTESTS

www.narrativemagazine.com/submit-your-work

Description: Biannual contests in a variety of categories, including short stories, essays, memoirs, poetry, and literary nonfiction. Entries must be previously unpublished. Length: varies by category.
Deadline: varies
Entry fee: varies
Prizes: vary by category

NATIONAL WRITERS ASSOCIATION CONTESTS

www.nationalwriters.com/page/page/2734945.htm

Description: Sponsors six contests: nonfiction, novel, young writers, poetry, short short, and David Raffelock Award for Publishing Excellence.
Deadline: varies by contest
Entry fee: varies by contest
Prizes: vary by contest

NEW MILLENNIUM WRITING AWARDS

newmillenniumwritings.submittable.com/submit

Description: Sponsored by New Millennium Writings. Fiction and nonfiction, 6,000 words maximum; flash fiction (short-short story), 1,000 words maximum; poetry, three poems to five pages total. No restrictions as to style or subject matter.
Deadline: November 30
Entry fee: $20, $35 for two entries, $45 for three entries, $60 for four entries, $80 for five entries
Prizes: $1,000 plus publication for each category

SOUL-MAKING KEATS LITERARY COMPETITION

www.soulmakingcontest.us

Description: Sponsored by National League of American Pen Women, Nob Hill, San Francisco Branch. Categories include flash fiction, short story, memoir vignette, humor, novel excerpt, intercultural essay, creative nonfiction, religious essay, young-adult

poetry, and young-adult prose.
Deadline: November 30
Entry fee: $5
Prizes: first place, $100; second place, $50; third place, $25 in each
category

TENNESSEE WILLIAMS/NEW ORLEANS LITERARY FESTIVAL

tennesseewilliams.net/contests

Description: Tennessee Williams gained some early recognition by
entering a writing contest. The festival that bears his name now
sponsors writing contests in poetry, fiction, very short fiction, and
one-act playwriting.
Deadline: varies according to genre
Entry fee: varies
Prizes: vary by category

THE WORD GUILD CHRISTIAN WRITING AWARDS

thewordguild.com/contests

Description: The Word Awards recognize the best work published
in the previous year in 35 categories of writing, including novels,
nonfiction books, articles, columns, poems, song lyrics, scripts, and
screenplays. Fresh Ink Student Writers Contest for never-before-
published student writers. In the Beginning for unpublished novice
and emerging writers. The Grace Irwin Prize for Canadian writers
who are Christians recognizes the best book published in the
previous year. The Leslie K. Tarr Award celebrates a major career
contribution to Christian writing and publishing in Canada. The
Partnership Award recognizes an individual or organization that
has shown exceptional support and encouragement for Canadian
writers and editors who are Christians.
Deadline: varies according to the award
Entry fee: varies according to the award
Prizes: vary according to the award

WRITER'S DIGEST COMPETITIONS

www.writersdigest.com/writers-digest-competitions

Description: Every other month, *Writer's Digest* presents a creative
challenge for fun and prizes, providing a short, open-ended prompt
for short-story submissions based on that prompt. Winner receives
publication in *Writer's Digest*. Also sponsors annual contests for

feature articles, short stories (multiple genres), poetry, personal essays, and self-published books (categories vary).

Deadline: varies according to contest

Entry fee: varies

Prizes: first place, $1,000; second place, $500; and more places for each contest; grand prize, $2,500

THE WRITERS' UNION OF CANADA AWARDS & COMPETITIONS

www.writersunion.ca/content/awards

Description: Short Prose Competition for Developing Writers: fiction or nonfiction by an author who has not yet published a book. Length: 2,500 words maximum. Danuta Gleed Literary Award for the best first collection of short fiction.

Deadline: Short Prose, March 1; Danuta, January 31

Entry fee: $29

Prizes: Short Prose, $2,500; Danuta, $10,000 plus two finalist awards for $1,000 each

NONFICTION

ANNIE DILLARD AWARD IN CREATIVE NONFICTION

bhreview.org/contest-submissions-guidelines

Description: Sponsored by Western Washington University's *Bellingham Review*. Unpublished essays on any subject. Length: 5,000 words maximum.

Deadline: submit between December 1 and March 15

Entry fee: $20 for first submission, $10 each additional one

Prize: $1,000

THE BECHTEL PRIZE

www.twc.org/publications/bechtel-prize

Description: Sponsored by Teachers & Writers Collaborative. For unpublished essays that explore themes related to creative writing, arts education, and/or the imagination. Length: 2,500 words maximum.

Deadline: January 15

Entry fee: $20

Prize: $1,000 and publication

EVENT NON-FICTION CONTEST
www.eventmagazine.ca/contest-nf

> **Description:** Unpublished creative nonfiction. Length: 5,000 words maximum.
> **Deadline:** October 15
> **Entry fee:** $34.95, includes a one-year subscription to *EVENT*
> **Prizes:** first place, $1,500; second place, $1,000; third place, $500 plus publication

GUIDEPOSTS WRITERS WORKSHOP CONTEST
www.guideposts.org/enter-the-guideposts-writers-workshop-contest

> **Description:** Contest is held in even years. Submit an original, unpublished, true, first-person story (your own or ghostwritten for another person) in 1,500 words or fewer about an experience that changed your life. Show how faith made a difference.
> **Deadline:** mid-June
> **Entry fee:** none
> **Prizes:** twelve all-expenses-paid, weeklong writers workshop in New York to learn about inspirational storytelling and writing for Guideposts publications

INTREPID TIMES TRAVEL WRITING COMPETITION
intrepidtimes.com/competitions

> **Description:** Sponsored by Exisle Publishing. *Intrepid Times* has a proud history of running narrative, travel-writing contests that focus on stories, places, and people.
> **Deadline:** varies
> **Entry fee:** free
> **Prizes:** first place, $150, publication on website, possible publication in anthology; runners up, $50

JOHN GUYON LITERARY NONFICTION
craborchardreview.siu.edu/submissions-annual-lit.html

> **Description:** Sponsored by Southern Illinois University Department of English. Annual competition. Literary nonfiction, 6,500 words.
> **Deadline:** submit between December 1 and January 31
> **Entry fee:** $2
> **Prize:** $500 and publication online

NEW LETTERS EDITOR'S CHOICE AWARD

www.newletters.org/editors-choice-award

Description: For unpublished essays. Length: 8,000 words maximum.
Deadline: October 18
Entry fee: $20
Prize: $1,000 and publication in magazine

RICHARD J. MARGOLIS AWARD

www.margolisaward.org

Description: Sponsored by Blue Mountain Center. Given annually to a promising young journalist or essayist whose work combines warmth, humor, wisdom, and concern with social justice. Submit at least two examples of published or unpublished work and a short biographical note, including a description of current and anticipated work. Length: 30 pages maximum.
Deadline: July 1
Entry fee: none
Prize: $10,000 plus a one-month residency at the Blue Mountain Center in Blue Mountain Lake, New York

SUE WILLIAM SILVERMAN PRIZE FOR CREATIVE NONFICTION

www.awpwriter.org/contests/awp_award_series_overview

Description: Sponsored by Association of Writers and Writing Programs. Open to published and unpublished authors. Book collection of nonfiction manuscripts. Length: 150–300 pages.
Deadline: submit between January 1 and February 28
Entry fee: $15 for members, $30 for nonmembers
Prize: $2,500 and publication with the University of Georgia Press

PLAYS/SCRIPTS/SCREENPLAYS

ACADEMY NICHOLL FELLOWSHIPS IN SCREENWRITING

www.oscars.org/nicholl/about

Description: International contest open to any writer who has not optioned or sold a treatment, teleplay, or screenplay for more than $35,000. May submit up to three scripts. Length: 70-160 pages.
Deadline: submit between March 3 and May 3
Entry fee: $50–$90, depending on submission date
Prizes: up to five $35,000 fellowships; recipients will be expected to

complete at least one original feature-film screenplay during the
fellowship year

AMERICAN ZOETROPE SCREENPLAY CONTEST

www.zoetrope.com/contests

Description: To find and promote new and innovative voices in
cinema. For screenplays and television pilots. No entrant may have
earned more than $5,000 as a screenwriter for theatrical films or
television or for the sale of, or sale of an option to, any original
story, treatment, screenplay, or teleplay. Prizes, fellowships,
awards, and other contest winnings are not considered earnings
and are excluded from this rule. Length: film scripts, 70–130
pages; one-hour television pilot scripts, 45–65 pages; half-hour
television scripts, 22–34 pages.

Deadline: September 16

Entry fee: $40–$50, depending on submission date

Prizes: first place, $5,000 plus consideration for film option and
development; ten finalists will also get this consideration

AUSTIN FILM FESTIVAL SCREENWRITERS COMPETITION

austinfilmfestival.com/submit

Description: Offers a number of contest categories, including
narrative feature, narrative short, documentary feature,
documentary short for screenplay, teleplay, and scripted digital
competition.

Deadline: varies by type

Entry fee: $35–$70, varies by type and submission date

Prizes: $1,000–$5,000

KAIROS PRIZE FOR SPIRITUALLY UPLIFTING SCREENPLAYS

www.kairosprize.com

Description: Sponsored by Movieguide. For feature-length
screenplays. Judges consider not only a script's entertainment value
and craftsmanship, but also whether it is uplifting, inspirational,
and spiritual and if it teaches lessons in ethics and morality.
Length: 87–130 pages; will accept scripts up to 150 pages (not
counting the title page) for an additional $20.

Deadline: October

Entry fee: varies, depending on submission date

Prizes: $15,000 each for first-time and professional screenwriters

MILDRED AND ALBERT PANOWSKI PLAYWRITING COMPETITION

www.nmu.edu/forestrobertstheatre/playwritingcompetition

> **Description:** Sponsored by Forest Roberts Theatre, Northern Michigan University. Unpublished, unproduced, full-length plays. Award to encourage and stimulate artistic growth among educational and professional playwrights. Provides students and faculty members the opportunity to mount and produce an original work on the university stage.
>
> **Deadline:** submit between October 1 and November 1
>
> **Entry fee:** none
>
> **Prize:** $2,000, a summer workshop, a fully mounted production, and transportation to Marquette, Michigan

MOONDANCE INTERNATIONAL FILM FESTIVAL COMPETITION

www.moondancefilmfestival.com

> **Description:** Offers a variety of awards for films, screenplays, librettos, and features that raise awareness about social issues.
>
> **Deadline:** October 31
>
> **Entry fee:** $25–$50
>
> **Prizes:** promotion to film companies for possible option

SCRIPTAPALOOZA SCREENPLAY COMPETITION

www.scriptapalooza.com/competition/how-to-enter

> **Description:** Any screenplay from any genre considered; must be the original work of the author (multiple authorship acceptable). Shorts competition: screenplays fewer than 40 pages.
>
> **Deadline:** submit between December 13 and April 18
>
> **Entry fee:** $50–$75
>
> **Prizes:** first place, $10,000; each genre winner, $500 (action, adventure, comedy, drama, family, science fiction, thriller/horror, historical), plus access to more than 50 producers through Scriptapalooza's network

SCRIPTAPALOOZA TV COMPETITION

www.scriptapaloozatv.com/competition

> **Description:** Scripts for television pilots, one-hour dramas, reality shows, and half-hour sitcoms. Length: pilots, 30–60 pages; one-hour program, 50–60 pages; reality show, one- to five-page treatment; half-hour sitcom, 25–35 pages.

Deadline: submit between September 6 and October 10
Entry fee: $45–$55, varies with deadline
Prizes: first place, $500; second place (4), $200; third place (3), $100, plus access to more than 50 producers through Scriptapalooza's network

POETRY

49TH PARALLEL POETRY AWARD

bhreview.org/contest-submissions-guidelines

Description: Sponsored by Western Washington University's *Bellingham Review*. Up to three poems in any style or on any subject.
Deadline: submit between December 1 and March 15
Entry fee: $20; international entries, $30
Prize: $1,000 and publication

ACADEMY OF AMERICAN POETS

poets.org/academy-american-poets/american-poets-prizes

Description: See the website for a list of multiple contests and prizes.

ANHINGA-ROBERT DANA PRIZE FOR POETRY

www.anhingapress.org/anhinga-robert-dana-prize

Description: Sponsored by Anhinga Press. For poets trying to publish a first or second book of poetry. Length: 48–80 pages.
Deadline: submit between February 15 and May 31
Entry fee: $28 per manuscript
Prize: $2,000, a reading tour, and publication by Anhinga Press

BALTIMORE REVIEW POETRY CONTEST

baltimorereview.submittable.com/submit

Description: All styles and forms of poetry, directed toward an announced theme. Maximum of three entries.
Deadline: November 30
Entry fee: $10
Prizes: $100–$500 and publication

BARBARA MANDIGO KELLY PEACE POETRY AWARDS

www.peacecontests.org/#poetry

Description: Sponsored by Nuclear Age Peace Foundation. Awards to encourage poets to explore and illuminate positive visions of peace and the human spirit. Poems must be original, unpublished, and in English. May submit up to three poems for one entry fee.

Deadline: July 1

Entry fee: adults, $15; youth ages 13–18, $5; none for ages 12 and under

Prizes: adult winner, $1,000; youth winner, $200; ages 12 and under, $200

BLUE MOUNTAIN ARTS POETRY CARD CONTEST

www.sps.com/contest-3

Description: Biannual contest. Poems may be rhymed or unrhymed, although unrhymed is preferred. Poems also considered for greeting cards or anthologies. No limit to number of entries.

Deadline: June 30 and December 31

Entry fee: none

Prizes: $350, $200, $100

BOSTON REVIEW ANNUAL POETRY CONTEST

www.bostonreview.net/about/contests

Description: Submit up to five unpublished poems; no more than ten pages total. Submit manuscripts in duplicate with cover note.

Deadline: May 31/June 30

Entry fee: $20, includes a subscription to *Boston Review*

Prize: $1,000 plus publication

CAVE CANEM POETRY PRIZE

cavecanempoets.org/prizes/cave-canem-poetry-prize

Description: Sponsored by Cave Canem Foundation. Supports the work of black poets of African descent with excellent manuscripts and who have not found a publisher for their first book. Offered every other year. Length: 48–75 pages.

Deadline: January 31

Entry fee: none

Prize: $1,000 plus publication by a national press and copies of the book, with a feature reading in New York City

COMSTOCK REVIEW CHAPBOOK CONTEST

comstockreview.org/comstock-writers-group-chapbook-award-for-2014

Description: Submissions must be unpublished as a collection, but individual poems may have been published previously in journals. Length: 25–34 pages. Poems may run longer than one page.

Deadline: submit between August 1 and October 31
Entry fee: $30
Prize: $1,000 plus publication and author copies

THE DONALD HALL PRIZE FOR POETRY

www.awpwriter.org/contests/awp_award_series_overview

Description: Sponsored by Association of Writers and Writing Programs. Open to published and unpublished authors. Length: 48 pages maximum.
Deadline: submit between January 1 and February 28
Entry fee: $15 for members, $30 for nonmembers
Prize: $5,500 and publication by University of Pittsburgh Press

FLO GAULT STUDENT POETRY PRIZE

www.sarabandebooks.org/flo-gault

Description: Sponsored by Sarabande Books. For full-time Kentucky undergraduate students. Submit up to three poems.
Deadline: submit between October 1 and December 1
Entry fee: none
Prize: $500 and publication

HOLLIS SUMMERS POETRY PRIZE

www.ohioswallow.com/poetry_prize

Description: Sponsored by Ohio University Press. For an unpublished collection of original poems, 60–95 pages. Open to both those who do not have a published book-length collection and to those who do.
Deadline: December 31
Entry fee: $30
Prize: $1,000 plus publication in book form by Ohio University Press

JAMES LAUGHLIN AWARD

www.poets.org/academy-american-poets/james-laughlin-award-guidelines

Description: Sponsored by Academy of American Poets. To recognize a second full-length print book of original poetry by a US citizen, permanent resident, or person who has DACA/TPS status, forthcoming within the next calendar year. Author must have published one book of poetry in English in a standard edition (48 pages or more) in the United States or under contract and scheduled for publication during the current calendar year; publication of chapbooks (less than 48 pages) does not disqualify. Length: 48-100 pages.

Deadline: submit between August 1 and October 1
Entry fee: none
Prize: $5,000 plus publication

KATE TUFTS DISCOVERY AWARD

www.cgu.edu/tufts

Description: Sponsored by Claremont Graduate University. Award presented annually for a first poetry volume published in the preceding year by a poet of genuine promise.
Deadline: June 30
Entry fee: none
Prize: $10,000

KINGSLEY TUFTS POETRY AWARD

www.cgu.edu/pages/6422.asp

Description: Sponsored by Claremont Graduate University. Presented annually for a published book of poetry by a midcareer poet to both honor the poet and provide the resources that allow artists to continue working toward the pinnacle of their craft.
Deadline: June 30
Entry fee: none
Prize: $100,000 and one week residence at Claremont Graduate University

MURIEL CRAFT BAILEY MEMORIAL POETRY AWARD

comstockreview.org/annual-contest

Description: Sponsored by *Comstock Review*. Unpublished poems up to 40 lines. No limit on number of submissions.
Deadline: submit between April 1 and July 15
Entry fee: postal, $5 per poem for up to five poems; online, $27.50 for five poems
Prizes: first place, $1,000; second place, $250; third place, $100

PATRICIA CLEARY MILLER AWARD

www.newletters.org/patricia-cleary-miller-award-for-poetry

Description: Sponsored by *New Letters*. A single poetry entry may contain up to six poems, and the poems need not be related.
Deadline: May 18
Entry fee: $24 each entry; if entering online, add a $5 service charge to entry fee; includes a one-year subscription to *New Letters*
Prize: $2,500 for best group of three to six poems

PHILIP LEVINE PRIZE FOR POETRY

cah.fresnostate.edu/english/centers-projects/levineprize/index.html

Description: Sponsored by California State University Department of English. An annual book contest for original, previously unpublished, full-length poetry manuscripts. Length: 48–80 pages with no more than one poem per page.

Deadline: submit between July 1 and September 30

Entry fee: $25 online, $22 postal

Prize: $2,000 and publication by Anhinga Press

POETRY SOCIETY OF VIRGINIA POETRY CONTESTS

www.poetrysocietyofvirginia.org/adult-contests

Description: More than twenty-five categories for adults and students. Form and length limit of entries vary according to the contests. All entries must be unpublished, original, and not scheduled for publication before the winners of the competition are announced.

Deadline: submit between November 1 and January 19

Entry fee: $4 per poem for nonmembers

Prizes: $100, $50, $30, $20, varying according to specific competition

SLIPSTREAM ANNUAL POETRY CHAPBOOK COMPETITION

www.slipstreampress.org/contest.html

Description: Sponsored by Slipstream Press. Entries may be any style, format, or theme. Length: 40 pages maximum.

Deadline: December 1

Entry fee: $20

Prize: $1,000 plus 50 published copies of chapbook

SOUL-MAKING KEATS LITERARY COMPETITION: JANICE FARRELL POETRY PRIZE

soulmakingcontest.us/contests/poetry

Description: Sponsored by National League of American Pen Women. Three poems per entry. One poem per page; one-page poems only. Free verse, blank verse, and prose poems.

Deadline: November 30

Entry fee: $5 per entry

Prizes: first place, $100; second place, $50; third place, $25

TOI DERRICOTTE & CORNELIUS EADY CHAPBOOK PRIZE

cavecanempoets.org/prizes/toi-derricotte-cornelius-eady-chapbook-prize

Description: Sponsored by Cave Canem Foundation. Dedicated to the discovery of exceptional chapbook-length manuscripts by black poets. Presented in collaboration with the O, Miami Poetry Festival and The Center for the Humanities at the CUNY Graduate Center.

Deadline: September 15

Entry fee: donations optional

Prize: $1,000, publication, ten copies of the chapbook, and a feature reading

TOM HOWARD/MARGARET REID POETRY CONTEST

winningwriters.com/our-contests/tom-howard-margaret-reid-poetry-contest

Description: Sponsored by Winning Writers. Poetry in any style or genre. Published poetry accepted. Length: 250 lines maximum.

Deadline: submit between April 15 and September 30

Entry fee: $12 per poem

Prizes: Tom Howard Prize, $3,000 for poem in any style or genre; Margaret Reid Prize, $3,000 for poem that rhymes or has a traditional style; $200 each for ten honorable mentions in any style

UTMOST NOVICE CHRISTIAN POETRY CONTEST

www.utmostchristianwriters.com/poetry-contest/poetry-contest-rules.php

Description: Sponsored by Utmost Christian Writers Foundation. Unpublished poems may be rhymed or free verse, up to 60 lines. Need not be religious in content. Maximum of five entries.

Deadline: February 28

Entry fee: $20 per poem

Prizes: $1,000, $500, $300; ten honorable mentions, $100; best rhyming poem, $300; honorable-mention rhyming poem, $200

VIOLET REED HAAS PRIZE FOR POETRY

www.snakenation.press/contests

Description: Sponsored by Snake Nation Press. Length: 75–100 pages. Previously published eligible.

Deadline: March 31

Entry fee: $25

Prize: $1,000 plus publication

WERGLE FLOMP HUMOR POETRY CONTEST

winningwriters.com/our-contests/wergle-flomp-humor-poetry-contest-free

Description: Sponsored by Winning Writers. Submit one published or unpublished humor poem up to 250 lines.

Deadline: April 1

Entry fee: none

Prizes: first place, $2,000; second place, $500; ten honorable mentions, $100; plus the top twelve entries will be published online

RESOURCES FOR CONTESTS

These websites are sources for announcements about other contests.

DAILY WRITING TIPS

www.dailywritingtips.com/25-writing-competitions

FREELANCE WRITING

www.freelancewriting.com/writingcontests.php

FUNDS FOR WRITERS

fundsforwriters.com/contests

NEW PAGES

www.newpages.com/classifieds/big-list-of-writing-contests

POETS & WRITERS

www.pw.org/grants

THE WRITE LIFE

thewritelife.com/writing-contests

DENOMINATIONAL PUBLISHERS

Note: Not all of these houses and publications are owned by denominational publishing companies, and some publish for a broader audience than the denomination.

ANGLICAN
Anglican Journal

ASSEMBLIES OF GOD
God's Word for Today
Influence
LIVE
My Healthy Church
Take Five Plus

BAPTIST
B&H Kids
B&H Publishing
The Brink
CommonCall
HomeLife
Judson Press
Light
Mature Living
Parenting Teens
ParentLife
Point

Randall House
The Secret Place

CATHOLIC
America
American Catholic Press
The Arlington Catholic Herald
Ave Maria Press
Catholic Book Publishing Corp.
Catholic Sentinel
Celebrate Life Magazine
Chrism Press
Columbia
Commonweal
Franciscan Media
LEAVES
Ligouri Publications
Liturgical Press
Living Faith
Living Faith for Kids
Loyola Press
Our Sunday Visitor, Inc.

Our Sunday Visitor
Paraclete Press
Parish Liturgy
Pauline Books & Media
Paulist Press
Resurrection Press
Scepter Publishers
St. Anthony Messenger
U.S. Catholic

CHARISMATIC/PENTECOSTAL

Charisma
Charisma Media
Chosen
Emanate Books
testimony/ENRICH
Whitaker House

CHRISTIAN CHURCH/CHURCH OF CHRIST

Christian Standard
College Press Publishing
Leafwood Publishers

CHURCH OF GOD

Bible Advocate
Gems of Truth
Now What?
Warner Christian Resources

EPISCOPAL

Church Publishing Incorporated
Forward Day by Day
Forward Movement

EVANGELICAL COVENANT

The Covenant Companion

LUTHERAN

Augsburg Fortress
Beaming Books
Broadleaf Books
Café
Canada Lutheran
The Canadian Lutheran
Christ in Our Home
Fortress Press
Gather
The Lutheran Witness
Northwestern Publishing House
The Word in Season

MENNONITE

Canadian Mennonite
Ink & Quill Quarterly
The Messenger
Rejoice!

MESSIANIC

The Messianic Times

METHODIST

Abingdon Press
The Upper Room

NAZARENE

The Foundry Publishing
Holiness Today
Reflecting God
Standard

ORTHODOX

Ancient Faith Publishing
Chrism Press

PRESBYTERIAN
byFaith
Flyaway Books
Presbyterians Today
These Days: Daily Devotions for
    Living by Faith
Westminster John Knox Press

QUAKER/FRIENDS
Friends Journal
Fruit of the Vine

REFORMED
Christian Courier
P&R Publishing
Tulip Publishing

THE SALVATION ARMY
Faith & Friends

Just for Kids
New Frontier Chronicle
Peer
SAConnects
War Cry

SEVENTH-DAY ADVENTIST
Guide
The Journal of Adventist Education
Ministry
Our Little Friend
Pacific Press
Primary Treasure
Vibrant Life

WESLEYAN
Light from the Word

PUBLISHING LINGO

My first week working in a bookstore I learned a valuable lesson. I had a stack of books in my arms that I had taken from a shipment in the back room. My boss walked by; said, "Steve, please put those in the dump"; and kept walking.

I paused and thought, *Why should I throw these away? They are brand new books!* To my chagrin, I discovered that, in bookstore lingo, a dump was a cardboard display in the front of the store.

The lesson I learned is that knowing the lingo can keep you from being confused or potentially misunderstanding some instructions. Like bookstores, writing and publishing have their own lingo. The following definitions will acquaint you with some of the more important terms.

ABA: American Booksellers Association. This acronym has come to mean the general market, as opposed to CBA, the Christian market.

Advance: Money a publisher pays to an author up front, against future royalties. The amount varies greatly from publisher to publisher and is often paid in two or three installments (on signing the contract, on delivery of the manuscript, and on publication).

AE: An abbreviation for Acquisitions Editor. Not all publishing houses use this abbreviation, but they all have people who acquire in their editorial departments.

All rights: An outright sale of a manuscript. The author has no further control over any subsidiary rights or reusing the piece. You must sign a contract for this agreement to be legal.

Anecdote: A short, poignant, real-life story, usually used to illustrate a single thought. It need not be humorous.

ARC: Advance Reader Copy. An early paperback (or ebook) version of a book sent out for reviews around four to six months prior to publication.

Assignment: When an editor asks a writer to create a specific manuscript for an agreed-on price.

As-told-to story: A true story you write as a first-person account about someone else.

Audience: The people who are expected to be reading your manuscript, in terms of age, life experience, knowledge of and interest level in the story or subject. Editors want to be sure writers understand their assumed audiences well.

Audiobooks: Spoken-word books available by streaming via the Internet, on compact disc, or MP3 file.

Backlist: A publisher's previously published books that are still in print a year or more after publication.

Bible versions:
AMP–*Amplified Bible*
ASV–*American Standard Version*
CB–*Confraternity Bible* (Catholic)
CEB–*Common English Bible*
CEV–*Contemporary English Version*
CJB–*Complete Jewish Bible*
CSB–*Christian Standard Bible*
ESV–*English Standard Version*
GNB–*Good News Bible*
GW–*GOD'S WORD Translation*
HCSB–*Holman Christian Standard Bible* (replaced by CSB)
ICB–*International Children's Bible*
KJV–*King James Version*
KJV21–*21ˢᵗ Century King James Version*
MEV–*Modern English Version*
MSG–*The Message*
NAB–*New American Bible*
NABRE–*New American Bible Revised Edition*
NASB–*New American Standard Bible*
NCV–*New Century Version*
NEB–*New English Bible*
NET–*New English Translation*
NIrV–*New International Reader's Version*

NIV–*New International Version*
NJB–*New Jerusalem Bible*
NKJV–*New King James Version*
NLT–*New Living Translation*
NRSV–*New Revised Standard Version*
PHILLIPS–*J.B. Phillips New Testament*
RSV–*Revised Standard Version* (replaced by NRSV)
TEV–*Today's English Translation* (aka *Good News Bible*)
TLB–*The Living Bible*
TNIV–*Today's New International Version*
VOICE–*The Voice Bible Translation*
WEB–*World English Bible*

Bio: Brief information about the author.

Bluelines: The last printer's proofs used to catch errors before a book or periodical is printed. May be physical pages or digital proofs in PDF.

BOB: Back-of-Book ad for the author's previous book(s) or a similar book released by the publisher. It uses the blank pages in the back of a book or extra pages at the end of an ebook.

Book proposal: Submission of a book idea to an agent or editor. It usually includes a hook, summary and purpose of the book, target market, uniqueness of the book compared to similar ones in the marketplace, chapter-by-chapter summaries or plot synopsis, marketing and promotion information, your credentials, and delivery date, plus one to three sample chapters, including the first one.

Byline: Author's name printed below the title of a story, article, etc.

Camera-ready copy: The text and artwork for a book that are ready for the press.

Category romance: Novels of around 50,000-60,000 words that are published in categories and according to strict guidelines. For example, Love Inspired novels, the Christian division of Harlequin.

CBA: Christian Booksellers Association. The acronym has come to describe the Christian market as opposed to ABA, the general market. As an entity, CBA folded in 2019, but the acronym still applies when referring to the Christian publishing industry.

Chapbook: A small book or pamphlet containing poetry, religious readings, etc.

Circulation: The number of copies sold or distributed of a periodical.

Clips: Copies of articles you have had published in newspapers or magazines.

Colophon: The publisher's emblem or imprint used on the title page or spine of a book or a statement at the end of a book with information about its production, such as the type of font used.

Column: A regularly appearing feature, section, or department in a periodical with the same heading. It's written by the same person or a different freelancer each time.

Comp copies: Complimentary copies given to the author by the publisher on publication.

Comps: Shorthand for "comparable." The publisher may have comps on cover designs or titles to help position the book in the marketplace.

Concept statement: A 50- to 150-word summary of your proposed book.

Contributing editor: A freelance writer who has a regular column or writes regularly for the periodical.

Contributor's copy: Copy of an issue of a periodical sent to an author whose work appears in it.

Copyedit: The editor checks grammar, punctuation, and citations to make sure the work is accurate. More detailed than a developmental edit. Some publishers refer to this as the line edit.

Copyright: Legal protection of an author's work. A manuscript is automatically copyrighted in your name when you produce it. You don't need to register it with the Copyright Office unless you are self-publishing a book or other publication since a traditional publisher registers it for you.

Cover copy: Or "copy." The text on the back cover of a book, in the online description, or in marketing materials. For a hardcover, it can also include flap copy, the text on the inside dust-jacket flaps.

Cover letter: A letter that accompanies some article submissions. Usually it's needed only if you have to tell the editor something specific, to give your credentials for writing a manuscript of a technical nature, or to remind the editor that the manuscript was requested or expected. Often used as the introduction to a book proposal.

Credits, list of: A listing of your previously published works.

Critique: An evaluation of a manuscript.

Defamation: A written (libel) or spoken (slander) injury to the reputation of a living person or organization. If what is said is true, it cannot be defamatory; but that does not prevent the injured party from bringing a lawsuit.

Derivative work: A work derived from another work, such as a condensation or abridgment. Contact the copyright owner for permission before doing the abridgment, and be prepared to pay that owner a fee or royalty.

Developmental edit: Usually the first round of editing done on a manuscript. The editor helps "develop" the book by shaping its content and structure. Also called a substantive edit or line edit.

Devotion: A short manuscript based on a Scripture verse or passage that shares a personal spiritual discovery, inspires to worship, challenges to commitment or action, or encourages. A book or periodical of devotions is called a devotional.

Ed board: Editorial board meeting. The editors meet to discuss the new proposals they received to determine which ones should go to the pub board.

Editorial guidelines: See "Writers guidelines."

Em dash (—): Used to create a break or set off nonessential material or extra information in a sentence instead of using commas. *The Chicago Manual of Style* calls this punctuation mark "the most versatile of the dashes."

En dash (–): An en dash is longer than a hyphen but shorter than an em dash. Often used between numbers and dates to show a range. It was called the "en" dash because in the early days of typesetting it was the same width as the capital letter N.

Endorsements: Flattering comments about a book, usually printed on the back cover or in promotional material.

Epub: Term for a specific file format used for ebooks. Mobi is used for Kindle (Amazon). Epub is used by everyone else (Nook, Kobo, Apple, Google Play, etc.).

Essay: A short composition expressing the author's opinion on a specific subject.

Evangelical: A person who believes that one receives God's forgiveness for sins through Jesus Christ and believes the Bible is the authoritative Word of God. This is a broad definition for a label with broad application. Often mistakenly used as a synonym for "Christian."

Exegesis: Interpretation of a Scripture passage.

Feature article: In-depth coverage of a subject, usually focusing on a person, an event, a process, an organization, a movement, a trend, or an issue. It's written to explain, encourage, help, analyze, challenge, motivate, warn, or entertain, as well as to inform.

Filler: A short item used to "fill" a page of a periodical. It could be a joke, anecdote, light verse, short humor, puzzle, game, etc.

First rights: A periodical editor buys the right to publish a manuscript that has never been published and to do so only once.

Foreign rights: Selling or giving permission to translate or reprint published material in another country.

Foreword: Opening remarks in a book to introduce the book and its author. Often misspelled as *forward*.

Freelance: Supplied by freelance writers.

Freelancer or freelance writer: A writer who is not on salary but sells his or her material to a number of different periodicals and publishers.

Galley proof: A typeset copy of a book or magazine used to detect and correct errors before printing.

General editor: Usually, the person who oversees a large work that has multiple authors writing individual chapters for a book or a series of books. This person is not an employee within a publishing house.

General market: Non-Christian market, sometimes called secular market.

Genre: Refers to a type or classification, as in fiction or poetry. For instance, westerns, romances, and mysteries are fiction genres.

Glossy: A photo with a shiny, rather than matte, finish. Also, a publication printed on such paper.

Go-ahead: When an editor tells you to write or submit your article.

Hard copy: A printed manuscript, as opposed to one sent via email.

Independent book publisher: A book publisher who charges authors to publish their books or buy a certain number of copies, as opposed to a royalty house that pays authors. Some independent publishers also pay a royalty. Sometimes called a subsidy, vanity, self, or custom publisher.

ISBN: International Standard Book Number, an identification code needed for every version of a book.

Journal: A periodical presenting information in a particular area, often for an academic or educated audience.

Kill fee: A fee paid for a completed article done on assignment that is subsequently not published. The amount is usually 25–50 percent of the original payment.

Libel: A published false statement that is damaging to another person's reputation, a written defamation.

Line edit: See "Developmental edit" and "Copyedit." Check to see how your editor defines each process.

Little/literary: Small-circulation periodicals whose focus is providing a forum for the literary writer, rather than on making money. Often they do not pay or pay in copies.

Mainstream fiction: Other than genre fiction (such as romance, mystery, or fantasy). Stories of people and their conflicts handled on a deeper level.

Mass market: Books intended for a wide, general market; produced in a smaller format, usually with smaller type; and sold at a lower price. The expectation is that their sales will be higher.

Matte finish: A nonglossy, nonreflective finish on a book cover. Has a textured feel.

Mobi: Term for a specific file format used for ebooks. Mobi is used for Kindle (Amazon). Epub is used by everyone else.

Ms: Abbreviation for manuscript.

Mss: Abbreviation for more than one manuscript.

NASR: Abbreviation for North American Serial Rights. Permission for a periodical targeting readers in the US and Canada to publish a manuscript.

New-adult fiction: A developing fiction genre with protagonists ages 18–25. In the general market, these novels often explore sexual themes considered too "adult" for the YA or teen market. They tend to be marketed to older teen readers.

Novella: A short novel, usually 20,000–35,000 words. The length varies from publisher to publisher.

On acceptance: Editor pays a writer at the time the manuscript is accepted for publication.

On assignment: Writing a manuscript at the specific request of an editor.

On publication: Publisher pays a writer when his or her manuscript is published.

On speculation/spec: Writing something for a periodical editor with the agreement that the editor will buy it only if he or she likes it.

Onetime rights: Selling the right to publish a manuscript one time to more than one periodical, primarily to nonoverlapping audiences, such as different denominations.

Over the transom: Unsolicited manuscripts sent to a book editor. Comes from the old transom, which was a window above the door in office buildings. Manuscripts could be pushed "over the transom" into the locked office.

Overrun: The extra copies of a book printed during the initial print run.

Pen name/pseudonym: A name other than your legal name used on a manuscript to protect your identity or the identities of people included or when you wish to remain anonymous. Put the pen name in the byline under the title and your real name with your contact information.

Perfect binding: When pages of a paperback are glued together (bound) on the spine and the cover is then attached.

Periodical: A magazine, journal, newsletter, or newspaper.

Permissions: Asking permission to use text or art from a copyrighted source.

Personal experience: An account based on a real-life experience.

Personality profile: A feature article that highlights a specific person's life or accomplishments.

Plagiarism: Stealing and using the ideas or writing of someone else as your own, either as is or rewriting slightly to make it sound like your own.

POD/Print-on-demand: A printing process where books are printed one at a time or in small numbers instead of in quantity. The production cost per book is higher, but no warehousing is necessary.

POV: Point-of-view. A fiction term that describes the perspective of the one telling the story, such as first person or third person.

Press kit: A compilation of promotional materials for a book or author, used to publicize a book.

Pub board: A formal meeting where people from editorial, marketing, sales, finance, and management meet to discuss whether or not to publish a book.

Public domain: Work for which copyright protection has expired. Copyright laws vary from country to country; but in the US, works published more than 95 years ago have entered the public domain. Because the US copyright law has changed several times, check with the Copyright Office (*copyright.gov*) to determine if a work is in public domain or not. Generally, since 1978, copyright endures for the author's life plus 70 years.

Query letter: A letter sent to an editor about an article or book you propose to write and asking if he or she is interested in seeing it.

Recto: The right-hand page in printing.

Reprint rights: Selling the right to reprint an article that has already been published. You must have sold only first or onetime rights originally and wait until it has been published the first time.

Response time: The number of weeks or months it takes an editor or agent to get back to you about a query, proposal, or manuscript you sent.

Review copies: Books given to reviewers or buyers for bookstore chains and online sellers.

Royalty: The percentage an author is paid by a publisher on the sale of each copy of a book.

Running head: The text at the top of each page that can show the author's name, book title, chapter, or page number.

SASE: Self-addressed, stamped envelope. Always send it with a hard-copy manuscript or query letter.

SASP: Self-addressed, stamped postcard. May be sent with a hard-copy manuscript to be returned by the editor to indicate it arrived safely. Rarely used.

Satire: Ridicule that aims at reform.

Second serial rights: See "Reprint rights."

Secular market: An outdated term for the non-Christian publishing market.

Self-publisher: See "Independent book publisher."

Serial: Refers to publication in a periodical, such as first serial rights.

Sidebar: A short feature that accompanies an article and gives additional information about the topic, such as a recommended reading list. It is often set apart by appearing within a box or border.

Signature: All books are printed in 16-page increments or signatures (occasionally in 32-page increments for large books like Bibles). A large sheet of paper is printed, then folded multiple times. Three sides are cut (top, side, and bottom). The fourth side holds eight double-sided pages. The signatures are compiled and bound into the finished book.

Simultaneous submissions: Sending the same manuscript to more than one editor at the same time. Usually this action is done with nonoverlapping periodical markets, such as denominational publications or newspapers in different cities, or when you are writing on a timely subject. Most periodical editors don't accept simultaneous submissions, but they are the norm in the book market. Be sure to state in a cover letter or on the first page that it is a simultaneous submission.

Slander: The verbal act of defamation.

Slanting: Writing an article to meet the needs of a particular market.

Slush pile: The stack of unsolicited manuscripts that arrive at an editor's desk or email inbox.

Subsidiary rights: All the rights, other than book rights, included in a book contract, such as translations, audiobooks, book clubs, and movies.

Subsidy publisher: See "Independent book publisher."

Substantive edit: See "Developmental edit."

Synopsis: A brief summary of a work, ranging from one paragraph to several pages.

Tabloid: A newspaper-format publication about half the size of a regular newspaper.

Take-home paper: A small periodical given to Sunday-school students, children through adults. These minimagazines are published with the curriculum.

Think piece: A magazine article that has an intellectual, philosophical, or provocative approach to a subject.

Trade book: Describes a 5½" x 8½" paperback book (sometimes 6" x 9"). This is a typical trim size for a paperback. Mass-market books are smaller, around 4" x 6".

Trade magazine: A magazine whose audience is in a particular business.

Trim size: The size of a book after being trimmed in the printing process. (See "Signature" for more information.)

Unsolicited manuscript: A manuscript an editor did not specifically ask to see.

Vanity publisher: See "Independent book publisher."

Verso: The left-hand page in printing.

Vignette: A short, descriptive literary sketch of a brief scene or incident.

Vita: An outline of one's personal history and experience.

Work-for-hire: A manuscript you create for an agreed payment, and you give the publisher full ownership and control of it. You must sign a contract for this agreement to be legal.

Writers guidelines: Information provided by an editor that gives specific guidance for writing for the publication or publishing house. If the information is not offered online, email or send an SASE with your request for printed guidelines.

INDEX

NOTES

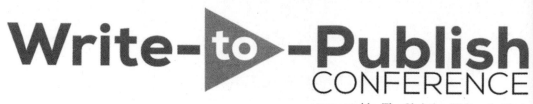

Write-to-Publish CONFERENCE

sponsored by The Christian Writers Institute

JUNE 13-16, 2023

WHEATON COLLEGE, WHEATON, ILLINOIS

Not a function of Wheaton College.

REGISTER ONLINE
WRITETOPUBLISH.COM

Since 1971, Write-to-Publish has been training, inspiring and encouraging writers like you, connecting them with editors and publishers who are looking for good books, articles, and other types of manuscripts; with literary agents who can represent them; and with well-published authors who can help them improve their craft.

WritetoPublish.com